LATE
INDUSTRIALIZATION,
TRADITION,
AND
SOCIAL CHANGE
IN SOUTH KOREA

KOREAN STUDIES
OF THE
HENRY M. JACKSON
SCHOOL OF
INTERNATIONAL
STUDIES

Clark W. Sorensen / Editor

YONG-CHOOL HA

Late Industrialization, Tradition, and Social Change in South Korea

University of Washington Press / *Seattle*

Late Industrialization, Tradition, and Social Change in South Korea was supported by grants from the 2024 Korean Studies Grant Program of the Academy of Korean Studies (AKS-2024-P-007) and from the Korea Studies Program of the University of Washington in cooperation with the Henry M. Jackson School of International Studies.

The open access edition was made possible by a grant from the Atsuhiko and Ina Goodwin Tateuchi East Asia Library Endowed Fund at the University of Washington Libraries, Seattle.

Copyright © 2024 by the University of Washington Press

Design by Mindy Basinger Hill

Composed in Parkinson Electra Pro by Integrated Composition Systems

The digital edition of this book may be downloaded and shared under a Creative Commons Attribution Non-Commercial No Derivatives 4.0 international license (CC-BY-NC-ND 4.0). For information about this license, see https://creativecommons.org/licenses/by-nc-nd/4.0. This license applies only to content created by the author, not to separately copyrighted material. To use this book, or parts of this book, in any way not covered by the license, please contact the University of Washington Press.

UNIVERSITY OF WASHINGTON PRESS   uwapress.uw.edu

LIBRARY OF CONGRESS CATALOGING-IN-PUBLICATION DATA
Names: Ha, Yong-ch'ul, 1949- author.
Title: Late industrialization, tradition, and social change in South Korea / Yong-Chool Ha.
Description: Seattle : University of Washington Press, [2024] | Series: Korean studies of the Henry M. Jackson school of international studies | Includes bibliographical references and index.
Identifiers: LCCN 2023040792 | ISBN 9780295752266 (hardcover) | ISBN 9780295752273 (paperback) | ISBN 9780295752280 (ebook)
Subjects: LCSH: Industrial policy—Korea (South) | Economic development—Korea (South) | Social change—Korea (South)
Classification: LCC HD3616.K62 H33 2024 | DDC 338.95195—dc23/eng/20230913
LC record available at https://lccn.loc.gov/2023040792

∞ This paper meets the requirements of ANSI/NISO z39.48-1992 (Permanence of Paper).

IN MEMORY
OF MY PARENTS,

W. M. Yuliana Lee and Su Won Ha,

WHO UNDERSTOOD
THE IMPORTANCE
OF EDUCATION.

Contents

Preface and Acknowledgments / ix

Introduction / 1

1 The Sociology of Late Industrialization / 13

2 The Colonial Origins of Neofamilism / 27

3 The State and Tradition / 61

4 Hollowing Out Bureaucracy / 102

5 Civil Society and Democratization / 127

6 Daily Practice of Neofamilism / 160

7 The 1997 Financial Crisis / 183

Conclusion / 202

Notes / 213

Bibliography / 249

Index / 299

Preface and Acknowledgments

The background of this book begins in the 1980s, when I returned to Seoul after a decade of study in the United States. The first thing that struck me was a contrast between what Korean social scientists said and wrote and what I observed in Korean society as a Soviet specialist. To most scholars, Korean society was viewed as "modern" largely because it was already highly industrialized. Employing Marxian or Parsonian paradigms, they were discussing workers, labor movements, and the middle class or strata. But similarities between Soviet and Korean societies were clear. Various informal ties—and the exchange of favors based on them—were ubiquitous in both societies. These ties were indispensable in accessing banks for loans, securing doctors' appointments, getting promotion in public and private bureaucracies, and in election campaigns. Korean society in the 1980s still showed strong signs of the persistence of traditional group identities. Elementary school alumni associations gatherings had become more common, and meetings among people from the same hometown were more frequent. My casual counting of the growing number of these primary organizations, which were commonly announced in newspapers, confirmed my observation, even as the industrialization process deepened.

In contrast to observed daily life, rife with "neofamilial" (as I call them) practices crucial to conducting business and social interactions—such as securing financial resources, information on economic educational opportunities, and access to medical services—Korean intellectual circles still clung to a defunct Marxian paradigm. Rampant regionalism within labor unions or labor-management relations did not draw much attention. The anti-authoritarian struggles of "progressive intellectuals" borrowed from Marxism, Leninism, Maoism, Stalinism, and even Kim Il Sungism. These ideologically tinted frameworks were retrofit onto Korean society not only to bolster anti-regime movements but also frequently to explain Korean society at large. However, conventional functionalism was widely applied to explain social changes in Korea after more than two decades of industrialization. Beyond these divergent worldviews, other macro and mid-range theories and frameworks were introduced to explain socio-political phenomena, such as world system theory, dependent development, and bureaucratic authoritarianism. Korean intellectual terrain was muddled with these conflicting frameworks, leaving distinctive aspects of Korean society relegated to a residual category after the universal aspects of it were "explained" by imported paradigms.

Addressing this lacuna was not a priority for academic research, either because Korean society wanted to be viewed as modernized or because the neofamilism that intellectuals themselves practiced was so natural a part of their lives that they were not so conscious of it. Such a tendency to ignore reality might have reflected wishful thinking that socio-cultural catch-up had happened, commensurate to the national economic achievements known as the "Miracle on the Han River." But more importantly, behind such wishful thinking is the prevalent Western sociological presumption that industrialization brings about universal social consequences; this epistemological influence had been deeply rooted in South Korean intellectual circles long before the Han miracle. It is only natural that the combination of wishful thinking and prevailing social science paradigms prior to economic development brought about a strange intellectual vacuum in which distinctive aspects of Korean social changes have been left out. This book seeks to understand these social phenomena that are so personal and familiar that they have been taken for granted.

A significant paradigm shift toward political economy was also occurring during the 1980s in the American social sciences, with the state enjoying a new limelight. Curiously, however, the developmental state was not analyzed in terms of its own dynamics: whether embeddedness changes over time and thus whether the developmental state undergoes institutional changes in the course of economic development. Given my past experience as a bureaucrat, I began to pay attention to this when reviewing archival data on the Ministry of Commerce and Industry of South Korea. I had a rare opportunity to look into the ministry's recruitment, decision-making, and implementation. Through numerous interviews with former bureaucrats and high-ranking chaebol managers, I was able to better understand how embeddedness-based interactions between the state and business had occurred and with what institutional consequences. It was an effort to analyze the institutional evolution of the developmental state itself.

This insider's view of the institutional dynamics of the South Korean developmental state revealed that Korean bureaucracies, from the beginning of late industrialization in the mid-1960s, were increasingly based on both examination (merit) and regionalism. Regionalism, in turn, encompassed school ties as prominent regional high school graduates were conspicuously overrepresented in passing the civil service examination. Business sectors, too, emulated the state's recruitment patterns. The reason for this was sought in the top leader's urgent pursuit of industrialization, which drove business sectors to adopt mimetic patterns of recruitment. But these synergistic patterns of recruitment based on regional and high school ties were not merely necessities for business survival. Had, and how had, the developmental state changed over time? The current literature on this question is not only sparse but also largely structural: shifts in the balance of power between the state and business are typically analyzed over time rather than based on closer examination of changes within the state itself. Close examination of state-business relations reveal subtle and complicated dynamics of this relationship, showing that Korean bureaucracy gradually lost its coherent decision-making power and that its bureaucratic integrity diminished.

Analysis of the evolution of the Korean developmental state led me to search for the origins of high school ties, which in turn led to comparative work on neighboring Japan and Taiwan. As I suspected, the social significance of high school ties emulated Japan during the colonial era, but surprisingly, these ties did not play as important a role in Japan as they had in Korea. The pervasiveness of high school ties, originating in colonial rule, is unique to Korea and became the basis for the embeddedness of the developmental state; Park Chung Hee relied on these ties as an important recruitment source. Tracing the origins of high school ties through research on students' anti-colonial protest movements during colonial rule led me to think about the nature of colonial Korean society. Japanese colonial rule affected Korean society not only economically; it also entailed lost opportunity for Koreans to invent traditions, which has had a lasting impact on Korean society.

Empirical understanding of interactions between the state and business through neofamilial ties led me to question the macro implications of the interactions. With chaebols (conglomerates) in the Korean economy so preponderant, it was a short step from the political economic considerations of state-business interactions to search for broader social and institutional implications. Neofamilism obviously was not limited to business-state relations.

In searching for relevant literature on social change in state-led late industrialization, it quickly became clear to me that theorizing social change under state-led industrialization was not well developed in comparison to analyses based in political economy. The political economy paradigm presented an alternative approach to market-based economic development by highlighting the role of the state but did not say much about social change in general. Chaebols turned out to be more than economic actors; they are a microcosm of Korean society in terms of the evolution of neofamilism.

The analysis of the role of high school, blood, and regional ties in Korea's late industrialization led me to think about the role of tradition in late industrialization—an important clue in understanding the macro social consequences of late industrialization. That tradition could play a positive role, and not be merely an impediment, has been addressed in the critical literature on post-modernization paradigms. Less known are the specifics of an apparent irony of late industrialization: why, when, how, and by whom tradition is introduced and plays a role in late industrialization—a research terrain that until now had not been clearly developed. A comparative review of the roles of tradition in different countries such as Japan, the Soviet Union, and Germany make it clear that traditional institutions and values play different roles in different contexts. In late industrialization, they play an essential facilitating role, giving rise to an irony in terms of macro social consequences. I found that traditional institutions and values play a critical role in shaping society. This book is an effort to demonstrate how to think about diverse paths to social change in different cases of late industrialization by looking at how tradition plays different roles, depending on timing, location, and leadership.

Thus, study of late industrialization is bound to take a multi-disciplinary approach as it needs to examine the state, business, culturally specific traditions, history, and international aspects. A closer examination of the social implications of state-business interactions requires careful cross-disciplinary readings. Over the course of my research, discovering how compartmentalized specialization inhibits free thinking was an important revelation.

This book was developed and completed over many years. Along the way I have accumulated much intellectual debt to many institutions and individuals.

First of all, I would like to thank Professor Steven R. Brown at Kent State University, who taught me the importance of typology in looking at human behavior and social change from early on in my intellectual career. Most of all, I learned so much from my teachers at the University of California, Berkeley. Ken Jowitt's lectures were always inspiring in developing conceptual thinking. His notion of neotraditionalism stimulated my interest in the role of tradition in industrialization. Reinhard Bendix alerted me to the danger in equating industrialization with modernity. My adviser, George Breslauer, taught me the importance of empirical evidence. His careful readings of the draft chapters greatly helped me in conceptual clarification. Aaron Wildavsky constantly reminded me of the importance of critical thinking. Robert Scalapino never failed to support me during my stay at Berkeley. I am also heavily indebted to the late Professor Hong Yung Lee, who understood the importance of my study and rendered constant support to the development of a neofamilial approach to Korean society with his detailed comments and guidance.

Conducting research and writing started in earnest when I began teaching at the Department of International Relations, Seoul National University from 1986 to 2007, where I greatly benefited from so many colleagues and students. Discussions with Professors Choi Jueong Un, Yoon Young Gwan, Lim Hyun Chin, and Chang Kyung Sup provided invaluable insights in understanding Korean society. Professors Baik Chang Jae and Sohn Yul provided careful readings of the manuscript on the dynamics of the strong state. Many undergraduate and graduate students who later became full-fledged scholars on their own provided not just research assistance but also faith in the importance of my work at a time when my research was in inchoate form. Yumi Moon, Bong Jun Ko, Myung Koo Kang, Sunil Kim, Jung Whan Lee, Young Ho Yoon, Kyung Jun Choi, Han Seok Cho, Heyjung Cho, Yeo Jung Yoon, Choong Ku Lee, Yong Mi Ryu, Nah Hosung, Hong Yerim, and Lim Bonkyu were willing to join me in interviewing former bureaucrats and businessmen and helped me record the interviews and collect data. I am especially indebted to Yumi Moon at Stanford University and Myung Koo Kang at CUNY. Wang Hwi Lee at Ajou University, Kyung Joon Choi at Konkuk University, and Ian Oates, associate director of the Center for Korean Studies at University of Washington, offered careful readings of the various chapters of the book and provided valuable feedback over the years.

My intellectual indebtedness continued when I moved to the Henry M. Jackson School of International Studies, University of Washington in 2007. There I met with eminent colleagues, such as Anand Yang, Don Hellmann, Ken Pyle, Gary Hamilton, Joel Migdal, Robert Pekkanen, Steve Pfaff, James Lin, Susan Whiting, Scott Radnitz, Jonathan Warren, and Hajin Jun. They appreciated the significance of the book project and encouraged me whenever I met challenges in writing. They were also gracious enough to participate in a seminar to discuss the different chapters of the book. I also express my special thanks to the Center for Korean Studies and its chair, Clark Sorensen, who have been supportive of my book writing from early on with careful readings and advice on publication, along with Hyokyoung Yi, Korean librarian at Tateuchi East Asia Library, University of Washington, for her assistance in locating important materials.

Beyond my affiliated institutions, I must thank several individuals and institutions, without whose help I could not have completed this book. Korea Research Foundation, Samsung Electronics, Korea-Japan exchange programs, and One Asia Foundation provided research funds at various stages of research for this book. My special thanks go to Professors Beom Shik Shin and Chae Sung Chun for their facilitation for research funding at the Asia Center at Seoul National University during my sabbatical year from 2014 to 2015 (SNU Asia Center Research Grant 2015). Special thanks also go to Professors Hyun Chin Lim, Myung Koo Kang, and Su Jin Park, who were directors of the center throughout my visits for the past 10 years. The writing support fund was invaluable in drafting chapters 4 and 5, collecting supplementary data, and conducting interviews by traveling around South Korea. My gratitude goes to Dr. Sang Hyon Lee of the Sejong Institute, who provided a comfortable environment to finish the book during my sabbatical leave for Fall 2021. I also would like to express my gratitude to Professors Wada Haruki of Tokyo University, who invited me to the Institute of Social Science at Tokyo University, and Hagen Koo of the University of Hawai'i, who did a careful reading of the introduction and chapter 3 and provided detailed advice for revision. Professors Se-jung Oh and Jong Woon Kim, former presidents of Seoul National University, understood the importance of Korean studies abroad and played an important role in helping me with fundraising and conducting research. Professor Unchan Jeong, who later became Prime Minister of South Korea, has shown constant support to my research and Korean studies in general. Finally, my thanks go to Lorri Hagman and Joeth Zucco at the University of Washington Press, the copy editor Alja Kooistra, and my personal editor, Brian Folk, for their extensive and detailed editorial advice.

Last but not least, I do not know how to express my thanks to my family, who endured so much over the years while I was preparing this book. My wife, Yangwon, has been a constant source of support, and my son, Justin, actively participated in the book preparation with careful reading and editing contributions. Although this book is a product based on assistance, cooperation, and collaboration with so many people and institutions, for any mistakes and misinterpretations in the book I am solely responsible.

LATE
INDUSTRIALIZATION,
TRADITION,
AND
SOCIAL CHANGE
IN SOUTH KOREA

Introduction

There are three sources that hinder the unity of our nation. First is class conflict based on economic interests. Second are pseudo-political parties that are solely preoccupied with private interests. Finally, unreasonable and absurd factionalism . . . people are organized around family connections, clan organizations, regionalism, and school ties. These groups are organized to occupy powerful positions in order to secure opportunities to aggrandize their wealth and to fill their stomachs. They are interested solely in enriching themselves without considering other people. Such factionalism and partisan struggles, which have been the sources of national misfortunes and tragedies throughout our history, ultimately brought about the downfall of our country and the loss of our nationality at the end of the Chosun dynasty. Reflecting on our historical records and experiences, we should not tolerate them. —*Park Chung Hee, 1969*

Once groups are organized based on school, regional, and family ties, they easily develop into particularistic entities beyond friendship. They divide us from them and fall into exclusivism by distinguishing friends and enemies. Thus, those who do not belong to the same school, or hometown, are hated, and if they are hated, their parents and siblings are also hated. The practice of being exclusive is what Korean society is right now. —*Park Chung Hee, 1965*

Every country absorbs industrialization into its own tradition; every country assimilates the process in a manner peculiar to it alone; in every country there emerges an amalgamation of cultural tradition and ramifications of industrialization characteristic of it alone. There are as many modes of industrialization as there are industrializing countries, and every one of them needs to be understood in its own terms. —*Ralf Dahrendorf, 1967*

Korea's economic development appears to contain a paradox: an ultra-modern industrial economy alongside traditional networks of obligation and solidarity, such as blood, school, and regional ties, which profoundly affect fundamental aspects of Korean politics and socioeconomic relations. But this situation is not actually a paradox, for the course of Korea's late economic development deliberately entrenched these ties into Korea's politics, society, and economy. Analysis of the persistence and predominance of what I call "neofamilism" reveals distinct social phenomena that arose through interactions between the developmental state, traditional institutions, and economic tasks.

Why could Korean president Park Chung Hee (1963–79) not avoid the chronic familism, regionalism, and other cliquishness that he hated so much and wanted to eliminate, even in the aftermath of the rapid industrialization that he himself launched? Contrary to Park's expectation, the social characteristics of which he was so critical were reinforced by the imperatives of late industrialization. Late industrialization is understood as an attempt to catch up with a country's earlier-industrializing counterparts, and its main features are speed and high economic growth. Why and how does late industrialization incorporate traditional institutions and values? As we will see, something unusual happened in Korean society during the critical period of economic development during the 1960s and 1970s.

Ulsan, a port city in the southeastern part of South Korea, is an example of how rapid industrialization brought change to a typical urban area. Before 1962, when the city was designated as a special industrial zone, Ulsan had a populace of 85,000, but with the infusion of heavy industries, such as shipbuilding, chemical, and auto industries, the city became one of the most industrialized areas in the country. By 1982, the population had grown to 476,000 (mostly industrial workers) due to in-migration. However, rapid urbanization did not diminish primary tie-based forms of organization. On the contrary, organizations such as clans, hometown associations, and school alumni associations emerged as important sources of identity.[1] Moreover, in the heavily working class–based area, the son of the founder and chair of Hyundai Heavy Industries was an elected member of the National Assembly from the Eastern District of Ulsan City from 1988 to 2004.[2]

On the political question of how kin-like or family-based ties affected elections of the president and National Assembly in Korean society in general, in a 2015 survey, 37.8% (40 out of 106) of respondents said they enormously influenced elections, 48.1% said considerably influenced, and 9.4% said somewhat influenced. Altogether, 95% said social ties affected elections one way or another.[3] Actual election results reflect the survey findings. In the 1987 presidential election, the first free democratic election since 1960, Kim Dae Jung received 88.4% of the vote from his home region in the southwest and only 2.5% and 6.9% from the two southeastern provinces.[4] In 1992, Kim picked up 91% of his own region and only 10% and 8.7% from the two southeastern provinces.

A survey in South Korea conducted in the early 1980s—two decades into industrialization—intriguingly showed that more than 70% of the respondents said school and regional ties were essential for survival in Korean society.[5] Another survey affirms the same societal trend, with more than 85% of the respondents saying that blood, school, and regional ties play some role in making important decisions in Korea.[6] A labor relations survey from the early 1990s indicates that only 11.8% regarded labor-management relations as being based on equal contract—that is, freely chosen by autonomous individuals—while 28.6% said they were modeled on pseudo-father-son relations.[7] The same survey found that familism served as a constraining factor on the formation of class consciousness and participation in labor union activities. More strikingly, a labor union official said in an interview that 90% of his daily life revolved around regionalism, such as meeting with labor union members with the same regional ties, contacting relatives in different sub-regions of the province in which he lived, and visiting clan organizations in the same region.[8]

Are these phenomena merely anecdotal, circumstantial, and transient in nature? Are they essentially informal and residual, as the school of modernization would lead us to believe?[9] This book contends that these are in fact the consequences of late industrialization and that they show how traditional institutions and values are introduced and reinforced through the mediation of the state. How did South Korea's industrialization assimilate Korean traditions? What are the patterns of the amalgamation of cultural tradition and ramification of industrialization? Did these processes produce distinct, socially meaningful units other than class in South Korea's late industrialization? While the singular path of South Korea's rapid economic development has been well documented, the distinct impact that late industrialization brought to Korean society remains an understudied terrain of research.[10] This book analyzes the macrosocial implications of the impact of late industrialization.

SOCIAL AND INSTITUTIONAL IRONIES OF LATE INDUSTRIALIZATION

South Korea's successful pursuit of late industrialization invoked and reinforced traditional institutions and values, regarded as resistant to change, to achieve rapid economic success. The distinct social and institutional changes in late industrialization cannot be properly understood without exploring these social and institutional ironies of economic success in late industrialization. The huge gap between political economy and sociology is a persistent anomaly in studies of late industrialization. The state has been considered to be of primary importance in achieving rapid economic development, as it provides various institutional and policy incentives for business in capital formation and technological development.

The social implications of what the state does, however, have seldom attracted attention. An example is the literature on embedded autonomy, which considers how the state is embedded in society through various networks such as school ties but simultaneously maintains sufficient autonomy to draft and implement policies, despite societal resistance.[11] Such autonomy is regarded as the key to economic success. Social and cultural factors have been drawn on to explain economic success, but no effort has been made to explicate what happens to society in the process of industrialization because of this embeddedness. The complexity of society under state-led industrialization has thus seldom gotten due attention. Moreover, when the state has been "brought back in" to social science analysis, it, too, has been only in the context of debates within political economy theory. Bringing the state back stopped short of reaching a deeper sociological level.[12] Conventional sociological categories, such as class and stratum, are heavily relied on in studies of nations that are latecomers to industrial development, including the case of South Korea.[13]

Although late industrializations share structural similarities, such as economic backwardness and the role of the state, structural features differ, making it impossible to anticipate similar social consequences. This nature of late industrialization requires highlighting historical specificity and considering contextuality of industrialization and social consequences.[14] Only through such an approach is it possible to discern and explain alternative dimensions of social change beyond class or stratum.

NEOFAMILISM AS SOCIAL CONSEQUENCE OF TRADITION–LATE INDUSTRIALIZATION NEXUS

Social and institutional ironies arise from the need to facilitate late industrialization. Feelings of backwardness, insecurity, and inferiority within the psyches of the leading elite induce a sense of urgency. Traditional institutions and values are then reintroduced as tools to address this by providing familiarity in communication and institutional operations.[15] Thus, traditional institutions and values can be seen as institutional imperatives of late industrialization, manifesting in different forms, depending upon domestic social and historical contexts.[16]

In the case of South Korea, familial, school, and regional ties were incorporated and reinforced through the state's recruitment and relations with business, a dynamic that can be defined as neofamilism. *Familism* is not limited to a conventional family; it incorporates broad primary ties based on kinship, school, and region. The prefix *neo* is meant to emphasize that traditional relationships have been revived and changed in an industrial setting, making neofamilism different from the traditional familism found in agrarian settings. Thus, neofamilism denotes the dynamic process of reinforcement of social ethos and relations based on primary ties that occurred during Korea's industrialization. These processes addressed issues of identity, provided a strategy for survival, and shaped the operations of institutions.

Neofamilism has an outward and mobility-seeking orientation commensurate with Korea's export promotion strategy. It also denotes a narrower and thus more specific structural configuration than broader concepts such as traditionalism.[17] Overlapping familial, school, and regional ties are used separately and together to seek access to incentives from the state.[18] What needs to be emphasized here is not that traditional elements persisted during and after industrialization, or that they are universal in time and space, but rather that certain traditional primary ties were reinforced and strengthened during the course of state-led industrialization. Neofamilism is also different from clientelism in that the former can take many different forms of relations, one of which can be clientelism. For instance, school ties can be invoked almost any time and any place without any conscious effort to manage them, and they can take contractual, noncontractual, or clientelistic formats.

Neofamilism can be understood as a part of network analysis, but the term *neofamilism* is chosen to denote the social ethos and structural features unique to Korea, such as the corporate family; regional solidarity; and the link among family, school ties, social mobility, and status. Autonomous, individual-based network analysis is limited in understanding neofamilism, which is based on corporate and familial units. The term also serves to clarify the dynamic process of reinforcement of these ties in the course of industrialization, which is usually taken for granted in network analyses.

Thus, neofamilism can be understood as the social consequences of the state's introduction of pre-industrial social patterns that were reinforced in the process of late industrialization. Neofamilism has become an important, deeply institutionalized source of identity, a key survival strategy, and the basis for organizational operations in South Korea. Neofamilism further emerged as a distinct social structure coexisting with and mitigating class relations, and this requires a serious and systematic inquiry within the context of Korea's late industrialization. This book is an attempt to clearly define the conceptual status of neofamilism and its theoretical implications for social change, recognizing specific forms as unique to Korea in terms of substance, although the pattern of interactions between industrialization and tradition has broader applicability.

LATENESS, THE STATE, AND SENSE OF BACKWARDNESS

The distinctive features of social change in late industrialization can be understood through an analysis of interaction between late industrialization and tradition through the mediation of the state. This requires examining the aspects of late industrialization that are conducive to the persistence of tradition and how the state is related to this process. The first observation to make is that late industrialization starts with the awakening of elites about the backwardness of their own countries.[19] Why, when, and how elites begin to perceive the lateness of their countries is an important question in understanding patterns of late industrialization.

What is universal in elites' perception of backwardness is the feeling of relative underdevelopment vis-à-vis their neighboring countries, region, and the world. At the same time, in most cases elites are in a precarious position in terms of legitimacy with regard to other elite groups and larger society. Japanese elites, for example, felt a deep sense of backwardness vis-à-vis the West at the time of the Meiji Restoration and were under pressure to establish a new order in terms of administrative and economic system building.[20] Likewise, Stalin, right after the establishment of the Soviet Union, felt a relative backwardness vis-à-vis Europe and was under constant pressure from the capitalist world.[21] South Korea's president Park Chung Hee was also fully conscious of relative backwardness vis-à-vis not only North Korea but also Japan and the West.²²

The perception of backwardness also arose due to personal insecurity or regime instability. Meiji leaders faced the urgent task of nation-building; Stalin had to demonstrate the validity of the new ideology of communism; and Park Chung Hee had to justify his military coup d'état to the masses and the old political elites. As such, the sense of backwardness accompanies the sense of inferiority.²³ The sense of inferiority, in turn, leads to the sense of urgency, which causes leaders of late industrialization to be overly ambitious in setting the goals of industrialization and to be highly conscious of the speed at which industrialization is pursued. Leaders of late industrialization often urged early accomplishment of economic targets and a high economic growth rate.²⁴

Ironically, the greater the sense of backwardness, inferiority, and urgency, the more likely traditional institutions and values are introduced. This seems ironic because rapid industrialization would entail the disappearance of traditional institutions and values, as modernization theories assume. Yet the more leaders pursue rapid economic growth, the more they are likely to depend on familiar institutions and values. Thus, in order to generate a high economic growth rate with a high sense of urgency, it is rational to take advantage of familiar institutions and values so the populace experiencing this transition would feel more comfortable. This explains the apparent paradox of late industrialization: the speedier late industrialization is pursued, the greater the dependence on traditional institutions and values.²⁵

A related question is whether and to what extent leaders of late industrialization are conscious of the use of traditional institutions and values and view them positively as a way to facilitate industrialization process. Put differently, a crucial factor in understanding social changes of late industrialization is the extent of the invention of traditional values and institutions.²⁶ On the one hand, leaders may adopt a "harnessing" strategy, whereby they adopt tradition to facilitate industrialization, frequently without consciously thinking about the need for the "invention" of tradition. Even though leaders may not be aware of traditional practices, or even view them in negative terms, traditional institutions and values may be still operating—and ultimately affecting social and institutional changes in late industrialization. This may be termed the introduction of tradition through the backdoor.²⁷ The second strategy involves the invention of tradition. Leaders are fully prepared for a comprehensive invention of tradition, the full scope of which can affect social change on two levels: modes of recruitment of officials who are actually involved in daily implementation of industrialization tasks and social institutions that are related to the management of social conflicts.[28]

Late industrialization involves the strong role of the state, and its impact goes beyond the economic level. Sociologist Reinhard Bendix, for example, remarks that government is an integral part of the social structure and that the state has the capacity to change society.[29] What sociologist Theda Skocpol refers to as the Tocquevillian perspective of the state also speaks to the state capacity to change society, culture, and beyond:

> This second approach (sociopolitical impact of the state) might be called "Tocquevillian," because Alexis de Tocqueville applied it masterfully in his studies *The Old Regime and the French Revolution* and *Democracy in America*. In this perspective, states matter not simply because of the goal-oriented activities of state officials. They matter because their organizational configurations, along with their overall patterns of activity, affect political culture, encourage some kinds of group formation and collective political actions (but not others), and make possible the raising of certain political issues (but not others).[30]

As Bendix and Skocpol mention, in most non-Western developing countries it is the government that needs to be seriously considered in understanding social and institutional changes. Functionally, in the cases of late industrialization, the state can exercise its influence on the economy in multiple ways through capital formation, production, and distribution. The state may exercise strong influence in the financial sector either by directly establishing a development bank, sponsoring loans, or heavily regulating financial transactions. The state may also directly participate in basic industries such as steel, coal mining, and socioeconomic infrastructure building and may make inclusive or exclusive policies in the area of social welfare.[31] The implications of different state roles in different areas for social changes are clear. State intervention brings about different rules of the game than those of the market, and the coexistence of the market and the state means a continuation of multiple sources of identity and loyalty. The various sources of identity not only lead to multiple forms of organizations and institutions, but they also affect the nature of the modus operandi of newly created industrial organizations.

Modes of recruitment of officials constitute another important factor in changing patterns of late industrialization as these officials will actually formulate and implement economic and other policies related to industrialization through interactions with non-state actors. Crucially, this entails whether and to what extent leaders feel competent in securing reliable, trustworthy, and capable people they can mobilize. Furthermore, whether recruitment is based on merit or particularistic grounds is important in that each mode of recruitment has different implications for human groupings, as state-led industrialization involves frequent interactions between state officials and business sectors. As such, modes of recruitment of state officials may also affect those of business sectors. When particularism in recruitment of officials is predominant, outside influence on the officials can be stronger than when recruitment is based on merit. Thus, state modes of recruitment are bound to affect business modes of recruitment.[32]

The invention of tradition at the social-institutional level refers to the coordination and management of social conflicts that result from industrialization. Here the question is whether and to what extent leaders utilize traditional institutions to determine the forms of business organizations and to prevent and resolve social conflict. One example is labor-management relations: leaders invent traditional social institutions, such as paternalism, in coordinating labor-management relations. Thus, leaders may be conscious of the need for invention but end up with a different level of invention of tradition, depending on how they perceive the extent of social conflicts that may emerge in the course of late industrialization. When leaders may be less acutely aware of the need to manage social conflict, traditional institutions may affect social and institutional changes more or less spontaneously, without much invention.[33]

An important social implication of the strong role of the state is the persistence of an already established social structure in the process of late industrialization. Political economist Joseph Schumpeter stated that once social structures are formed, they persist, possibly for centuries, and different structures and types display different degrees of this ability to survive. Bendix was much more specific in terms of context in which established social structure does not disappear. He mentioned that even after a considerable degree of economic change, the consequent social structure will not take on universal forms; instead, it will depend on the "pre-industrial conditions, the particular impetus to develop, the path which modernization takes, the significant differences that persist in developed economies, and finally with the impact and timing of dramatic events."[34] He further observed that the roles and functions of traditional groups, such as kinship ties and collectivism in the pursuit of late development, played a positive and compatible role with modernization.[35]

Here, as Bendix emphasized, another important factor to consider for social change in late industrialization is whether traditional social structures remain and to what extent they exercise political, economic, and social influences.[36] If a traditional social structure is still strong, social consequences will be affected by the degree to which the dominant group resists or participates in industrialization. Also, the traditional institutions will affect social consequences by the degree to which they serve as a source for the recruitment of bureaucrats.[37] However, where traditional structure breaks down without any dominant hegemonic social group or class, the social consequences of state-led industrialization will greatly depend on the top leadership's attitude toward traditional values and institutions. That is, social consequences will depend on whether leadership positively views tradition as a way to promote industrialization or negatively views (or has a lack of awareness of) tradition. A negative orientation can take the form of either rejection of tradition without any alternative idea of how to build a new society or an attempt to make economic and social changes by reinventing tradition. Thus, the social consequences of late industrialization will be greatly affected by the leadership's orientation toward tradition.

Following Bendix, our overarching concern in this study is to determine what makes each case of industrialization and also late industrialization distinct, if not unique. What are the context and ways in which tradition interacts with industrialization? The essential contextual factors particular to different countries are the status of traditional social elites and the degree of the state's autonomy.

Assessment of the kinds of social units that may emerge from late industrialization requires that the following issues are specified: First, when and why did leaders of late industrialization begin to feel the sense of backwardness? Second, to what extent does the sense of backwardness lead to the sense of inferiority and urgency in pursuing late industrialization? Third, how ambitious are economic goals, and with what speed is late industrialization implemented? Fourth, do leaders have both the motivation and personnel pipelines to recruit loyal and competent people whom they can mobilize to implement industrialization tasks? Fifth, the degree of particularism in implementing industrial policies will affect patterns of interactions not only between state officials and business sectors but also between state officials and the rest of society. Finally, whether traditional social structure persists needs to be considered, and at the same time the orientation of leaders toward traditional institutions and whether they invent traditional institutions to manage social conflict in particular and social interactions in general need to be analyzed.

While conventional sociological categories assume a clear demarcation between political, economic, and social arenas, in societies undergoing state-led industrialization, the boundary lines between different institutions are at first unclear and systems are only slowly differentiated. The social impact of industrialization in these societies can be properly understood by looking into the complex interplay between the state and other actors involved in industrialization and by carefully examining state economic policy.

With empirical evidence from the mid-1960s through 1980 in South Korea, this book analyzes the role of the state in reinforcing traditional social relations in Korea during this period of rapid industrialization. The analysis of state economic policy and the interactions among government, industry, and society during this period demonstrate (a) that certain traditional primary social ties, such as blood, school, and region, were unintentionally reinforced rather than weakened; and (b) that in place of class, new social units—amalgams of modernity and tradition—were created. This outcome can best be understood as neofamilism. Most importantly, because these new social units were systemic—not intermittent, partial, or anecdotal—understanding how they arose and functioned is essential in understanding the development of Korea both socially and economically.

The Sociology of Late Industrialization

CHAPTER 1

Industrialization has long been understood as the essential transformation in societies' entrée to modernity: an archetypal sociopolitical project that has at the same time fundamentally shaped the course of social science theorizing. Changes related to industrialization involve social structures, sectors, institutions, psychology, and culture.[1] The central question explored by social scientists has been how to understand the scope and patterns of such changes, with late industrialization becoming the order of the day in the postwar era.

The most controversial question in sociology in the 1950s and 1960s was whether industrialization would bring about universal consequences regardless of different historical, social, and political contexts. Concerns for contextualization were absent in the major Western paradigms in sociology. Marxism and functionalism, regardless of their fundamental differences in perspectives on social conflict, converged on the unilinear development pattern based on Western historical experiences.[2] The developing world was viewed as a sphere for modernization that would bring democracy in politics and capitalist development in the economy.

The emergence of the Communist Bloc and the expansion of US hegemony played important roles in validating the Marxism and functionalism paradigms; however, challenges to these paradigms came through cultural and institutional turns. Marxism based on economic determinism came to be challenged by cultural turns in class analysis wherein complexity of human behaviors is understood in cultural and traditional terms beyond economic interests, while modernization theories based on functionalism also showed limitations, faced with diverse paths to success and failures of modernization in different parts of the world.[3] Mechanistic paradigms of universalism were rendered obsolete, giving rise to the turn to culture and tradition. Multiple paths to modernity began to be recognized, and the positive value of tradition was invoked.[4]

Sociology in North America lost interest in macrosociology, which focuses on social structural changes, in the 1980s, and institutionalism emerged as the major paradigm.[5] The state, which had not been regarded as an important variable for social change, was again regarded in sociology as an important institution.[6] Regardless of different orientations in institutionalism, however, a macrosociological perspective was not a major concern. Even in the case of historical institutionalism, the primary focus has been political economy, as seen in the "varieties of capitalism" literature.[7] Divergent paths to capitalist development were explained by incorporating tradition and culture as an important basis for path dependence in historical institutionalism. Different contexts of industrialization are given serious consideration, but contextualization remains at the level of economy, short of engaging in macrosociology. Thus, the path to abandoning universalism has been uneven: while universalism has been questioned, the old habit persisted in institutional prescription, termed "institutional monocropping."[8] The state has been brought back and diversity in industrialization has been recognized, but with a heavy tilt toward political economy.

Some scholars have suggested alternative ways of approaching social changes through units other than class. Social anthropologists have proposed focusing on "non-groups" for analysis, and, at the same time, anthropologists have demonstrated the significance of persistent family and quasi-family units in modern settings.[9] In the meantime, relational sociologists have proposed a relational approach to society in which static and substance-based approaches are rejected.[10] Rational actor and norm-based models, diverse holisms and structuralisms, and statistical "variable" analyses are rejected. But these alternatives to structural units or analysis seldom question the pattern of industrialization; instead, they are considered under the assumption that there is only a single pattern. In short, although many alternative views of the non-Western world have been suggested and much effort to contextualize different facets of modernization has been made, contextualized approaches to social change under different patterns of industrialization have not received due attention.[11]

The current research on social change presumes that industrialization brings about universal consequences, whether in the West or wherever industrialization occurs. This assumes that industrialization is a powerful force that generates considerable standardization without leaving much room for variation.[12] Lack of differentiation of social consequences or the assumption of universal social consequences is closely related to the lack of differentiation of patterns of industrialization.

POLITICAL ECONOMY, THE STATE, AND THE CONTEXTUALIZATION OF INDUSTRIALIZATION

This neglect of interest in late industrialization among sociologists has multiple intellectual sources: the lack of differentiation of patterns of industrialization; lack of attention to the possible role of the state in social change; assumption of universal consequences of industrialization; and the ambiguous conceptual status of tradition in theories of industrialization.

Contextualization or differentiation of industrialization in respect to social change did not receive serious academic attention until the 1970s, when the political economy approach became a dominant paradigm of research. Neither the prevalent Marxian perspective nor structural-functionalist approaches paid much attention to the question, largely because market-based industrialization and economy were taken for granted. Thus, structural-functionalism and modernization theory regard social differentiation as a requirement that Third World countries must satisfy.[13] Similarly, Marxian thinking views the industrialization that occurred in the West as a model for underdeveloped economies.[14]

Interest in different paths to capitalism started with the political economy interpretation of late industrialization in the late 1970s and early 1980s, when a number of scholars reworked the Marxist conception of the state to show that its bureaucratic apparatus was different, and partially autonomous, from the interests of the capitalist ruling class.[15] A number of these young, left-leaning scholars wanted to "bring the state back in" as the prominent factor contributing to social and economic change.[16] They argued that the relative autonomy and administrative capacity of the state was an important feature in achieving societal stability and economic growth.[17] A number of scholars of Asia who borrowed these ideas empirically applied them to explain East Asian industrialization.

The first to do so was political scientist Chalmers Johnson, who posited the idea of the "developmental state," arguing that Japanese industrialization could be explained largely by the active intervention of the state in the economy.[18] Other scholars soon elaborated on this thesis for other rapidly industrializing East Asian economies, especially South Korea and Taiwan.[19] Sociologist

Peter Evans, who first suggested the importance of the state regime in Brazilian economic development, conceded that East Asian states were "stronger" than Latin American states and thus could industrialize faster and more successfully.[20]

The study of late industrialization was a clear departure from the past in terms of contextualization of industrialization. The most significant theoretical contribution of the political economy approach was the shift of analytical focus from society to the state. The relative autonomy and administrative capacity of the state was seen as important to achieving economic development, especially in newly industrializing countries such as South Korea and Taiwan.[21] Regarding social change in late industrialization, the political economy approach with its focus on the role of the state (vs. market) made expecting different patterns of social change possible by recognizing different patterns of industrialization. The dominant political economic perspective, from the view of the developmental state to the recent "varieties of capitalism" debate, has focused mostly on the state as an all-encompassing institution, on government policy incentives, and on state-business relationships.

However, in most studies of political economy, society is an object of analysis only insofar as it influenced economic changes. The political economy approach thus unwittingly left social and cultural aspects in the process of industrialization largely conceptually underdeveloped.[22] Institutionalism has not shown how the state's strong role in the course of economic development affects society. Indeed, society, tradition, and institutions have been frequently drawn on to explain economic institutions and development without much attention to macro-social implications.[23] The challenge in the field of political economy to the notion of universal patterns of industrialization was not matched by a similar one in sociology due to the declining interest in macrosociology in America in the 1980s.[24] What is needed is now is a sociological conceptual framework for understanding social and institutional changes in different types of industrialization.

INDUSTRIALIZATION AND SOCIALLY MEANINGFUL UNITS BEYOND CLASS

Class analysis as a heuristic tool has been assumed to be universally applicable to societies, regardless of the pattern of industrialization. Furthermore, with the spread of Marxism-Leninism in the postcolonial world, class analysis was uncritically adopted by non-Western intellectuals as a basis for explaining social change.[25] In the 1960s, this economic determinism began to be challenged by micro-historical-national analysis.[26] Historian E. P. Thompson defined class and class formation as a "social and cultural formation" that needs to be understood in relation to other classes through time and by works based on the specific experiences of workers in European countries during the 19th century.[27] Similarly, sociologist Michael Mann analyzed the impact of many different social, economic, political, and international factors on the formation of workers' image in major European countries.[28] He concluded that the image of workers had been affected by such macro political and social changes as economic fluctuations, religion, nation-building processes, militarism and war, and ideologies. Identity based on economic status had to compete in workers' consciousness with many other images: direct rivals such as deference, sectionalism, and a cautious pragmatism toward the employer and the multiple undercutting images of everyday life, derived from gender, age, family responsibilities, religion, region, and so on.[29]

The two approaches, despite differences in focus and the level of analysis, were critical of economic structuralism.[30] Both assert that class is not a fixed reality; rather, it is historically and culturally contingent on historical and cultural contexts in which people live. Class consciousness is formed not only at the workplace but also at home, in the community, and in social clubs and through leisure activities. Furthermore, the formation of class consciousness needs to be approached both synchronically at a certain place and diachronically at different time points. Workers thus began to be viewed from the perspective of their work environment and worker-centered experiences. Also, the premodern cultural and traditional legacies are important diachronically in the course of industrialization. Related to this is the understanding that society is composed of a "totality of social relations."[31]

The contextual interpretation approach to labor history and working-class movements in the West is also different from that of older economic structuralism. This emergent paradigm was critical of the conventional view that a working-class movement per se was regarded as an important indicator for formation of the working class. Not all workers participate in such movements as much as is assumed in economic structuralism, and thus the movements should not be considered as the critical expression of class consciousness.[32]

A Thompsonian framework is also applied to the study of working-class formation in South Korea. Nationalism, familism, national security, and harmony were identified as factors that the industrialized state mobilized to suppress the formation of class identity and class consciousness. The state inculcated Confucian values as a way to reinforce patriarchal relations in which docility and submissiveness to authority are encouraged, while anti-communism for the sake of national security discouraged class formation based on horizontal ties among workers. At the same time, workers' reinterpretations of Korean history and mass movements of intellectuals such as the *minjung* movement, which worked to build solidarity among workers, countered state influence on class formation.[33] While the Thompsonian framework recognizes class formation in South Korea's late industrialization in terms of the state's propensity to leverage such anti-class-forming factors as inculcated Confucian values, anti-communism, and paternalism, these factors are external to late industrialization. Put differently, the main question was whether to pursue social change while keeping class as a socially meaningful unit or whether meaningful units other than class could occur due to the institutional imperatives of late industrialization.

All the views take industrialization for granted, without specifying types within it. Even when the analysis of social change is conducted in the context of late industrialization, the social impact of lateness is understood within the confines of class. This book identifies and analyzes neofamilism as a distinct, socially meaningful phenomenon that resulted from interactions between economic developmental tasks and traditional institutions that had been brought back by the Korean state.[34]

TRADITION AND SOCIAL CHANGE

Tradition, according to sociologist Edward Shils, is something that is "handed down" and can take various forms. Tradition can be concrete, such as material objects, buildings, monuments, landscapes, sculptures, paintings, books, tools, or machines, or it can take form of cultural constructions, such as beliefs, images of persons and events, practices, and institutions.[35] Cultural constructs become tradition only when a pattern of assertion or action has entered into social memory over time.

Tradition concerns the relationship between the past and the present, especially the impact of the former on the latter. Approaches to the relationship between tradition and social change have undergone remarkable change over the past few decades, related to three different approaches to understanding tradition: structuralist, modernist, and postmodern. The structuralist approach highlights continuity from the past to the present and is indifferent to change or time. This view assumes that once structure is established, it seldom changes. The distinction between the past and the present is not regarded as significant. The modernist perspective is predicated on the discontinuity or disconnect of the present from the past. Modernity is about something new. The postmodern approach to tradition assumes neither continuity between the present and the past nor the abrupt rupture of the present from the past. It is open to various possibilities in terms of interactions between the past and the present and of their consequences.[36]

The definition of tradition varies across the three perspectives. The modernist and the structuralist approaches share a fixed notion of tradition. They differ in that the modernist perspective views tradition as being incompatible with modernity and thus assumes the ultimate fading away of tradition.[37] The structuralist perspective, however, assumes continuity without much change.[38] Tradition assumes the involvement of agents that are responsible for the continued succession from one generation to the next at least for three generations.[39] The agent can vary in form, from individual or family to the community and the state, depending on the nature of the tradition and the scope of its impact. Tradition connotes neither positive nor negative implications; in contrast, traditionalism refers to reliance on the past.[40] In this book, tradition is represented in institutions and values in which the state is the main agent in bringing them to the present. The postmodern approach has become prevalent, largely due to its flexibility in understanding interactions between the past and the present and for its focus on actors and projects in linking the past to the present, thus allowing a variety of patterns, such as creation, reinvention, and negotiation.[41]

MODERNIZATION AND TRADITION

In earlier versions of modernization theory, tradition is viewed as a hindrance to modernity, with modernity and tradition considered mutually exclusive;

thus, modernity is realized through the breakdown of tradition.[42] Tradition is thereby regarded as something to be mitigated (if not eradicated), leaving no room for tradition to play any positive role in modernization (industrialization). Earlier versions of modernization had been heavily criticized for reifying ideal types, based on the oversimplification of Western experiences. They were not attentive to historical contexts where traditional institutions, such as the family, played a role in the course of Western modernization.[43] Later versions of modernization theory focus more on historical contexts in which industrialization and modernization occur. Pluralities of tradition are recognized. Closer examinations of modernization revealed not only that the breakdown of tradition did not necessarily bring about modernity but also that breakdown of the family, community, or even political settings tended to lead to disorganization, delinquency, and chaos. Tradition, in fact, turned out to be conducive to modernization.[44] Further modernization may not bring about modernity, and even if it does, modernity can be partial or uneven.[45] Modernization ceases to be viewed as necessarily Western or American and is recognized as non-unilinear.[46] At the same time, the influence of traditional systems and values is understood as not necessarily receding with industrialization, and cultural change is viewed as path dependent. Modernization paths are accepted as diverse and not universal.

The emergence of newly industrializing countries (NICs) was empirical proof that industrialization and modernization can take various paths different from the West and that traditional institutions and values could be conducive to the acceleration of late industrialization in East Asian countries, as seen in literature on "Asian values" and "varieties of capitalism." Arguments that address tradition in relation to late industrialization stress that traditional Confucian values were conducive to generating economic wealth under state-led industrialization.[47] The role of the state in mobilizing these values has been acknowledged, but the main problem with this framework is how to approach values in relation to industrialization. Treating the values as an independent variable juxtaposes values and industrialization without analyzing the specific process and context in which values interact with industrialization through the mediation of the state. Furthermore, arguments that invoke so-called Asian values Orientalize those cultures and make them static, since such values are seen as timeless and unrelated to historical development. This imagined stasis cannot explain why the same values became the sources of developmental problems. Research on varieties of capitalism recognizes the role and persistence of traditional institutions in late industrialization.[48] Such literature focuses on institutions rather than only on markets and claims that markets operate within the confines of institutions. The institutions are the products of historical evolutions, and economic actors are constrained by the institutions. For example, labor relations are understood to have developed based on traditional institutions of a country (e.g., lifetime employment in Japan and centralized bargaining in Northern Europe). These historically evolved institutions are path dependent, so that institutions are not only mutually interdependent but also difficult to change.

Closely related to the varieties of capitalism is the invention of tradition, which concerns the redefinition of traditional institutions and values in the present context by certain social and political groups. The notion of invention transcends temporality and recognizes intentional human actions in dealing with traditional institutions and values. The invention approach recognizes various projects of political and social actors, including industrialization. Thus, this notion is particularly relevant to the understanding of social change in late industrialization. For example, inventions of tradition in Japanese industrialization include the redeployment of the Japanese traditional societal unit *ie* (家), or household, to the sphere of Japanese modern institutions, such as the factory, and the invention of paternalism for labor relations.[49] Other than the case of Japan, little study has been conducted on the role of tradition in late industrialization through interactions with the state's role and industrialization tasks.[50]

Modernization theories have thus evolved to recognize multiple paths to modernization and industrialization, considering historical and cultural contexts.[51] Multiple paths are based on the understanding that modernization (industrialization) is an effort by elites to mitigate their nations' "inferior" economic status and move toward equivalence with "well-placed" nations. Thus, the domestic environment, dispositions, and capabilities of elites are important in understanding modernization.[52] Also, the roles of traditional institutions and values vary, depending on the historical contexts and how and how quickly nations industrialize, as decided by elites. However, while the functional aspects of traditional institutions and values are recognized in different industrial sectors and institutions, little analytical attention has been given to how the state incorporates traditional institutions and values at the macro level, which gives rise to distinct social and institutional consequences.

TRADITION IN KOREAN SOCIETY

Structural-traditional approaches to the Korean case have in fact examined the role of traditional social relationships in shaping values and institutions in the process of industrialization and the implications of these relationships for class formation. One variation of this approach analyzes the responses of Korean society to the market, noting the persistence of collectivism based on the traditional concept of mutual help, rather than the rise of individualism and class identification.[53] The patrimonial modernization view of Korean society focuses on the continuation of traditional patrimonialism in political, administrative, economic, and social arenas.[54] In this model, Korean society is composed of privileged officeholders who dominate unorganized non-officeholders. This model draws a distinction between modernization, any attempt to improve a society's economic performance, and development, the maximization of a society's potential. Since Korea industrialized with its patrimonial institutions intact, according to this model, it is modernized but not developed. A similar model understands Korean society as one in which the masses stand alone and isolated from state authority.[55]

Korean scholars have noted the continuous existence of regionalism, school ties, and familism as a distinct feature of Korean society.[56] Micro-traditional approaches to the question of Korean social organization help reveal the role of personal ties in Korean society. Studies on Korean social networks have identified how familial, regional, school, and neighborhood ties are formed for specific purposes.[57] Anthropological studies have demonstrated the continued existence of traditional ties and behaviors throughout industrialization.[58] Studies of the urban poor have shown how traditional networks serve as a means of survival through supplementing income sources in construction and factory work.[59]

These approaches, whether the focus is micro or macro, have the following characteristics: Most of the studies are static, in that they take the existence and operation of Korean traditional institutions for granted, without specifying how and why these institutions persist in the context of late industrialization. Due to this lack of contextual consideration, these studies are limited to sectoral analysis without being able to consider structural implications of the persistence of the traditional institutions. What is important and relevant to this study is not the mere persistence of traditional institutions but why and how the traditional institutions had been reinforced in the process of late industrialization, with implications for macro social change. It is only through that clarification that the structural implications of the persistence and reinforcement of traditional institutions can be understood.[60] The alternate view presented here understands Korean society not in terms of class or stratum, or a state-society division, but in terms of neotraditional personal relations. State-led industrialization in Korea thus served to reinforce and strengthen primary groups, leading to a society best understood in terms of neofamilism.

SOCIAL CHANGE IN LATE INDUSTRIALIZATION

Late industrialization and its social, institutional, and political implications have a very lengthy scholarly pedigree, although they are not coherently approached. The initial focus on late industrialization began with the case of Germany. For example, the early 20th-century economist and sociologist Thorstein Veblen, who recognized the technological advantages of latecomers through borrowing from early industrializers, was also concerned with social, political, and institutional consequences of late industrialization. He highlighted urgency as an impetus for hurried state intervention in economic development, given the threats from warring European nation-states; in turn, the state is likely to emphasize strengthening military force. In regard to Germany's experience with late development, Veblen thought state intervention and initiatives to spur industrialization brought about dependency of the populace on the state, resulting in their passivity vis-à-vis the state.[61]

Economic historian Alexander Gerschenkron provided a more systematic view of institutional features related to late industrialization. Latecomers are bound to go through a path of development that is constrained by lack of capital and technology. In order to overcome these deficiencies, they are likely to adopt institutional forms and policy measures that are different from those of early developers, such as the roles of the state and banks, which establish ties with industrial enterprises as a way to mitigate risks that fledgling firms cannot otherwise afford to take. Although Gerschenkron also demonstrated that late industrialization requires ideologies for overcoming backwardness, his focus was limited to economic institutions.[62]

The strong role of the state in late industrialization goes beyond the economic level. An important factor in considering social implication of the strong role of the state is the persistence of already established social structures in the process of late industrialization. Once they are formed, social structures persist, possibly for centuries, and different structures and types display different degrees of this ability to survive.[63] Bendix specified that even after a considerable degree of economic change occurs, the consequent social structure will not take on universal forms, but will depend on the "pre-industrial conditions, the particular impetus to develop, the path which modernization takes, the significant difference that persist in developed economies, and finally with the impact and timing of dramatic events."[64] He further observed that the roles and functions of traditional groups, such as kinship ties and collectivism in the pursuit of late development, were compatible with modernization.[65]

Identifying why and how traditional social institutions and values, as Bendix observed, interact with late industrialization is crucial to understanding social implications of late industrialization.[66] Although the connection between late industrialization and traditional institutions has not been clearly analyzed, it is generally assumed that the involvement of non-market factors, such as the state, would make possible the continuity of traditional institutions. Or more generally, as Dahrendorf remarked, "each country assimilates industrialization into its tradition."[67]

Analyzing cases of late industrialization mandates careful attention to contextual factors such as the status of traditional social elites and the degree of the autonomy of the state. In Germany, strong opposition groups to industrialization such as Junkers existed, whereas in Japan, Korea, and the Soviet Union, opposition was either weakened or destroyed. In Germany, Junkers held many important bureaucratic positions, which set limits on developmental priorities and other policies.[68] In Japan, Korea, and the Soviet Union, bureaucrats were the main movers in industrialization without much resistance from society. In Japan, samurai-turned-bureaucrats enjoyed a high level of insulation from politics and society, derived from the state's exam-based merit system of recruitment. While there was no salient opposition group to industrialization in Japan, state officials, politicians, and intellectuals made judicious efforts not to lose Japanese traditional social structures and values in the course of industrialization. In contrast, in the Soviet Union and

Korea, the traditional groups and classes were either deliberately destroyed or lost political significance (due to the colonial rule), respectively.[69]

The state thus plays a key role in effecting group formations, and to the extent that the state is involved in late industrialization, non-market factors such as ethnicity, traditional ties, and nationality influence patterns of social change. When the market is the only operating institution in economic transactions, the ultimate object is "to acquire a certain object (amount of money); and the interest in the other person is minimal."[70] Class emerges purely as a consequence of market-based economic relations. When non-market factors are involved in economic relations, forms of human interactions and social formation go beyond purely class-based social ones. In short, state intervention in the economy brings about different rules of the game from those in market-based ones, and these different rules mean that human interaction patterns and institutional operations will differ accordingly, and in culturally distinctive ways.

A second observation of the literature is that social structures and ethos prior to late industrialization may persist and even play a positive role, contrary to what modernization theories have advocated. The literature also shows that late industrialization involved traditional institutions and values through state actions, although the specific mechanisms of the process and interactions between late industrialization and tradition are not clear. The peculiarities of social consequences of late industrialization have been insufficiently studied, while social and institutional histories of Germany and Japan have been treated as sui generis and not studied comparatively.[71]

Third, because of the paucity of successful late industrialization cases in the 1960s and early 1970s, debates between adherents of the modernization paradigm and its critics took on an abstract character, with few concrete references to actual cases. The inconclusive end of this debate was overwhelmed by the new paradigm of political economy in the 1970s, which focused more on economic outcomes at the expense of adequately capturing societal effects. This gap between studies of political economy and of the social consequences of late industrialization has widened and persists today.

Social science analysis has focused on the variations of class, avoiding consideration of alternatives to class as a unit for social change. More significantly,

German sociologist and political economist Max Weber's critical observation that class as a social outcome is based on market-based economic changes has not been heeded; rather, class analysis has been liberally applied to the cases of late industrialization with insufficient consideration of the role of the state in social change.[72] The same can be said about studies of tradition, which have stalled since the modernization paradigm was criticized in the mid-1970s and political economy studies began to focus on the roles of institutions and policies in explaining economic success of late industrialization. The role of tradition in social change at the macro level in late industrialization has thus remained unexplored; rather, tradition has been approached either in the context of management and industrial sectors or is considered external to the actual industrialization process. This book, building on studies that recognize and consider tradition, explores the social implications of state actions in the economy through the case of South Korea's late industrialization.

The Colonial Origins of Neofamilism

CHAPTER 2

Two diametrically opposed paradigms—orthodox and revisionist—have long dominated the study of Japanese colonial rule in Korea (1910-45). The orthodox interpretation, well known for its nationalist coloration, focuses on political dependency and arbitrariness, social control, discrimination, repression, economic exploitation, and the loss of cultural identity. Here the Korean Peninsula is considered nothing but a source of grain supply and industrial resources for Japanese economic development, as well as cheap (forced) Korean labor.[1] The orthodox approach argues that Korean traditions and cultural practices were suppressed under colonial rule, to the extent that Korean identity was severely threatened.[2] Any change in the colonial economy was thus "development without development," which was not relevant to Korea.[3]

The revisionist approach focuses on positive economic change, along with modern sociocultural influences spurred by Japanese rule. This view started against the background of South Korea's economic development since the mid-1960s with an intent to look for the colonial sources of development. Colonial rule is thus seen as the period in which modern capitalism was introduced and in which, regardless of the political context, the Korean economy developed.[4] Criticizing the orthodox interpretation as too nationalistic, revisionists argue that colonial rule left such legacies as capital and infrastructure accumulation, as well as a strong state and its modern bureaucracy, all of which became instrumental in designing and implementing Korean economic development plans during the 1960s.[5]

Despite fundamental differences, the two approaches share common methodological and substantive assumptions. The binary opposition between colonial exploitation and development does not allow room to understand the macro picture of the colonial Korean society and institutional developments, with its contradictory and uneven effects. Also, both are monosectoral in their scope of analysis focusing on a single sector, whether economic, social, or political issues, although they are primarily focused on economics. Each has also conducted a "war of case studies," typical of monosectoral analysis, in which one case of exploitation is countered by another case of development.[6] The two approaches lack a theoretical framework within which to understand the broader institutional and social consequences of colonial rule.

The exploitation-centered orthodox approach rightly emphasizes the suffering imposed by discrimination and physical and psychological controls, but it is not clear what the enduring psychological, institutional, and social consequences of this suffering are. In fact, most such studies are limited only to the colonial period itself.[7] Problems with the revisionist approach are equally serious. Revisionist research proceeds as if dealing with the economic sector per se is tantamount to dealing with the societal whole. It is overly reliant upon Western sociological concepts and categories to characterize Korean colonial society and thereby fails to acknowledge the unique aspects of Korean colonial society.[8] By linking the institutions of the colonial era to those in present-day Korea—that is, a strong state, economic development, and the emergence of management styles—revisionists commit the error of "reverse teleology," or reading history backward.[9] The studies cannot do justice to the complex nature of colonial institutions and societies as they actually existed because their interest in the colonial society of Korea is limited to explaining postcolonial economic development. It is not surprising, therefore, that revisionist studies have not paid attention to social institutions developed during the colonial era and how they have affected both society and subsequent patterns of economic development in Korea.

Efforts have been made to overcome the dichotomous views of colonial Korea by focusing on the more complex interplays of the colonial rule and society as a whole. Some studies have sought to understand colonial complexity in which different forces interacted, frequently causing unintended consequences.[10] This approach focuses on these interactions within colonial Korea and criticizes the orthodox school's exclusive focus on nationalistic interpretations of colonial social changes. These studies argue instead that colonial society was involved in constant negotiations and contestations among the national, colonial, and modern arenas. It attempts to show how the Korean people, though limited in leverage as individuals, were not simply coerced but interacted on their own volition with the other spheres. Thus, Japanese hegemony was viewed as not completely based on force.[11]

Being critical of the exploitation-development dichotomy, the trichotomy approach is more open and less deterministic in assessing the impact of colonial rule; by trying to understand the complexity of the colonial rule through interactions between the colonial, national, and modern arenas, this approach acknowledges the primacy of one of the three elements depending on sectors and situations and is sensitive to the occurrence of unintended consequences. As one author states, the analysis of the consequences of industrialization under the colonial rule "liberates us from nationalistic bias and the illusion that modernization was unilaterally positive. It makes us think how nationalism, modernity, and colonialism functioned in colonial society, not just in political, anti-imperialistic terms, but as a more complex process of social, economic, and cultural change fostered by emerging colonial modernity."[12]

The trichotomy approach provided a framework to understand colonial complexity, but as the approach is based on case studies to demonstrate the interactions among the national, colonial, and modern arenas, the analytical priority among the three is contingent and indeterminate, so it is not possible to formulate a macro conceptual framework. Since the interactions need to be analyzed in each case, such as education, labor relations, and administration, in terms of which among the three was predominant, this framework cannot provide a holistic picture of colonial society. That is, what is problematic in the trichotomy approach is the failure to recognize the centrality of the colonial compared to the modern and the national. It is clear from the previous discussion that Korean society under colonial rule has been understood and presented based on fragmented realities, and thus institutional legacies have not been systematically analyzed. This chapter, building on past monosectoral analyses, highlights the primacy of the colonial, rather than weighing it equally with the national and modern, and formulates a new conceptual framework to understand the distinct social changing patterns under colonial rule.

A CONCEPTUAL FRAMEWORK: COLONIAL SPACE

Approaching the complexities of colonial experience requires a clear understanding of what exactly constitutes the colonial situation. Sociologist Georges Balandier's remarks on Africa are still useful: "Any present-day study of colonial societies striving for an understanding of current realities and not a reconstitution of a purely historical nature, a study aiming at a comprehension of the condition as they are, not sacrificing facts for the convenience of some dogmatic schematization, can only be accomplished by taking into account this complex we have called the colonial situation."[13]

Balandier itemizes the components of the colonial situation as follows:

1. Domination imposed by a racially (or ethnically) and culturally distinct foreign minority in the name of racial and cultural superiority.
2. The linking of radically different civilizations into some form of relationship.
3. A mechanized, industrialized society with a powerful economy, a fast tempo of life, and a Christian background imposing itself on a non-industrialized, "backward" society.
4. The fundamentally antagonistic character of the relationship-between two societies resulting from the subservient role to which the colonial people are subjected as "instruments" of the colonial power.
5. The need to retain essential dominance both by outright coercion and the creation of a system of pseudo-justification and stereotyped behavior.[14]

This summary contains accidental and essential elements, with only the latter being applicable to the Korean case. Thus, while "Christianity" is accidental, the essential elements of Japanese colonialism in Korea include foreign dominance, in which the domestic majority is controlled by a foreign and numerical minority with the intent of economic and strategic exploitation, based on overwhelming coercive force.

Balandier's main concern—to remind us that ethnic components are crucial in understanding the colonial social whole in the African context—can be easily extrapolated to more general terms: to maintain discrimination through control, colonial authorities reserve the right to launch arbitrary interventions in any area of human action as the need for control arises. As a consequence, system boundaries among political, economic, and sociocultural activities become unclear and blurred under colonial control. Put differently, in the colonial situation, any activity can be made political through the colonial authorities' pervasive politicizing of even mundane issues. Such formulations underscore the unique aspect of colonial social changes, particularly social distortions caused by a foreign minority's rule over a local majority, discrimination, and an overwhelming reliance on force to maintain control.[15]

The blurring of system boundaries is closely related to colonial disequilibrium—the artificial blockage of intersystem spillover—which arises when conscious efforts are made to avert or forestall the flow of institutional change from one area into another. Without such efforts, control over the colony itself becomes difficult, if not impossible. For instance, colonial authorities permit economic activities only through prior considerations of political control and block the spontaneous emergence of social groups based on economic interactions. Thus, noncolonial differentiation among political, social, and economic sectors is artificially disrupted by an overarching imperial imperative and arbitrary political intrusion. According to sociologist P. Mercier, the most important factor in understanding postcolonial African society is the dilution of class relationships by the superimposition of the colonized/colonizer axis upon the subordinate society.[16] In the African context, tribal and kinship ties are the most salient factors affecting social relations.[17]

Blurred system boundaries and the consequent artificial blockage of intersystem spillover mean that system boundaries can shift, and thus we have the difficulty of understanding colonial society in single macro-structural terms. Put differently, colonial society is potentially so fluid that it cannot be conceptualized by any single "total concept."[18] To approach the colonial situation as a whole means understanding that colonial society is based on this fluidity. Thus, efforts to understand any one element—particularly such essential elements as foreignness, imposition, control, and unnaturalness—and to generalize the whole therefrom will not produce an accurate picture. We cannot expect predictable social consequences under colonial rule due to the whimsical nature of colonial power. Religion, for example, under the non-colonial situation is a matter of social and cultural domains, but under the colonial situation it could easily become a political issue. This is what I refer to as blurred system boundaries. Extending this logic, under the colonial situation it is not easy to anticipate social changes out of economic actions as is the case under the non-colonial situation. The abnormally fragmented nature of colonial society emerges here as a conceptual constraint on the discussion of colonialism by postcolonial scholars, diverting understanding of the essential dysfunctionality of colonial/postcolonial society into endless and sterile intellectual debate on accidentals. Thus, it is necessary to examine the intended and unintended social and institutional consequences of blocking change from one sector to another.

While all colonial societies share colonial disequilibrium, the contents of social consequences are unique to each colonial society because of their different historical contexts and colonial experiences. The artificial blockage of flows between sectors forces the analyst of colonialism to forsake many standard social science concepts and formulate new and context-specific social categories to understand a given colonial society. Colonial control may prove to be the link, for example, between the introduction of an apparently modern institution and a totally different consequence in another area. Thus, if class formation were seriously skewed because of anticolonial nationalism, the situation might require a different conceptualization applicable to a skewed class society. The concept of "class" either is subsumed by a higher-level, colonialism-specific category or acquires new and variable meanings depending on the individual characteristics of the precolonial indigenous society. What is treated as an independent variable elsewhere becomes a dependent variable here. In addition, the fragmented nature of colonial society ensures that concepts of social cause and effect can no longer be taken for granted. Instead, causal determinants become a highly empirical enterprise.

Taking into account the factors of colonial situation, disequilibrium, and totality, our general framework here may be expressed as constituting a colonial space. In this context, *colonial* denotes the fact that the colonial power sets the priorities, makes decisions, and implements them according to its goals, which may or may not be relevant to a colonial society, and *space* indicates the general field of human interactions where systemic boundaries are fluid and blurred. The term *colonial space* is used to help us to understand the colonizer's perception and imperative that colonial control involves and requires the uninhibited crossing of boundaries, in the same sense that a computer operator can freely erase and redraw his creations in cyberspace. Thus, in the non-colonial situation we may justly speak, for example, of political, social, or economic systems with relatively firm and definable boundaries. That is, space is used to denote a totality of living patterns where predictable system differentiation is inconceivable.

Colonial space therefore implies the usurpation of coherent structuration and system building through purposeful fragmentation and disequilibrium. Although there may be surface resemblances to economic or political space, these subordinated spaces are neither fixed nor stable. Whereas the non-colonial system is recognized and defined by its spontaneity, logic, and coherence, colonial space is recognized and definable by its artificiality, discontinuity, and arbitrariness. External coercion and control are substituted for integral necessity and organic development; force replaces the logic of cultural appropriateness. In colonial space, one cannot automatically rationalize or model any outcome according to necessary cause or effect. It is independent of human need and satisfies the latter only intermittently and accidentally. For this reason, it is meaningless to point to isolated instances in which indigenous populations may benefit accidentally from the arbitrary mechanisms and functions obtaining within colonial space.

In colonial space, foreign authorities manipulate system boundaries at will whenever their focus of interest and attention shifts, leaving the indigenous population helpless to affect the most fundamental conditions of their lives; colonial control is inconsistently and unevenly extractive, coercive, instrumental, and invidious, with shifting areas of benign neglect. At the same time, colonial authorities maintain artificial boundaries between one system and another depending on the outcomes of interactions with the colonized population. Colonial space in this sense is highly dynamic and volatile. Especially in the Korean context, where the old social structure was rapidly disintegrating, it was easier to block the emergence of such large-scale social units as class. Thus, colonial space produces groupings of people who share similar experiences but no organizational connections: they are arbitrarily grouped or regrouped according to their shifting functions within spaces defined by, and furthering the interests of, the colonial power.

The cumulative effect of such overwhelming arbitrariness on individuals, society, culture, and national and ethnic identity cannot be overestimated. More generally, the arbitrariness of colonial space preempts the possibility of acquiring a rational sense of cause and effect, divorces people's actions from results, and preempts almost every possibility of developing a meaningful sense of self-as-actor. All of these are the legacies of every once-colonized people, including Koreans.

THE FUNCTIONAL STRUCTURE OF COLONIAL SPACE

Given the colonialism-specific logic just described, colonial space can be divided into three areas: colonial superstructural space, colonial functional space, and colonial social space. These spaces differ primarily in (1) the changing threat perception of the colonial authorities with respect to such elements (i.e., does a given element comprise a greater or lesser degree of accommodation or resistance?); and thus, (2) the scope and intensity of direct colonial control over the relevant elements, in which control is equivalent to arbitrary interference and thus increased disequilibrium within the affected element.

Colonial superstructural space (CSUS) is the space in which colonial authority attempts, within the inevitable constraints of material possibility, to establish its hegemony over the colonized and to inaugurate institutional, societal, and ideological arrangements to implement and maintain such hegemony. Examples of efforts to further Japanese hegemony include the Japanese equivalent of the "white man's burden," the concept of the Greater East Asia Co-Prosperity Sphere, tendentious distortions of Korean history, the attempt to assimilate the Korean people into Japan through Japan-Korea unity and identity, anthropological studies treating Korean people as "natives," forcing Koreans to use Japanese names, and the imposition of Japanese emperor worship and the use of the Japanese language. Bureaucratic and other organizations that support such ideological impositions are also elements of CSUS. Acts associated with CSUS are undertaken where an element is crucial to the mechanisms of colonial control or where relatively less-essential elements are perceived to contain a relatively high degree of potential threat. In this sense, CSUS is the most colonial and least indigenous aspect of colonial space. Moreover, because high levels of surveillance and control over "normal" elements of an indigenous society are required to establish colonial hegemony, CSUS is innately hostile to indigenous institutions. CSUS is highly pragmatic and opportunistic, and thus its boundaries are exceptionally fluid and arbitrary, admitting blatant contradictions. For instance, the contradiction between treating Koreans both as cultural brothers deserving assimilation and as inferior "natives" never occurred to the Japanese colonizers, as indeed it need not have as long as the conclusion (the colonization of Korea) remained the same, irrespective of the premises.[19]

Colonial functional space (CFS) is the space in which the functional arrangements necessary to accomplish the primary goal of economic exploitation by the colonial power are made. It exists where the mechanisms of colonial society are either routine or the perceived threat level is low, or both. Here belong familiar phenomena, such as coerced economic policies and institutions, along with a coerced educational system and curriculum. CFS resembles sociologist Peter Ekeh's category of migrated institutions in that it often combines such foreign structures as centralized educational systems or modern production practices with indigenous traditional systems or divisions of labor.[20] Thus, this is a space that differs little on the surface from similar structures in non-colonial situations. What makes CFS colonial, however, is that the functional goals and means of implementing policies are those of the colonizers, who are again those empowered to make such decisions. The overriding goal is to maximize economic exploitation within a highly controlled and thus stable and friendly environment. The means involve incentives to engage colonial people in economic efforts but within an overarching logic of discrimination and material control. The colonial power needs to educate the colonized population to pursue its economic goals cheaply, and it limits the goals of colonial education to suit this need. As one former French principal of an Algerian school expressed it, the goal of French colonial education was neither to transform Algerians into true French nor to permit them to remain true Algerians, but to land them in a nowhere zone somewhere in between.[21]

Since arbitrary intrusions of coercive power are relatively rare in this space and the perceived threat potential of its elements is tolerable, maximum interaction and dialectic between colonizer and colonized occur under CFS. Here objective functional needs common to all societies contend and conflict with the imperative of colonial control. Regardless of the given colonial situation, both the colonized and the colonizer must engage each other in this space, either for survival or for exploitation. The need for colonial control frequently contradicts the logical consequences of functional activities, such as industrialization and education. The unintended emergence of colonial modernity raises thorny issues of control. The colonial power has to deal with workers in materially modern factories and graduates of modern educational systems. Colonial education, however tightly or expertly controlled, inevitably creates challenges arising from the cognitive disjunction between colonial discrimination and universalism acquired through education.

Colonial social space (css) can be regarded as a residual space that the colonial power leaves least controlled after carving out its position in the other two spaces. Empirically, css contains the traditional sector, but as Ekeh points out, even if the degree of control is relatively minimal, the remaining traditional orders suffer qualitative changes. Thus, what constitutes css must be empirically defined in terms of time and place. In the Korean case, the family system is a good example of css. As will be discussed, Japanese colonial authorities left the Korean family system virtually intact, not because they wanted to protect it but because it was much more beneficial in terms of colonial control to do so.

BOUNDARY BLURRING, CATEGORICAL VARIABILITY, AND ACCOMMODATION/RESISTANCE

These three categories—csus, cfs, and css—constitute the logical abstractions most suitable for expressing the peculiar nature of colonial space. In employing them, it is above all necessary to avoid the trap of conceptual rigidity. Attempts to categorize instantly confront the blurring of boundaries discussed earlier, which is an intentional and invariant feature of colonial systems. It should be stressed that the colonial power alone is the ultimate definer of the specific content of colonial space. Depending upon the colonial power's perception of colonial reality, spatial boundaries can move arbitrarily. This fluidity of boundaries makes it difficult to apply fixed sociological categories to the elements and makes each of them (e.g., religion) potentially a csus category. It is either the new goals set by the colonial power or the reactions of the colonized that determine new boundaries between the spaces without changing the fundamental imperative of economic exploitation. The fluidity defined by the colonial power is what prevents coherence between socioeconomic actions and socio-institutional consequences.

As noted, csus, cfs, and css are distinguished primarily by their innate importance to the colonizers and/or the perception of potential threat within subordinate colonial spaces. This raises the question of what constitutes the perception of threat in a colonial context. It is clear that colonial systems create a wide continuum on the axis of power, from the near powerlessness of the colonized to the vastly overextended power of the colonizer. In fact, within such systems there is only one primary category in which the colonized are guaranteed power to effect changes within the colonial system: the axis of accommodation/resistance. If the colonized accommodate, they ensure the stability of the colonial status quo (given that this stability is defined as the continuance of the colonizer's ability to effect arbitrary systemic change unimpeded by consideration of the colonized). If they resist, they force the colonizer to address their resistance, thus adding another level of control to that characterizing the status quo and possibly increasing the cost of maintaining the colonial system. This is the only invariant axis along which the colonized may be ensured anything resembling "power" in a colonial system.

Accommodation among the colonized is defined as accepting the premises of colonial rule and thus not creating the need for negative sanctions from colonial authorities. Resistance is defined as refusing to acknowledge colonial rule and thus either launching a struggle against it or remaining aloof from it. *Accommodating resistance* involves a willingness to participate in colonial spaces but with the ultimate goal of resisting or rejecting colonial rule; *resisting accommodation* means accommodating reluctantly because one has no other choice or to exert passive resistance. Thus, each space has two types of social consequences: institutions that function to support the space and human groups surrounding the institutions. Following Ekeh, the nature of institutions can take traditional, migrated, and emergent forms.[22]

In each kind of colonial space, responses are more or less clearly limited. CSUS, for example, largely empowers elite groups as it is defined by the colonial power. In this space, the colonized have limited options for reaction—either resistance or accommodation (collaboration)—largely because of the sensitivity of the colonial authorities to this space. From this space emerge nationalist groups who resist colonial control and collaborators who accommodate the colonial power. Here many different kinds of colonial institutions serve to promote justification of colonial rule, but all can be reduced to the category of colonial bureaucracy because almost all were implemented under its auspices.

In CFS, one can theoretically imagine four different kinds of reactions by the colonized: collaboration, accommodating resistance, resisting accommodation, or resistance. The predominant reaction pattern, however, is accommodating resistance. Since this space is about daily survival and gaining status, the colonized are obliged to accept reality. Once they are engaged in CFS, however, their reaction patterns among these four possible responses may vary, depending on their socioeconomic positions prior to colonial rule and their relationship with the colonial power. Even among capitalists under colonial rule there can exist different groups and orientations toward the colonial power. A uniquely conflicted and ambivalent ethos of Korean capitalists under colonial rule may also emerge, something not imaginable in a noncolonial situation: the feeling that they are betraying the nation, for example, is overshadowed by the justification that what they do ultimately serves to strengthen the nation. Workers whose jobs were created as a result of colonial economic changes are prevented from uniting to follow certain ideologies that may threaten colonial rule, and thus these workers' organizations become fragmented. Workers themselves also develop a colonial ethos that requires them to consider national liberation and their own interests simultaneously.[23] Because there are different kinds of capital and worker groups, making generalizations about workers is extremely difficult. The institutions of capitalist and market systems are strongly colored by colonial control.

Colonial education produces an ironic predicament. Those who accept colonial schooling show accommodation in doing so, but a modern education gives them the tools to resist the colonial power, either overtly or covertly. Likewise, the colonial power needs educated people but cannot support the institutional principles that modern education purportedly supports, such as equality, justice, and autonomy. The result is a seemingly modern educational system that is strongly influenced by colonial control: separate from the progressive curriculum, it features punishment and a strong authoritarian relationship between teachers and students.

CSS encompasses those traditional social elements to which the colonial authorities are indifferent. This might be called *resistant traditionalism*, in which the colonized use elements of tradition as symbols of resistance while the colonial authorities use those same elements for purposes of control. If CSUS and CFS facilitate challenges to many traditional values and institutions, CSS reinforces tradition unintentionally, a fact that is normally not well understood in most nationalist historiography. In everyday life, it may take what sociologist Erving Goffman called "secondary adjustment" in the context of total institutions, such as prisons and mental hospitals, in which, without directly challenging the authorities, "forbidden satisfactions [are obtained or permitted] by forbidden means."[24] CSS encompasses a majority of rural inhabitants, as well as the family system and the rural authority structure.

We have seen how complexity in the interactions between colonial rule and traditional institutions and values embodies numerous indeterminacies and contradictions. At a micro level, understanding the impact of colonial rule on tradition requires close examination of the intentions of the colonial rule and its consistency in relation to each case of traditional values and institutions. The macro picture regarding the relationship between colonial rule and indigenous traditions will take on a mosaic form in terms of degree of control and consequences.

EDUCATION IN COLONIZED KOREA

In analyzing education under colonial rule, the focus is not on detailing historical facts, but on how the colonial situation changed the institution. Colonial control constantly created contradictions between CSUs and CFs— that is, between colonial control and colonial modernity—and brought about long-lasting social consequences. In addition, traditional family ties, as discussed later, were paradoxically strengthened despite apparent socioeconomic changes. These examples help to explain the institutional legacies of the colonial era, especially in relation to Korean economic development. During rapid industrialization, strong high school and family ties were reinforced in Korean society and cannot be understood without examining their historical link to the colonial past.

Colonial Education, Colonial Control, and the Emergence of High School Ties

Within the threefold model outlined here, CSUs expresses most intensely the essential contradiction of the colonial situation. Colonial contradiction occurs wherever the strategies necessary for achieving the primary goal of economic exploitation automatically produce an increase in resistance from the colonized. Such contradictions are inevitable artifacts of the logic of colonialism. Contradiction is therefore the locus of conflict and transformation in the colonial context and the most obvious mechanism for generating unintended social consequences. An outstanding example of the contradictions inherent in CSUS is the institution of colonial education. In the Korean context, both the colonizer and the colonized needed formal education, but the educational enterprise took on contradictory significance for both sides. Education inevitably became one of the most intense fields of perceived threat to the Japanese authorities, as demonstrated by the broad scope of repressive measures taken against students and schools. This repression is what justifies locating education firmly within CSUS. More crucially, it was within the institution of education that the most uniquely Korean of postcolonial social artifacts was forged and refined—a network of social ties of mutual cooperation, trust, and assistance generated not between university students, as in Japan, but within high schools.

The colonizers needed an educated workforce to increase the usefulness of selected colonized persons and schools that would teach unquestioning respect for authority.[25] The colonized needed a modern education because it was one of the few paths to an economically successful life open to Korean people. The fact that the colonial power limited the number of educated Koreans speaks to Japanese sensitivity to the potential threat inherent in the educational process. Even though this strategy was designed to counter the contradictions of the colonial educational enterprise, it merely localized and intensified the paradox: "In fact, one of the functions of school selection was to make education scarce, thus increasing its value and the demand for it."[26] Unsurprisingly, selection was biased in favor of colonial loyalty over academic excellence. For the colonial authority to maintain "proper social distance" from the colonized for colonial control along with explicit discriminatory measures, neither too much acculturation nor too much local orientation was allowed in selecting students. Thus, there existed inherent limits to any assimilation policy.[27]

Nevertheless, the increased perceived value of education generated by this policy of creating an artificial scarcity could not help but also increase the perceived value of its unintended artifacts: knowledge of the wider world and increased political sophistication, both of which were intellectual tools suitable to affirming or debunking Japanese colonial ideology. By artificially limiting the number of educated persons, the Japanese unintentionally enhanced the perceived charisma and authority of persons who elected to use their newly educated minds in the service of Korean nationalism and anti-Japanese resistance.

Like the Japanese colonizers, the Korean colonized were ambivalent toward colonial education. They were fascinated by new knowledge generally and by knowledge of housing, agriculture, hygiene, and health in particular. Furthermore, they understood the need for knowledge in resisting the colonial power. However, the decision to receive a colonial education meant acknowledging colonial rule, a typical example of contradiction between accommodation and resistance.

The goals of technical education and raising loyal "servants for the emperor" in colonial Korea were persistently pursued despite several changes in the Educational Edict and Laws.[28] But the educational opportunities given to the Korean people were severely limited both in number and in content. In 1939, only 2 per 1,000 of the Korean population were enrolled in primary school, while the enrollment figure in Japan was three times as high; in high schools, 14 times; in universities, 111 times.[29] According to Gregory Henderson, a specialist on Korea, "In thirty-one years the number of students at all levels increased over sixteen times, from 110,800 in 1910 to 1,776,078 in 1941. Over 50% of Korean children were not receiving compulsory education. Only 5% of Korean children went beyond the primary education. At liberation little over 20% of Koreans had received any formal schooling, as opposed to three quarters of the Japanese population of colonial Korea; some ten times the proportion of resident Japanese as of Koreans had secondary education."[30] In addition, the geographic distribution of high schools is significant. As table 1 shows, only one or two high schools were established in each province. Limited educational opportunities in non-vocational high school can also be seen in the regional distribution of high schools.[31]

Over time, the attitudes of Koreans toward colonial education shifted from an initial general denial and resistance to gradual acceptance. In the early 1910s, when public primary schools were opened, the authorities had a hard time recruiting students because Korean parents refused to send their children to the new schools, partly from lack of understanding but mainly because of their resistance to Japanese rule.[32] This phenomenon was especially widespread among upper-class Koreans, who still insisted on the curriculum taught in traditional schools, such as national history and language; most students thus came from the middle or lower classes.[33] Thus, public primary schools were called the "schools of the poor."

TABLE 1. High schools (not vocational) in Korea, 1937

PROVINCE	PUBLIC		PRIVATE	
	M	F	M	F
Kyŏnggi	2	3	6	6
Ch'ungbuk	1	1	0	0
Ch'ungnam	1	2	0	0
Chŏnbuk	1	3	1	0
Chŏnnam	1	2	0	0
Kyŏngbuk	1	2	0	0
Kyŏngnam	2	3	1	1
Hwanghae	1	3	0	0
P'yŏngnam	2	2	1	1
P'yŏngbuk	1	1	1	0
Kangwŏn	1	1	0	0
Hamnam	1	3	1	2

Source: Chōsen Sōtokufu, Gakumukyoku, *Chōsen shogakkō ichiran.*

The situation shifted rapidly in the 1920s, however, when people began to show more interest in sending children to the new schools.[34] As the number of applicants increased, schools were able to begin selecting the students they wanted. This was a dramatic contrast to the previous decade when they had to make an effort to recruit students. There are three reasons for this change. First, at the end of the March First Independence Movement in 1919, most people began tilting toward the new ideology, which emphasized the need for self-strengthening to save the country (a compromise to full resistance). Second, because Korean society, regardless of Japanese colonial rule, was facing social turmoil with the decline of the old ruling class, the *yangban* order, people tried to reestablish their social identity through education. As Henderson aptly put it, "The hectic years of late Yi over, education came to be the only path for ambition, and all the schools were oversubscribed several times. For the young, forming one's ambitions in terms of the Japanese world and one's career within Chōsen became almost inevitable, even where resentment and hurt lasted."[35] Third, Korean society had maintained a long tradition in which education equaled a shortcut to governmental positions, giving people a high level of motivation to acquire it.[36]

High Schools and the Development of Resistance

Educational opportunities in colonial Korea were especially limited beyond the primary school level. Remarkably, throughout the colonial period, no more than 3% of primary school graduates went on to high school. Even as late as 1942, the number of Korean middle school and high school students was about 25,000, which was less than 2% of primary school graduates. Of the 1,218,367 Korean primary school graduates (girls and boys), only 28,878 were allowed to attend high school.[37] The number of public and private high schools increased from five in 1910 to 45 in 1935 (girls' schools included) and 142 in 1942 (including middle schools and Japanese schools).[38] High school graduates, especially public high school graduates, were nationally or regionally selected and well positioned to play important roles regardless of whether they received a college education. The importance of high school thus increased in Korea far beyond its corresponding value in Japan or China.

In this way schools, especially high schools, naturally evolved to become centers for the organization of Korean colonial society. This trend was strengthened by default, since on-campus associational organizations were difficult to establish under the strict Japanese regime and were often quickly suppressed once established. In addition, Korean high school students shared with their noncolonial peers all the customary traits of youth: a new awareness of the importance of social groups and the desire to participate in activities according to their own interests, undistracted by outside interests. The relative scarcity of university students, and particularly university graduates, meant that high school students were by default the most well-educated group in Korean society; they were among the privileged elite who learned "new knowledge," such as math, science, history, and geography.

As a result, high school graduates thought most keenly about, and most often articulated, the colonial contradiction, and they came to internalize the colonial contradiction in an acute and personal manner.[39] Having accommodated the colonizers in participating in this education, they found that the same education was equipping them with the knowledge and organization necessary to resist both this educational system and the colonial system as a whole. High schools were a theater of conflicting values, strains, and double standards. It must also be said that the crude Japanese propaganda dispensed in the schools, and the oppressive and heavy-handed manner in which ideologically doctrinaire teachers inculcated it, was often an education in itself, and the lesson taken by its recipients was one entirely unintended by the Japanese.

Student Movements during the Colonial Period

Several scholars provide a detailed recounting of the anti-Japanese Korean student movements.[40] It is sufficient here to provide a brief survey of these movements as they relate to the institutional and social consequences of high school education in Korean colonial and postcolonial society. Both the patterns and the content of student resistance changed over time in response to the transforming colonial environment. This environment is empirically quantifiable as educational policy and patterns of police surveillance, organizational suppression, and arrests change, but on a more immediate level, the transformation came down to the level of individual students and teachers and the increasing tensions between them. A crucial artifact of external organizational and policy changes was a corresponding transformation of high school students' sense of identity—what it actually meant to be a high school student. Increasingly, their identity began to formulate itself along the axis of resistance.

The March First Independence Movement was the first opportunity for students to demonstrate the significance of their political and social role. After that uprising, students played a leading role in nationwide political movements against Japanese rule in the June 10th Movement for independence incident in 1926 and the Kwangju student uprising in 1929. But as time went on, student movements became less centralized and began to be organized around local school groups. Before the March First Independence Movement, student organizations took the form of mutual friendship societies among students from various parts of the country who stayed in Seoul: for example, the North-West Student Friendship Society and the Honam (South-West) Student Organization.[41] During the 1920s, communism and nationalism became two ideological pillars, though the two were not easily distinguishable. During the 1920s and early 1930s, however, organized groups and slogans made the communist influence more visible. As colonial control intensified from the late 1920s until the end of colonial rule in 1945, the student movement, regardless of ideological orientation, became narrowly focused on school and secret organizations. Open protests organized by nationwide organizations gradually gave way to local high school and secret organizations.

The most popular form of student protest in this period was the strike, in which high school students refused to attend school until their demands were heeded. About half of the strikes between 1921 and 1928 were staged by high school students. More important, high schools throughout the provinces of the country participated: Kyŏnggi (77 strikes); South Hamgyong (51); Hwanghae (42); South Kyŏngsang (38); Kangwŏn (29); North Chŏlla (29); South Chŏlla (28); North P'yŏngan (24); South Ch'ungch'ŏng (20); South P'yŏngan (20); North Ch'ungch'ŏng (17); North Hamkyung (15); and North Kyŏngsang (13).

Student demands embraced various issues: educational facilities, the rejection of teachers, school administration, and ideological and nationalistic issues. Among them, the rejection of teachers and ideological and nationalistic issues loomed largest. From 1921 to 1928, there were 434 instances of teacher rejection and 74 ideology-related strikes.[42] Because most of the teachers were rejected for discriminating against Koreans or making derogatory remarks about Korean culture and Koreans personally, practically all strikes carried a strong anti-Japanese message. In the July 1927 strike, students of Hamhung Public High School issued the following statement to the school authorities demanding the removal of three Japanese teachers:

> Not only these teachers, but the rest of the faculty are merely preaching the superiority of Japan and the inevitable disappearance of Korean people. We do not regard this as a true education which would satiate our zeal for knowledge. For those of us who are dependent upon our parents for school, our hope has turned to despair. Schools have become forts; teachers behave as if they were military police and secret agents and plant fear into our minds. We come to school every day with a feeling that we are falling into a hole. As Pestalocci showed, educators should educate students transcending national boundaries, based on a humanitarian spirit.[43]

In addition, students were challenging parochial discrimination by way of universal principles, such as equality and human rights, which they had gained through colonial education, a clear contradiction of colonialism.

Student strikes continued throughout the 1930s. There were 107 strikes in 1930 and 102 in 1932, but as Japanese pressure and surveillance on students became more severe after the Manchurian invasion, the number began to decline, decreasing to 36 in 1935.[44] In the first half of the 1930s, students adopted the new strategy of establishing secret organizations, most of which, regardless of ideological orientation, were composed of high school students and graduates. It is likely that communist organizational skills, such as strict discipline, impersonalism, and secret contacts, were used by socialist and communist-oriented students in organizing secret organizations, but even nationalist-oriented students had to go underground because of heightened colonial control and surveillance of all organizations, communist or not, since the last half of the 1920s. Among 50 known secret organizations, 43 were organized around high schools. The same trend continued in the second half of the 1930s. Thirty-three out of 34 known secret organizations were organized by high schools all over the country.[45]

One regional situation and one specific organization will illustrate how secret organizations were formed and operated. The regional example is of Kyŏngsangbuk-do (Northern Kyŏngsang Province), between 1928 and 1945. There were 11 cases of secret student organizations that were suppressed by the police; their members were later prosecuted and sentenced (see table 2). Five different local high schools were involved in the Taegu student secret organization. The case became known to the outside world in 1928, when the police arrested 105 students. The organization was started in 1927 as a secret lecture series that nine Taegu high school students attended. After three lectures, 15 members organized the Sinudongmaeng (New Friend Alliance); thereafter, the group kept changing its name to secure secrecy, first to Hyŏgudongmaeng (Revolutionary Friend Alliance) and again to Chŏgudongmaeng (Red Friend Alliance). Ideologically communist in orientation, this organization was dedicated to the anti-imperialistic struggle against Japan.[46] The local example was the arrest of twelve members of the so-called Sangnokhoe (Evergreen Group) of Chunchon High School in 1939. All were graduates of Chunchon High School, all but one were classmates, and all were from either the same city or province. The main charge against them was organizing a secret organization and a reading group to promote nationalistic spirit through reading books and discussions. After four classmates agreed to start the organization, they recruited their junior students at the same high school. All were sentenced to jail terms from one and a half to two and a half years for violation of the Public Order Maintenance Law.[47]

A regional analysis tells us that in most cases secret organizations were formed by a single high school but rarely by several schools jointly. In the case of the Sangnokhoe, it can be surmised that personal connections based on trust were the link rather than schools themselves. The data show that none of the secret organizations could last long under the watchful eye of the colonial police. Most organizations were small in scale, ranging between two and 40 members, so as to evade surveillance of the police, and most were started by classmates of the same year, again to secure trust. Thus, even though they were dealing with national and international issues, their regional backgrounds were narrow and uniform. When these groups were forced to limit membership to close schoolmates, they inevitably took on a local or regional focus—yet another aspect of the colonial paradox.

Placed in a wider perspective, the institutional significance becomes clearer. The colonial situation in Korea was an environment in which associational, publication, and speech activities were severely limited by various regulations, such as the Police Law, the Domestic Security Law, the Newspaper Law, the Publication Law, the temporary order for carrying subversive documents, the Assembly Order, and so on. Violations of the notoriously restrictive Domestic Security Law, which covered political activities, increased substantially.[48] Under such circumstances, modern associational groupings were rare, and it was difficult to find large-scale social units as sources of identity. As Henderson remarked, "Underneath the top level, the long history of Japanese surveillance with its war finale worked its own will on the form of those organizations outside governmental mobilization. The Japanese were superbly informed and had excellent distribution of information within their hierarchies. Korean groupings were in constant fear of infiltration and discovery. In self-defense, the small group, the friendship circle, the gang, sworn in brotherhood, became the social unit."[49]

High school ties cemented under colonial rule added special meaning to the fact that students shared these formative years in their lives. They also shared a sense of mission, aspirations, frustrations, and guilt about what they could or could not do about their colonial situation, regardless of whether they participated in the secret student movements. Furthermore, given the limited sources of identity foundation outside school, solidarity based on

TABLE 2. Secret student organizations in Kyŏngsangbuk-do

SCHOOLS	TYPE OF GROUP	DATE OF ARREST	NUMBER OF ARRESTS
Taegu High School Taegu Commerce Vocational School Taegu Agricultural High School Taegu Middle School Private Kyŏngnam school	Taegu Secret Student Coalition	April 6, 1928	105
Kyŏngbuk Taegu Normal School	Teacher and student secret association	January 26, 1932	37
Kyŏngbuk Provincial Normal School	Secret organization	March 30, 1933	6
Kyŏngbuk Ŭisong Primary School	Secret organization	August 28, 1933	2
Kyŏngbuk Public Agricultural School	Red Students Vanguard	December 2, 1933	27
Kyŏngbuk Taegu Normal School	Tahyok Party study group	August 1, 1941	300
Kyŏngbuk Taegu Normal School	"CareFree Garden"	June 29, 1943	2
Kyŏngbuk Taegu Public Commerce School	Taeguk Dan	May 23, 1945	36
Kyŏngbuk Andong Public Agricultural High School	Korean Independence Restoration Study Group	March 1, 1945	41

Source: Kyŏngsang-buktosa P'yŏnch'an Wiwŏnhoe, *Kyŏngsang-buktosa*, 457.

common school experiences and locality became a much stronger basis for trust and mutual help. In this regard, it is important to note that even local landlords tried to establish school networks to protect their own interests.[50]

The suppression of nationwide student organizations led to the gradual narrowing of the organizational and political space for anti-colonial resistance. The fact that general and universal issues had to be discussed in secret local organizations illustrates the important theoretical point of colonial disequilibrium: colonial control produced students with modern knowledge who had to rely socially on very restricted school and regional ties to express their views. This case also points out the dangers of monosectoral analysis because it illustrates dramatically how colonial modernity combined with the need for control can bring about one consequence in one sector and a different one in another. Within the concept of colonial space, Korean colonial education started as a part of CFS, then challenged CSUS, and finally ended up in CSS with the institutional legacy of social relations based on high school ties. The long-term implications of this transformational dynamic can only be understood in conjunction with the consequences of colonial control.

YANGBAN AND COLONIAL RULE

Both nationalistic and revisionist interpretations share the perception that Korean society underwent many changes as a consequence of the introduction of new institutions and policies under colonial rule. Important institutions and policies were the introduction of new administrative mechanisms such as the *myŏn* (the lowest unit of administration), the land survey, new agricultural cultivation techniques, the new school system, industrialization, and urbanization. Among them, the impacts of the land survey were the most far reaching: land with ambiguous or disputed ownership was transferred to state ownership, further impoverishing the peasants and creating more migrant workers. The nationalistic approach highlights the exploitation and destruction of traditional cultures, whereas the revisionists emphasize development. Conspicuously absent in both interpretations, however, is any characterization of what survived these changes after colonial rule. After all, Korean society remained predominantly rural in terms of economic and population structures at the end of colonial rule: in 1938, 85.5% of the Korean population lived in rural areas, and agriculture accounted for 46.4% of the economy.[51] Those tenant farmers who could not be absorbed into industrial sectors remained in the rural villages.[52] How are we to understand this vast portion of the population in social and institutional terms?

Many studies have focused on the economics of the landlord-tenant relationship as it affected this majority of the Korean population.[53] There is no denying that this relationship was important to the survival of tenant peasants. But although their suffering was from time to time expressed in the form of landlord-tenant disputes, for the most part peasants had to endure and abide by the larger institutional mechanisms that the landlords and the colonial power jointly created and maintained. Those mechanisms were reinforced by the traditional family system that the *yangban* landlords perpetuated. For this reason, both the changes in and continuity of the Korean family system cannot be understood adequately without considering the adjustments that the old ruling class, the *yangban*, made in the context of the village. At the same time, the colonial power's strategy with regard to the traditional family system should be taken into account.

The *yangban* class had been disintegrating as a cohesive group since the late 19th century due to the limited land and the increased wealth of non-*yangban* class. Its decline manifested itself in a further "yangbanization" of society. For example, in the Taegu region at the end of the 17th century, *yangban*, commoners, and untouchables constituted 8.3%, 51.5%, and 40.6% of the population, respectively; in the middle of the 19th century, they were 65.5%, 32.8%, and 1.7%, respectively.[54] This drastic enlargement of a once-exclusive status effectively meant a "cheapening" of status value. Officially, the *yangban* system based on official positions and land ownership was abolished in the 1895 Kabo Reform, and colonial rule arrived in the midst of status confusion. With the weakening connection of the *yangban* to the land, middle-class people and the commercial class began to emerge as new landlords. Thus, the extent to which the old *yangban* survived as landlords is very important in understanding the continuity of *yangban* domination during colonial rule. One survey shows that during the colonial period, 73.8% of the large landlords came from the *yangban* class, demonstrating a high rate of successful adaptation to a new situation, whereas commoners and merchants constituted 17.1% and 7.3%, respectively.[55] But because many official titles were bought up at the end of the Yi dynasty, the non-*yangban* proportion could have been much higher than 25%.

Thus, Korean colonial society can be characterized as undergoing a confusing shift in that the *yangban* were politically meaningless (at the central level), surviving economically but undergoing shocks, yet socially still influential, as one Japanese source described: "With annexation, the old status differentiation was abolished, and the trend is gradual disappearance of class distinctions, but the *yangban*, who used to enjoy privileges and respect, are still respected, maintain influence, and are scattered around various places in the local areas."[56] Because social categories and economic categories frequently did not match, the colonial authorities used both economic and social categories in approaching Korean colonial villages: landlords versus tenants, on the one hand, and *yangban* villages versus commoners and other types of villages, on the other.[57]

The degree to which the concept of *yangban* ceased to function differed widely depending on the area. At new schools, for example, the concept was rapidly fading.[58] Many public high schools kept detailed records of their students' status backgrounds until the 1930s; thereafter, economic criteria became more important. Following our concept of colonial space, it can be surmised that in CFS the disappearance was faster, while in CSUS and CSS it was quite slow. From the perspective of young students, for example, their world must have been confusing enough: at school they learned modern knowledge, and in the village, their identity was traditionally defined by which family they belonged to. The *yangban* landlords in the villages throughout Korea maintained this notion of the Korean family.

The phenomenon of *yangban* resilience is well documented by many Japanese sources. Most often cited is the extent and persistence of clan villages and extended families during the colonial period. One study pointed out that Korea, unlike China and Japan, was unique in the predominance of clan villages, which numbered 15,000 in 1940.[59] The extended family was an important component of these clan villages. Usually large, up to more than 20 members, the extended family was based on strict patriarchal power and blood ties; in 1930, the number of extended families was 4,747.[60] These clan villages and extended families underwent many changes as a consequence of economic changes and war mobilization during the 1930s and 1940s, but they did not disappear completely—not surprising considering the size of the rural population at the end of colonial rule.

These clan villages were under the strong influence of *yangban* landlords because they had been established by prominent *yangban* several centuries earlier. Clan villages were viewed as conducive to the colonial rule by the Japanese authorities. Although clan villages had negative aspects, such as exclusiveness, conservatism, and concealment of crimes, these demerits were outnumbered by their merits: unity based on clear leadership, progressive education, facilitation of agricultural policies, and *kye* ("rotating mutual help").[61] In short, "clan villages are excellent self-governing entities."[62] This reputation did not come without some effort from *yangban* landlords, who were actively involved in local political, administrative, and economic affairs. The *yangban* served on various advisory committees and associations related to schools, forestry, the Red Cross, fire stations, and farmers' associations and were leading members of financial institutions and *myŏn* chiefs. They utilized their positions to strengthen their status in clan villages by promoting clan activities, such as clan assembly and the publication of books on clan genealogy.[63]

The *yangban* contribution to clan organizations served several purposes. First, it protected *yangban* interests in that the trust they gained helped them to play an intermediary role between the colonial power and the villages, thereby enhancing their status in dealing with the colonial power for their own gain. Second, their activities took on a facade of preserving Korean tradition and a quasi-anti-Japanese outlook and also consolidated clan cohesiveness. And sometimes they performed social welfare functions that were not available outside clan villages. It is no wonder that one Japanese visitor in 1922 observed that "looking at the *myŏn* system, one cannot but feel that there is a clear confusion between Korean tradition and the new colonial system. Although I have not visited many places, it is impossible to deny that *myŏn* officials are members of the big extended families of the local areas. It is especially so in the southern part of the country. Changing local decentralization into clan-based decentralization is against the true spirit of the *myŏn* system."[64]

The *yangban* landlords' adaptation strategies may not have been possible without the colonial authorities' judicious calculations as to how to treat Korean traditional institutions. The colonial authorities chose landlords as their social base, and the overlapping of landlords and the *yangban* class meant that the colonial authorities already permitted the continuity of the tradition in the service of economic interests.[65] In fact, the colonial authorities were extremely cautious about changing Korean customs, being wary of possible reactions and resistance from conservative forces in Korea. Therefore, they decided to take a gradual approach that was particularly visible in the introduction of new civil codes. Thus, except when absolutely necessary, Korean customary laws were permitted to continue.[66] The core elements of the Korean family system prohibited the changing of family names, marriage between a couple with same family name, and the adoption of a child with a different family name from the adopter. Attempts were made to change these statutes in 1940, but no fundamental changes were made to the old system.[67]

There is much evidence to support the notion that Japanese colonial authorities had decided to take advantage of the old system to maintain control. According to one contemporary Japanese account, the village Alliance for National Mobilization, *ku* (subunits of *myŏn*), and various *gye* organizations were based on village organizations that were frequently part of, or related to, clan organizations; in many cases, one person occupied multiple leadership positions in these organizations. In *ku* meetings, village elders and Confucian scholars were invited and seated ahead of officials.[68] Also, in the selection of village leaders for the New Guidance for Villages project, family background was the second most important criterion. Those with *yangban* family background were preferred.[69]

FAMILISM IN COLONIAL KOREA

Average peasants other than the *yangban* landlords and those who went abroad or migrated to Manchuria had to survive mostly in the context of the extended family, and there are several reasons why they remained family centered under colonial rule. First, near-complete lack of alternatives meant that agriculture became much more labor intensive and thus demanded more family cooperation. The whole family, including children, had to work to survive: "In early spring poor peasant children had to plough, care for the cows, fertilize the crops, and feed the animals, all tasks forcing them to work so hard their bones did not grow straight. They could not go to school and had to spend their life illiterate."[70] Second, social welfare was poorly developed under colonial rule. Unlike in Japan, until 1944 emergency aid in kind and supplementary support were made only to those in need who lacked a family; therefore, family members had to support one another.[71] The customary range of support was extensive, reflecting the extended family system: parents, grandparents, spouse, sons, daughters, grandsons and granddaughters, brothers and sisters, first uncles and aunts on the father's side, nephews and nieces, cousins, second cousins, grandparents on the mother's side, and wife's parents, in that order.[72]

Another reason for the reinforcement of the family system among peasants was education. It is well known that Korean families sacrificed whatever they had to educate sons (especially the eldest son). During the colonial period, families below middle peasant status had a difficult time supporting even primary school attendance, unable to pay even 1 won a month for education.[73] Thus, they were frequently in debt. The other side of the coin was the perception of success. If one family member was successful after finishing his education, the success was regarded as that of the whole family, and the successful person was obligated to support the family. One Korean author of the 1920s commented that if one received an education, he could make money, achieve power, and let his family's name be known to the world: his family could enrich itself through his influence.[74]

Thus, for the average poor Korean peasant, village life during colonial rule probably meant that politically he had to be silent, economically he had to suffer under tenancy, and socially he could not liberate himself from the village-wide clan order and close family obligations. While he might have heard or read about (if he received an education) the outside world, in reality he was confined to his narrow village boundaries, feeling a great gap between the cognitive world and the world that he actually experienced because his radius of travel was limited. As modern Korea historian Andrew Grajdanzev notes, "The per capita annual average number of trips in Korea in 1937 was 2.1; that in Japan was 25.1, twelve times as many. If only 69,000 workers commuted to work every day, 341 days a year, this would account for the 47 million trips made in a year. This clearly shows how little the life of Koreans is affected by the railways. It is interesting to note that the average fare paid by passengers in Korea was 78 sen as compared with 22 sen in Japan."[75]

The Japanese colonial authorities clearly decided to promote their economic interests by not disrupting the traditional authority structure and family relationships they encountered in Korea. In fact, they exploited the preexisting social structure. This strategy is in marked contrast to the serious discussions underway in Japan about how to redefine the status of the Japanese family in line with pursuing modernization tasks since the early Meiji. The main issue was to what extent modern Western elements could be incorporated and, conversely, how Japanese traditional *bushi* (samurai) family norms and systems should be retained. At the end of this long deliberation, the final decision was to retain the basic tenets of the Japanese household unit—namely, the *ie*—as the first and fundamental element of Japanese society.[76] Further discussions involved how to reflect these values in schools. The social and economic status of the family was constantly revised and redefined to cope with new tasks, such as the labor movement and ideological currents. In short, family issues in Japan were viewed as a part of broader sociopolitical issues in redefining Japanese tradition.[77] This discussion started in 1870, and after two decades of preparation, a new civil code was finally put in effect in 1890. In contrast, no such discussions took place in colonial Korea, largely because maintaining the old system was beneficial in securing Japanese economic interests and control. For the Korean people, maintaining family traditions was regarded as an act of passive resistance to the colonial authorities. So, there was neither a conscious effort to change the family system, as there had been in Japan, nor, thanks to the colonial situation, any spontaneous flow of economic change into family structure and functions, as there had been in England. In short, the Korean family system is a case of colonial non-change par excellence.

POSTCOLONIAL AND POSTWAR KOREAN SOCIETY

After colonial rule, the Korean War (1950-53), as with other wars, provided forced opportunities for mobility as people were separated from the comfort zone of their villages and towns to mingle with those from other regions. It was especially so with soldiers who were drafted into the military and war. Also, land reform undermined the economic foundations of the former *yangban* and landlord class. However, that did not mean that they did not exercise influence at local levels. Based on their superior educational backgrounds, they were able to make their presence strongly felt in local and national elections. They thus were able to incarnate "re-traditionalization" of the past practices of maintaining familism at the local level.[78] Economic and political situations did not allow clan organizations to maintain their past pattern of solidarity based on land ownership and political influence. After the Korean War, clan organizations were considerably weakened, but they did not lose control altogether. They were able to gather their own strength by taking advantage of new political opportunities such as local and national elections.

For average people, life after the Korean War was hard, even for daily survival. Many people were dislocated during the war, especially those who came from the North to the South. However, in an economy without much industrialization most Korean people resided in rural areas. Even when they had to migrate far from their home turf, they ended up either in other rural areas or in impoverished urban settings. Although it was similar in rural areas, people in urban settings were especially left without state protection and mostly lived as nuclear families on a daily basis, although their perception of the family still remained broader than just the nuclear family. Politically they were put into a situation in which they had to directly confront bare state power without any intervening organizations mediating between themselves and the state.

Socioeconomically, Koreans were helpless in the absence of outside support, further reinforcing a family orientation whereby the sense that the family is the last resort for survival was quite salient. Of course, in this new type of familism, the scope of the family considerably narrowed to one close to the nuclear family. Although villagers participated in clan-based ancestor worships throughout the year, for their day-to-day survival they were left to fend for themselves. As such, the conception of family was differentiating in that the looser sense of a clan system and the stronger solidarity among immediate family coexisted. In this context individuals' identities were not strongly established. Rather, individuals lived with a strong sense of being a "family individual," indicating a strong sense of collectivity. It is no wonder in this context that family was the strongest source of trust, as one survey result showed. For example, to the question "whom do you trust most?" 53.8% of the survey respondents said it was immediate family, and only 14.2% said it was a neighbor.[79]

The nature of familism can be characterized as a result of passive adjustment to a new environment during and after the war. Many people experienced ideological division within the family as well as villages. Villagers had little choice but to trust family. Through this experience, the conception of family entailed a limited one, based on blood, which presumed mutual support for survival. In this sense, this sociocultural pattern of sociability can be understood as neofamilism. This new type of neofamilism took on a more negative quality in that rather than being based on community cooperation and moralities, it focused on securing the maintenance and protection of narrowly defined family interests.

However, Korean society in the run-up to the 1960s was not one based on fixed structure but rather one based on relationships. This is largely due to the colonial legacy of the blockage of social changes in one area from spilling over into other areas. For instance, due to the suppression of labor unions under colonial rule, economic changes did not significantly affect changes in labor and society in general. This aspect of colonial rule had a profound impact on the post-liberation Korean society. Liberation for Korean society meant liberation from the imposed colonial modern facade rather than internalized modernity, and with liberation Korean society released suppressed feelings against the colonial power, as expressed in spontaneous violent eruptions and group conflicts.

To be specific, about 80% of the population was engaged in agriculture in the 1950s. The land reform in 1952 brought about the shrinking economic and political influence of landlords and the *yangban* class, which in turn resulted in weakening of clan organization. However, as local election results indicated, the political influence of *yangban* and landlords did not completely disappear. Their social influence was quite considerable, to the extent that they were able to maintain social distance from underprivileged groups, such as former commoners and untouchables, through marriage among themselves. In the 1950s, marriages occurred mostly within the same village or adjacent ones, and thus mobility was limited. Economic activities were also limited to cooperation among relatives and family members.[80] Those who could not make a living in rural areas, those who were not inheritors, and northerners who came to the South flocked into Seoul. In consequence of the land reform and Korean War, the number of extended families (families with more than three generations living together) reduced from 30.4% in the entire population in 1930 to 11% in 1955. The number of households with fewer than 10 members increased to 88.7% from 67.3% in 1930. However, this change did not mean that the influence of the traditional family disappeared completely. Due to a weak social welfare system, strong educational aspirational hopes of parents for their children remained strong, based on familial ties. Nuclear families in urban areas and those migrants from rural areas still maintained ties with a base in their hometowns.[81]

Overall, until the 1950s Korea experienced a low level of economic differentiation, while politically and culturally Korean society remained largely unchanged. There did not exist a strong ruling class that could resist the strong state or exercise influence over it. Only groups based on school, regional, and blood ties contended for access to the state. Opportunities for economic and social mobility were quite limited, and most people lived in poverty. However, individuals' high aspiration for social mobility—the achievement of which would depend on neofamilial connections—were dormant and ready to erupt given the opportunity.

Colonial social changes are closely related to colonial control, causing colonial disequilibrium in which the social implications of change in one area are not fully played out in others. The concept of colonial space emphasizes how problematic it is to apply fixed conventional sociological concepts and categories to the colonial situation. The inherent contradictions within the new Korean educational system introduced to facilitate colonial rule caused students to challenge the colonial authorities, and the coercive responses of the colonial authorities in turn brought about unexpected social solidarity among a narrow school-based elite. In addition, the Korean traditional clan structure and family system were used to promote the interests of the colonial authorities. These cases clearly show the unsatisfactory nature of monosectoral analysis; we need to think instead about how changes in one sector affect the interspatial priorities set by the colonial power. The cases also show how difficult it is to make predictions about social change under colonial rule.

This chapter's analysis also leads to the following observations. First, from the perspective of traditional institutions, what is truly colonial is to deprive indigenous people of opportunities to invent traditions. Second, as such, the ways in which Korean traditional institutions were approached were inconsistent, uneven, and partial, as inventing tradition under the colonial rule was largely done for purpose of colonial control. What is truly colonial was that there was no systematic approach to reviewing and inventing traditional institutions and values. Consequently, results of efforts to invent traditional institutions varied from unintended consequence, transformation, confusion, and abolition.[82] The colonial approach to Korean traditional institutions left consequential legacies in the postcolonial Korean society, including the failure to invent Korea's own tradition by its own leading group, such as *yangban*; the confusion caused by the colonial power in which it was not easy to identify Korean traditional institutions and values; and the pervasive perception that undifferentiated sticking to traditions was regarded as a way to preserve Koreanness. Also, the breakdown of the *yangban*, as the leading group in Korean society prior to the colonization, entailed the absence of a coherent group that would lead the discussion of what constituted Korean traditions. Such postcolonial confusion was further aggravated by the premature importation of Western institutions and values because of Korea's incorporation into the Western world upon liberation in 1945. Korea's industrialization was implemented in the midst of such a complex historical background in which the top leader and Korean society had difficulty in identifying their traditions or tended to view traditions as something older, prior to colonial rule.[83]

Last, and most relevant to this study, are the theoretical and practical implications for postcolonial Korean society. We need to know, for example, how the institutional legacies of the colonial era have interacted with Korean patterns of economic development. Korean politics is played out in the regional arena; ownership of the Korean chaebols is notoriously monopolized by families; and most elite behaviors are based, as in the colonial era, on high school ties. Furthermore, high school ties are intrinsically regional, and the importance of the locality-bound family has serious implications for regional identity, especially given the scarce sources of multiple identities. High school ties, strong familism, and regionalism were the main sources of social trust at the time of liberation and provided the social conditions for the state-led economic development of the 1960s. Korean society was anticipating the emergence of "neofamilism," which developed during the economic development of the 1960s and 1970s from the interaction between the state and the social legacies of colonial rule. Thus, the social legacies of colonial rule led to path dependence in the course of postcolonial social and institutional development.[84] This is why we need to carefully trace the colonial sources of the present phenomenon of neofamilism and how they have interacted with Korean economic development rather than simply impose Western sociological categories on Korean society.

The State and Tradition

CHAPTER 3

Park Chung Hee, a lieutenant general with a complex personal history, came to power through a coup d'état in 1961. Born in 1917 as the last of seven children to a poor family in Kumi, a town in the southeastern region of the Korean Peninsula, he grew up under the Japanese colonial education system. He attended Taegu Normal High School, which trained elementary school teachers, and afterward entered the Manchurian Military Academy, which was run by the Japanese government. He also completed a short training course at the Japanese Military Academy in Japan and was appointed an officer in the Japanese army.[1] At the end of colonial rule, he reentered the Korean Military Academy and became an officer. He was soon thereafter implicated in the Yeo-Soon revolt in 1948, a communist-instigated uprising, and was released from active service. With the help of his military cohorts, he remained in the military as a civilian until he was reinstated in 1949. Park held a deep distrust toward and contempt for civilian politicians of the time for their corruption and cliquish behaviors and planned a military coup in 1960 but had to postpone due to the student uprising in April 1960 against election rigging by the Seung Man Rhee regime in March of that year. The Chang Myon regime, which came into power after the ouster of Rhee, could not exercise strong leadership, leaving the political situation extremely unstable. Park masterminded and successfully launched a coup d'état in May 1961 and took over the chairmanship of the Supreme Council for National Reconstruction. The military Junta issued the Six-Point Revolutionary Pledge to Korean society, the main themes of which were strong anti-communist posture, anti-corruption, strong commitment to economic development to overcome poverty, and pro-Western orientation.[2]

ECONOMIC BACKWARDNESS AND INFERIORITY

Park's sense of Korea's backwardness was grounded in his negative view of Korean history. He lamented that despite good natural and human endowments, the country had not been able to exert a visible international presence, largely due to domestic problems: "It is five thousand years since our founding father established the fatherland. Our nation is based on one of the few pure races in the world, but our history has been one of internal division, mutual hatred, and conflict in the midst of poverty and idleness. Although sharing pure blood, God-given land, and unique culture, we have not been able to establish a nation worthy of the name. Reflecting upon our past, our history has been one of insult and bloody tears. How could such a nation have dared to look outside?"[3] His view of 20th-century history highlighted the loss of independence and loss of self-reliance in economy and culture: "Our history beginning with the 20th century had been one of hostile external environments and currents, colonization for 40 years, import of decadent culture since the end of World War II, the Korean War and consequent confusion, poverty, and two revolutions . . . This disgraceful half-century of our history witnessed offenses against our good customs and ideological and political confrontation, lavish spending and waste, idleness, vanity, mutual hatred, and jealousy, which all gave rise to a society of instability and emotional harshness."[4]

Finally, Park addresses the psychological and social impacts of this negative history: "The masses, due to prolonged suffering, turned into expressionless semi-slaves and passive human beings who are used to idleness after many years of living with sadness and resignation. The pattern of land ownership that had dominated Korea throughout history dampened the idea of private ownership and dried up desire for reconstruction."[5] Park's negative view of Korean history and sense of national backwardness started with his observations of the domestic situation:

> Our five thousand years of Korean history from the Old Koguryo period through the Three Kingdom Period, the Unified Shilla, the post-Three Kingdom, the unified Koryo to the Yi dynasty of five hundred years were one of retreat, unsophistication and stagnation. When did we ever dominate others by crossing the border, seek for

reforms and change by bringing in ideas and materials from abroad, demonstrate and extend our unified power to the outside and exalt our autonomy through special industries and culture? We have been pushed and purposelessly assimilated into foreign cultures and could not make an inch of progress from the primitive economy. We spent most of our time on fratricidal infighting. It was a history of microcosm of the feudal society which was characterized by idleness, remissness and stagnation.[6]

He goes on to highlight Korea's relative backwardness vis-à-vis specific regions and countries, particularly in comparison to Western Europe:

What did our ancestors do then? At the end of the Chosun dynasty, factional struggles among *Yangbans* under Sunjong became chronic, the court was in chaos due to the intervention of the queen's family in politics, and bureaucrats were frantically engaged in exploiting masses. Peasant revolts were pervasive, the culmination of which was Hong Kyung Rae's rebellion in 1811. How could it not fall behind Europe? It would not be an exaggeration that Korea is falling behind Europe by more than 150 years. We should make a much greater effort to catch up for the 150 years. Are we indeed determined to do so? We should clearly remember that the rehabilitation of Germany is not merely a miracle. I urge our people to awaken at this point.[7]

It was obvious to Park that Korea was falling behind Japan and that Korea was relatively backward compared to most newly born Third World states.[8] He noted, "Fortunately, our patriotic forefathers and the victory of the united forces brought liberation sixteen years ago. However, indulged in the jubilation of being independent we failed to complete a self-reliant system. Instead, while we were wasting our time, more than forty underdeveloped countries gained independence and joined the UN. But we have not come out of backwardness, remaining underdeveloped and suffering from poverty, hunger and chaos."[9] Finally, he pointed to social impediments to modernization and industrialization in Korean history: "It would not be an exaggeration to say that we have lived in a particularistic society where we judge people by the level of wealth, better education, family backgrounds of the past and the present, religious identities and political party affiliation."[10]

These lamentations are well documented in Korean political historiography.[11] What bears emphasizing is that Park did not dwell on the backwardness of Korea but mentioned historical failings to heighten the sense of urgency to move forward:[12]

> There is no progress and prosperity in human life that can be achieved without shedding blood and sweat. At a historical turning point, the clouds of retreat that cover our fatherland and history of our nation will not clear up unless we who live today make life and death effort to free ourselves from the bridle of disgrace and backwardness.[13]

> One year to us is nothing but a moment in eternity. It is only a fleeting moment. But what we can do during the time will make a serious and critical impact on our journey to the modernization of our fatherland.[14]

> We are facing the threat of aggression externally, and internally we face the enormous national task of the modernization of our fatherland. Even seconds and minutes are precious and not to be wasted. Waste of an hour today may bring 10 years' underdevelopment. Unity today may bring about a great takeoff later.[15]

Park's sense of backwardness and urgency led to overly ambitious goal-setting in economic development.

AMBITIOUS ECONOMIC GOAL-SETTING

Politically, Park was in a hurry to establish and demonstrate his political legitimacy through tangible achievements after the military coup d'état. The Korean economy prior to the industrialization drive was in a dire condition, with the agricultural sector taking up 47.3% of the national economy. The proportion of industrial production was only 12% of the entire economy, and the bulk of it was in light industry (79%).[16] Personal GNP per capita was a meager 80 dollars. The number of production units was only 8,628, and the number of workers was 221,000.[17] The Korean War further devastated industrial facilities. The scale of damage was enormous: the number of enterprises that were damaged was 10,436, 24.9% of which was in manufacturing sector.

The total war damage in the industrial sector amounted to 40 billion won (in current prices) and more than 4,700 buildings were destroyed, with infrastructure damage reaching 19.8 billion won.[18]

Korean business prior to the mid-1960s relied heavily on the state for capital and technology. The state's influence on business had become strong since liberation, especially through the privatization of seized Japanese-owned properties. The scale of Japanese property was enormous: 822 Japanese companies employed 59.6% of the entire workforce.[19] As such, enemy properties drew interest from business sectors and beyond by using various ties to gain access to the state. The properties were privatized without following any systematic guidelines: personal connections and exchange for political support were used, with prices far below market prices.[20]

Likewise, foreign assistance was also allocated in an arbitrary fashion. Between 1945 and 1961, Korea received 3.1 billion dollars' worth of assistance from the International Cooperation Administration (ICA) and other agencies, some 30% to 40% of the national budget.[21] Along with a high level of dependence of business on the state, the import substitution strategies taken by the government worked to give rise to pervasive corruption throughout Korean society. Import substitution strategies involved various protection measures for the domestic market, such as differential custom rates, import licensing, and foreign currency allocation. The supply of loans at low interest rates was also rampant and constituted favoritism. Even before the industrialization drive in the 1960s the dependence of business on the state and the consequent corruption was well established.[22]

Under such circumstances Park set unrealistically high economic goals and emphasized achieving them quickly. Ambitious economic goals can be seen both at macro and micro levels. Park complained that the annual GNP growth during the first half of the 1950s was a meager 4% to 5%, while it was 6% for the second part of the decade. He then set much higher goals. The planned annual growth for the first five-year economic plan (1962–66) was 7.1%, but the actual growth was even higher at 8.3%. This pattern repeated for the second and third five-year plans: for the second five-year plan, the actual growth rate was even higher, at 11.4%, than the planned growth rate of 7%. For the third five-year economic plan, the planned growth rate was 8.6%, while the actual growth rate reached 11.2%.[23] Park's sense of urgency and ambitious goals are reflected in how quickly economic structure changed. While it took almost two centuries

TABLE 3. Structural change of the English economy

	1688	1801	1851	1901	1935
1. Agriculture	40	33	20	7	4
2. Industry	21	23	34	40	38
3. Trade and transport	12	17	19	23	30
4. Other	27	27	27	30	28

Agriculture: fishing and forestry; industry: mining, building, and manufacturing; other: government, defense, domestic service, professions, rents of dwellings, etc.
Source: Peter Mathias, *First Industrial Nation*, 315.

for the agricultural sector's share of the national economy to reduce to 20% in England, this transformation only took 20 years in Korea. Likewise, in England the industrial sector reached 34% of the economy in 1851 from 21% in 1688 (table 3). In the case of South Korea, the industrial contribution to the economy was 18.6% in 1961 but increased to 41% in 1980.

Park also sought to dramatically increase export volume. As tables 4 and 5 show, annual targets for export were constantly upgraded by Park's urging, without consideration of the previous year's record. This ambitious goal-setting is clearly seen in the gap between the upgraded export targets and the actual performance. Between 1962 and 1966, with only one exception for the year 1963, the actual export record was always below the targeted goals.[24] For example, the original plan for 1971 was 550 million dollars, but it was increased to one billion dollars at the export promotion meeting presided over by President Park in June 1966, despite voiced warnings that this was overly ambitious.[25] Testimonies of the officials who worked under Park also lend credence to his sense of urgency: "My nickname was export minister, and day and night I was preoccupied with the idea that export is only way to survive, and thus put all of energy into promoting export. But then what made all these miraculous records possible? First and foremost, it was possible due to the faith in and determination on export promotion. Without the monthly export promotion meetings in the presence of President Park it would not have been possible to achieve consecutively 30% annual growth of export."[26] Park not only expressed his ambitious goals in words; they were also reflected in his personal interventions in personnel issues and economic goal implementation that set the peculiar tones for state-business relations.

TABLE 4. Changes in export goals, 1962-65 (in million dollars)

YEAR	ORIGINAL PLAN TARGETS	CHANGED TARGETS	ACTUAL RECORDS
1962	60.9	–	54.8
1963	71.7	–	86.8
1964	84.1	120	119.1
1965	105.6	170	175.1

Source: Sanggongbu, Muyŏk chinhŭng 40yon, 189.

TABLE 5. Changes in export targets, 1970-80 (in million dollars and rates of growth)

YEAR	PLANNED TARGETS, AUGUST 21, 1970	REVISED TARGETS, FEBRUARY 20, 1972	REVISED TARGETS AFTER YUSHIN REFORMATION, NOVEMBER 7, 1972
1970	1,000 (42.3%)	–	–
1971	1,312 (31.2%)	–	–
1972	1,682 (28.2%)	1,750 (29.4%)	–
1973	2,119 (26%)	2,200 (25.7%)	2,350 (30%)
1974	2,583 (21.9%)	2,650 (20.5%)	3,000 (27.7%)
1975	3,076 (19%)	3,140 (18.5%)	3,750 (25%)
1976	3,522 (16.7%)	3,650 (16.2%)	4,600 (22.7%)
1977	4,091 (14%)	4,160 (14%)	5,600 (21.7%)
1978	4,584 (11.1%)	4,650 (11.8%)	6,800 (21.4%)
1979	5,007 (9.2%)	5,070 (9%)	8,250 (21.3%)
1980	5,356 (7%)	5,500 (8.5%)	10,000 (21.2%)

Source: O Wŏnch'ŏl, Han'gukhyŏng kyŏngje kŏnsŏl, 7:487.

ECONOMIC DEVELOPMENTAL STRATEGIES AND IMPLICATIONS FOR STATE-BUSINESS RELATIONS AND SOCIAL CHANGE

Based on Park's sense of the country's backwardness, it is necessary to closely examine state actions, business strategies, and interaction patterns between the state and business in order to understand the social and institutional implications of state-led late industrialization. State actions include the perceptions of general economic conditions, basic strategies to overcome backwardness, and specific interaction patterns between the state and business through implementation. More specifically, Park's specific strategies to develop the economy and major economic policies need to be analyzed in terms of their implications for social change.

What set Park apart from the previous regimes in South Korea were his personal interest and involvement in economic development.[27] Park's strong interest in economic development lies in part due to his general sense of the country's economic backwardness and inferiority and urgency, but it was also politically motivated in that because he took power by military coup, visible early economic achievement would consolidate and enhance his political legitimacy. However, given the corrupt and small-scale economy based on import substitution, Park was deeply concerned that Korean business was not up to the task of rapid industrialization in terms of the size of capital, management styles, and strategic capability and thus thought the state should provide the business sector with detailed plans and incentives. This strong commitment to and anxiety over business success set a general tone for economic decision-making and implementation. Such a protective posture over business also gave rise to a peculiarly close relationship between the state and business in Korea, which in turn had serious social and institutional consequences.

Park's prioritization of rapid economic development was put into specific economic plans.[28] The most consequential strategy for rapid economic development was the adoption of export promotion in the early 1960s.[29] Export promotion strategy was a clear departure from the import substitution strategy in the 1950s under the Rhee regime, and its social implications were, accordingly, quite different. Principally, export promotion strategy contrasts with import substitution strategy in economic opportunities, the state's role, and the degree of interaction between business and the state. With import substitution strategy, the market is primarily limited to the domestic sphere, and business opportunities thus have less potential for expansion. Naturally, the number and scale of business and workers employed in industrial sectors tend to be less under import substitution strategy than under export promotion strategy.[30] As a limited number of business enterprises compete for the domestic market, competition is fierce and businesses seek state favors even through illicit means, which tends to give rise to frequent corruption.[31] Due to a smaller scale of business, however, the scale of corruption under import-substituting industrialization (ISI) may be less than in economies under export promotion. The social impact of economic policies is also limited as fewer business enterprises compete for state favors.

Along with greater dependence of business on the state, ISI strategies taken by the government led to pervasive corruption throughout Korean society, although not at the scale seen in an economy based on export promotion. The ISI strategies involved various protection measures for the domestic market through such policy tools as differential custom rates, import licensing, and foreign currency allocation. Also, the supply of loans at low interest rates was rampant, and the fierce competition to get such loans engendered favoritism, as interest rates in the curb market were much higher than state-sponsored ones. Even before the industrialization drive in the 1960s, the dependence of business on the state and the consequent corruption was well established.

However, under export promotion strategy, business and job opportunities proliferate as the market expands to the international level. Thus, competition under export promotion strategy is not necessarily a zero-sum game around the domestic market. As such, economic policies have a much wider scope than those of ISI; they involve a larger number of enterprises and thus a larger portion of society. The state is much more open to society under export promotion than under import substitution, due not only to increase in business enterprises but also to much-expanded state activities. More important, participation in international markets through export sets certain standards in business behaviors, particularly in dealing with the state.[32] In providing state subsidies to business, the state can base its decisions on export records, an objective criterion for achievement. As under ISI, business competes for state favors—but the degree of arbitrariness is bound to be more limited, because export based on the international market sets limits to corruption, as business cannot easily control international market prices.

The problem that Park faced in promoting exports was that Korean industries were not ready for export in terms of scale and marketing capability. Thus, the state prepared extensive economic developmental plans in which the government and business closely cooperated, although "the principal engine" was private enterprise.[33] The state's perception that business is weak led to detailed measures to promote industries that could compete on the international market. The state's attention to enterprises to ensure their success did not stop at the level of initiation but extended to the resolution of possible operational problems. Timely intervention by the state was crucial in case enterprises face crisis, as one official who was closely involved in industrial policies remarked:

> Even after factories are built and start operation, the government needs to actively support them whenever they are in crisis. Without governmental support, factories in late industrialization countries cannot survive and need to be supported through various means, such as administrative guidance and measures and new legislation. Timing is critical in rendering support. Timing in the development of industries in late industrialization is like treating patients in an emergency room. Wrong timing is the same as seeking medicine for patients after they are dead. In Korea, monthly economic reports, export promotion meetings, and quarterly reviews of economic performance are prepared to monitor the economy. Also, the state head makes it a rule to attend ministry briefings at the beginning of the year and participates in-person in directly revising, supplementing, and supporting policies. There is no country in the world that takes more timely, strong, and effective measures for business than South Korea.[34]

The following testimony of a former official at the Ministry of Commerce and Industry (MCI) clearly indicates how the state perceived the capability of Korean business to compete on the international market when preparing development plans:

> Q: I heard that business people came to your ministry to ask for guidance in preparing business plans; what was the level of business in preparing plans and strategies?
> A: Whether big or small business, their level was quite below that of bureaucrats. They were not in a position to conduct plans on their own. They could not catch up with ministry officials, and they asked state officials to guide them.
> Q: How did they regard the ministry's policies?
> A: They just followed state policies, as their level of knowledge on

market management and access to technology is low. They followed the instructions of the minister, vice-minister, and doctorate holders in the ministry who had broader knowledge. Institutionally and administratively, business was completely dependent on the state, as business was not capable of planning. The role of business was to follow the state. The Ministry of Commerce and Industry was to play the roles of CEO and adviser and the role of business was just to follow it.[35]

The state's perception that business was not ready for international competition led to various far-reaching supporting measures for business, including in the areas of taxes (6), tariffs (5), financial incentives (11), and others (17).[36] In addition, many administrative incentives were adopted, such as special economic zones and utilities.[37] The fact that the state was ready to support business with so many incentives laid the foundation for close state-business ties, which was unique to Korea.

Prowess in exporting became a necessary condition to do business in Korea, as it guaranteed the government's support. Export policy was nothing but export support policy.[38] This had serious social and institutional implications. Under this broad export-first principle, bureaucrats of relevant ministries held consultative meetings with businesses and requested their cooperation while also offering various inducements, such as loans without letter of credit to cut export time and lowering consumption and corporate taxes. What was so distinctive about the Korean style of supporting business was that government export promotion measures were targeted not at industries as a whole, but at specific firms or enterprises within industries.

The enterprise-based approach to development refers to policymaking and implementation that targets specific companies. Due to limited financial resources, budgetary constraints, and shortage of foreign currencies, the state cannot take a comprehensive and balanced development approach where major industries are developed simultaneously. Instead, the state prioritizes industries in terms of early and visible success. Once certain industries reach a certain level and scale of export success, the state moves on to other industries. In the case of Korea, capacity to export was regarded as an important criterion in prioritization of industries. This targeted development strategy is based on the assumption that in countries where business cannot decide its own direction, due to lack of scale, know-how, and finance, the state ought to set the direction and provide means for development. The state decides which chaebols are to be awarded licensure of certain factories to be built, sets priorities for development, and prepares financial plans and measures to protect them after they are put into operation. On the specific process of enterprise-based approach to development, one former official remarked as follows:

> "Without export no support" will be the guiding principle. Those companies that cope with export targets will be supported and those that cannot will be excluded from support. As such, support should not target industry but specific companies. The number of companies to be supported was to gradually expand rather than start with a large number of companies. Once selected, companies are supported fully as long as they continue to export. If capital is needed, they will be supported either with Korean currency or with foreign currency. The state and business need to be one entity. Businesses will be exempt from tariffs for imported materials that are to be used for export. Interest rates will be lowered. Operation funds will be sufficiently provided. Technical support will be provided free of charge. Inspection tour abroad will be permitted. Finally, when export targets are met, there will be reward with medals and commendation.[39]

The modes of applying incentives adopted by the Korean government gave rise to distinct state-business relations that had serious social implications. Incentives can be either positive or negative—providing or withholding various material incentives, respectively—and can be applied either consistently or arbitrarily. Largely due to the sense of urgency and the need for rapid economic change, the Korean government's approach to distributing incentives was arbitrary.[40]

The enterprise-based approach was closely related to the state's (i.e., Park's) protective view of business: that rapid industrialization would not be possible without the state's direct role in planning, implementation, and protection measures. On this a former official at the time recalled that as projects were successfully implemented one by one, the cumulative linkage impact of those successes vitalized industries as a whole. It was akin to retaking military strongholds previously overtaken by an enemy. From this Korean model of late development, new businesses and industries were created. This model was applied to successive industries beginning in 1964, such as the development of small to medium-sized enterprises (SMEs), petrochemical industries, electronics industries, and heavy chemical industries.[41] Consequently, a uniquely close relationship developed between the top leader, state bureaucracy, and business under the so-called Korean-style economic developmental model in which the state monitored, assisted, and rewarded business to compete on the international market. On the overly protective state approach to business, one former official close to Park reminisced that "the state nurtured business as if a mother breast-feeds her child."[42] This peculiar state-business relationship in which business is autonomous and responsible for its own success while the state guides business with all possible support set the stage for the patterns of state-business interaction in decision-making and implementation, which in turn would have serious implications for social change.

DECISION-MAKING, IMPLEMENTATION, AND SOCIAL IMPLICATIONS

Social implications of state-business relations can be better grasped by examining how the general principles of planning and implementation were put into actual practice. The state's strong protective view of business manifested itself in different areas of economic planning, such as decision-making and implementation, as well as at different levels, such as presidential, ministerial, and business. Korea's economic developmental process was distinct in that President Park was directly involved in not only major decision-making, but his intervention was far reaching, even to the details of implementation.

One example of Park's role is his vision for the development of the auto industry as early as the late 1960s, and in the early 1970s, he hinted at the need to develop heavy chemical industries: "On May 30 in 1972, President Park participated in the monthly export promotion meeting where there was an exhibition of auto parts for export. After this meeting President Park called me in his office and asked, 'What should be the next industry for development?' I said that would be heavy chemical industries, and the first priority was auto industry."[43] Park proposed either unrealistic goals from the beginning or revised original goals upward both to enhance and consolidate the legitimacy of his regime and to meet the standards of the export market. For example, the idea to promote petrochemical industries was already decided at the time of Park's annual inspection tour of the MCI in 1965. A task force was organized to pursue the project in July 1966, and a panel for the development of petrochemical industries was established in November 1967, with a series of discussions conducted regarding the projection of demand, industrial sites, and scale of production. The key problem was that due to the narrow domestic market and capital constraints it was not easy to compete on the international market, even if industries were established. With the suggested production capacity of 30,000 tons for the domestic market, it was not possible to compete on the international market, where the standard was 300,000 tons.

Park decided to build factories with 100,000-ton capacity, beyond the 60,000 tons that was regarded as optimal, and set the prices of petrochemical product at 3.9 cents per pound, which was competitive vis-à-vis the United States (4 cents), Taiwan (5.5 cents), and Japan (4.5 cents). All the costs, including utilities, were adjusted to the production cost, which was arbitrarily set for international competition. All the measures for support, such as taxes, financial support, and other subsidies were provided to the fledgling industries. This is a typical example of how Park turned from the conventional economic thinking that factories should be built based on current level of demand. Instead, production capacity was determined based on the consideration of international competition.

Park's ambitious goal-setting was not limited to the scale of production capacity but was also salient in setting export targets. At monthly export promotion meetings Park made strong appeals for increases in export. The president's intervention was also quite extensive beyond export issues, largely because of the uncertainty facing a latecomer economy as well as the president's own sense of urgency. One indicator for this was the frequency of President Park's field inspection and guidance: from his inauguration in 1963 to 1965 he visited local sites 43 times, with the total elapsed time of his visits amounting to 109 days, which is more than one day per week on average.[44]

In addition to facilitating the initiation of new industries, Park played an important role in securing financial and other resources that were needed to implement the decisions already taken. One such example concerns the promotion of the electronics sector. Park strongly advocated for the need to develop electronic industries and encouraged the business community to participate in them. But Park also personally ordered the minister of economic planning to secure necessary funds to support the industries.[45]

The state was eager for economic change and thus regarded business as a means to reconstruct the state. The boundary between the state and business was quite thin. The state tried to support business with every possible means to expedite economic changes. In turn, the state mobilized human resources on behalf of the private sector by arbitrary means, intervening in staffing in the business sector to realize state goals through business. The private sector itself adopted state goals as its own, and thus the sense of identity in goals was established between the state and business, as a businessman testified:

> Q: How did the state-business relationship evolve as the two sectors worked closely together?
>
> A: Bureaucrats and business managers belonged to similar age cohorts in many cases and frequently shared the same sense of mission to modernize the country. They coexisted with the will to realize state goals. Bureaucrats were not so much preoccupied with their private interests. The sense of "cooperation" existed between the state and business. The general mood was that the two sides shared scarce resources.[46]

President Park's ambitious goal-setting was directly reflected in lower levels of decision-making. Park pushed ministers to raise economic goals, who in turn exhorted directors and section chiefs. Whenever the low rung of bureaucrats came up with reasonable goals to achieve, high-ranking bureaucrats had to revise them for higher ones, as the following recollection indicates:

> The first draft for the seven-year plan was based on safety, and I called in the department chief of the textile industry and told him, "You are a commander of special forces for export. If we cannot increase export, we will go bankrupt." The revised plan was truly ambitious. The export of sewing products for 1963 was 86,000 dollars, which was increased to 4.03 million dollars. The target for the seven-year plan was set at 50 million dollars. It meant a 12.5 times increase during the seven-year plan

period. . . . 50 million dollars was an amazing amount given the fact that it was almost a half of the total export in 1962.[47]

Park's constant upgrading of export targets is significant for understanding the social implications of this export promotion strategy. Park's ambitious goal-setting caused a high level of anxiety and scrambling on the part of bureaucrats in charge of export, who had no choice but to accommodate these orders. To achieve ambitious goals that Park set, bureaucrats became inextricably involved in firm-level production processes, as so many problems and obstacles had to be cleared for business: "In order to achieve excessive export targets, the head of the textile department had to set monthly targets and allocate the targets to different companies and went around to encourage and supervise them to realize the goals. Factory people and ministry officials frequently worked through the night, and ministry officials came to know details about factory operations."[48]

Pragmatism and Particularism in Implementation

President Park showed strong interest in the details of industrial policy implementation and played an important role in accelerating policy implementation by mitigating bottlenecks, especially in carrying out export targets. He issued detailed instructions and orders to make sure various export promotion measures were correctly implemented. For example, he urged bureaucrats to facilitate meeting export targets as quickly as possible by taking all necessary measures to support business. Accordingly, both business and bureaucrats were under scrutiny, based on actual export records. Thus, export performance became an important criterion to evaluate the merits of both business and bureaucrats.[49] At the same time, Park kept urging bureaucrats to be flexible in applying rules and regulations in dealing with business as long as it helps business increase exports. The flexibility in applying rules and regulations in turn gave room for capriciousness on the part of bureaucrats in dealing with business.[50]

Along with realizing export targets, the speed at which export targets were met was critically important. Virtually in every order he issued, Park always emphasized the speed of implementation. Revised policies and guidelines had to be completed in a matter of a few days.[51] This sense of and need for speed was strongly felt among bureaucrats who worked under Park. For instance, one high-ranking official recollected that under President Park, "it was better to finish on time with 70% completeness than being late with 100% completeness."[52] A businessman of that time echoed this ethos, noting that "there was no room to waste a second when it was so important to build factories with much speed, so that export can be achieved."[53]

Speedy decision-making took its toll in the course of implementation. Decisions made in haste had to go through frequent adjustments when they were implemented. Thus, it was natural to see frequent changes of policies in day-to-day practice. Such decision-making and implementation styles reflected the extremely uncertain environments in which both the state and business had to work. As one high-ranking official remarked, there were no precedents or guarantees for the state's decisions to succeed: "Nobody knew for sure what to do and how to do it and whether they were going to be successful. We did a life and death struggle to make things work. There were so many problems and a high degree of uncertainty."[54] There were several reasons why original decisions had to be changed frequently in the process of implementation: first, they were made out of the sense of urgency without full consideration of relevant factors; second, the original goals were unrealistically ambitious or upgraded higher; and third, the environment itself was so volatile that so many contingencies occurred.

Finally, the distinct approach to economic development that was adopted under Park was "enterprise-based" support. This approach in turn tremendously affected the mode of implementation—and ultimately, state-business relations. Under such circumstances, the style of implementation can be characterized as pragmatism and particularism. Pragmatism refers to the frequent changes in decisions to realize target goals. Frequent changes are inevitable due to unrealistically ambitious goals, which were set out of a sense of urgency and pressure for rapid implementation.[55] Frequent changes in Korean decision-making even caught the attention of a foreign journalist: "Korean bureaucrats in economic affairs are undoubtedly geniuses of extemporization. They come up with new measures, institutions and regulations in a dizzying speed only to change them almost daily afterwards. Korean bureaucrats deserve to be called actors of thinking while running."[56] Particularism frequently involves decisions with a low level of generality involving only a single firm at a particular time.[57] Particularism in the context of Korea's economic development occurred for similar reasons as pragmatism but was also closely related to the government's strategy, which was organized around enterprise-based support.

Frequent change in policies and certain company-targeted policies in the course of implementation can be found at the department level and below, where daily implementation occurred. According to one MCI official, frequent changes were bound to occur in the highly changing environment:

> Q: Everything moved quite fast then?
> A: Yes, it did.
> Q: Was original policy changed during implementation?
> A: Yes, it changed a lot.
> Q: In some cases, laws were prepared in a single day for a particular company. And with new laws introduced, enforcing ordinances were also changed, correct?
> A: I am not sure about laws, but ordinances were changed for particular companies when changes were absolutely necessary for those companies.
> Q: How often did it change?
> Q: Ministerial-level ordinances were changed quite frequently.

Regarding frequent changes in regulations, one businessman also concurred:

> Q: Did you not feel that government's regulations frequently changed?
> A: Yes, they did.
> Q: Why do you think so?
> A: It occurs either for the purpose of improvement of the regulations or for a particular company.
> Q: Do you mean that they change for particular companies?
> A: Yes, that is lobbying power. It is lobbying power of companies that can even change laws. It is often the case that regulations change through lobbying. That is why there are so many changes in regulations.[58]

Such enterprise-based policy is related to the top-down decision-making and implementation style led by the top leader. For example, when President Park issued a memo in the early 1970s on starting the auto industry, the ministry drafted a document to be sent to lower levels, and after Park handed down a memo to Hyundai chairman Chŏng Chuyŏng, through the deputy prime minister, the MCI drafted a plan and consulted with the company. These examples indicate the developmental logic of oligopoly or monopoly in late industrialization, where a late-industrializing country is willing to cultivate monopolies in certain industries, at least at the initial stage of development, and to support them—even when the government may be criticized for collusion with business and economic dictatorship.[59]

Changing Decision-Making and Implementation

There were three major institutional actors involved in decision-making and implementation in Korea's late industrialization: the president, the bureaucracy, and business. As mentioned earlier, the role of President Park in decision-making and implementation cannot be overemphasized, and the implications of his role for social and institutional change are enormous. First, his ambitious economic developmental goals, arising from the sense of urgency, led to frequent upgrading of economic targets. Second, his obsession with quickly realizing these goals caused continuous uncertainty and ambiguity. Third, his commitment to an export-based strategy provided a concrete standard in the midst of an uncertain environment. Finally, his protective support of business at the company level meant the provision of all possible incentives for business.

For bureaucrats, the circumstances set by Park meant they had to always be ready to meet Park's demands in the highly uncertain and volatile environment—but at the same time they faced constant scrutiny by Park in terms of meeting export goals. They had to constantly provide new information through contacts with business for ever-changing decisions and implementation. Enterprise-based support, combined with changing rules and environment, meant they had to frequently make discretionary and arbitrary decisions in dealing with business. The only constraints on their arbitrariness were Park's oversight and the level of achievement in export.

For bureaucrats this meant they had to make adjustments with new information. Bureaucrats had to realize ambitious economic goals set by Park in an environment in which "nothing can be done and anything is possible."[60] Under extreme pressure to demonstrate visible success, they had to mobilize every possible means inside and outside the state. Internally they needed to establish informal networks to cope with new information, and externally they had to maintain close contacts with business, either by providing necessary incentives or by collaborating on new plans and implementation. This led to blurring of the boundary between the state and business.[61]

Business, which faced a highly uncertain environment, lack of experience, shortage of capital, and ever-changing international markets in which it was not experienced, tried every possible means to gain access to state incentives. It needed state support for new projects and to mitigate short-term bottlenecks. Effort to gain access to state incentives was all the more intense as business was aware that the state needed their cooperation for success. According to one survey, 64.7% of respondents replied that relationship with the state is critical for business success, and 90.5% of respondents were of the opinion that government policies affect business strategies. Most important, 63.9% said they needed lobbying for successful business management, and 75.5% said governmental support was helpful for business growth.[62]

It is clear that both macro parameters set by Park and the micro level of implementation forced frequent contacts between the state and business. The state held incentives for business but needed cooperation from business to realize economic goals—while business desperately needed state support. The social base and patterns of interaction between the state and business are crucially important to understand the social implications of Korea's late industrialization. State-business contacts were made through human interactions, and the analysis of recruitment patterns in both the state and business sectors is the first step to understand their implications for social change.

MERIT, REGIONALISM, AND SCHOOL TIES IN STATE RECRUITMENT

Although Park was so eager to achieve rapid economic development through unrealistically high economic goals, it was not an easy task to implement the plans. President Park faced two serious problems. First, administratively he was bequeathed a corrupt bureaucratic apparatus. Second, politically he was heavily dependent on the military because he came to power through a military coup d'état.[63] Thus, Park's main challenge was to install a new administrative structure to cope with new economic tasks. In personnel changes, priority was given to competency and loyalty, both equally essential to fulfill the challenge of fostering rapid economic development. To have only the former would have risked the full implementation of policies, whereas with only the latter appropriate policies might not have been formulated and information distorted.

Park tried to solve this two-dimensional challenge by continuing the tradition of hiring middle-level bureaucrats through highly competitive examinations. At the same time, people from his native province were strongly favored. Park's recruitment pattern can be seen at the macro and micro level; the former refers to the recruitment of high-ranking officials of the entire government (see table 6), while the latter to a case from the MCI. At the macro level, regional representation from the southeast increased significantly from the 18.8% of all ministerial-level officials during the First Republic (1948–60) to 30.1% during the Park regime (1961–79). Considering the fact that the southeast was underrepresented under the First Republic, this constituted a tremendous change.[64]

Another survey also corroborates the trend of an increasing proportion of the high-ranking bureaucrats (above the fifth rank) coming from the southeastern region: in 1962, it was 20.8%, and it increased to 23.4% in 1971 and 31.6% in 1979.[65] This trend continued in 1982 (see table 7).[66] Kyŏngbuk Province, the core of the southeastern region, was overrepresented with the ratio of 1.6, whereas Chŏllanam-do (southwestern region) was significantly underrepresented with the ratio of 0.6. Such increasing recruitments based on regionalism was interpreted as evidence for the insufficient practice of the merit system and the overwhelming political influence in Korean public administration without considering that practice was related to the institutional imperatives of late industrialization.[67]

The single most significant phenomenon in recruitment at the MCI is the increase of regionalism at all ranks. Before 1961 there were no disproportionate regional preferences, based on analysis of the regional origins of those who were recruited. The proportion of career bureaucrats (who served above section chief level) and non-careerists (who served below the section chief level) from the southeastern region visibly increased only after 1961.[68] The proportion of MCI officials from the southeastern region was less than 20% before 1961, but it more than doubled during the 1960s and 1970s.

In particular, during the 1970s, about 40% of officials were recruited from the southeastern region. This regional bias becomes clearer when compared to that of officials from the southwestern region (see table 8). Before 1961, the

TABLE 6. Regional origins of high-ranking officials of Korean governments (in percentages and number of persons)

	SEOUL	KYŎNGGI	KANG-WŎN	CH'UNG-CH'ŎNG	YŎNG-NAM	CHŎLLA	CHEJU	HWAN-GHAE	P'YŎNG-AN	HAM-GYŎNG
First Republic (1948–60) (243)	48 (20)	13.5 (33)	6.1 (15)	16 (30)	18.8 (46)	6.2 (15)	0.4 (1)	3.7 (9)	9.8 (24)	5.3 (13)
Interim government (April 1960–June 1960) (33)	17.6 (6)	5.9 (2)	0 (0)	8.8 (3)	20.6 (7)	20.6 (7)	0 (0)	2.9 (1)	5.9 (2)	14.7 (5)
Second Republic (May 1960–May 1961) (196)	9.2 (9)	7.1 (7)	0 (0)	16.3 (16)	25.5 (25)	16.3 (16)	1 (1)	4.1 (4)	133 (13)	5.1 (5)
Third, Fourth Republic (429)	10.4 (45)	3.7 (17)	5.6 (24)	13.9 (60)	30.1 (130	13.2 (57	2.1 (9)<	6 (26)	8.1 (35)	6 (26)
Transitional government (1979–80) (56)	16.1 (9)	7.1 (4)	5.4 (3)	17.9 (10)	26.8 (15)	14.3 (8)	0 (0)	5.4 (3)	5.4 (3)	1.8 (1)
Fifth, Sixth Republic (1981–88) (505)	11.5 (58)	7.9 (40)	5 (25)	12.3 (62)	41.2 (208)	12.6 (64)	0.4 (2)	9.1 (46)		
Kim Young-sam government (1993–98) (197)	13.2 (26)	7.6 (15)	2 (4)	14.7 (29)	41.2 (81)	14.7 (29)	0 (0)	6.6 (13)		
Total (1,559)	12.9 (201)	7.6 (118)	4.6 (71)	14 (219)	32.9 (512)	12.5 (196)	0.8 (13)	14.7 (229)		

TABLE 7. Provincial origins of high-ranking officials (fifth rank and above) in Korean government, 1982

REGIONAL ORIGIN	RATIO[a]
Seoul	1.3
Kangwŏn	0.7
Ch'ungbuk	1.2
Kyŏngbuk (southeast)	1.6
Chŏnbuk (southwest)	0.6
Kyŏnggi	0.6
Ch'ungnam	1.4
Kyŏngnam (southeast)	0.7
Chŏnnam	0.6
Cheju	0.4

[a] The ratio refers to that between the percentage of bureaucrats from province above the fifth rank in Korean government and the percentage of the provincial population. A ratio of 1.0 means the provincial proportion of state employees is equal to that of the proportion of the provincial population.

Source: Ha Taegwŏn, "Han'guk insa haengjŏng," 108.

ratio of newly recruited officials from the southeastern region to the southwestern region was 1.2:1 (46:28). This roughly corresponded to the ratio of the population size of the two regions (1.36:1; see table 9). However, the gap greatly widened during the 1960s and 1970s, when the industrial takeoff occurred. In particular, the gap widened dramatically during the 1970s. As we can see in table 9, during the 1960s, 37 careerists and 48 non-careerists were recruited from the southeastern region, whereas 18 careerists and 31 non-careerists were recruited from the southwestern region. However, in the 1970s, only 15 careerists and 9 non-careerists were recruited from the southwestern region, whereas 58 careerists and 34 non-careerists came from the southeastern region. The ratio of the total number of the recruits from the southeastern region to those from the southwestern region was 3.77:1 from 1971 to 1979. This is twice the actual population ratio of 1.88:1 in 1980. This shows that regionalism operated at all ranks, contradicting the conventional observation that regional bias was weak at lower ranks.[69]

TABLE 8. Regional distribution of Ministry of Commerce and Industry officials, 1948–79 (all ranks)

Years	Ranking of first appointment	SEOUL/ KYŎNGGI		SOUTHEASTERN		SOUTHWESTERN		CH'UNGCH'ŎNG		OTHER REGIONS		SUBTOTAL	
		n	%	n	%	n	%	n	%	n	%	n	%
1948-60	Above 5th level	23	27.7	13	15.7	10	12	12	14.5	25	30.1	83	100
	Below 5th level	66	39.8	33	19.9	18	10.8	16	9.6	33	19.9	166	100
1961-70	Above 5th level	61	44.2	37	26.8	18	13	12	8.7	10	7.2	138	100
	Below 5th level	94	42.3	48	21.6	31	14	37	16.7	12	5.4	222	100
1971-79	Above 5th level	45	28.5	58	36.7	15	9.5	28	17.7	12	7.6	158	100
	Below 5th level	25	29.8	34	40.5	9	10.7	14	16.7	2	2.4	84	100
Total		314	36.9	222	26.2	101	11.9	119	14	94	11	851	100

Source: Yong-Chool Ha and Myung-Koo Kang, "Creating a Capable Bureaucracy," 85.

TABLE 9. Regional distribution of population, 1960, 1970, and 1980

	1960		1970		1980	
	n	%	n	%	n	%
Total	24,989,241		31,435,252		37,406,815	
Seoul/Kyŏnggi	5,194,167	20	8,878,534	28.2	13,280,951	35.5
Southeastern region	8,070,646	32	9,947,037	31.6	11,429,489	30.6
Southwestern region	5,948,265	23	6,436,724	20.5	6,065,497	16.2
Ratio of southeastern to southwestern regions	1.36:1		1.55:1		1.88:1	

Source: Office of Statistics, Republic of Korea; and Yong-Chool Ha and Myung-Koo Kang, "Creating a Capable Bureaucracy," 96.

Here a notable phenomenon is that the regional bias toward the southeastern region was more salient at high ranks. From 1948 to 1979, a total of 443 bureaucrats served in the MCI as officials above the section chief level. Of these careerists, 35 officials were recruited before 1948 and 29 bureaucrats served as either the minister or the vice-minister of the MCI. The single most interesting pattern of these 64 officials was that Seoul origins were the highest: 14 out of those 35 officials were recruited before 1948, and 13 out of 29 ministers or vice-ministers were from Seoul. Except for these 64 officials, 379 officials were recruited through four different routes: 135 (35.6%) of them were recruited through higher civil service examinations, 37 officials (9.8%) were ex-military officers, 90 officials (23.7%) transferred from other ministries, and 116 officials (30.6%) were recruited through special recruitments.

The regional bias is also clear when analyzed by the channels of recruitment. More people were clearly recruited from the southeastern region from which President Park originated, indicating that regional background was clearly an important source of securing loyalty. As table 10 shows, in every channel of recruitment, regional preference toward the southeastern region—or, by contrast, bias against the southwestern region—was strengthened since 1961. For example, out of 130 total officials recruited by higher service exams since 1961, 48 officials (37%) were from the southeastern region, whereas only 16 officials were from the southwestern region. More important, however, regional bias in recruitment through higher civil service exams increased during the 1970s. Out of the total number of careerists recruited through these exams

TABLE 10. Regional distribution of career bureaucrats, 1948–79

Category	Region	1948–55 n	1956–60 n	1961–65 n	1966–70 n	1971–75 n	1976–79 n	TOTAL n	TOTAL %
Civil service exams	Southeastern	—	—	5	6	23	14	48	35.6
	Southwestern	1[a]	2	4	2	5	5	19	14.1
	Seoul/Kyŏnggi	—	1	8	11	13	12	45	33.3
	Ch'ung	—	1	—	3	11	3	18	13.3
	Other regions[b]	—	—	1	—	2	2	5	3.7
Ex-military officers	Southeastern	—	—	3	1	—	5	9	24.3
	Southwestern	—	—	1	—	—	2	3	8.1
	Seoul/Kyŏnggi	—	—	10	1	1	3	15	40.5
	Ch'ung	—	—	1	1	1	1	4	10.8
	Other regions	1	—	4	—	—	1	6	16.2
Transfer[c]	Southeastern	4	—	1	7	8	3	23	25.6
	Southwestern	4	—	5	—	—	2	11	12.2
	Seoul/Kyŏnggi	9	—	7	3	3	3	25	27.8
	Ch'ung	5	—	1	1	3	5	15	16.7
	Other regions	8	1	2	—	4	1	16	17.8

Special recruits[d]								
Southeastern	5	4	9	5	5	—	28	24.1
Southwestern	3	—	5	1	—	1	10	8.6
Seoul/Kyŏnggi	10	2	15	6	6	4	43	37.1
Ch'ung	4	2	5	—	3	1	15	12.9
Other regions	14	1	3	—	1	1	20	58.8
Total								
n	68	14	90	48	89	69	378	
%	18	3.7	23.8	12.7	23.5	18.3	100	

[a] The percentage of the region is the ratio of each category of each time period.
[b] Includes Kangwŏn, Cheju, and North Korean provinces.
[c] Those who were transferred from other government ministries to the Ministry of Commerce and Industry.
[d] Those who were recruited by higher civil service exams, military background, or transfer.

Source: Yong-Chool Ha and Myung-Koo Kang, "Creating a Capable Bureaucracy," 89.

from 1961 to 1979, 48 officials (36%) were from the southeastern region. But of these, 23 officials (43%) and 14 officials (39%) were recruited in 1971 to 1975 and 1976 to 1979, respectively, surpassing the average population ratio of the southeastern region. This implies that the pattern of increasing regional bias could be undetected under the increasing trend of merit-based exam recruitment.

It is, of course, true that the examination itself does not produce a regional bias. However, the regional bias was more visible in the process of assigning posts and promotion. The blending of regionalism and the merit-based principle started as early as the ministerial assignments stage of the newly recruited officials. Usually, newly recruited bureaucrats from the southeastern region were assigned to the more prominent posts. Moreover, people from the southeast were more frequently promoted to important positions. The process worked as follows: During a typical promotion practice, five section chief candidates were recommended to form a promotion pool and competed for one department head position. They had to be qualified in terms of length of service and work experience for a given post, and in most cases candidates for promotion usually passed the higher civil service examination. It was perfectly legal for higher officials who made the promotion decision to choose any one of the five qualified candidates. It was only natural to expect that higher officials from the southeastern region would prefer those with the same regional origins. This meant that regional backgrounds served as the deciding factor for promotion among the strictly merit-based candidate pool, subtly combining merit with regionalism. Given this mode of promotion, it was technically difficult to register any formal complaints against the final decisions.

As a former ministry official in charge of personnel matters reflected:

> More often than not, those who were recruited into the MCI either took the higher civil service examination or were graduates of the law school of Seoul National University. While we were formally committed to the merit system, in reality regionalism was a determinant. When section chiefs were promoted, those from the southeast were selected even when they were not ranked first in standing. It was possible because most people at the higher level were from the same region. The virtuous cycle goes like this: those from the southeast were assigned to important posts and could thereby demonstrate their work abilities better than others could.[70]

Regional bias provided employees with good standing and a better chance for getting promoted. Although technically it does not seem unfair, regionalism is intricately linked to the promotion process. As for political positions, such as minister, vice-minister, and assistant minister, where external influences are visible, those from the southeast were absolutely dominant. Among the 11 who were promoted beyond the assistant secretary level between 1965 and 1975, seven were from the southeast region. This overrepresentation of the southeast region continued throughout Park's regime, and the tendency increased over time, regardless of the levels and modes of entry.

Regional bias was also intricately related to regional high school and college ties. Regional and high school ties formed in the formative years of individuals were preserved when they entered colleges in Seoul. For example, out of total 379 careerists, a quarter of officials graduated from regionally famous high schools, and except for those famous high schools in Seoul, the majority of them graduated from the locally famous high schools in the southeastern region. Specifically, more than 40% of career bureaucrats of the MCI graduated from Seoul National University (SNU) during 1948 to 1979. Regardless of regional backgrounds, graduates of SNU were the absolute majority. Since 1961, the proportion of SNU graduates increased greatly from only 8 graduates of SNU recruited to the MCI before 1961 to roughly 50% of officials (149) graduates of SNU, and among them, 45 officials (30%) graduated from the law school of SNU in 1978. In particular, between 1966 and 1975, more than 55% of newly recruited careerists were SNU graduates. Meanwhile, 27 officials (9%) were graduates from Korea University, and 16 officials (6%) were from Yonsei University. In short, between 1961 and 1979, about 65% of newly recruited careerists were graduates of these three schools.[71]

More interestingly, we can observe an increasing regional bias among recruited SNU graduates as well. The overall proportion of SNU graduates from the Seoul/Kyŏnggi area was slightly higher than the southeastern region. In particular, in the 1960s, SNU graduates from the Seoul/Kyŏnggi region were much more overrepresented than the population size of the region. But if we look at the trend during the 1970s, SNU graduates from the southeastern region surpassed the total number of officials from the Seoul/Kyŏnggi region (31 to 25). Meanwhile, SNU graduates from the southwestern region decreased greatly after 1966. This phenomenon shows that regionalism was intermingled with the merit-based principle in recruitment.

Such deepening regional bias is attributable to the ways in which loyalty to President Park was secured. President Park took political power by military coup, and he justified his illegitimate rule by promising rapid economic growth. He needed both competent and loyal people for rapid economic growth, and his choice was constrained by the institutional setting of the period. In short, it is clear that for the Park regime, recruiting loyal and competent personnel to build capable bureaucratic organizations was essential not only for its political survival but also for expediting the industrialization process. The strategy chosen by President Park was to combine regionalism and merit, ultimately securing the loyalty that he desired.

FAMILY-SCHOOL-REGIONAL NEXUS IN THE BUSINESS SECTOR

Park's sense of urgency for economic development and the distinct view that Korean business was not up to the task of export promotion led to an extensive list of incentives to businesses to facilitate economic development and exportation. Under such circumstances, a business had ample reason to seek state support to bolster its own advantages. What further facilitated individual companies to actively seek state incentives was the company-specific mode of distribution of state incentives.[72] Under such circumstances it could not be more rational for companies to adopt mimetic recruitment patterns similar to those of the state, and in turn such mimetic recruitment patterns between the state and companies had consequential implications for social and institutional changes.

The Korean business sector has three features particularly relevant to the approach taken here. First, ownership is heavily concentrated in the hands of family members of the company founders. Second, the next management level is recruited from university graduates who frequently have regional ties with top owners. Finally, the workers at the lowest echelon are closely bound by regional ties. Korean chaebols, the central business group during industrialization, are owned and managed by family members of the founders. One survey shows that out of 137 big enterprises with employment more than 300, 121 (88.3%) were family owned and managed.[73] Other data corroborate this. Among 100 sons of 34 chaebols, 40 were presidents, managing directors, executive directors, or directors and another 10 were department chiefs of affiliated companies.[74]

Among white-collar employees who entered chaebols and later became high-ranking managerial members of these conglomerates, most of them were graduates of Seoul National, Yonsei, and Korea Universities. Among the 3,987 who were high-ranking managers above the level of board member of the 347 member companies of the Korean Federation of Industrialists, 35.2% of them were SNU graduates, whereas Yonsei and Korea Universities each had 8%.[75] These proportions roughly correspond to elite distribution within the government bureaucracy as well. Among bureaucrats above department chief in 1980, 42.9% were SNU graduates, whereas 5.6% and 7.3% came from Yonsei and Korea Universities.[76] College ties are important, but what is significant is that high school ties constituted the core subcategory of grouping among college graduates.[77] Also remarkable are the high regional affinities between the owners and the high-ranking managers of the 100 chaebols. Among the 2,243 high-ranking managers who were not blood related to founders or owners who were from the southeast, 57% were from the southeast, and in the companies whose owners were from the southwestern region, 60.7% of them were from the southwest.[78] The same pattern was visible among SMEs. Among 69 manufacturing SMEs, 55 (79.7%) of them were family owned.[79] As of 1975, 59.2% of the financing sources of the SMEs were family and relatives.[80] SME recruitment favored workers who shared same regional origins.[81]

Finally, at the lowest tier, average workers found solidarity with others from the same region. Among factory workers, especially at production lines, regional ties were also strong, partly because of the recruitment patterns based on regional ties. That is, once workers of a certain region were recruited, they also brought in persons who shared their regional origin.[82] Such regional gatherings were regarded as a survival mechanism. During the 1960s and 1970s, most factory workers were without a state welfare net. Consequently, workers, especially female workers, organized various means for self-support, such as rotating financing (*kye*), sharing housing and meals, and group purchasing, based on regional ties.[83]

NEOFAMILISM IN INTERACTIONS BETWEEN THE STATE AND BUSINESS

Structural configurations of neofamilism became clear. As each company tried every possible means to secure access to state incentives, deeply rooted extensive and intensive human interactions based on regional and school ties formed a foundation for close ties and collusion between the government and business, which developed into a government-business "mingling" phenomenon. The following interview materials show the mutual perceptions between bureaucrats and business, as well as the reasons for and patterns of the mobilization of neofamilial ties.

First, business was fully aware that bureaucrats were hard-pressed to realize export goals set by President Park and that they were bound to support business:

> Q: How were bureaucrats at that time, especially those of the Ministry of Commerce and Industry?
>
> A: They thought without export the country would collapse and thus thought export as an issue where life or death is at stake. Successful implementation of export targets was regarded as a way to demonstrate patriotism. Bureaucrats' determination to fulfill export targets was much stronger than now.[84]

Under such circumstances business followed bureaucrats as the former was well aware of the dedication of the latter to export to maximize their interests:

> Q: How did the business community view the government's support for export?
>
> A: As the government lent every possible support to business, had to follow decisions on support for business precisely, without making any changes. As President Park was so occupied with export, we could not but actively support it. However, bureaucrats dipped their hands in policy support to products for domestic market, let's say, .5% for personal gains while 5% for political slush fund.[85]

On the uncertain situation of the time one businessman said the following:

> Q: Was the situation during the industrialization so uncertain that business people felt that everything was possible and at the same time that nothing was possible?
>
> A: This was due to ambiguity in laws and regulations. The interpretation of laws and regulations varied, depending upon the situation.

As such, officials tended to decide in favor of business. However, there were also situations that could not be subject to arbitrary decisions of officials.[86]

According to the following testimony of a former MCI official, efforts to penetrate the ministry were palpably felt inside the bureaucracy:

> Q: There was a saying that companies locate and maintain various personal ties within the ministry to contact them whenever problems arise.
> A: It was quite natural. Most companies could not survive without them. They carefully cultivate the ties.
> Q: Were school ties and regional ties mobilized?
> A: If they decide to do so, they use school and regional ties as a way to open communication channels. In my case I have a lot of people who are connected through school and regional ties, and managerial people in companies mobilize whatever they have, and that was the normal practice of the time.[87]

This means that business judiciously and carefully mobilized school, blood, and regional ties to secure information and financial support from the government. Such all-out efforts to secure channels within the state did not stop at the ministry level; they even reached the national assembly and top level of power:

> Q: How did you contact the government?
> A: Is it not true that there was no person in the presidential house and secretariat who could not be connected, not only through my own ties but also through school and regional ties of my friends and the friends of my friends? Companies systematically use these ties. When you become a high-level manager of company you are requested to submit a list of people in major institutions that you know, including all the people in political, administrative, and financial fields. When problems occur, a total mobilization of human contacts is launched with the MCI. The CEO calls for an executive meeting, identifies target officials in the ministry, and entrusts a certain executive to take charge in fulfilling the mission. The designated person discusses the scale of money to be spent for the mission and mobilizes every possible tie,

sometimes succeeding in influencing more favorable regulations. From a business perspective it is a sort of investment. There are cases where a long-term investment is done through travel support and sending them abroad for training.[88]

As such, companies tried to mobilize all possible ties to set up a "bridge" with the government. On this phenomenon one former high-ranking bureaucrat stated as follows:

> Q: How did companies try to set up a communication channel with the ministry?
> A: It would not be far-fetched to say that they tried to hang on to every possible "string" (tie).[89]

Such practice in contacting the government was a well-known phenomenon. Companies especially took lobbying through various ties for granted because the state was seen as the source of all the support that business needed:

> Q: How important was the connection with the state in doing business?
> A: The connection with the government was most important in building new factories and doing business. State-business collusion started from this. There is nothing that exists without reason. Since the state held all the financial sources, the connection with the government was quite essential for business.
> Q: How about a specific example?
> A: When companies tried to secure special access to low-interest loans, each company tries their best in lobbying . . . naturally, regional and school ties become important. For me I am a graduate of a college of business and of a vocational high school. Since the number of graduates was not large, we knew each other well among the graduates of the college, and seniors and juniors knew each other well.

From the perspective of an official the situation was not that much different:

> Q: If so, were there cases where business used school and blood ties in securing information from the state?
> A: Yes, companies did so.

Q: If so, what was most effective?
A: In my case I do not have strong regional ties, and thus school ties worked better. In general, it was either school ties or regional ties. Is it not?

Having seen in rich empirical detail how neofamilial connections developed historically, we can now address neofamilism in more general conceptual terms.

NEOFAMILISM AS PHENOMENON AND ITS DIFFUSION

Neofamilism denotes the dynamic process of reinforcement of social ethos and relations based on primary ties that occurred during Korea's industrialization. It can be understood at three levels: as identity, as a survival strategy, and as social modes of institutional operation. Neofamilism in terms of identity designates the act of individuals defining their social relations and their identity primarily in terms of familial, school, and regional ties. Familial ties can vary widely from immediate nuclear family to clan ties; school ties can take various forms, from primary to university levels (although high school ties are perceived as strongest); and regional ties include the village network. In Korea, class identity, functional identity, or role identity are overshadowed by neofamilial identity bases. On the level of individual strategy, people take for granted the uses of neofamilial ties to promote their socioeconomic interests. The mobilization of neofamilial ties, rather than playing by rules, to promote personal interests negatively affects the application of universal norms and predictability in administrative and legal operations. Finally, neofamilism at the institutional level is a non-Weberian phenomenon. For example, bureaucracy gradually lost its operating principles, such as legality and professionalism. Individuals operating by neofamilial mores weaken the operation severely by distorting structural configuration. Neofamilial institutional practice is partly affected by individual survival strategies in relation to institutions, but it is mainly driven by institutions' own historical legacies in terms of their origins and historical development.

Neofamilism was thus perceived to be stronger than individualism. The ethos that neofamilism carries is "privatism." In distinction from individualism, privatism denotes lack of respect for individuality and of keeping "proper" interpersonal distance.[90] Contrary to the conclusions of many Western sociological studies on informal organizations, Korean-style industrialization brought about a society in which neofamilial units were reinforced. Moreover, they are unlikely to disappear. Neofamilism in Korea has become a source of identity and survival.[91]

The neofamilism approach sheds important light on social and political phenomena in Korea. At the micro level (in public bureaucracies), transfers and promotions were based largely on school and regional ties. In business, blood, school, and regional ties were also salient features in the management structure. It also leads us to reconsider (a) the prevalent assumptions about the existence of a coherent middle class, (b) the emergence of a civil society, and (c) bureaucratization as a causal result of industrialization. Members of the Korean middle class shared only an income level, and otherwise they were isolated from one another. In fact, the whole society was divided by degrees of accessibility to state power. This raises a larger question. At the macro level, identities, survival strategies, and the prevailing institutional modus operandi based on neofamilism discourage class-based identities. This is seen in the rampant regionalism in Korean elections at all levels (legislative and presidential).[92] Moreover, the institutional impact of neofamilism was equally serious. Due to the constant penetration of neofamilial ties into the internal workings of the bureaucracy, Korean bureaucracy came to lose its boundary with business and was eventually hollowed out (see chapter 4).

The core neofamilial relationships formed between business and the state were emulated and expanded into the rest of the society by two mechanisms. One, in the economic sphere, involved the structural linkage between chaebols and SMEs. As of 1975, 46 chaebols made up 13.4% of GDP and 36.7% of manufacturing GDP.[93] In 1982, the number of SMEs with 5 to 299 employees constituted 97.3% of the total number of industries, but their contribution in terms of value-added GNP was only 36.2%.[94] With such overwhelming economic concentration in the large conglomerates, the SMEs were highly dependent on the chaebols. In 1982, 38% of the business of SMEs involved subcontracting with the chaebols, and this had increased to 74% by 1991.

This high level of dependency forced SMEs to endure various exploitative business practices by the big industries, such as delays in payment and forced price reduction.[95] Each chaebol had a huge number of subcontracts with SMEs, and one byproduct was the transference of the neofamilial ethos to

SMEs from chaebols.⁹⁶ The following interview with a small enterprise CEO is quite revealing:

> HA: What do you think about the impact of chaebols on small-medium industry in terms of business practices?
>
> HAN: Chaebol had a great deal of impact on small-medium industries. The latter tried to learn from the former in mobilizing various connections to approach chaebols to obtain contracts. Small-medium industries envied chaebols' access to the state through the mobilization capacity of chaebols through school, blood, and regional ties. Small-medium industries learned from big business the need to mobilize various ties as chaebols set the tone for business practices for the entire economy. Small-medium industries during the 1970s also relied on blood ties and other ties in securing personnel and financial resources.⁹⁷

The second source for diffusion was the peculiar political and economic role of white-collar workers of chaebols. White-collar workers constitute the core middle class. In April 1975, the total number of workers nationwide was 1,404,399, of which 29.3% were in enterprises with more than 500 employees.⁹⁸ The social and institutional implications of this fact are quite consequential. Though white-collar workers are middle class in economic terms, their identity basis was so narrow and bounded by the three neofamilial ties that they became the main agents for spreading neofamilism in Korean society.

Through the chaebols' ties with the state, these white-collar workers were also the primary beneficiaries of state resources. The background and orientation of chaebol white-collar workers was widely emulated by the rest of society, partly with some contempt but mainly in earnest. As business and employment opportunities multiplied with the shift to export strategy, the popular perception of the state changed from that of exploiter to that of provider. In one survey, 50% of the respondents said that money and personal connections were more important in obtaining a desirable job or status than individual efforts (40%).⁹⁹ The web of neofamilism was thus perceived to be stronger than individualism. Accordingly, chaebols' practices of neofamilism became an importance source of spreading neofamilism to Korean society, trickling down to SMEs and thus to the rest of society.

PARK, NEOFAMILISM, AND TRADITION

The emergence of neofamilism in conjunction with Korea's economic development shows a distinctive aspect of the interaction between tradition and late industrialization. That is, there was no conscious and explicit effort on the part of Park Chung Hee to invent traditional institutions. Rather, it was a sort of unintended consequence of the effort to recruit competent and loyal sources of manpower that can be entrusted with industrialization tasks. Park was not committed to any specific ideology except for nationalism and pragmatism, which did not entail recruiting personnel based on ideological predilection. Given Korea's social and cultural tradition of the time, it was only natural for Park to combine merit-based examination and regional ties as the major principles of recruitment. It is ironic that Park ended up relying on school and regional ties, given the fact that he was repeatedly critical of them as negative legacies of Korean history.[100] In a sense unlike what happened in Meiji Japan, the way in which Korean traditions were brought back into industrialization was situation driven and totally unintended, thus constituting a case of tradition coming back through the back door.

This unintended aspect of neofamilism begs the larger question of whether and to what extent Park was conscious about Korean tradition. At the early stage of his power, Park held a negative view of Korean history and tradition. Furthermore, he thought that the colonial rule had essentially destroyed Korean traditions. Past research on Park's use of tradition shows the total lack of evidence for his use of tradition as a way to think about managing social conflict arising from late industrialization.[101] This does not mean, however, that he did not mention Korean traditional institutions and values. While he constantly referred to negative traditional institutions and values, he was, at the same time, fully aware of positive examples. For instance, he mentioned *hyangyak* (village covenants), *kye* (rotating financing system), *ture* (communal labor sharing), patriotism, and *sirhak* (pragmatism) as positive elements of tradition.[102] However, there is no evidence to support the notion that Park was consciously inventing Korean traditions, especially in managing social conflicts and linking them to industrial institutions, such as labor relations and governance structure.

Park's approach to tradition was so distinct in that while he was not so much interested in inventing Korean traditional institutions for economic development, he constantly emphasized the importance of spirit or values. For example, even in addressing labor relations he simply highlighted the importance of the spirit of cooperation rather than being interested in institutionalizing a distinctively Korean style of labor relations. This is a typical case of harnessing, where traditional values are opportunistically applied as opposed to inventing them. This applies to various cases, such as the New Village Movement, education policy, and the Second Economy Campaign.[103] This tendency to heavily lean on rhetorical invocations of values and spirit was reinforced as the regime character became more authoritarian since the introduction of the Yusin (Reform) regime in 1972.[104] He invented various traditional values, such as filial piety, patriotic loyalty, and the concept of nation to foster values among Korean people congruent with his authoritarian regime. This was a shift from his original negative view of tradition to a more utilitarian one.[105]

This raises the question of why Park's interest in Korean tradition was heavily tilted toward not so much institutions as values and spirit. One reason was the prevalent negative perception of Korean traditional institutions, which were seen as having been either distorted or destroyed during the colonial period. Put differently, Korean traditional institutions were deprived of opportunities to be upgraded due to the loss of authority of the ruling class of Korean society.[106] More specific to Park, his sense of urgency was so intense that he did not have much time to think about the issue. This is in line with testimony given by one of his close confidants, who observed that "Park did not have any coherent philosophy, nor did we see the use of traditional institutions consciously."[107] According to the testimony, Park was simply occupied with how to create new jobs for a hungry populace. One objective condition also might have worked against any conscious effort to invent Korean traditional institutions. By the 1960s, Korean society had already been under the strong influence of Western institutions and values in politics, education, and the cultural sphere and, unlike in Meiji Japan, was already an amalgam of Western and Korean institutions, no matter how the latter was defined. Under these circumstances Park was more likely to end up emphasizing spiritual aspects of Korean traditions, and the upshot was that despite all the campaigns, declarations, and admonishment efforts to revive Korean culture and tradition, such projects ended up being incoherent, unsystematic, and transient in terms of long-lasting impact on Korean society.

SOUTH KOREA AS BOILING POT

An important implication of this analysis is that the unique content and background of tradition in specific late industrialization cases makes straightforward comparisons difficult. For example, South Korean state-led industrialization was unique in terms of its social implications. Although it shared with other late-industrialization cases such as Germany and Japan a high sense of backwardness and a sense of urgency for rapid change using heavy state involvement in economic development, the societal results were different. Korean industrialization did not face strong social forces that resisted industrialization, as in Germany. Korean bureaucrats were not tied to any strong social groups or classes, as in the German case of Junkers. Members of the Korean bureaucracy were formally recruited by merit based on examinations, but in contrast to Japan, the resulting administrative structure was bureaucratic only in a weak sense, with regional ties being an important factor for recruitment. With the breakdown of traditional social structure in Korea, political leaders and intellectuals were not overly conscious of the influence and impact of traditional values and institutions. This created the myth that as traditional structures (e.g., landlordism) broke down, industrialization would lead directly to modernity.[108] However, what really happened was that the mode of recruitment of bureaucrats combined merit with regionalism, unintentionally bringing neofamilism into the industrialization process.

The image of Korean society in the aftermath of economic development based on neofamilism can be compared to the Tadohae, an archipelago off the southern coast of South Korea: although all of the islands appear to be joined, they are in fact isolated bodies of land. The apparent homogeneity and unity of Korean society is similarly deceptive. Once the old social structure was destroyed by colonial rule, by the Korean War, and by the division of the country, South Koreans scrambled like isolated bubbles in a boiling pot searching for a higher social position in the rapidly changing environment. As South Koreans struggled for their positions in this new order by seeking out personal connections, there is little evidence that they developed a sense of class consciousness based on horizontal links among members of the same economic status.[109]

The Korean case challenges the prevailing assumption that industrialization brings about universal social and institutional consequences. It shows that it may not be sufficient to apply conventional sociological analysis to understand the social consequences of late industrialization in South Korea. Fresh interpretations are needed to replace conventional narratives that explain bureaucratization as a causal result of industrialization, the existence of a coherent middle class, the potential for developing "civil society," and the structure and dynamics of legal and business institutions involved in the process of industrialization.

Hollowing Out Bureaucracy

CHAPTER 4

The developmental state in Korea in the 1960s was disaggregated in terms of the top leader, ministries, and specific bureaucrats as they are involved in recruitment, decision-making, and implementation. Yet analysis of it over time allows us to trace what happens to the developmental state in the course of economic development. The top leader's perceptions of backwardness, recruitment patterns, decision-making, and implementation styles all carry long-term implications.[1] The current literature on the developmental state, regardless of its focus on macro-structural or functional aspects, does not capture changes within the state. For example, in understanding how the developmental state changes over time, the status at T0 is compared to that of T1 without a concrete trace of dynamics that might have occurred between the two time points. For instance, studies of state-business relations assume a dependent relationship of business to the state at T0, where business follows the state; changes at T1 then show that state interventionist functions are reduced while the scale of business grows to challenge the state. The conclusion from this model is that business has grown to challenge the state.[2]

However, such arguments contain serious logical flaws as they are based on the simplification of dynamics of the relationship between the weak and the strong. Even within a dependent relationship, the commanding side—or the side with more resources—is not necessarily always in a commanding position and fully free from the influence of the weaker side.[3] Also, without a specific analysis of mutual impact through interactions between the two sides, it is not possible to conclude that the strong-weak relationship is reversed, simply due to changes to the initial conditions. As weak business does not necessarily mean a strong state; a weak state does not necessarily bring about strong business. At the same time, strong business does not necessarily result in a weak state. Such juxtaposition between the state and business makes it difficult to understand the specific process of the emergence of the weak state through time and leaves little room for a possible situation where both can be weakened.[4]

In addition, closely related to the lack of a dynamic approach to the state is the treatment of the state as an abstract entity. It may be a natural consequence of approaching the state in static terms. The static approach is easily seen in a macro-structural approach to the state where the state is understood in terms of how the status of the state changes in the contexts of social and political changes. As such, the micro-level internal changes of the state over time have not drawn much attention.[5] Even micro approaches to the state do not deal with internal dynamics of the state as they primarily focus on economic functions of bureaucratic organizations.[6] It means that understanding the dynamic process of change in the internal aspects of the state requires a disaggregate approach to the state rather than treating it as abstract entity. The disaggregate and dynamic approach to the state inevitably focuses on interactions between state agencies, on the one hand, and those between these agencies and external actors, including business, on the other.[7] Most theories on the state or studies of the state neither establish disaggregate units nor analyze the interactive aspects in detail.[8]

An interactive approach to the state involves analyzing interactions between the state and actors outside the state and the mutual influence of such interactions; these influences encompass not only the state itself but also social actors outside of the state and sometimes society as a whole. This observation comes from the larger concern that in state-led industrialization, where inter-systemic boundaries are not clear, it is necessary to understand how major institutions and society in general are also impacted from interactions between the state and business.[9]

Neofamilism provides a unique lens to observe the dynamics of the Korean developmental state. The dynamic approach here refers to the analysis of changes within the Korean bureaucracy through the process of industrialization from 1963 to the 1980s, including the origins and characteristics of Korea's strong developmental state, how it has changed over time, and the consequent changes in state-business relations. The case of the MCI's recruitment, decision-making, implementation, and interactions with business illustrates how the state underwent changes.

The emergence of neofamilism influenced changing aspects of the developmental state in the process of economic development. The developmental state was disaggregated into the top leader, ministries, and specific bureaucrats, and interactions between the disaggregated state actors and business were analyzed as part of forming neofamilism. What happens to the developmental state during the course of economic development? Consideration of the top leader's perceptions of backwardness, recruitment patterns, decision-making, and implementation styles shows that the Korean style of late industrialization brought about a weakening of bureaucracy (*debureaucratization*) and ultimately hollowed out bureaucracy.[10]

IMPACT OF PERSONNEL POLICY

Recruitments within the MCI were based on the combination of merit and regional ties, which overlapped high school ties. The combination was an institutional imperative to launch late industrialization out of the sense of urgency. President Park Chung Hee, the top leader, needed people who were both competent and loyal. Competency was secured by merit-based recruitment and loyalty by recruiting those who shared regional ties with the president (southeastern region). The most serious consequence of such regionalism-based recruitment for the stability of bureaucracy was the emergence of pervasive informal organizations based on regional and school ties. The formation of informal groups within the MCI was most visible among those from the southeastern region of Korea. Those who were alienated from southeastern region groups also followed suit, forming their own groupings.[11]

Those from the southeast were organized based on regional and school ties such that they comprised the majority. Those who felt alienated from and resistant toward the southeastern region grouping, especially those from the southwestern region, organized informal groups.[12] Informal organizations of those from regions other than the southeast were not as visible, and their existence was not taken seriously by those from the southeast. Thus, the influence of informal groups without ties to the southeast drew little attention. Nevertheless, solidarity among the members of the ministry and their identity as one entity weakened while identities based on school and regional ties strengthened. Such informal identities came to affect not only day-to-day operations but also personnel policies.[13]

Informal organizations further facilitated the formation of identity based on school and regional ties and reinforced the combination of regionalism and merit in personnel policies, resulting in weakening organizational integrity and consistency. Accordingly, the ministry became vulnerable to outside efforts to infiltrate decision-making and implementation processes.[14]

Business owners entrusted family members, relatives, and school friends with issues that may involve illegality and corruption, while college graduates were recruited through open competition. As a result, people from the southeastern region and graduates of SNU worked within the business sector.[15] Business owners thus recruited former generals as board members to establish access to state incentives and also sought former high-ranking bureaucrats. Recruitment patterns within the MCI facilitated company penetration into the ministry. Sharing common networks between state officials and business managers provide a fertile ground for collusion and laid the foundation for a deeply structured pattern of "mingling" between the state and business.[16] It is clear that the combination of merit and regionalism in recruitment to facilitate late industrialization brought about sources for informal groupings and opened the door to the penetration of business into state bureaucracy.

PENETRATION FROM POLITICAL POWER

Organizational stability and integrity of the bureaucracy are essential in deterring attempts by business to penetrate the bureaucracy. Organizational stability was easily compromised as bureaucrats had to cope with improvised policies, unrealistic goals, and frequent changes by informally coordinating with business to realize goals. Bureaucrats were evaluated by their ability to achieve such goals. When they did not meet said goals, bureaucrats were replaced without predictability. At the same time, a "parachute" style of recruitment took form, in which people from outside the bureaucracy were brought in to expedite the implementation of policies.[17]

The minister of the MCI took improvised measures to achieve goals, including contests for export ideas and improvement of the ministry's administrative process, and used the results to decide promotions and transfers. For example, in 1976, the minister issued an order that required 300 bureaucrats, made up of section chiefs and below, take a qualification test and used the test results for personnel decisions.[18] Lateral entries were frequently given to those possessing certain degrees and technical knowledge as a form of motivational pressure to the regular bureaucrats and to spur short-term goal achievement.[19] Such measures damaged solidarity among bureaucrats and had a severely destabilizing effect upon personnel-related matters. Unsystematic and improvisational evaluation of bureaucrats and frequent outside hiring brought about destructive outcomes in terms of organizational stability. Under constant rumors about personnel changes and organizational reshuffling, bureaucrats could not concentrate on their work as they had to seek outside sources to secure their position and prospects for promotion. In short, all these gave rise to the "politicization" of bureaucracy.[20]

Furthermore, President Park's direct intervention in personnel decisions weakened organizational stability. Such intervention was closely related to his obsession with promoting exportation. As a former bureaucrat observed, Park frequently replaced bureaucrats who could not meet export targets:

> Q: Was there pressure on departmental heads and directors of bureaus from President Park?
> A: Ministers, vice-ministers, and deputy vice-ministers enjoyed stability if they performed well.
> Q: How did pressure on the minister affect the ministry as a whole?
> A: It manifested itself in terms of promotion and assignment of tasks. If the minister trusted some people, they stayed on. When I was director, I remember how often directors were replaced. They were fired for poor performance shortly after they were appointed.
> Q: You said personnel changes were quite frequent. How frequent were they?
> A: For those who were deemed incapable, replacement occurred every six months, and this was the case even with the minister. Minister Park Choong Hun himself was replaced after six months and later brought back to serve eight years, based on good export records. President Park never hesitated to cut people but did not completely abandon them and often brought them back again.[21]

The president's instructions regarding personnel matters were issued when he received reports and was conducting frequent on-the-spot inspections. For example, in 1970 when the export target was set to $1 billion, he urged the MCI to achieve the target during his annual inspection at the beginning of the year and specifically instructed staff to conduct the status inspection twice a year and ordered the replacement of those who were responsible but failed to achieve the goals.[22]

However, as export promotion was the most important concern of the top leader, exports were the most important standard whereby bureaucrats were evaluated; in addition, the tasks ordered from the president became the raison d'être and operational principles for the MCI. Under such circumstances, the ministerial level of personnel policies and bureaucratic stability gradually deteriorated. That is, the incessant imposition of tasks and the pressure to realize them, constant infusion of outsiders into the ministry, repetitive purges, and reshuffles and transfers caused chaos within the ministry. Personnel policies gradually became divorced from principles and predictability due to irregular staffing policies. In consequence, increasing penetration of the ministry by outsiders brought about the weakening of bureaucratic autonomy.

PRESIDENT-CENTERED DECISION-MAKING AND IMPLEMENTATION

President Park was more than just a commander in the style of the Japanese who sets the direction and oversees military units; he was involved in the details of decision-making. In his annual year-opening speeches, in addition to announcing new goals, he issued concrete directives as well as bringing up problems related to his decisions. Thus, he practically made decisions for ministries, and analysis and evaluations were conducted four times a year regarding progress on the president's decisions.[23] Consequently, decision-making is highly centralized around the president; all the major decisions either originated from him or could not succeed without his support. Such a dependence upon the top leader gave rise to serious negative consequences for bureaucratic stability. Decision-making was greatly influenced by the level of trust that could be secured from Park by ministries and stakeholders, including the deputy prime minister, officials at the secretariat to the president, industry commissions (heavy chemicals, for example), or others close to the president. Groups that secured the president's support garnered favorable decisions.[24]

In addition to president-centered decision-making, bureaucrats had to work in a highly uncertain environment, as most of the projects were pioneering experiments in production and export. This rendered bureaucrats vulnerable to failure.[25] Such vulnerability led to increasing dependency on the president for certainty through necessary funding and personnel, based on quick-changing market opportunities. Adding to the uncertain environment were the frequent changes of goals, as seen in the constant boosting of export targets. Such frequent changes led to close contact between bureaucrats and business as new information necessitated consultation. The fact that such contacts were primarily based on individual enterprises rather than industry as a whole increased frequency for individual companies to penetrate into the ministry.

Finally, the most damaging among the negative impacts of president-centered decision-making upon the ministry was the enabling of business to intervene in decision-making via the president. Such chaotic, undisciplined, and abrupt intervention by business based on earning the president's favor was dubbed the "wild horse phenomenon," in which the regular process of decision-making is bypassed completely. The result was a top-down style of decision-making that frequently left ministries and ministers ignored, with higher-level decisions being simply imposed upon them.[26] It is clear that the prominent role of the president in decision-making caused dependency of the ministry on the top leader in various ways, shrinking autonomy of the ministry; the president's personal initiation of policies, detailed intervention in decision-making, and frequent changes in decisions made are the main factors driving this dependency.

President Park also was as deeply involved in implementation as he was in decision-making. Even when decisions were made extemporaneously, he was willing to draw upon every means to speedily ensure expected outcomes. His obsession with detailed intervention during implementation was perhaps most clearly visible in the promotion of exports. He urged bureaucrats to apply rules and regulations flexibly when they were thought to be impeding exports; even then, speed was paramount.[27] These guidelines had serious implications for bureaucratic integrity and state-business relations, as they became the standards of daily administration of the MCI. Exports were the main priority in rendering state support to companies. So strong was the shared preoccupation with meeting targets among bureaucrats and businesspeople that colluding to falsify reports and export records frequently occurred. It reinforced target-oriented administrative behaviors and consequent "arbitrariness" in policy implementation, giving rise to an arbitrary application of rules and regulations while engaging in the international market through export.

The president's intervention in implementation could be also observed in his strong encouragement of close cooperation and sharing responsibility between relevant ministries. He tried to reduce confusion by eliminating inter-ministerial differences, which led him to be closely involved in the details of implementation. Such intervention was not limited to export issues; rather, it encompassed virtually every industry. There are many examples for the sense of urgency and speed in decision-making and implementation, which led to the president's crossing official administrative boundaries. For instance, an order issued on September 30, 1966, even mandated that the Central Intelligence Agency mobilize to facilitate implementation. Park also expressed deep concern about the delay in building the Hankook Fertilizer Company and ordered the KCIA to intervene to ensure that construction would be completed on schedule.[28]

Another example is the development of the Changwon National Industrial Complex. The project was hurriedly implemented by presidential order starting in October 1973. In November of the same year, the leading agency for the project was changed from the Water Resources Management Corporation to the Industrial Complex Development Corporation. There was little idea as to the scale of the complex, land use, or location of factories. It was typical of the 1960s and 1970s style of development that lacked preparation of concrete plans.[29]

Personnel policies of ministries were negatively impacted by such a sense of urgency. Interorganization boundaries were diluted from violations of boundaries among sub-units of the ministry, and all personnel resources of the ministry were concentrated in meeting export goals. As one former official of the MCI remarked, all sub-units of the ministry had to join in meeting export targets, regardless of their original official functions: "All of the departments of the ministry other than those in charge of textile and small-medium industries (which were directly responsible for exports in textile) scrambled. Under the minister who was assigned to meet export targets, the entire ministry needed to be united in achieving the singular goal of meeting export targets. The motto was 'think while you run.' And even though it was only six months, the results were remarkable."[30]

Naturally, companies inherited this pressure to export as state and business were put into constant contact during the process of implementation.[31] Such pressure ultimately worked to change the nature of state-business relations in the long run.[32] Business not only tried to secure maximal support from the state for exports but also went beyond by trying to expand the domestic market. Over time, moral hazard became rampant, particularly in the form of falsely inflating export records or including defective products. Some businesses secured permits under the guise of exporting in order to start new ventures unrelated to exports.[33]

The president's influence upon the implementation phase of key decisions via such capricious intervention led to the arbitrary breakdown of bureaucratic boundaries. The emphasis on exports begat unintended institutional consequences as international markets, which were beyond state intervention, limited administrative arbitrariness. The drive for exports at all costs resulted in arbitrary implementations of rules and regulations. Finally, the resulting constant and close contact between the state and business sowed the seeds for inescapable changes in the relationship dynamics between state and business. It is clear that the president's sense of urgency gave rise to the dilution of administrative boundaries and more frequent and closer contacts between state officials and business, compromising bureaucratic autonomy and principled implementation.

STATE-BUSINESS INTERACTIONS AND HOLLOWING OUT BUREAUCRACY

The formation of neofamilism entailed serious institutional consequences for the dynamics of the developmental state itself. In a nutshell, neofamilism resulted in a weakened bureaucracy, which lost such bureaucratic characteristics as organizational autonomy, legalism, professionalism, and impersonalism. The hollowing out of the bureaucracy all began with President Park, who set ambitious goals with a high level of urgency.

Park's recruitment strategy of combining merit with regionalism was a structural cause for intra-ministerial instability, reproduced through informal groups that were formed based on regional and school ties. Additionally, the top leader's detailed intervention in goal-setting, decision-making, and implementation further impeded bureaucratic autonomy. The president's sense of urgency also gave rise to ignoring boundaries between sub-ministerial units, as well as those between ministries. In addition, bureaucrats had to foster close relations with business as they moved expeditiously to meet stringent deadlines, set by a president who did not hesitate to penalize those who failed to meet his expectations. In fact, bureaucrats had to accommodate business's efforts to penetrate bureaucracy through neofamilial ties to secure state incentives and render every possible assistance to ensure their business success. Without business success, bureaucrats' careers would be endangered.

As for business, aware of the availability of financial, technical, and administrative incentives controlled by the state, executives resorted to every possible means in getting access to the incentives to open, maintain, and expand business. They sought to leverage every possible neofamilial tie, such as school and regional ties, from inside and outside of business to secure state incentives. What aggravated business penetration into state bureaucracy was the uncertain and volatile environment created by the president. Neofamilial ties played a bridging role between business and the state bureaucracy. The upshot of business-state interactions was a hollowed-out bureaucracy: rules and regulations were frequently violated with impunity, due to strong goal-attainment orientation. Thus, such mutual dependency blurred boundaries between bureaucracy and business and other social influence based on neofamilial ties.

Analyzing the impact of Park's personnel policies on long-term institutional dynamics reveals that merit principles were intricately combined with regionalism and other ties, which in turn played important conduit roles between the state and business. Political influence upon personnel policies gradually undermined bureaucratic stability. In short, the ministry was faced with two sources that penetrated its own decision-making and implementation, rendering bureaucratic autonomy to be precarious. Internally, the embedded regionalism and school ties in personnel policies gave rise to undermining of bureaucratic stability through the formation of informal groupings inside bureaucratic organizations, affecting promotion and transfer policies based on regionalism. Externally, state personnel policies were emulated by business sectors, and state bureaucracies were constantly penetrated by outside influence, especially business, ultimately causing hollowing out of bureaucracy.

DEBUREAUCRATIZATION

The hollowing out of bureaucracy is a form of "debureaucratization."[34] It is one of the three patterns of dynamic interactions between bureaucratic organization and environment: continuation of the original relationship, bureaucratization, and debureaucratization. The first type refers to the continuation of equilibrium; the second to the expansion of the original bureaucratic boundary to the outside environment, and the third to the compromise of bureaucratic autonomy due to the influence of the outside environment.[35] There are internal and external factors that affect the long-term consequences of bureaucratic organization. Internally, personnel policy is an important mechanism. Externally, how a bureaucratic organization approaches and manages the outside environment determines the organization's long-term institutional consequences.

In the first two cases of maintenance and bureaucratization, universal values, power equilibrium, and the principle of competition are secured in interactions with outside environment, and bureaucratic organizations actively engage the external environment to realize the goals set by them. In the case of debureaucratization, the bureaucratic organization is influenced by external environments and institutions.

Western literature on bureaucracy assumes a clear divide between inside and outside the bureaucracy, and cases deviating from this model are regarded as abnormal. From this perspective, debureaucratization is viewed as a stage in which the organization's goals are vulnerable to change and penetration from the outside. Thus, the question on debureaucratization hinges on the degree of dependency that the bureaucracy has upon the external environment. Does the assumption of the lack of shared goals apply to the case of the MCI type of hollowed bureaucracy?

The state and business in South Korea share the same goal of industrialization in the context of late industrialization. The state needs business and business needs the state. Unlike the assumption set by sociologist S. N. Eisenstadt, the setting of strict boundaries is unclear in the case of the Korean bureaucracy. For instance, the economic goals of the MCI had to be realized via private business. The state maintained a superior position over business by providing various incentives, but the successful implementation of economic policies relied on private business. This can be characterized as "commanding dependency," where a high degree of interlocking goals exists, a frequently observed characteristic of late industrialization. However, interlocking does not necessarily mean the goals are identical; it merely refers to some degree of sharing. The core issue is how to manage situations in which the respective expectations of the state and business toward each other diverge. Each case of late industrialization has its own way of handling the discrepancy between the expectations of the state and business.

From the perspective of bureaucracy, personnel policy and interaction patterns with business are important. In the case of Japan, strict merit-based personnel policies, internal consensus, and institutionalized relations with business are firmly established to prevent outside influence on bureaucracy.[36] The opposite case is the Soviet Union, where the state arrogates social interest to itself. The case of South Korea is distinct in that, unlike in Japan, personnel policy and interaction with business is not institutionalized, and thus goal identification and sharing between the state and business quite often fluctuates between the state and business. The arbitrary application of merit-based incentives—based on the degree of meeting export goals, ambitious goal-setting, implementation based on a high sense of urgency, and blurring boundaries with business—all contributed to the hollowing out of the bureaucracy.[37]

Squeezed between political pressure from above and penetration from below, the MCI was divided into a three-tiered organization. The upper level tier beyond the bureau director severely suffered from political pressure and ultimately became politicized, while the low-level tiers below the department fell victim to capricious bureaucratization based on frequent arbitrary decisions. The middle tier had to bear pressure from the other two tiers. The resulting bureaucratic chaos has frequently been regarded as a sign of bureaucratization that resists external pressure and tries to secure bureaucratic interests and becomes indifferent to outside influence (*pokchibudong*).[38]

However, what happened to the Korean bureaucracy is not so much conventional bureaucratization in terms of formalism, legalism, and collective resistance to outside influence; rather, Korean bureaucracy is suffering from bureaucratic chaos that comes from the lack of predictability in personnel policy, passivity in decision-making, and arbitrary implementation. What is interesting about this phenomenon is that on the surface it closely resembles bureaucratization in terms of the lack of policy initiative and indifference to the outside due to its passivity, but debureaucratization stemming from the hollowing out of bureaucracy should be distinguished from bureaucratization.[39]

DYNAMICS OF STATE-BUSINESS RELATIONS

The analysis of state dynamics and of interactions between the state and business in the process of industrialization sheds new light on how state-business relations evolved over time. The state's perception of business at the beginning of industrialization, business approaches to the state, the modes and patterns of interactions, and ultimately the hollowing out of the state itself are important factors that need to be considered in understanding the changing aspect of state-business relations.

Explanatory frameworks differ on the reason for a shift in state-business relations. One view is that the state effectively became a hostage to business as it could not abruptly stop supporting business, mainly due to the growth of business influence and partly due to the path dependence of past behaviors.[40] Another view highlights the exhaustion of state roles and functions in relation to business. Here the overlapping functions of the state with those of business are highlighted in that as the business grew in size and scope, the functions of the state became obsolete.[41] Besides, with democratization the developmental state had to face challenges from new political actors, such as labor.[42] A third view is that the image of business challenging the state is based on the phenomenal growth of business in terms of volume and scope. Indeed, Korean chaebols grew phenomenally: in 1979, the total assets of the 30 largest chaebols were 52.9% of GDP of South Korea, which jumped to 56.5% in 1986 and 66.7% in 1994.[43] Such expansion of the chaebols was quickly interpreted as a source of autonomy upon which chaebols even came to challenge the state.

This transformed image of business is all the more remarkable considering the historical backdrop regarding business dependency on the state. First, the image of business's lopsided dependency on the state has historical origins. When the military took power in 1961, it issued a special law punishing illicitly gained wealth in the past. Businessmen were arrested and forced to comply with state demands. Such measures contributed to the perception that business was subject to political control. Second, the state's perception of business was that business was not ready to develop on its own to compete, especially in the international market for exports. This perception in turn led the state to take a strongly protective approach by providing a wide range of incentives to business.[44]

Although business undeniably shifted from being weak and dependent to becoming bigger and stronger, we still lack a more nuanced picture of state-business relations in terms of the specific changing dynamics of the developmental state and their mutual impacts upon each other. Whether the developmental state ended up being constrained by strengthened business, or the state graduated from its own functions and thus business came to substitute for the state, or state autonomy was challenged by new actors, what is needed is a close examination of the dynamically changed institutional character and ethos of both the state and business over time. To do this, it is necessary to go beyond functional logic, to transcend a structural dichotomy between a strong state and weak business or between strong business and a weak state. There is more to state-business relations than a purely zero-sum logic, which can only be understood through analyzing the microdynamics of state-business relations over time.

Even in a one-sided relationship of command and subjection, the strong side is not completely free from influence of the weak side, nor is the strong side always superior to the weak. Furthermore, the existing approaches do not pay close attention to the process and consequences of mutual impact between the strong and the weak over time. Without understanding such processes, it does not logically stand that those mere changes in original conditions reversed the relative positions of the strong and the weak over time. How did the business sector affect state dynamics, and in turn how did those dynamics affect state-business relations? Strategies of business in dealing with the state also need to be analyzed. Without attending to interactions between the state and business over time, the changing nature of the state-business relations cannot be properly understood.[45]

State-business relations evolved within the context of business's extreme level of dependence on the state from the outset. Dependent relations are not a static or monolithic concept; they can manifest in different forms over time. At the same time, dependency once established seldom disappears completely.[46] We should not assume the weakening state and ascending business without understanding interactions between the two over the course of industrialization; a dependent relationship takes on different forms over time.[47]

COMMANDING DEPENDENCY AND DEPENDENT MANIPULATION

Dependence on Business for Goal Achievement

At the initial stage of industrialization, the state enjoyed a commanding position in state-business relations, whereas business was dependent, in that it had to follow the state. This situation began to quickly change as implementation progressed. A new dynamic between commanding and dependence emerged through state-business interactions that focused on exports. The MCI had to promote exports at all costs by mobilizing every possible means.

Against this backdrop, the MCI executed export promotion policies to meet targets set by the president. Favoritism frequently became a controversial issue but was not taken as seriously when rampant pragmatism drove implementation. Violation of regulations were tolerated if targets were met, as shown by one case that happened in the mid-1960s. The MCI opposed inspecting the taxes of trading companies as it might negatively affect export promotion. When criticism arose surrounding favorable treatment in relation to big enterprises' cartel issues, the MCI changed its ministerial decree before the law for the coordination of SMIS (small-medium industries) was made. These demonstrate that procedural measures, legal or otherwise, could be liberally applied when exports were at stake.

Meanwhile, contact between the state and business further increased and became more institutionalized. Since 1965, the president began overseeing export promotion meetings on a monthly basis and export goals were scrutinized.[48] The president issued orders and received feedback every month. Within the MCI, monthly consultative meetings with business examined export-related problems and obtained concerns from business. Thus, private businesses involved in exporting came to be involved in institutionalized processes and held regular contact with the president and related ministries, including the MCI.[49] Under intensifying pressure to export, the ministry's coordinating power began to weaken. For example, in the second half of 1966, the minister of the MCI called in businessmen and encouraged them to achieve export goals.[50] Initially the MCI put pressure on companies that were unable to meet export targets but shifted over time toward methods of persuasion and ultimately entreaty when the situation became urgent and difficult.

Bureaucrats at the MCI busily pleaded to companies to meet export targets. At first, they threatened to cut support to business unless export targets were met by a given deadline. Where this approach failed, an alternative attempt promised incentives for realizing targets, namely a recommendation for a presidential citation. When even this did not work as intended, bureaucrats were ultimately forced to defer to companies by asking about the bottlenecks to increasing exports. In response, companies issued every detailed complaint and bureaucrats had to listen. Thus, companies held the upper hand in promoting exports.[51] In order to realize export targets, companies had to comply with commands from the state and yet tried to take advantage of state bureaucrats who were constantly under pressure from the president to realize export goals. Knowing the vulnerability of state bureaucrats, companies' perceptions of the state changed visibly to take advantage of it.

Beginning in 1975, the MCI pursued a policy to establish large-scale comprehensive trading companies as a way to secure export bases. Once granted permission to operate a trading company, a company could receive guaranteed state support in the form of financial, tax, and foreign currency incentives.[52] The introduction of comprehensive trading companies meant a larger portion of big business involved in exports and greater room to secure incentives from the MCI, making it more difficult for the MCI to control companies. "Business grew indifferent or insensitive to government policies. A situation developed where it became difficult to hear even words of appreciation from business."[53] The scale of "trading companies" grew in the course of specialization and growth through export.[54]

Comprehensive trading companies took every measure, legal or not, to maximize state support. Rather than improve competitiveness or productivity, their primary goal was to demonstrate visible export results regardless of legality: "The state provided incentives based on export volume regardless of profitability. Thus, there was no difference between a company making a 99-dollar profit with one dollar cost and another making one dollar profit with a 99-dollar cost. Under such circumstances, which companies would choose the first way with all the troubles and effort?"[55] The government strongly demanded export increases in return for the incentives provided to business. This encouraged the practice of dumping, or exporting a product at a loss, and even the purchasing of export records from other companies to meet state expectations.

Policy Learning and Manipulation of Business

Business circles learned how to increase their influence on the MCI. They learned that it was quite effective to go through political channels to influence the ministry, and when involved in projects of high priority to the state, this approach allowed business to obtain additional benefits. The best example of this was a presidential ordinance to freeze private loan markets on August 3, 1973, from which the business sector learned that the state would still continue supporting them despite their mediocre performance.[56] Such confidence led all the major companies to participate in the government's large projects under the Heavy and Chemical Industries (HCI) program without much critical thinking or planning. Business also learned that the most effective means to exercise influence on bureaucracy was through high-level political channels rather than through legal and rational bureaucratic channels.[57]

Squeezed between political influence and business sectors, bureaucrats gradually lost their coordinating power. Regular meetings between business and the president provided new grounds for political approaches to business matters. Decisions made by bureaucrats were frequently changed due to external influence, as seen in the cases of investment coordination and exiting underperforming business.[58] When many companies ended up with large debts due to unrealistic expansion, the government tried to apply special measures to correct the situation, yet companies used political connections to try to avoid sanctions. In turn, the capacity for government to correct the situation weakened.

The government adopted a policy to promote the HCI sector by guaranteeing all possible supporting measures after selecting individual companies. A good example is the shipbuilding industry. The government urged Hyundai Construction Co. to conclude a contract with a Greek shipbuilding company and used it to obtain loans from British banks to establish Hyundai Heavy Industries. Also, in an attempt to develop the heavy chemical industry by inviting related companies to industrial sites, different sites for different industries were decided on: the second steel plan in the end of Nakdong River; nonferrous metals in Onsan; machinery in Ch'angwŏn; shipbuilding in Kŏje; electronics in Kumi; and chemical industries in Yŏsu and Kwangyang.[59]

Based on such investment plans by the government, it was presumed that strong supporting measures would follow. In fact, special support was given to all the major firms in the HCI sector. In the case of Hyundai's Ulsan shipyard construction, the government directly adopted a plan to construct port facilities. The opposition party at that time criticized the plan as being a special favor to Hyundai, but the project was carried out.[60] Thus, businessmen were well aware of their influence on government. That is, they learned through experience and assumed that if they started big projects, the government had to support them. The more the government emphasized certain projects, the easier it was to get support from the government. This led to a dilemma: the government, once committed, was put into a position in which it could neither render continuing support nor stop supporting business.[61]

To summarize, at the beginning of industrialization, the MCI or the state was able to mobilize business with support from the president. However, faced with ambitious export targets imposed by the top, the MCI lost control over business and their autonomous position vis-à-vis business began to erode. However, this does not signify a fundamental change in the relative position between the state and business. Instead, it meant the state's dependence on business expanded and intensified during industrialization. That is, the state's command over business became more dependent on the latter for success, reaching the point of *commanding dependency*. Business, however, embraced state projects with a high degree of confidence that the state would support them. In a mutually dependent situation, business learned how to maximize state support. Business responded to the state's commanding dependency through what could be termed *manipulative dependency*: a shift from the one-sided dependence of business on the state to business manipulating the state at both political elite and bureaucracy levels. As the president's top-down decision-making intensified, bureaucrats had to comply with increasingly over-ambitious targets, which in turn increased contact between the state and business. Bureaucrats had to command business while being dependent on it (commanding dependency), whereas business learned to affect internal decision-making of the state (manipulative dependency).

THE CHANGING NATURE OF STATE-BUSINESS RELATIONS

With the state bureaucracy undergoing a hollowing out, the nature of state-business relations evolved from business merely taking advantage of resources and opportunities given by the state to business more actively mobilizing the state to their benefit through resistance and threats to change state policies. The forced restructuring of underperforming companies is a good case in point. Overinvestment and redundant investment had become a serious problem by the mid-1970s. The ambitious and urgent implementation of heavy chemical industries ended up with excessive facility investment, resulting in the proportion of "policy-related finance" constituting 80% of total bank loans.[62] Companies ended up overinvesting without considering actual demand, under the expectation that there will be ample state support behind state-promoted projects. Such investment dysfunction gave rise to excessive competition and decreased productivity, to the point where the situation could not have improved without forced restructuring.

In 1979, the government announced the so-called Comprehensive Economic Stabilization Policies of April 27 to deal with overlapping investments, especially in the areas of shipbuilding, generation facilities, petrochemicals, construction machinery, and specialty steel.[63] The Investment Adjustment Measures of May 25 focused on generation facilities and Daewoo's overinvestment in shipbuilding. Investment in generation facilities was divided into two groups, Hyundai and Daewoo/Samsung. Hyundai Heavy Industries particularly presented various demands, such as support for investment, operation funds, and administrative support, and was passive in taking over the Hyundai Yanghaeng, so that it only took over the assets while excluding debt.[64] Later, investment in generation facilities was divided into three companies under the investment adjustment for the HCI sector. Hyundai took over automobiles while Daewoo absorbed Hyundai Yanghaeng. Daewoo came to ask the government for 700 billion won in support, and the deal could not be completed at the ministerial level and was brought back to the drawing board.[65]

Under the new military government in 1980, all previous polices were nullified and a new plan for investment adjustment was prepared for generation facilities, automobiles, and heavy construction machinery. Daewoo was supposed to take over Hyundai Yanghaeng but was not able to come up with even half of the 200 billion won that was needed for the takeover. Therefore, Daewoo ended up asking for the rest of the amount from the government. Ultimately, Hyundai Yanghaeng, renamed Hanguk Heavy Industry, was reorganized as a public corporation.[66] Another typical example is the case of Daewoo Shipbuilding, which complied with President Park's order to take over Okp'o Shipbuilding and established Daewoo Heavy Industries in 1978. The president promised 250 billion won of support in return for the takeover.[67] However, additional support did not arrive smoothly after Park was assassinated in 1979, so when Daewoo completed the shipyard in 1981, it faced worldwide depression and came close to bankruptcy. Chairman Kim Woochoong threatened the government with bankruptcy unless the government provided additional support.[68]

The Daewoo case demonstrates that to the state, a takeover of a troubled company meant the acquiring company would rely on itself. Yet, from the acquiring company's perspective, a takeover was understood as a guarantee of state support. Business followed state policies, but when things became difficult, they asked for state support. That is, business reasserted claims based on what they had learned in the process of industrialization, indicating the business sector's improved bargaining power.

Business has succeeded in overturning government decisions to their benefit in other ways. On June 28, 1980, the government adopted financial reform to abolish preferential interest rates for policy funds that the government renders to business.[69] The measure also prohibited fake names in financial transactions to enhance transparency (real name reforms). The business community successfully blocked this measure through lobbying.[70] Another significant case involves the decision for the Sunkyong Group's entry into the mobile communications industry in July 1992. The MCI originally wanted to postpone the decision, arguing that the designation of companies for the second mobile communication industry would negatively impact the trade deficit. However, the Ministry of Communication advocated pursuing the project in the name of developing communications services. The Economic Planning Board (EPB) sided with the MCI, citing the same reasons about the trade deficit. However, President Roh Tae Woo made a political decision to complete the decision before his term was over. The chaebols originally supported the Ministry of Communication, but once Sunkyong was designated as the main company, they politicized the issue and tried to link it to the presidential election in December 1992. Sunkyong ultimately returned its business permit.[71]

The most salient example of a business's persistent effort was Samsung's announced intention to enter the auto industry in January 1990.[72] The Korean Automobile Industry Association and the existing auto companies strongly opposed the plan, arguing that the move would create excessive competition. Considering the opposition, the MCI delayed making a decision until August 1990, when the MCI further postponed the decision until the second half of 1991.[73] Samsung once again expressed its intent to enter commercial vehicle production, and existing auto companies continued to collectively strongly oppose Samsung's decision. The MCI once again took a cautious reserved position and did not make a definitive decision. Existing automakers also launched political lobbying. In the meantime, Samsung Heavy Industries announced that Samsung was planning to start auto production. The MCI refused to open public hearings, a procedure required by law, and finally in July 1991 permitted Samsung's entry into the auto industry.[74]

The implications of these cases are that the bureaucracy, which had been hollowed out due to excessive penetration of external influence, had more difficulty in making autonomous and consistent decisions. Decision-making capacity based on technical and rational criteria was hampered due to increasing influence from the outside, including the political sphere. In this respect, the hollowed-out bureaucracy that emerged in Korea is distinct in nature from what happened in Western Europe. In the latter case, hollowing refers to the weakening of central state power due to the liberalization of state functions to the private sector; in Korea, however, state bureaucracies eventually came to lose bureaucratic functions based on laws and lose professionalism due to the penetration of external influences.[75] A key problem was that the state had become so accustomed to wielding state initiatives to support business during industrialization that they could not sufficiently perceive the extent to which business had learned to exploit state support. Even when the government threatened to stop support when business didn't comply with demands for investment adjustment, business knew that the government was ultimately bound to take over investment losses.[76]

HOLLOWED COMMANDING AND BARGAINING DEPENDENCY

Due to the many irregular measures and constant revision of decision matters, business perceptions toward the EPB and the MCI had already changed. Business, through various contacts with the state, fully learned how to turn even disadvantageous situations to their advantage. Under such circumstances bureaucrats had to change the measures that they took due to the manipulations by political and business circles. The repeated practice of such behavior gave rise to *hollowed commanding*, in which state decisions lost their effectiveness due to weakened state capacity. Meanwhile, with state policymaking and implementation becoming ineffective due to this hollowed commanding, the chaebols' approach to the state evolved to actively manipulating the state beyond merely receiving advantages and resources in a dependent manner.

Such an overly aggressive and demanding posture of business can be viewed as challenging a weak state. For example, Kim Eun Mee observed that the fact that chaebols were deeply involved in major economic decisions about chaebol consolidation in the early 1980s is proof for a compromise between strengthened chaebols and a weakened state.[77] To fully understand the institutional legacy of dependency characterizing chaebols or business, an analogy is in order. State-business relations are analogous to father-son relations: when a grown son tries to be independent of his father, he is bound to cause friction or disagreement with his father. Yet the son may ultimately return to his father for help, in which case the father cannot but help the son. In the 1980s, business tried to avoid state control but attributed any troubles to the state—and ultimately expected the state's protection and support. Accordingly, business frequently does not attribute its troubles to itself, with the majority of responsibility attributed to the state. It was not easy to locate businessmen who were willing to take risks; why take risks when there were easier ways? Business pointed fingers at the state, expected special favors, and denied the state's attempt to oppose chaebol initiatives: "Chaebols wanted limitless state support . . . chaebols wanted favors without state and political intervention. What they want is a laissez-faire environment along with state favors and the suppression of labor."[78]

Business during industrialization can be compared to a child who pilfers money from the father's pocket; business pursued its own interest through the state's industrial policies. The chaebols, which grew in scale and scope over the course of industrialization, took advantage of the state in increasingly sophisticated ways. However, what is important is that the growth of the chaebols did not bring about a fundamental change in state-business relations. As a son returns to a father when he is in trouble, so did chaebols return to the state with their woes, asking for special favors, as one former high-ranking bureaucrat testified:

A: From the perspective of the government, supporting business was regarded as "incubating." The state tried to push out business to stand on its own as there was a limit to what the state could do.

Q: When did the government take such a position?

A: It was when the heavy chemical industries were started. The government tried to drive out chaebols and encourage them to be independent. The reason for the failure to do so is simple. There was a time when the government provided special favors to business mainly to concentrate capital, which was scarce. The government used that as leverage over business for some time. Now the government urged chaebols to fight against bureaucracies to become independent of state influence. The position at higher levels was that it was time to wean.

Q: What was the chaebols' response? They did not like to be weaned?

A: Of course, they did not want to. They wanted to do away with government controls while holding on to the special favors that they received.[79]

As pointed out earlier, the current literature on the relationship paints a dichotomous picture for state-business relations. In contrast, our analysis demonstrates how the strong state–weak business dynamic at the beginning of late industrialization changed to one of strong business–weak state. The reference for such a dichotomy comes from a state-society confrontational model drawn from Western experiences. As shown all along, state-business relations were not simply one between the strong and the weak in which the order simply reverses over time. In late industrialization, goals are shared and the state has to support business for success. The state maintained a superior position over business with its incentives. This relationship can be characterized as commanding dependency on the part of the state and dependent manipulation on the part of business, in which business tries to maximize state benefits within the context of dependency.

With time, the state came to lose control over business due to this hollowing-out process, not only due to business challenging the state from a position of greater size and strength. This weakened capacity of the state can be called "hollowed commanding." For business, a better understanding of how to take advantage of the state without fully overcoming dependency or still maintaining a willingness to depend on the state creates *bargaining dependency*, in which business wants to exercise greater bargaining power with the state but continues to be dependent on the state. The underlying assumption of this analysis is that dependency once established cannot be easily shed, and thus a mechanistic approach to state-business relations based on size and scale needs to be reviewed critically.

The top leader's sense of national backwardness and urgency to industrialize had a decisive impact on setting goals as well as on the style, substance, and speed of decision-making and implementation. This in turn affected the modes of operation of the ministry and ultimately led to changes in bureaucratic integrity. The president's ambition was a considerable source of pressure upon bureaucrats, making bottom-up decision-making virtually impossible. Dependence on the top leader in decision-making and initiation of new policies gave rise to heated competition among bureaucrats to secure the president's trust and support, along with the so-called wild horse phenomenon in which outsiders sought direct contact with the top leader, bypassing bureaucrats. All these brought about the politicization of public bureaucracy.

Decision-making from a sense of urgency also heightened the need for information from outside the bureaucracy. However, more importantly, the president's drive to export forced bureaucrats to develop closer relationships with business. Such mingling inevitably led to arbitrary decisions and situational responses due to company-specific policy not based on institutionalized procedures. Related to these outcomes are the double-faced consequences of export-oriented policies. On the one hand, export volume worked as an objective standard for evaluating bureaucrats and a constraining force on corruption, as exports depend upon the international market. On the other, obsessive export promotion permitted loosening standards in applying rules and regulations, giving rise to arbitrariness in decision-making and implementation.

Last, president-centered decision-making patterns easily crossed boundaries between administrative agencies and hampered institutionalized interactions between administrative units. The MCI's ability to coordinate different units within the ministry crumbled. President Park's regional background and sense of urgency to industrialize created an organizational culture combining regionalism and merit in personnel policy. Through use of the merit system and regionalism, the top leader secured loyalty and enhanced effectiveness and efficiency of economic developmental policies. Consequently, the proportion of MCI officials from the southeastern region of Korea created informal organizations based on regional backgrounds. Such a phenomenon was not unique to the MCI and spread to business and the rest of society.[80] Such mimesis of state by society in turn exposed the bureaucracy to greater risk of being penetrated by external social actors, particularly business. In addition to such structural factors, the president's frequent warnings and punishment of failure to meet export targets through personnel changes further undermined organizational stability.

In terms of decision-making, rapid economic development meant decisions had to frequently change, resulting in pragmatism where every possible means had to be mobilized to realize goals. During implementation, the phenomenon of particularism emerged, in which governmental policies were aimed at specific companies, which further reinforced mingling between bureaucrats and business in decision-making. Pervasive particularism in policy implementation indicates an extremely volatile environment with a high degree of uncertainty, as there is much ambiguity in daily decision-making and implementation.[81] Thus, the merit system lost its effectiveness when combined with regionalism, and overly ambitious goals and their hasty implementation blurred internal and external boundaries. As a result, the organization of the MCI was not bureaucratized; rather, the bureaucratic nature of the MCI was hollowed out over time from constant penetration of outside influences.

Civil Society and Democratization

CHAPTER 5

Discourses on civil society have, over their long history, evolved in different directions, depending on time, place, and sociopolitical contexts.[1] Yet there has been a tendency to indiscriminately apply a universal and ahistorical concept of civil society to describe different settings. An example of this trend is the idea that civil society is a part of society with a life of its own, different from the state and largely autonomous from it. Civil society thus has been envisioned to lie beyond the boundaries of family, clan, and locality.[2]

This typical illustration of autonomous society and limited state, based on market economy and legal institutions that protect individuals, has been widely adopted and used regardless of regional and historical differences. However, this view is merely an extrapolation of British or French cases, or "a privileged moment in the history of England, Scotland, and France."[3] As sociologist Adam Seligman observes, "it should be clear by now that however admirable the idea of civil society is as a political slogan, we should have serious doubts as to its efficacy as a concrete model for social and political practice. These doubts arise both from the inadequacy of the idea itself, along with the contradictions that inhere to it, and from the fact that it reflects not only a particular stage of historical development in the West but the particular conditions that are obtained there and not necessarily in other parts of the world."[4] When this image of civil society—which spans macrostructural levels down to individual psychological characteristics as components of civil society—is extrapolated to the non-Western world, it is either adopted as an ideal, highly abstract model lacking in detailed historical analysis or conveyed as ideal weapons in anti-authoritarian struggles.

At the same time, the discrepancy that the concept of civil society causes between the ideal and reality easily leads to frustration or an inferiority complex among political activists in the non-Western world. More specifically, when the concept was extended to Eastern Europe, Asia, and Africa, it became associated with democratization. In these newly democratizing countries, the term *civil society* was adopted not because of existing or available conditions for a civil society but rather because of its freshness and novel symbolic value for mobilizing people around anti-dictatorial movements.[5] Such a political use of the definition of civil society has led to confusion and myths surrounding the relationship between democratization and civil society. Equating civil society with democratization leads to a misconceived notion that wherever there is democratization, there is civil society.

While it would be misleading to think of democratization and civil society as being unconnected, the prevailing conflated view cited above tends to uncritically regard oppositional forces arrayed against non-democratic regimes as necessarily constituting civil society. As philosopher Axel Honneth remarks, "This concept served to tie together all the spheres of social action not belonging to state institutions, insofar as these spheres could serve as a basis for the construction of a democratic opposition."[6] Opposition forces are composed of various groups, whose natures and orientations can only be understood in relation to the wider social context and to leading political groups. That is, depending on features of the structure and ethos of a society, opposition forces that merely engage in democratization movements may or may not develop into civil society. As one expert on the issue pointed out, without holistically considering general characteristics of society or ordinary citizens, literature tends to focus on elite-led or dominant democratization movements at the top rather than at the level of society and its ordinary citizens.[7] The general literature on civil society misses this point.

This elite-oriented approach tends to view the number of opposition groups and civil organizations as an indicator of civil society development. The sudden mushrooming of civil organizations during or after democratization is certainly a big change that is not to be ignored, but the sheer number of organizations do little to describe the depth and extent of civil society. Weber aptly comments that "the quantitative spread of organizational life does not always go hand in hand with its qualitative significance."[8] Related is the tendency to identify social movements with civil society. The fact that social movements have been instrumental to toppling non-democratic regimes is significant in understanding the nature of civil society. However, there is a rift between anti-regime movements and the development of civil society. Whether social movement leads to civil society depends on many other factors, such as general societal features and the nature of the relationship between political elite groups and the masses.

The confusion and myths originate from the fact that elite-led democratization movements in Eastern European and Asian countries adopt the same definition of civil society as seen in prototype cases such as Great Britain and France without considering historical contexts. In latter cases, civil society originally had more to do with social order than political order, where gradually political democracy grew based on social conditions. In contrast, in non-Western cases, political democratization was initiated and led by elite political groups that were not necessarily joined by social groups in the form of social movements. Political sociologist Luis Roniger's remark on this point is germane: "Whereas the concept was phrased originally in connection with the nature of modernity, in the last decade the revival of interest in civil society has been connected with the process of democratization. This has created a widespread conceptual identification between civil society, democracy, and equality."[9]

New ways of understanding civil society reflect such frustration and limitations of the conventional use of civil society and seek possibilities of diverse paths to civil society framed by context. Historian Frank Trentmann's remarks in this regard are revealing and significant: "Rather than crystallizing into a single master definition, then, the modern history of civil society is an unfolding dialogue between different imaginaries of the social. The dialogue rests on a shared recognition that society has its own life with roots outside the state and a shared interest in the mechanisms and values that make society work, not on any programmatic, let alone ideological, agreement on its relationship to state and economy."[10] Trentmann's remarks raise interesting and important comparative questions. For instance, regarding the autonomy of civil society in relation to the state, one might question the different degrees and thus different patterns of autonomy, depending on the historical and institutional development of a society. Another point to consider is whether individualism is a necessary condition for civil society and, if so, whether we can imagine different degrees of individual autonomy as a basis for civil society.

Such concerns about avoiding a historically specific conception of civil society led to relatively more open and dynamic definitions. Sociologist Jeffrey C. Alexander, for instance, defines civil society "as the arena of social solidarity that is defined in universalistic terms. It is the we-ness of a national community, the feeling of connectedness to one another that transcends particular commitments, loyalties, and interests and allows there to emerge a single thread of identity among otherwise disparate people."[11] Such broad definitions are meant to go beyond historically specific cases of civil society and open possibilities to accommodate different paths of civil society development. However, it is important to accept different patterns of state-society relations and thus varying degrees of social autonomy in different contexts as well as to come up with a typology of different cases of social changes in the world, based upon which a comparative framework can be formulated.[12] Korean scholarship on civil society is thus due for re-examination through the lens of neofamilism.

KOREAN STUDIES OF CIVIL SOCIETY

Most of the problems and weaknesses as seen in the general research on civil society are evident in studies of Korea. For instance, it is generally assumed that democratization is closely related to civil society. Civil society is viewed either as (a) an important contributing factor for democratization or (b) its consequence. In many cases, the relationship between the two views is not clearly stated. Scholars who adopt the former view approach civil society as a way to explain democratic transition and consolidation, while the latter camp focuses on expansion and development of civil society.[13] The exact nature of the relationship has seldom been questioned. Impressed with the number of organizations that were formed during democratization, civil society is presumed to have existed to oppose the authoritarian regime and was assumed to have bloomed further with successful democratization. Ultimately, a strong continuity is assumed to exist between civil society and social movements for democratization. Establishing such a mechanistic connection between civil society and democratization makes it difficult to question the nature of social movements prior to democratization and to discern whether, why, and how social movements necessarily lead to civil society.[14]

This lack of clarity is, however, not accidental; it reflects the lack of understanding the complex relationship between socioeconomic changes and democratization (political changes).[15] Democratization initiated by politicized activist groups, successful industrialization, and an emergent middle class and workers led to an easily assumed conclusion of the existence of civil society. Mass participation in the democratization process is regarded as being tantamount to civil society. Democratization is viewed as a joint effort by both elite activists and the masses (*minjung*). Social movements are understood to develop almost automatically into civil society.

Here the aforementioned pitfalls of the current literature repeat themselves. Absent are concrete analyses of historical patterns of the emergence of civil society; the typical state-versus-society model is imposed on the Korean case, and opposition at the elite level is assumed to be shared by the masses without a detailed analysis of the relationship between the two. As will be shown, it is true that the elite and the masses held certain shared interests in opposing authoritarianism in the process of Korean democratization, but that says little about the relationship between the two groups or about the extent to which such a sentiment of opposition against the authoritarian regime was shared. In short, the Western model was imposed without a concrete analysis of social structure and ethos at the societal level at the time of elite-initiated democratization after liberation.[16]

Indeed, a review of major works on civil society in Korea reveals how such an automatic assumption of civil society leads to awkward explanations of the nature of Korean civil society. Frequently quoted peculiarities are cultural and historical in nature, such as civil society without civic rights, lack of pluralism, family orientation, network orientation, inability to develop civil values and inner moralities, amalgamation of modern and traditional values, and regionalism. Within this cultural perspective where cultural characteristics of Korean society are shared, there are some variations.[17] One view argues that despite the distinctiveness of state-led economic development, the Korean middle class emerged as a pillar of civil society as in the West. In this view, negative factors such as a strong central state power; statism; a state, capital and mass media tripartite alliance; cronyism; a politicized civil society; the weak foundation for the welfare state; and the weak link of civic organizations to the grass roots in Korea are attributed to state dominance.[18]

A slightly different set of views within this Korean tradition of studying civil society contends that cronyism and authoritarianism were the problems with the state, while a different pattern developed at the societal level through capitalistic development and education.[19] These views, despite differences, share the flaw of mistakenly presuming the separation of state, economy, and society—with little understanding of how the state, economy, society, and tradition all interacted to cause distinct patterns of cultural and social changes and state dynamics during Korea's late industrialization.

Put differently, these views suffer from the assumption that industrialization brings about universal social consequences. From this perspective, it becomes extremely difficult to understand how the emergence of the middle class in Korea occurred under strong traditional and non-modern cultural values.[20] At the same time, as long as they hold assumptions of universal industrial social changes, there is no way to consider how culture interacts with industrialization, and therefore cultural values are viewed as remaining static and treated as separate from the industrialization process. These approaches attempt to mitigate this pitfall by attributing "negative" cultural values to state dominance or dependent development patterns. However, they do not explain why and how the state or dependent forms of development were related to these traditional values without affecting society and particularly the economy. In short, it is futile to posit the assumption of universal industrial social changes regardless of the patterns of economic development. Thus, without an adequate framework to explain how tradition and culture interacted with economic development in which the state plays a strong role, it becomes difficult to synthesize cultural and economic changes. The absence of a framework to understand how culture and tradition interact with the economy led to a strangely optimistic view that regionalism can be conducive to rejuvenation of civil society.[21]

In fact, it is almost fashionable to try to understand distinctive features of Korean civil society by models developed in Western contexts. Korean Marxists argue that civil society is too ambiguous to locate the true social base for democratization and that the true base is *minjung*, a synonym for all oppressed forces under authoritarian rule.[22] Other views adopted a trichotomized model of state/political society/civil society, with political society inserted between civil society and state. These efforts to understand distinctive aspects of Korea's civil society reinforce the universalistic view of civil society by treating distinctiveness within universal frameworks. Furthermore, such model-based approaches of trying to fit realities into models fail to suggest frameworks for understanding distinctive aspects of interactions among state, economy, and society.[23]

One of the interesting points of confusion in Korean literature is the treatment of chaebols from the perspective of civil society. Marxists consider chaebols as a part of the state, while another view describes chaebols as agents for confronting the state. Most literature is silent about the chaebols' theoretical status and relation to civil society. As much as this indicates confusion in the field, it is important to note that we lack an adequate political sociology of late industrialization.

The state is significantly absent in the discussion of civil society in Korean literature. It is only logical when we consider the Western orientation of the models and arguments. However, given the state's strong role in industrialization and other matters, it is necessary to consider how the state evolved institutionally during and after industrialization and democratization. First, while shedding assumptions of universal industrial social changes, a conceptual framework and empirical analyses are needed to determine the structural features and distinct ethos that emerged in the course of industrialization. Second, the relationship between the political activist groups and the masses needs to be better differentiated. Third, the state and international factors need to be considered in terms of their roles and impacts in relation to civil society.[24]

In short, the Korean case is complex in that at the political levels there was sharp confrontation between opposition groups and the regime, while a completely different structure and ethos emerged among the masses, resulting in serious implications for the emergence of civil society in Korea. Neo-familism is crucial in understanding the dual aspect of Korean masses: on the one hand, they were sympathetic toward anti-authoritarian struggles; on the other, their daily lives were run based on neofamilial practices for survival. The next task is to explore these complex interaction patterns.

STATE-SOCIETY RELATIONS IN A COMPARATIVE PERSPECTIVE

The following analysis is aimed at demonstrating the distinct patterns of state-society relations; they are not intended to historicize each pattern, and therefore they are ideal-typical in highlighting fundamental differences among the four different types of state-society relations: state-versus-society, state-in-society, state-over-society, and state-leading-society.

State-versus-Society Model

Great Britain is an exemplary case for the state-versus-society model. It is well known that Britain experienced spontaneous industrialization in which the market played a major role and thus the state's presence was negligible.

Class rose as a new basis of social identity, and individualism became the primary mode of personal existence. To the extent that British civil society was against the state in this implicit sense (as opposed to the active oppositional stance of the French bourgeoisie), the state's role was limited to legal provisions for charity, incentives for workers to establish self-help savings banks, promoting fraternal societies, retail and industrial co-ops, and legal guarantees for labor unions.[25]

Such perception of state and society by the bourgeoisie led to a proliferation of voluntary organizations at the rural as well as urban levels. The fact that voluntary organizations spread through the entire nation distinguishes the British case from late developers, where civil organizations are usually organized at the central or urban levels. The voluntary organizations in Great Britain were operated on democratic principles, providing a high level of affinity with the political democratization process that was to follow.[26]

One important factor in the growth of civil society in Great Britain was the role of political parties. Local party organizations went beyond their role in elections to become instrumental in political education and inculcation of values: local parties implemented regular lectures and discussions of political issues and programs to understand the requisites of a good government. They also implemented projects to teach people how to read newspapers critically and develop critical ways of thinking, offered recreation programs, and suggested habits to abide by laws.[27]

The most important implication of the British experience for other cases is its gradual transition from economic changes to political ones. Social instability was avoided due to the democratic transition that occurred amid economic plenty. The British pattern of democratization is distinguished from many non-Western cases where democratization was launched by certain elite groups. In Great Britain there was considerable affinity between economic changes based on the market and patterns of social change. Civil society was implicitly linked to market principles in terms of individualism and universalism, an aspect that cannot be easily applied to other cases of social and political changes.

State-in-Society Model

The state-in-society model is one in which the state is disconnected from social organizations; thus, social organizations are autonomous from the state and have no engagement, or the state cannot reach them.[28] In the African context, state boundaries do not necessarily coincide with traditional tribal boundaries due to colonial control, rendering the state's reach among villages difficult. Traditional villages are left autonomous and thus resistant to state influence. Migdal calls this situation strong society versus weak state and characterizes it as a "web-like society" in that once the state reaches the villages, it cannot move or get out.[29]

There are three different forms of social organization in a web-like society in terms of their orientations toward the state. One group is basically survival oriented in nature. Urban migrants organize themselves based on regional and blood ties to survive harsh urban settings. Naomi Chazan calls them "a medley of local improvement societies, farmers' and women's cooperatives, and spiritual churches."[30] These groups are isolated from the state and do not undermine the state's power. The second group is more threatening to the state in that they contend and supersede and thus try to take over the state. Fundamental groups, ethno-national movements, and ideological associations belong to this category. The third group includes trade unions, student organizations, and women's organizations. Chazan calls them pseudo-civil society as they resemble civil society but are actually strongly influenced and manipulated by the state, primarily via patron-client networks. The state lacks the discipline and consistency to deal with these organizations, which frequently invoke particularistic access to state power.[31]

These three groups are not conducive to the development of civil society. The first group is withdrawn from the state, the second challenges it, and the third internally undermines state authority. In particular, the phenomenon of withdrawing from the state is quite serious as people protect themselves by relying on their own survival mechanisms at the local level. Chazan explains in the context of Africa that "with state agencies unable or unwilling to assume responsibility for the welfare of their citizens, individuals and groups had to devise methods of fending for themselves in conditions of growing impoverishment. A variety of survival strategies, ranging from migration and passive resignation to self-encapsulation in local or religious communities and parallel market activities, were refined and elaborated during the early 1980s."[32] Behavioral consequences range from "passive departicipation, repression or empty form of controlled participation."[33] People tend to rely on primary groups and narrow communities for survival, leading to "abdication from the public sphere" and "a virtual exit" from the state."[34]

In short, the social and political legacies persisted in a slightly different form under the undisciplined mode of African state operation. While the state is arbitrarily strong, it lacks institutional integrity or discipline and is thus in actuality weak and unpredictable. Society had to adjust to such state behaviors and isolate from the state. The African situation provides two important lessons in our understanding of civil society. First, autonomy of social organizations alone is insufficient for civil society unless the autonomy is engaged with the state. Second, a weak state is not necessarily good for civil society, and the mode of state operation affects civil society formation.

State-over-Society Model

The state-over-society model is based on the political, economic, social, and international experiences of the former socialist countries, including the Soviet Union and those of Eastern Europe, in which the state absorbed political, economic, and social functions. The highly overcentralized system did not function properly from the start.[35] One of the institutional consequences of the malfunctional socialist system was an increasing gap between formal and informal institutions. Amid hardships such as extreme shortages of goods arising in the formal sector, socialist societies had to rely on informal social relations to survive.[36] Informal practices meant subversions of official goals, rampant false reporting, and lying, which further widened the gap between official and private realms.

Opposition toward the communist system had to hide underground or face severe surveillance. With the sudden death of the communist system in Eastern Europe countries such as Poland, Czechoslovakia, and Hungary, opposition groups developed during severe state control resurfaced but were faced with the serious task of overcoming legacies. These groups found themselves mired in a deep sense of elitism and status based on hierarchy. Being recruited into these opposition groups, which evolved into pro-democratic forces, became a daunting task for which the right contacts were needed to be a member. The monopoly that opposition groups held was heavily tilted toward unity within the groups, and thereby they lacked effective conflict management. Gradually, fragmentation of opposition groups led to political division as different groups struggled for resources and members. Under such circumstances, political parties formed without much linkage to society. Consequently, their representation function was weak if not nil, and they were quite disconnected from the interests of people. Civil organization bridged this disconnect between political parties and society at large. The weakening of the state's roles in state-society relations and the enforcement of laws exacerbated the situation; non-political or trivial issues became easily politicized.[37]

State-Leading-Society Model

This model is based on cases of late capitalist industrialization, mainly from Germany and partly from Japan, and is thus the most relevant to understanding the emergence of civil society in Korea. One common element among late industrialization cases is that the state played a major—if not the most important—role in industrialization; the contents and extent of the state's role vary by case, in turn affecting modes of social changes. However, in all cases the state was supportive of business, which held ownership and was responsible for economic outcomes. The way in which the state affects social changes in late industrialization is determined by the social-structural conditions at the time of industrialization and the degree of the state's manipulation of traditional values, behaviors, and institutions.

Although the social-structural consequences of late industrialization vary, a common element among the late industrialization cases of Germany, Japan, and Korea is a strong statist or elitist tradition, where state exists above individuals or society and is perceived as playing a leading role. As such, the state is entrusted to do good for society. Such perception of the state was reflected in the ethos and growth of civil society in Germany and Japan. In Germany, significant growth of civil organizations occurred during the late eighteenth and nineteenth centuries. On the surface, there were numerous civic organizations ranging from hobby groups to charities that resembled those in Great Britain. In fact, this time was called a period of civil organizations.

However, such apparent similarities beguiled the state's strong influence on German civil society. First was the tradition of following the state or ensuring a harmonious relationship between state and society. Second, during Bismarck's period such a harmonious relationship denoted an increasing influence of state on society. Amid increasing workers' organizations and political activism, the state interfered to slow down the development of civil society and blocked horizontal linkages among civil organizations through various social protection laws and policies. This depoliticization effort by the state toward civil organizations gave rise to peculiar features of German civil society. German civil organizations, though numerous, were apolitical in that they avoided confrontation with the state.[38] Such a harmony-oriented stance of civil organizations was a fundamental difference between German society and French and Anglo-American ones. Unlike the latter, German civil organizations were not based on individual autonomy and lacked freedom from state interference.[39] There were persisting feudal influences of the Junkers, whose lifestyle was emulated even by the new middle class.[40]

German political institutions were not conducive to the development of civil society either. German bourgeois political parties remained aloof from the masses as they were initially elitist and thus disconnected. Parties' social bases were narrow and particular; workers, large landowners, large industrialists, Catholics—these groups all had their own parties. As Sheri Berman notes, "instead of reconciling the interests of different groups or creating a sense of national unity, therefore, parties reflected and deepened the divisions within German society."[41] As for bourgeois parties, their elitist organizational style was a failed attempt to develop grassroots linkages.[42] Such weak nationwide political institutions further drove people into their narrow civic organizations during the hard years of the 1870s and the 1920s. Citizens' activities were confined to their own organizations rather than crossing interorganizational boundaries, until Hitler overcame this pattern.

Although Japan shared Germany's deferential attitude to the state, Japan's path of social change in the course of late development was different in that there were no powerful, old social groups like the Junkers. Instead, the political elites made every effort to redefine Japan's tradition in terms of values and institutions. They found and reinforced affinity between organizational prerequisites for industrialization and *ie*, the traditional social unit. Japan worked judiciously to combine the principles of *ie* with the notion of individuality in modern civil codes and family law. In the area of social welfare, family obligations were given priority over those of the state. Efforts were made at the local level to revive the neighborhood system of premodern Japan and to teach self-help and self-management methods. The government intervened in labor-capital relations to ensure class conflicts were contained.[43] All of these efforts amounted to a reinvention of tradition. As a result, the state was regarded as an agent of progressive change for traditional society, and the boundary between the state and society was often blurred. Ultimately, the goals of the state and society were viewed as identical.[44]

Among the four patterns of state-society relations, one can discern two distinct modes of civil society formation: one is the bottom-up socioeconomic model and the other is the top-down political model. The state-versus-society model represents the first type, while the state-leading-society and the state-over-society models describe the second. In the bottom-up socioeconomic model, emergence of civil society was gradual and thus a rather even and comprehensive pattern of change developed at the social and economic levels. At the same time, the discussion of civil society covers as low a level as individuals in terms of personal autonomy. In contrast, in the top-down political model, the discussion of civil society is made in conjunction with how to derive a relatively autonomous arena out of the state-dominant institutions and everyday practices. The Korean case clearly belongs to this model. The state led industrialization, whereby Korean society followed the state's leading role in economic development. Neofamilism was a social consequence from interactions between the state and society through economic development. In the political field, democratization was initiated by anti-authoritarian political activists. Thus, Korea's case shows a mixed pattern: the attitude of Korean masses who lived in the strong neofamilial environment toward democratization and the disjunctive relationship between them and the political activists are crucial in understanding the emergence of civil society and democracy in Korea.

BEYOND LOCATING SOUTH KOREA'S STATE-SOCIETY RELATIONS

From a comparative perspective, the four types of state-society relations help us contextualize Korean civil society. First, the ideal-type cases highlight the importance of understanding general social structure in discussing the nature of emerging civil society. The former socialist cases and the German and Japanese cases direct our attention to the nature of social structure before or at the time of democratization. A complex mixture of formal and informal organizations and fragmented aspects of former socialist societies need to be considered in understanding the process and nature of civil society.

Relatedly, the mere emergence of the middle class or the formal existence and number of civil organizations should not be taken as evidence per se of civil society, let alone a strong civil society. If voluntary organizations resign themselves only to their own survival, without connection to the state and other organizations, they cannot be said to constitute civil society. German and Japanese cases show that the ethos of the middle class and civil organizations as well as the patterns of interactions among civil organizations all need to be taken into consideration. Autonomous organizations need to be interactive and communicative with one another to facilitate the development of civil society. Autonomy without engagement negatively impacts the prospects for development of civil society.[45]

Second, the cases of the state-leading-society model indicate the importance of examining the role of the state in social change, particularly in how it takes advantage of traditional values and institutions, and to analyze the variegated social structures arising from late industrialization. Germany had to struggle to reconcile the increasing formation of the working class with the traditional Junkers. In Japan, there was no immediately visible traditional group like the Junkers and thus it was able to redefine Japanese tradition with much ease. In both cases, states played a strong and active role in shaping their intended social structure, in contrast to the case of England, where there was a hampering effect upon the spontaneous emergence of civil society.

African cases show that a weak state is not necessarily conducive to the development of civil society. Arbitrary intervention or oppression by the state certainly does not facilitate the development of civil society. A general perception has been that a strong state is not conducive to civil society.[46] Relaxation of state control is needed but should not be understood as weak. Furthermore, the state needs to function predictably and provide incentives to the development of civil society. Thus, the notions of "weak" or "strong" are best understood in terms of describing the scope and depth of state control over society; a strong level of control should signify the state's capacity to maintain institutional boundaries with society and maintain a certain level of predictability. Capricious or arbitrary state actions cause confusion and chaos, which are inconducive to civil society. A weak state not only militates against civil society; as demonstrated in the African case, it may further destroy emerging civil society due to its lack of legal discipline and ability to provide equal protection. Finally, modes of state operations, such as personnel policies and distribution of incentives, can affect the nature of organization and social groupings in societies where civil society is yet to emerge. For instance, patrimonial modes of operations in the state may encourage society to move in that direction.

Regarding the relationship between civil society and democratization, the four cases highlight the need to understand the relationship between opposition groups and society in terms of the extent to which the wider society affects, both formally and informally, the structure and ethos of opposition groups. As is clear in the case of the Solidarity movement in Poland, opposition groups could not exist without the protection of intricate informal networks of wider society. Also important is the extent of cooperation and protection and the common values shared between the two sides, as well as the internal structure of opposition groups in terms of hierarchization, internal cohesion, and general ethos.

The relationship between civil organizations and political parties needs to be carefully analyzed in terms of affinity, differences, backgrounds, and orientations. Related important issues include the degree of linkage between society and political parties, relations among political parties in terms of communication and compromise, and the tradition of political parties and the degree of their connection with society. For instance, the extent of elitist orientation, the nature of the social base, and patterns of interparty rivalry need to be closely analyzed before drawing a conclusion about the role political parties play in the attainment of civil society or democratization.

NEOFAMILISM AND ITS IMPLICATIONS FOR KOREAN CIVIL SOCIETY

The three key aspects of neofamilism—identity, individual survival strategies, and institutional consequences—impinge on civil society. Neofamilial identity describes how these ties define an individual and prove highly consequential in designing one's life strategies for survival. The quality of various neofamilial connections also determines the degree of access to state power.

Neofamilism as a strategy refers to the use of neofamilial ties to promote socioeconomic interests; rather than "playing by the rules," people mobilize such ties to promote their own interests. This behavior interferes with the application of universal norms and predictability in administrative and legal operations. Neofamilism at the institutional level is the consequence of the other two aspects: identity and survival strategy. It refers to the effects that neofamilial identities and survival strategies have on institutions. The social consequence of the development of small, neofamilial units is that society loses its structural configuration and institutions are rendered vulnerable to outside penetration based on neofamilial ties.

In fact, neofamilism operates at both macro and micro levels. At the macro level, neofamilism discourages the creation of class-based units, as seen through rampant regionalism in Korean elections at all levels (legislative and presidential).[47] At the micro level, transfers and promotions in public bureaucracies are based largely on school and regional ties and are also observed in the business sector; blood, school, and regional ties are salient features in management structures. These characteristics necessitate reconsidering other institutional consequences of Korea's industrialization; prevalent assumptions about the existence of a coherent middle class, the emergence of civil society, and bureaucratization require serious revision. The Korean middle class shares only an income level; its constituents are otherwise segregated from one another according to their means of gaining access to the state. In fact, the entire society is stratified by the degree of accessibility to state power. As for bureaucratization, contrary to prevalent thought, the Korean bureaucracy has been hollowed out, its bureaucratic elements diminished.

The pervasiveness of neofamilism in Korean society becomes apparent through the lens of the neofamilial structure and its practices and extends to political, administrative, social, and cultural areas. It has become a significant part of defining one's identity and a means for survival. Widespread neofamilial practices have serious implications for civil society, however defined. For instance, neofamilial practices show how social trust is limited to small groups based on school, blood, and regional ties. Thus "real communication" and information flows do not fully circulate throughout society. People seek "real" information, the value of which is only confirmed through neofamilial ties; trust is established based on the degree of trust attributed to the person providing the information. Consequently, information is not fully shared. The range of people for contact is also limited to those who share neofamilial ties, and those who are connected are treated differently. Inter-neofamilial group boundaries are very rigid. This raises serious issues regarding legal universalism, in that laws are not always applied predictably and equally. It is obvious in this context that the modular citizen is quite inconceivable.[48]

Neofamilial ties have also been used primarily to get access to state power to secure incentives provided by the state. This important fact illustrates attitudes and behavior of dependency upon the state, which is quite contrary to autonomy from the state, as is the case with the state-versus-society or state-in-society models. Indeed, Korean neofamilial practices gave rise to one type of state-leading-society model in which both state and society were weakened in the process of industrialization: the state was hollowed due to constant penetration by neofamilial groups while there lacked a sense of a larger abstract notion of society beyond small group identities.

CIVIC MOVEMENT GROUPS OR ORGANIZATIONS VERSUS CIVIL SOCIETY GROUPS

We now analyze how neofamilism interacted with ruling opposition groups (elites) involved in democratization, social movements, and political parties to clarify the relationship between democratic transition and civil society. The Fifth Republic of South Korea was born in 1981, through a military coup d'état in 1980 after the assassination of Park Chung Hee, marked by amending the constitution to adopt an indirect selection of the president. The collapse of the authoritarian regime was a spectacular process that involved a large coalition of various social and political forces in Korean society: the "June Democratic Uprising," from June 10 to June 29, 1987, drew ever more diverse and larger sectors of Korean society, reaching the point where the police could not control the situation. The 17-day run of demonstrations ended on June 29 with the Declaration of Democratic Reform by Roh Tae Woo, the ruling party presidential candidate. It was proclaimed by the anti-authoritarian forces that the victory was won by the participation of various sectors of Korean society, such as students and both white- and blue-collar workers, representing a victory of the masses. The June Democratic Uprising was unprecedented in recent Korean political history in terms of the range and scale of participation in democratization, its success the result of long struggles by organized anti-regime groups. Because detailed analysis on anti-authoritarian struggles has been done elsewhere, it suffices here to provide a short overview concerning questions about Korean civil society.[49]

Political relaxation under the Chun Du Hwan regime began in 1983, giving rise to new alliances among students, workers, and church leaders. The

Minch'ongyŏn (Youth Coalition for Democracy Movement, YCDM) was launched in 1983 and the Han'guk Nohyop (Korean Council for Labor Welfare, KCLW) was established in 1984. Two national umbrella organizations appeared: the Council of Movement for People and Democracy (CMPD), which emphasized a more radical orientation, and the National Congress for Democracy and Reunification (NCDR), with a more moderate orientation, organized in 1983 and 1984, respectively. These two organizations were consolidated into Mint'ongyŏn (People's Movement Coalition for Democracy and Reunification [PMCDR]) in 1985. In May 1987, the people's movement groups organized the National Movement Headquarters for Democratic Constitution (NMHDC), 24 groups and organizations that represented labor and peasant organizations, various religious leaders, journalists, writers, and other intellectuals.[50]

Thus, the number of organizations that participated in democratization movements in Korea is quite numerous and impressive and at least provides sound evidence for activism in civil society. It is only reasonable to assume that civil society in Korea contributed to the emergence of democracy and that democratization further facilitated the development of civil society. How can we differentiate Korea's pattern of civil society development from other cases? The answer depends on how to characterize the nature of the relationship between civil society groups and broader society. One view is that the distinctiveness of Korean civil society, unlike what happened in the state-versus-society model, lies in the fact that the Korean bourgeoisie was under strong state influence even after Korea was considerably industrialized. At the same time, unlike elite-based democratization, in which links with the masses are not closely established, the anti-authoritarian groups who struggled for democratization constantly claimed their connection to Korean masses. This view, while accepting the positive role of civil society in democratization, places the Korean case of the relationship between civil society and democratization as neither a state-versus-society model of the West nor one in which elitist orientation is quite strong, as in Latin America.[51]

By recognizing the positive role of civil society yet leaving the Korean case in conceptual limbo, this view does not address the basic problems facing Korean civil society. Even when this view points out the dangers of state influence over and politicization of civil society, it does not adequately explain them. Overcoming such a conceptual limbo requires clear distinctions to be made between an abstract and a macro level of concept such as civil society and the nature of civic organizations within it, on the one hand, and between civic organizations and larger society beyond civil society, on the other. As shown in the four models, civil society groups and civil society either overlap, or the former emerges from the latter only in the state-versus-society model, which describes spontaneous socioeconomic changes following political changes.

The nature of the relationship between civil society groups and larger society needs to be specified depending on the context. For instance, scholars observed that various sectors of Korean society, including the middle class, participated in anti-authoritarian regime struggles and thus supported democratization.[52] A logical conclusion from this premise is that there was almost no gap between political elite groups and larger society. However, one view is that there existed widespread political groups called masses (*minjung*) that were not only economically but also politically oriented against the upper class. More specifically, it is believed that a sort of collective mass consciousness exists in Korean society. The widespread feeling according to this view is that the masses are separate from upper layers of society and that the latter cannot understand the former. Also strong is the perception that masses should not blindly follow upper layers of Korean society but that they should be autonomous.[53]

Therefore, the masses are those who are not composed of any singular economic class but are rather an amalgamation of trans-class orientations sharing a similar political orientation against a common enemy (illegitimate ruling groups). An implication of this view is the presumed existence of strong ties between the masses and the anti-authoritarian activist groups. Apart from the question as to the true orientation of the masses—whether they are real entities or describe sentiment—this view does not explain the following conflicting survey results. While about half (49%) were in favor of economic development over democratic reform in 1993, about a quarter (26%) chose democratization over economic development. In 1997, however, less than a tenth (9%) replied that democratization was more important than economic development for their nation. As a result, their desire to live in a greater democracy remains, by and large, an abstract political ideal signifying few of the concrete practices of democratic change.[54]

In practice, there has been little decline in the propensity to which Koreans, whether democrats or non-democrats, are committed to authoritarian means of dealing with national problems, as demonstrated during the first democratic government. A large majority (66%) remains subscribed to the belief that a powerful dictator, such as former General Park Chung Hee, is more effective than a democratic government in handling those problems; a majority (58%) rejects the democratic method of conflict resolution in favor of the authoritarian method.[55]

Thus, the complexity lies in the Janus-faced political orientations of the Korean masses, which supported and even participated in the democratization process while maintaining anti-democratic tendencies as described. Rather than assume the congruence of perspectives between masses and the opposition groups, this complex relationship needs to be explained. One explanation is economic in nature. As political scientist Doh C. Shin concludes, "adherence to such authoritarian practice remains linked to the economic gains that many Koreans personally experienced during three decades of military rule."[56] This view may explain the undemocratic tendency but not the pro-democratic side of the masses' orientation.

A more plausible explanation is provided by historian David Steinberg when he says that democracy may have been taught as "an abstract concept in schools (conformity was taught in practice), but was clearly undercut by observable events outside the classroom."[57] According to this view, democratic principles learned at a cognitive level are opposite to the realities of practice, possibly explaining the double-faced orientations of the masses. However, it cannot explain why the masses decided to participate in demonstrations in the late 1980s in particular. In other words, while this view seems reasonable, its universal validity itself is its weakness, thus serving merely as a background variable.

A more crucial variable is the existence of a high level of cognitive dissonance between college life and post-college life. While in college, the majority of students experienced an acute collective guilt that they did not actively participate in student movements.[58] This psychological burden became exacerbated as they entered the business world after graduating, as they had to accept and follow neofamilial practices for survival. Under such circumstances, cognitive dissonance emerged between real life and the dictates of their consciences. This process served as a base for a psychological and sentimental bridge between salaried white-collar workers and opposition groups, especially student groups.

Another significant situational factor is the Kwangju massacre of 1980, which deeply affected many Koreans. The results of one survey show that the masses were most supportive of "punishing the military leaders who plotted a coup in 1979 and ordered the massacre of Kwangju residents in 1980."[59] A high level of concern and propensity to be involved in anti-military regime demonstrations are therefore quite conceivable, given the aforementioned cognitive dissonance already embedded in the minds of many college graduates and the recent memory of the Kwangju incident. In addition, the enhanced economic status of those who joined the struggles must have played some role by providing a sense of confidence. Thus, an array of structural, psychological, and situational factors came into play in the process of the collapse of the authoritarian regime.

A critical note is that the link between the political activists and the masses was based on sentiment, not on any institutionalized mechanism. That the masses targeted the regime rather than the entire system is also important. This means that in both political and civil society, opposition groups are not systematically linked to the general masses once anti-regime struggles are over, and strong neofamilial practices persist at the societal level. This situation can be demonstrated more vividly when attention is directed to problems of Korean civil society formation, as outlined below.

The current status of Korean civil society is better understood by focusing on civic movements and the extent of the gap between civic movement and larger society. The gap vividly manifests in "civic movement without citizens." This phenomenon can be understood from two perspectives: first, the degree of participation in civic movements can be an indicator at the mass level. As expected from neofamilial structures and ethos, the majority of Korean people conduct their lives in neofamilial settings. As one finding shows, over seven in 10 (73%) are affiliated with at least one of the primordial associations built on fraternal, neighborly, or religious ties. In contrast, only one in six (15%) belongs to any business or communal institutions that symbolize civil life in modern society featuring high levels of industrialization and urbanization.[60]

This means a low portion of Korean people is affiliated with institutions related to civil society. A large majority (85%) is not affiliated with any modern type of mass organizations that directly seek to influence the governing process. Among those affiliated with these types of associations, which serve as channels of representative democracy, a small minority (38%) join multiple and diverse civic associations. This indicates that Korea is still a nation of numerous elements that are closed off from one another.[61] Consequently, the proportion of the population that is affiliated with modern civil associations is 9%, and just 4% is affiliated with interest groups or business associations.[62] The findings are clear: beyond the organic boundaries of the personal ties deeply rooted in the pre-industrial age, a vast majority of Koreans remain unconnected with one another; they still refuse to join hands with strangers.[63] Other survey results roughly show a similar tendency. Among 817 Seoul residents, only 6.2% replied they were participating in civil activities; 17.7% were actively participating 17.7%; and 11.2% stated that they contributed.

From a second perspective, the organizational structure and mode of operations of civil movement organizations indicate a gap between larger society and civil movement groups. First, most civil movement groups are run by former political activists. According to one survey, Korea's new civic movement is primarily led by civic activists and professors (59%), full-time professional workers (21.3%), volunteers (16.4%), and general membership (3.3%). The proportion of civic activists is much higher in the case of "voice" types of civic organizations (67%), which advocate for change, than in the case of service type organizations (48%), which promote knowledge or engagement.[64] Personal networks are also important to promoting membership and recruitment of leaders and activists (as opposed to cognitive recruitment in the West) in Korea's new social movement.[65] These characteristics reflect that Korea's civic movement has been top-down in nature, led by professional groups such as social activists, professors, and lawyers. Also, the fact that civil organizations have grown faster in the area of publicity that focuses on raising social, economic, and political issues further reinforced the leadership role of civic activists and professors.

Such organizational features raise several related issues. The weak social basis for civil organizations naturally means a low degree of financial autonomy, which in turn indicates dependency on support from state, business, individual donations, and profit-making projects. The low level of citizen participation leads to decision-making that is largely dominated by a handful of top leaders or permanent staff.[66] More important is the tendency for civic organizations to expand their focus of interests, which dilutes professional competency. For instance, Korea's Citizens' Coalition for Economic Justice

(KCEJ) originally covered a range of areas, including unification issues, information and science, environment, women's issues, urban planning, government reforms, agricultural issues, and international exchanges. The organization has grown to 20 committees and councils, four auxiliary organizations, and 30 regional branches. The expansion of organizational scope is not limited to the KCEJ. As discussed below, virtually every organization has experienced the expansion of organizational scope.

Another noteworthy consequence of the weak social foundation is "attention-seeking" behaviors of these organizations as a way to demonstrate their raisons d'être.[67] Many civic organizations raise issues to get attention from society, focusing on politically sensitive topics including medicine-pharmacy differentiation, driving out unfit candidates for the National Assembly, and the minority rights movement. Again, this issue-oriented behavior means weak continuity and long-term strategy. Shifting attention from one issue to another sometimes causes the "fallacy of no error." Civic organizations are faced with issues for which the long-term implications or solutions are uncertain, as they were either poorly understood or prepared.[68]

POLITICIZATION OF KOREAN CIVIC ORGANIZATIONS

Politicization is the most serious consequence of civic movements and organizations without citizen participation; Korean civil organizations have been criticized for being too involved in the political process. The tendency toward politicization takes form in different ways, including excessive attention to political issues, attempts to reorganize into political organizations, and the leadership of civil organizations entering politics. Civic organizations' tendency to pay heavy attention to political issues is closely related to seeking attention from the general public.[69]

In terms of an oversensitive orientation toward political issues, civil society groups or civil movement groups were primarily concerned with political goals and means, irrespective of socioeconomic conditions. Prior to the 1980s, the major political goals of student movements included anti-Korean-Japanese normalization, an anti-constitutional amendment, opposition to the dispatch of troops to Vietnam, and autonomy from dependence on foreign powers. Recent issues include the reduction of the number of National Assembly members, the revision of political party law, and implementing hearings for high-ranking officials (in doing so, some activities questioned the legality of campaign activities involved in driving out unfit candidates).[70]

The second aspect of politicization is the securing of entry to political positions by civic activists, a tendency supported by several cases. Under the government of Kim Young-sam (1993–98), several leaders of the KCEJ joined either the cabinet or the ruling party.[71] The final aspect of politicization of civic organizations is an inclination to organize separate political parties. Within the KCEJ, the Korea Environment Movement Coalition, and other organizations, there have been serious debates concerning the desirability of converting the civic movement into a political movement. These debates started after the local election in 1995 when some leaders of the KCEJ openly proposed the idea for "political reforms through politicization of civil movements."[72] Yet another similar debate came up several months before the 17th National Assembly election in July 2003. Representatives of various civic organizations issued a joint declaration that urged the need to form a new political force for political reforms.[73]

The reason the anti-authoritarian political activists targeted the regime was that basic political rights, such as voting rights and freedom of association, were granted without struggles in the founding constitutions in 1948 under the influence of the United States. As the target was the regime, not individual rights per se, a growing gap developed between the general masses and the political activists who later became the backbone of civic organizations. That is, the struggles were "upward" against the regime as the political activists did not need to secure basic individual political rights. Such distance from the general masses and upward struggle against the regime led to a situation in which their struggles were closely related to and influenced by the main oppositional political figures, such as Kim Dae Jung and Kim Young-sam. In fact, different groups of activists supported either of the two prominent political figures of the time.

The people's movement groups were split into three different camps. The first camp argued for "critical support" (*pip'anjŏk chiji*) of Kim Dae Jung, who succeeded Kim Young-sam as president and was "relatively progressive." The PMCDR was aligned with many student organizations, and the YCDM took this position. The second camp called for talks to resume between the two Kims and insisted on negotiating a single candidate. This camp argued that the important issue was not progressiveness but the "electability" of a candidate. The Seoul Labor Movement Coalition and various student groups belonged to this camp. The third camp, composed of many labor unions and radical student groups, deeply distrusted political society and proposed an independent "people's candidate." This camp argued that it was time for the people's movement groups to organize themselves as a meaningful political force.[74]

In this regard it is important to note that even the labor movement was viewed as a part of the political struggle rather than being specifically for the interests of workers, such as strengthening labor unions. While labor leaders were very cautious toward elevating labor disputes at the political level out of fear of political retaliation, students-turned-workers were much more willing. On this difference in perception of the significance regarding labor movements, one former labor activist remarked that "students sometimes do not appreciate how precious our unions are and how many sacrifices we had to make in order to establish these unions."[75]

Political choices that anti-authoritarian activists made after the breakdown of the authoritarian regime revealed not only the distance between workers and themselves but also where their motives lie. Based on the activists' affinity for opposition leaders such as Kim Young-sam and Kim Dae Jung, former civic movement leaders joined political groups. In choosing political camps, their personal or regional connections were more important than ideological or policy affinities, as one former activist testified:

> It was at the end of 1987 or the beginning of the year 1988 when intellectual groups entered the political world in large numbers. More than 100 of them joined the first opposition party, the Pyongmin Party, between the 1987 presidential election and the April 26 general election. More than 100 intellectuals joined the party if my memory serves me correctly. Most of them entered college between 1974 and 1981. Ten of them ran for office and the rest became party functionaries. Kim Dae Jung promised that if he failed in the presidential election, he would organize a good quality party. We joined him with the thought we could build up a regular party. Put differently, we joined the party as if we were launching a political movement. But now the situation is quite different. Now the new "386" generation does not enter the party as party functionaries.[76]

In fact, it is customary in Korean politics to classify student activists turned politicians in terms of their entry point into politics: for example, the

April 19 student uprising group, the June 3 generation of the mid-1960s, the Yushin generation of the 1970s, and "Generation 386" of the 1980s.[77] What is institutionally significant about Generation 386 of the 1980s and early 1990s democratization is that they are not only large in numbers but are also well organized: their organizations are even called "families," based on the solidarity founded upon longtime participation in secret ideological circles. As prestigious high school alumni associations constituted major human networks, these "family" organizations have become a major source of political solidarity and groupings. Due to their historical background as secret organizations, they are exclusive and closed to outsiders, as was the case with the Solidarity movement in Poland. Of course, such clandestine organizations existed largely in isolation from the general masses. One former student activist described the situation as follows:

> The notion of family is not only limited to explaining student movements in the early 1980s. We need to pay attention to the active "family" alumni associations with the emergence of "Generation 386" as a political force. As well known, high school associations were the main sources of human connections. What is happening now is that informal groups ("families") are organized based on members of past student movements and are becoming a major source of human connections. In the early 1980s, the core of the Seoul National University underground student movement was called "family" or "team." The origins of these units vary, but most of them started in 1971, when campus circle activities were banned by special military order, going underground when the circles were disbanded by force. Major underground circles at Seoul National University were "Apple," "Aka," "Gate," "Guggyong," "Nongbop," "Kyongbop," and "Hugyong," which are acronyms or abbreviations.[78]

The factors above contributing to the distance between political activists and the general masses should be understood in a wider and longer historical perspective that accounts for a strongly embedded tradition of elitism. Elitism here refers to the belief among the intelligentsia and political elites that they should lead society and the masses. When elitism is combined with the senses of backwardness and urgency, elites tend to think that they are the ones who should plan for the future on behalf of society and that whatever they do would be viewed by the rest of society as legitimate and positive. This belief assumes that elites are self-sacrificing and do whatever they can for the future of the country. As such, elites' behaviors and thoughts have never been empirically scrutinized. Normally, the thoughts of leading groups developed into programs that map the future of the country. Given the push from the West at the end of the 19th century and ensuing colonial rule, ideas of the elite have been seldom tested empirically until the 1960s. Ideas and thoughts of political activists of the 1980s and 1990s were no exception to this pattern. Although the real gap between the elite and the masses narrowed considerably in the 1980s due to industrialization and social and cultural changes, the trend still persisted, as discussed earlier.[79]

Given this perspective, Korean society is faced with two problems: One is building a new political process based on compromise and tolerance in interactions among political elites. The other is establishing a relationship between the masses and political elites, based on a sense of representation rather than responsiveness. Democratization brought about change in political elites; former political opposition groups were given a chance to rule based on a mandate from the people. In the Korean case, groups both old and new mingled, with little concern about policy and political differences. Such a political marriage of convenience has not been conducive to creating new interaction patterns among different political groups. As old wounds and grudges erupted, revenge politics virtually became the dominant pattern of interaction among political elites where mutual backbiting occurs regularly. Such mudslinging among political elites brought about constant revelations of corruption and scandal. The two former presidents were imprisoned for corruption scandals as well as their previous wrongdoings; the sons of presidents were arrested for illegal exercise of influence; and a multitude of corruption and improper behavior by political leaders in the form of "gates" and "winds" captured the eyes of the public incessantly throughout the 1990s.[80] The ruling elites aired too much dirty laundry to the public largely due to inadvertent fighting among themselves. Invective and acrimonious exchanges of words and behaviors among politicians led the general public to become extremely cynical about politics, ultimately undermining the legitimacy of public authority.

Since the late 1980s, political parties have continued to manipulate regionalism as a way of garnering electoral support (see tables 11 and 12). Just as the

TABLE 11. Presidential elections by region (in percentages)

ELECTION (YEAR OF ELECTION)	CANDIDATE (POLITICAL PARTY)	REGIONS								NATIONWIDE
		Kyŏnggi	Ch'ung-ch'ŏng	Honam	Yŏngnam	Kyŏngbuk	Kyŏngnam	Kangwŏn	Cheju	
13th (1987)	Roh Tae Woo (DJP)	34.4	33.1	9.9	48.8	68.1	36.6	59.3	49.8	38.6
	Kim Young-sam (RDP)	28.7	20.1	1.2	41.6	26.6	53.7	26.1	26.8	28
	Kim Dae Jung (PPD)	28.4	8.9	88.4	5	2.5	6.9	8.8	18.6	27.1
	Kim Jong Pil (NDJP)	8.4	34.6	0.5	2.5	2.4	2.6	5.4	4.5	8.1
14th (1992)	Kim Young-sam (DLP)	36	36.2	4.2	98	61.6	72.1	40.8	15.2	42
	Kim Dae Jung (DP)	34.8	27.3	91	10	8.7	10.8	15.2	32.9	33.8
	Chung Joo Young (UNP)	19.8	23.8	2.3	12	17	8.8	33.5	15.4	16.3
15th (1997)	Kim Dae Jung (NCNP)	39.3	43.5	93.5	12.3	13.7	11	23.8	40.6	40.3
	Lee Hoe Ch'ang (NKP)	35.5	26.7	3.8	58.4	61.9	55.1	43.2	36.6	38.7
16th (2002)	Ro Moo Hyun (NMDP)	50.7	51.5	92.5	24.5	21.7	27.1	41.5	56.1	48.9
	Lee Hoe Ch'ang (GNP)	44.2	42.1	5.4	70.3	73.5	67.5	52.5	39.9	46.6

Source: Central Election Management Committee, South Korea, cited in Yi Chŏngjin, "Chŏngdang yŏnhap," 119.

Note: DJP: Democratic Justice Party; RDP: Reunification Democratic Party; PPD: Party for Peace and Democracy; NDJP: New Democratic Justice Party; DLP: Democratic Liberal Party; DP: Democratic Party; UNP: Unification National Party; NCNP: National Congress for New Politics; NKP: New Korea Party; NMDP: New Millennium Democratic Party; GNP: Grand National Party.

TABLE 12. Turnout in national assembly elections

ELECTION (YEAR OF ELECTION)	POLITICAL PARTIES	REGIONS									NATIONWIDE
		Kyŏnggi	Ch'ungch'ŏng	Honam	Yŏngnam	Kyŏngbuk	Kyŏngnam	Kangwŏn	Cheju		
12th (1985)	DJP	30.2	45.1	35.9	35.9	38.6	33.9	46.1	31.6		35.3
	NDP	38.1	20.5	24.8	25.3	20.6	28.7	11.1	5.6		29.3
	(DJP)	30.4	34.7	22.8	41.4	49.9	36.1	43.6	36		34
13th (1988)	PDP	22.3	3	69.1	1.2	0.8	1.5	4	6		19.3
	DP	23.7	15.3	0.9	37.1	26	45.6	21.6	27.1		23.8
	RDP	16.7	42.1	1.6	11.1	14.9	8.6	20.2	3.4		15.6
14th (1992)	DLP	35.5	40.1	24.4	48.5	48.2	48.6	41	34.1		38.5
	DP	34.8	22.6	62.1	11.8	8.8	13.9	12.4	20		29.2
	KNP	19.4	19	4.7	18.1	22	15.4	30.7	0		17.4
15th (1996)	NKP	34.5	27.8	18.1	41.3	30.5	50.6	37.3	37.2		34.4
	KNC	31.4	8.4	71	3.1	1.5	5.7	6.7	29.4		25.3
	LDC	14.1	47	0.7	12	20.1	5.3	23.6	1.2		16.5
16th (2000)	GNP	39.1	23.2	3.9	53.1	52.5	53.7	38.6	44.2		39
	KDP	40.9	30.6	65.9	13.2	14.7	11.8	36.4	49.4		35.9
	LDC	12.4	35	2.4	8.6	14	3.3	10.2	0.7		9.8

Source: Central Election Management Committee, South Korea, cited in Yi Chŏngjin, "Chŏngdang yŏnhap," 120.

developmental state was hollowed out by "dysfunctional" personalistic/tribal/ neofamilial allegiances, so the development of a more rational and mature policy/political system was hobbled. Political parties failed to present alternative policy options and new ways of understanding politics, society, and international relations. Instead, they continued to assume an elitist stance, using elections simply as a formal way of securing power.

Political elites frequently reshuffled among different parties in the form of merges and splits, with little regard for the general public. Between 1948 and 1999, there were 150 attempts to merge parties involving 249 parties.[81] Also, the mergers occurred right before and after elections. These figures illustrate the political opportunism of Korean political parties. As with the case of Eastern Europe, Korean political parties played their games without regard for the interests of society, failing to uphold the principle of representing the sentiments of the public. A tendency of Korean political parties to remain particularly attached to regionalism has not contributed to diluting traditional institutions like neofamilism at the societal level; on the contrary, they have exploited them. It is clear from this analysis that neither interaction patterns among political elites nor the political parties' relationship with the masses has been conducive to the development of civil society; if anything, they have negatively affected it.

STATE AND CIVIL SOCIETY IN KOREA

What was the nature of the Korean state in relation to civil society at the time of democratization? Institutional consequences of state-business interactions based on neofamilism in the process of industrialization eventually caused the "hollowing" of Korea's bureaucratic structure rather than bureaucratization, as has been argued in Western sociological literature.[82] The impacts of democratization on an already hollowed-out bureaucracy have been disastrous, as seen in growing and overt political influence on state administration in terms of decision-making and personnel policies. With the system's weakened ability to limit political influence in staffing major administrative posts, frequent regime changes have meant increasing irregularities in personnel policies. As each new regime attempts administrative reform, the administrative structure has considerably destabilized.

Adding to these factors are frequent revelations of corruption among bureaucrats. In 1991, the number of bureaucrats penalized for misdeeds was 3,996; in 1992, 4,092; in 1993, 7,116; in 1994, 6,223; in 1995, 5,061; and in 2000, 4,507. About 30% to 40% of the cases involved negligence on the job, and in 2000, misconduct at the top was followed by violations of operational codes and bribery. These statistics indicate a low sense of responsibility on the part of individual bureaucrats, enabled by lax organizational discipline.[83] The spillover effect from the political arena made matters worse. The negative view of politics as previously described easily extended to public perception of bureaucrats, reinforced by revelations of corruption in both arenas. This has fostered a distrust of state authority among Korean people and has developed into state bashing in which people challenge the state's decisions. Examples range from everyday situations, such as confronting the police on the street, to bigger issues in which the state's role of arbitration and coordination are questioned.[84]

Finally, international factors also impinge on prospects for civil society in Korea. Democratization proceeded along with the breakdown of the Cold War international system in the mid-1980s. However, the dismantling of the Cold War in the Korean Peninsula has been rocky and uneven compared to the rest of the world, largely due to the continuity of the North Korean socialist regime. As a result, South Korean views toward North Korea have become highly polarized, and opinions unthinkable during the Cold War are beginning to receive new attention, as evidenced by the Sunshine Policy, which opened up dialogue and interaction between North Korea and South Korea. Adding in the emotional politics of the elite, South Korean policies toward North Korea have become increasingly contentious and divisive.

There are two large trends in Korean society: rapid industrialization in the absence of reinventing tradition has caused insecurity and identity crises alongside a feeling of overconfidence that has manifested into the desire to be recognized by the international community. Compounding these two factors are a sudden loss of confidence in and existential fear about the sustainability of the Korean economic system, expressed in a defensive posture against external "intruders" during and after the financial crisis of the late 1990s. These complex cognitive and psychological dynamics are a fundamental source of institutional and social anxiety, which is closely related to emotional responses to various situations.

These phenomena have taken on a collective nationalistic facade. The nationalistic tendency has made compromise and rational thinking about foreign policies extremely difficult, as seen in the formulation of new policies with the United States. While new patterns of debates on foreign policies have begun to develop, such a nationalistic facade is inconducive to civil society in that it does not easily allow pluralism or tolerance, which is needed in any form of civil society.

Civil society has been a goal to be achieved in and of itself, especially in the forming of a democracy. In the West, it has been a differentiating symbol in comparison with the non-Western world, and in the East, it is a symbol of modernity to be constructed. However, idealizing the concept has created myth and confusion. The main source of confusion comes from a lack of understanding of contextual differences in developmental paths between different regions. A different way of contextualizing historical experiences suggests the possibilities of different patterns of state-society relations, situating the Korean case in that conceptual framework.

Four different models for state-society relations illustrate different paths of social changes and thus civil society, each model determined by different patterns of industrialization and democratization. First, by rejecting the assumption that industrialization brings about universal social consequences, the framework easily differentiates Western cases such as Great Britain from other cases such as South Korea. Spontaneous industrialization brings about social and institutional consequences that differ from state-led industrialization in terms of social units and modes of institutional operation; this in turn affects paths of civil society. In the case of South Korea, neofamilial units have emerged as a result of Korean state-led industrialization, thus affecting the state apparatus and even institutions of anti-authoritarian political groups. In a nutshell, Korean-style industrialization has had the effect of weakening both state and society.

Democratization led by opposition groups occurs in varying social contexts. In this regard, understanding the larger social context in which democratization occurs is important. In contrast to the bottom-up model in Great Britain, a complex relationship exists between opposition groups and the rest of society in terms of general ethos and goals to be achieved. This illustrates a need to reconsider the seemingly automatic relationship between democratization and civil society; democratization may start with some support from society, but that should not assume a simple path for development of civil society from democratization. The sources that support democratization, the institutional dynamics of state and political institutions like parties, the legacies of anti-authoritarian struggles, and international factors are important in this regard. Currently, what is impeding the development of civil society in Korea is politics, namely the political elite and their modes of behavior.

The emotional and vengeful pursuit of political hegemony and a consequent lack of compromise between different parties and strong legacies of regionalism have seriously hampered the facilitation of civil society. In the meantime, the Korean people have undergone tremendous psychological and institutional upheaval. Since the outbreak of the financial crisis in 1997, Korean people and society have experienced the clashes of economic institutions between embedded values, behaviors, and institutions, on the one hand, and Western institutions that have been adopted en masse in various fields, including finance, business practices, state bureaucracy, and labor issues, on the other. What sort of equilibrium will eventually emerge remains to be seen. However, Korean neofamilial embeddedness will not disappear. The form and content of Korean civil society will be determined at two levels. The speed and extent to which institutionalization of new political processes will have a significant effect on society will be key factors at the elite level. At the societal level, a new equilibrium between Korean traditions and Western institutions will determine how Korean civil society will take form. Korean civil society will not look the same as civil societies of the West. After all, civil society is neither static nor shrouded in mystery; rather, it is the attempt to grapple with the central problems of modern society. If the question of civil society for the West has been about the atomization of competitive society and a state-dominated existence, the Korean case highlights the imperatives of balancing the constraints needed for survival and the need for participation in Korean political and economic contexts.

Daily Practice of Neofamilism

CHAPTER 6

How were the components of neofamilism perceived in daily personal experiences? And how was neofamilism practiced as a part of individual survival strategy? Surveys inform analysis of the perceptional aspects and behavioral consequences of neofamilism, going beyond the analyses of its institutional consequences. In a 2015 survey, respondents were asked about the importance of neofamilial ties at three levels: in Korean society in general, in personal life, and in the workplace. An overwhelming proportion (98 out of 106, 92%) indicated that neofamilial ties were extremely influential, considerably important, or somewhat important in Korean society. Only eight persons (8%) stated that neofamilial influence was not significant. When asked about the influence of neofamilial ties on society, notably 99% said neofamilial ties were paramount.[1]

When asked the influence of familial, school, and regional ties on personal life, the basic pattern stands, with 66% of respondents saying neofamilial ties were seriously influential in their personal lives. It is interesting that the influence of neofamilial ties at the personal level is lower than respondents' perception of the influence of neofamilial ties on society. When asked specifically on the influence of neofamilial ties at the workplace, 70% of the surveyed said the ties seriously and considerably influenced their business activities at workplaces. It is clear the influence of neofamilial ties is important in all contexts.

When asked to rank the importance of the three components of neofamilial ties—blood, school, and regional—in their personal life, 64% (45 out of 70) of respondents indicated that blood ties were most important. Twenty-six percent said school ties were most important, and 10% stated that regional ties were most important. When asked to identify the second-most important form of neofamilial tie, 22% indicated blood ties, 44% school ties, and 34% regional ties. For the third-most, regional ties stand out at 56%, school ties at

30%, and blood ties at 14%. Overall, these figures show that blood ties ranked as the most important of neofamilial ties, followed by school then regional ties.[2]

NEOFAMILISM AND POLITICAL BEHAVIORS

On the general question of how neofamilial ties affected the election of the president and members of the National Assembly, 40 out of 106 respondents (37.8%) expressed that the level of influence on elections was enormous, whereas 48.1% indicated that there was considerable influence, and 9.4% said that elections were somewhat influenced. Overall, 95% of respondents said neofamilial ties affected elections one way or another. However, a quite different pattern emerged when asked how the ties actually affected their personal choices in elections: 9.4% indicated an enormous level of influence, 26.4% expressed a considerable level of influence, and 34% indicated that they were somewhat influenced, yet 30.2% said almost no influence. That is, about 70% of total respondents indicated that ties affected their personal choices in elections.

The regional variations on the same question of how neofamilial ties affect personal political decisions show an interesting pattern, where those from the southeastern and southwestern regions are much more affected by neofamilial ties: 53% (Ch'ungch'ŏng Provinces), 8% (Kangwŏn Province), 74% (southeast), and 67% (southwest). It is significant to note that there was little difference (7%) between the southeastern and southwestern regions, while the central regions, Seoul (56%), and Kyŏnggi (53%) were relatively less affected by neofamilial ties than were the southeastern and southwestern regions.

Among of those who did not vote based on neofamilial ties, a majority said this was based on candidates' ideological orientations. Nineteen out of 32 (59.4%) indicated political ideology as a determining factor, while 28% went by candidates' election pledges at the central and local levels. Although the extent of its impact upon election behavior varies, it is safe to say that neofamilial ties are very important in determining political choices.

NEOFAMILISM AND ECONOMIC ACTIVITIES

A general question is posed in the 2015 survey as to how the neofamilial ties affected various economic decisions and behaviors in Korean society during the 1960s and 1970s; these include decisions and behaviors related to the purchase of goods, procuring real estate, management, investment, saving, and insurance purchases.[3] Survey responses roughly confirm the overall assessment of the impact of neofamilism, with close to 90% saying neofamilial ties affected economic behaviors, but with some differences. The proportion of respondents who considered neofamilial ties to have an enormous influence on economic matters turned out to be significantly lower, at 11%. This was followed by those who indicated that neofamilial ties considerably influenced (42.5%) and somewhat influenced (34.9%) economic decisions and behaviors. To the question regarding the influence of neofamilism in their personal life or decisions, the pattern was different: only 3.8% of 106 respondents indicated an enormous influence, 17% a considerable influence, 46.2% somewhat an influence, and 32% not much influence. Although they perceived Korean society and the economy to be under the strong influence of neofamilial ties, respondents felt that this influence did not extend as much to themselves. Nevertheless, the overall patterns remain the same in that the ties were significant in economic areas as well.

Respondents were asked about the circumstances under which neofamilial ties mattered to their economic behaviors. Forty-nine percent said neofamilial ties were a factor only when their interests were served. Twenty-eight percent said they mobilized neofamilial ties when economic interests were difficult to calculate. Twenty-three percent opined that there were more occasions when neofamilial ties took precedence over their personal economic interests. Finally, only 6% said neofamilial ties were respected even when their economic interests were infringed upon. These results indicate that people were more calculative and cautious in relying on neofamilial ties as related to economic behavior, but it is also clear that neofamilial ties played an important role in this sphere.

A related question was posed to identify the areas of economic decisions in which neofamilial ties were used, including the purchase and management of real estate, purchase of goods and insurance, finance and investments, and obtaining loans. Neofamilial ties were most employed as follows: purchasing goods and insurance (22%), getting bank loans (20%), finance and investments (11%), and real estate purchase and management (9%). Neofamilial ties were thus instrumental in gaining access to financial resources, but, strikingly, 44% of respondents said that they did not rely on neofamilial ties at a personal level, once again revealing the gap between general perceptions and the personal use of neofamilial ties. However, a different pattern emerges when respondents expressed the second-most utilized area of economic activity: real estate purchase and management (49%), goods purchase and insurance (28%), financial investment (23%), and bank loans (6%). As for the third-most used area, purchase of goods and insurance come first at 22%, followed by bank loans and financial investment (20% and 11%, respectively). Forty-four percent said they did not consider any neofamilial ties to be relevant, even as a last resort option in securing information or other help in economic decision-making.

Two follow-up questions were posed: How did the neofamilial ties affect decisions when they were the most important source for making decisions on economic matters, and how did the ties affect decisions when they were the second-most important source for their decision on economic matters? Three different situations were offered as options. First, "Information was secured through the neofamilial ties, but decisions were made independently based on the information"; second, "Although economic outcomes of the decisions were uncertain, I just joined those who shared neofamilial ties"; and third, "Even when economic loss was foreseen, I followed people who shared neofamilial ties." When neofamilial ties were regarded as the most important sources, 53.2% said they made independent decisions only by using information secured through neofamilial ties; 40.3% said they followed the decisions among those who shared the ties, even when they were not sure about future outcomes; and only 4% said that they followed those who shared the ties, even when loss was foreseen. When neofamilial ties were regarded not as the primary source of information but as being of secondary importance, 48.5% said they followed those who shared the neofamilial ties although there was uncertainty in outcome. When neofamilial ties were the third priority to consider in their decision, 72.6% said they followed those who shared the ties, even when outcome was uncertain. This outcome indicates the importance of neofamilial ties as information sources as well as the level of trust in the ties. Put differently, the majority of people resort to neofamilial sources when they make critical decisions, and they go along with group decisions among those who shared same ties regardless of outcomes.

As to the outcomes of economic decisions made based on neofamilial ties, 57% (39 out of 62) indicated that both positive and negative outcomes occurred more or less evenly, while 19.4% (12 out of 62) replied that the outcomes were mostly positive, and 17.7% (11 out of 62) stated that results were negative most of the time. Relatedly, 43.4% (46 out of 106) had served as a guarantor when someone they shared neofamilial ties with was obtaining financing, while 56.6% (60 out of 106) did not; among those who were guarantors, 78% (36) said they experienced financial loss, while only 22% (10) did not. A distinctive regional pattern regarding experiences of serving as loan guarantor due to neofamilial ties is that those in the southeastern region had many more experiences in serving as a loan guarantor than those in other regions, where a far smaller proportion of the respondents said they had served as a loan guarantor (58% vs. 39% [Seoul]).

PRINCIPLES VERSUS NEOFAMILISM

The respondents were questioned about their perceptions of Korean society in terms of the extent to which blood ties, school ties, and regional ties were considered in legal implementation and economic policies. Nearly 19% said that almost all cases were affected by those ties, 58.5% answered that the ties were important on many cases, while 21.7% indicated that cases were frequently affected. Nearly all (99.1%) acknowledged the influence of neofamilial ties in the implementation of laws and economic decision-making. It is striking that the remaining proportion, composed of only one person, said that ties bore almost no influence on these matters. This indicates a pervasive lack of universalism, especially in the application of laws. When asked about whether they sought to utilize neofamilial ties when they were in violation of the law or facing economic loss because of neofamilial ties, the responses contrast with the general perception that acknowledges the pervasive influence of neofamilial ties. Only 6.6% said they tried to rely on the ties on many occasions, 10.4% said not infrequently, 36.8% indicated a few times, and 46.2% said almost never.

The respondents were given a more specific situational question: whether they have contacted state bureaucrats for their own personal economic purposes, such as new information gathering for business, inquiries related to state decisions on their business, and interest coordination. Their responses were consistent with their answers to the general question whether they ever asked for favors through neofamilial ties. Forty-six percent said they contacted state bureaucrats for various purposes as in the question, while 54% said they almost never did.

ECONOMIC CHANGES AND NEOFAMILISM

On the questions regarding to what extent the degree of dependence on school, blood, and regional ties has been changing since the financial crisis at the end of 1990s and how they think the influence of school, blood, and regional ties has been changing since the democratization, 28.3% of respondents said considerable change occurred, 50.9% stated a little change, and 20.8% expressed that there was little change. Asked whether neofamilial relations changed due to economic structural changes arising from industrialization in the 1960s and 1970s, all three groups said there had been changes, but most expressed that the degree of change was slight. The second-largest proportion of responses indicated that considerable changes to neofamilial relations had occurred. Responses that there was no fundamental change and only slight change contained the greatest proportion of respondents with higher levels of formal education. Another contrast to note is between higher- and lower-income levels; responses indicating that there was no or only slight fundamental change to neofamilial relations contained the greater proportion of respondents in the highest income brackets.

When questioned on the degree of social conflict due to industrialization, 24% of respondents said it was serious, 50% responded that it was gradually growing, 22.6% indicated that it was not that serious, and only 1.9% expressed that there was almost no social conflict. When considering the two questions (Q11 and Q12) together, it is reasonable to interpret that as the economy had been showing unprecedented scale of change and was thus quite overwhelming, respondents must have assumed the presence of unknown or unforeseen changes of varying magnitude.[4] At the same time, in relation to changes in neofamilial ties, respondents were likely to think that economic change would be sure to affect even neofamilism-based human relations; yet, despite these conceptions, neofamilism continuously functioned within the social fabric of Korean society, as reflected in the respondents' awareness that neofamilial ties had an overwhelming influence in Korean society during industrialization.

Such conceptual schizophrenia is well reflected in responses to the following question: "In the 1960s and 1970s, were you able to mingle well with those with whom you shared blood, school, and regional ties but were much richer or poorer than you? Or were you uncomfortable with them?" Of the responses, 12.2% said it was very uncomfortable, 30.0% indicated that it was getting increasingly uncomfortable, 28.3% expressed that it was not uncomfortable, and 20.8% said there was no discomfort at all. The distribution of the answers reveals an interesting dynamic within Korean society at the time. Although those who did not have much problem mingling with those from a different economic status (49.1%) are slightly more than those who felt uncomfortable (42.2%), the answers show that Korean society was quite divided in terms of social distance between classes. When inquired about their overall assessment of how the significance of neofamilism has trended from the 1960s to 1970s to the 2010s, slightly over half of the respondents (51.9%) said that it is still significant, 46.3% said it has changed little by little, and only 1.8% said the significance of neofamilial ties is almost nonexistent. This finding illustrates the continuing importance of neofamilial ties in Korean society, although signs for gradual change are also visible.

To explore the resiliency of neofamilism, another question asked how they assessed the impact of the abrupt financial crisis in 1997-98 on neofamilial ties and their influence in Korean society. About 24% of respondents thought neofamilial ties were further reinforced; 53% expressed that Korean society came to depend less on the ties, and 17% said there was no change or no relevance. These responses are interesting in that they illustrate the persistence of neofamilial ties; not a single person thought the shock of the economic crisis itself would bring about immediate, drastic change to the influence of neofamilial ties. What is more interesting is that a considerable number of respondents (77%) seemed to have the view that in the wake of the financial crisis, they relied on neofamilial ties, probably for the sake of surviving the crisis.

Finally, respondents were asked to provide their view about the future of neofamilial ties in Korean society: "What do you think of the importance of blood, school, and regional ties in the future?" To this question, 4.7% of respondents said the ties would further be reinforced, 50% said they would continue to exist if not be reinforced, and an equally significant proportion (41.5%) said these ties would gradually weaken. Just 3.8% said neofamilial ties would disappear very soon. The picture that emerges from these responses is one of divided attitudes in Korean society, although the notion that the ties will remain important is still significant.

The following three questions turn to specific personal experiences in neofamilial practice in the 1960s and 1970s, as well as during and after the financial crisis in the late 1990s. The first asked whether respondents themselves had used neofamilial ties. The second inquired whether they had been approached by someone through neofamilial ties for special consideration. The third pertained to whether they had observed the preceding two situations during the financial crisis in the 1990s. Responses illustrate how extensive and pervasive neofamilial practice was during industrialization in the 1960s and 1970s, especially as a key survival strategy: 64% had relied on neofamilism for personal benefit. Among the respondents, 59% indicated that they had been contacted to do something for other people through neofamilial ties, and 47% had observed such neofamilial practices beyond their own experiences. The figures indicate that neofamilial practices were actively performed, while the lower proportion of responses confirming others engaging in neofamilial practices suggests that neofamilial activity was not as overt or visible to third parties.

Neofamilial practices run the gamut of life but are centered mainly on economic areas, indicating that neofamilial ties were then seen as critical survival strategies for average Korean people. The following are more specific areas of neofamilial practices in the daily lives of Korean people: emergency economic assistance; job-related help such as job seeking, transfers, and promotions; and access to financial institutions.

MAPPING OF NEOFAMILIAL BEHAVIORS

It is clear from the survey results that neofamilism was widely practiced during the period of industrialization in the 1960s and 1970s. Whether at the macro level of Korean society, at the personal level, or in the workplace, neofamilism was an important part of the lives of Koreans. Responses provide empirical confirmation that neofamilism was important to individual identity and for personal survival. As table 13 shows, blood, school, and regional ties covered an extensive range of aspects of life. Although all three ties were extensively mobilized for a variety of purposes, blood ties stand out compared to the other

TABLE 13. Types of activities and distribution of neofamilial ties

	TYPES OF TIES	ASKING FOR FAVOR	ASKED FOR FAVOR	OBSERVATIONS OF OTHERS	TOTAL
Personal economic assistance	Blood	11	4	5	20
	School	3	2	7	12
	Regional	4	4	2	10
Finance-related matters	Blood	10	11		21
	School	4	11		15
	Regional	5	2		7
Job-related matters	Blood	4	5	4	13
	School	4	2	3	9
	Regional	4	3	1	7
Other matters (election, licensing, military service, etc.)	Blood	2		1	3
	School	2	4	1	7
	Regional		1	1	2
	Total	53	49	24	126

Source: Data from author's 2015 survey.

ties as being present in almost all the categories of human life: personal economic assistance, financing, employment, and other activities for survival. Next came school ties, which were also widely used, particularly for job-related matters such as recruitment, promotion, and transfers. Regional ties also came into play but were described by many respondents in terms of employment and sales networks, including financial products such as insurance.

Several of the respondents' statements indicate the importance of blood and school ties and their pervasiveness in everyday life: "Blood ties, school ties and regional ties are as natural as breathing; school ties and regional ties are always to be confirmed as if looking for necessities in life. Blood ties are undoubtedly like insurance or savings."[5] On family and relatives: "I can open myself to family members and relatives regarding my problems and those of my family. I can share secrets and be open about my weaknesses and problems." On school alumni: "They can render all kinds of mental and physical support on both public and personal matters." On regional ties: "Closer than coworkers but slightly less important than school alums." On school ties, another survey participant wrote, "I regard school alumni in the workplace and society as if they are my brothers. Among alums, seniors can freely call juniors by first name without using honorifics in a way that signals, perhaps even boastfully, the closeness of the relationship."

One respondent conveyed the following as the atmosphere during the industrialization: "I still remember I used to take care of people with the same regional background as mine, and that I did not feel comfortable since my regional background was different from that of the owner and that the owner himself paid unusual attention to those who came from his own hometown."

On regional ties, one typical example is as follows: "Serving as guarantor for someone else's bank loans is risky for me, so it is not easy to consent to the request; but when asked for example to purchase insurance by way of regional ties, there was not much choice but to accept although the product was no better or different from what could be purchased elsewhere. The times were such that it was not easy to refuse requests for favors based on regional ties even when backgrounds are so different."

Neofamilism was practiced most extensively and intensively in the case of economic activities. This is understandable, given rapidly changing economic circumstances that presented prospects of upward social mobility. Economic activities based on neofamilial ties can be broadly classified into those characterized by "giving" or "taking." On the taking end:

- Until recently I received financial support from my brothers.
- I received financial assistance from blood relations because my own family situation was so bad.
- Because my older brother was rich, I used to call upon him for help whenever I had difficulties.
- I asked brothers and friends (school ties) for favors in financial matters.
- I have experienced getting employment through the connection of my brother-in-law (husband of my sister).
- I got a job after my brother asked his friend.

Compared to the taking end, much more diverse responses are recorded on the giving side of economic activities:

- I helped people who were connected by blood and school ties.
- I purchased insurance policies when asked by a school classmate.

- There were endless calls for help from blood relations, so much so that not much was left of my salary. I helped those who were homeless and could not afford food or school tuition to the best of my abilities.
- I ended up in debt from supporting relatives.
- Because I guaranteed personal loans of friends, I ended up losing my home when I had to take over debts. It took more than 15 years to recover from it, and there is still outstanding debt.
- As my personality was such that I could not say no when asked for a favor, I complied to requests based on blood, school, and regional ties. However, every time I had to swallow financial and other damages. Due to the distrust and sorrow of repeated betrayals, I confined myself to home and avoided people, not attending school alumni meetings.

It is clear that people responded by citing more unfortunate cases due to neofamilial ties and obligations from the ties. What is also clear is that there were frequent interactions resulting in positive economic gains and mutual assistance. One current example is that of guaranteeing the loans of others, personally or institutionally. While fewer respondents guaranteed loans for family members, relatives, and school friends than those who did not, the proportion is still significant at 43%. Of this group, a majority (78%) ended up having to repay debts.

Given the frequency of reports on financial losses from personal guaranteeing, it is clear that neofamilial interactions brought about difficulties for many Koreans. The main reason for the need for guaranteeing was the lack of institutional mechanisms in the 1960s and 1970s for guaranteeing and checking creditworthiness. Furthermore, capital was in short supply. Such circumstances led to a scramble for loan guarantors through neofamilial ties in securing institutional or private sources for capital. The rapid industrialization projects that were unfolding at the upper echelons of the economy—also based on neofamilial recruitment in business and in the state bureaucracy—created the need for sources of trust to identify and secure new business opportunities. With a scarce base of trust within a highly volatile environment and at a time in which hopes were mixed with rapid success and abrupt failures, people either grudgingly or with some degree of anticipation engaged in a certain level of risk; only when things turned sour did they realize they had made a mistake.

The majority of the respondents said neofamilial considerations were given priority over laws and regulations. This response in part reflects the speed at which decisions had to be made and implemented. People relied on neofamilial ties to secure information quickly, and the ability to get access to state incentives was a critical factor in determining business success. Given such conditions, combined with the top leader's (president) orientation, which tended to be lenient toward violations of laws and regulations as long as export goals were met, it is not surprising to observe that expediency, attainable via neofamilial ties, was prioritized over laws and regulations at lower levels of Korean society on a daily basis.[6]

The findings provide an interesting implication for the relationship between social conflict and class consciousness. On the one hand, most people generally sensed that social conflict was growing, due to industrialization of the 1960s and 1970s. On the other hand, there was a split between those who were uncomfortable with members of a higher economic status and those who did not feel as such. At the same time, the majority of survey participants acknowledged that neofamilial ties have been significant in Korean society since the 1960s and 1970s. It can be interpreted that neofamilial ties played a role in mitigating class tensions for respondents who expressed that they did not feel uncomfortable with people of higher economic status, with whom they shared neofamilial ties. Even for those who felt uncomfortable, frequently resorting to neofamilial ties for opportunities of upward social mobility must have created enough hope and expectation for an improved economic future sufficient to mitigate present discomfort. The finding indicates that rather than directly applying class analysis, a more nuanced approach is required to understand social change in late industrialization, where interaction between industrialization and tradition gives rise to distinct social units (neofamilial networks) and life expectations.

The survey respondents provide interesting observations of neofamilism's emergence and its future prospects. On the question of why neofamilism became so significant in Korean society, the following remarks are particularly germane:

Blood, school, and regional ties played an important role largely because the labor market lacked systematized processes of employment. The rights of recruiters were unusually strong and there was no systematic control over the use of school, regional, and blood ties.

The reason blood ties and regional ties were mobilized is because small-medium industries were the backbones of industrialization; trust was absolutely needed between owners and employees. Since trust between superiors and subordinates was necessary, blood, regional, and school ties—the emotional bases of Korean society—were the foundation for business in the 1960s and 1970s.

In the case of small-medium enterprises, accounting and finance are crucial for financial stability. Thus, the persons in charge of these two areas were filled with people based on blood ties. They were also needed for the sake of saving labor costs and for managing and ensuring the secrecy of the CEO's slush fund. In the case of big business, regional ties and blood ties were important from the time of recruitment. Regional background was an absolute criterion in recruiting for Kyŏngsang- and Chŏlla-based companies. School ties were a dominant factor for securing trust from superiors and getting promoted.[7]

The remarks above indicate that trust was limited in Korean society during industrialization, a characteristic amplified by the rapid pace at which industrialization was pursued. As the top leader needed competent and loyal bureaucrats, so did entrepreneurs, although loyalty seemed to be given more weight in order to keep business secrets. Furthermore, there was no well-functioning labor market from which employees could be freely recruited due to labor market segmentation. Under such circumstances, blood ties were important for the SMI sector while regional ties played as important a role as school and blood ties for the recruitment of big business, particularly for the sake of securing company-wide loyalty.

On the continued influence of neofamilial ties, 55% of respondents said that such ties will either be reinforced or continue to exercise influence in Korean society. At the same time, 45% stated that they would either weaken or soon disappear. However, their written statements on the future of neofamilism reveal a much more complicated picture:

As society becomes more transparent, is run more exactingly, and information is increasingly shared, blood, regional, and school ties may play some role in securing access to people, but they may not be of much help in fundamentally solving problems.

A positive change in the aftermath of the financial crisis is the emphases on merit and competitiveness. Competitiveness (merit) should come first before school, regional, and blood ties. Social connections should not take precedence over merit. This is a change in a desirable direction.

Due to globalization and the upgraded scale of business that requires system-based operation, a change has occurred from considering blood, school, and regional ties to what is required of jobs and general ability. Ability is the top priority to secure competitiveness in domestic and international markets.

In order to get out of the financial crisis, more innovative and creative ways are required in which case people will be judged more by ability than connections.

We will be facing a new society where ability is ultimately needed for the resolution of problems.

Individualism will be pervasive; there will be no permanency in trust in human relationships. Repetition of one-shot associations and dissociations will be the norm. Neofamilial ties will be of limited help as dependence on them will weaken and ultimately disappear.

Simple affection-based school, regional, and blood ties should be replaced with ones based on ability, so that exiting from past practices is sure to come.

There is less dependence on school ties, regional ties, and blood ties, but the dependence itself has not disappeared. Especially so in the political circles.

In the case of private companies, if the owners of companies adopt strict controls against school, regional, and blood ties, dependence on them will be greatly reduced and transparency will be strengthened.

But unless politics changes and the general public realize the possibility of the change, fundamental changes will be difficult.

From the moment people feel that they cannot depend on other people, all the relations will be severed, and the current financial crisis is the entry point to the severance of the relationships. The severance phenomenon will be more severe for the middle and lower classes.

Most important is rampant individualistic thinking and selfishness. School, regional, and blood ties were based on trust and credibility. With the rapid economic development and ensuing mammonism, distrust among people is becoming a serious issue. It may be a natural consequence when efficiency and ability are the main consideration, but trust is being lost among people. It is a problem to lose humanness.

There will not be a fundamental change in the roles of blood, school, and regional ties as they are the emotional backbones of Korean society.

I do not expect any basic changes to neofamilial ties; going through difficult times under the financial crisis brought about an important lesson that blood, school, and regional ties are not the whole thing, rather ability and self-standing power is more important. In that sense there was clearly a change.

With the increasing insecurity due to changes in retirement and making a living, people will look more for those whom they can trust. As such, a deepening sense of crisis will increase dependence on traditional human relations.

There has not been visible change in dependence on school, regional, and blood ties since the financial crisis. Dependence on these ties has deepened in seeking for jobs and financing related to maintaining a household.

Dependence on blood ties has been strengthened.

The primordial emotional base is bound to affect business although the new circumstances and the scale of economy will dictate somewhat to secure efficiency. But it will depend on whether the owner decides to secure ability-based operations.

School ties will continue if not be reinforced. Regional ties will continue for a considerable time. Blood ties will be visibly weakened.[8]

The above statements express two possible views: one describes weakening neofamilial ties and their influence, while another depicts neofamilial ties either strengthening or maintaining the status quo. A differentiated picture emerges for the first trend: shared among the statements are the fundamental challenges that are brought to neofamilism by the eruption of the financial crisis of 1997-98. The crisis had an undermining effect on neofamilism. Neofamilism, in this view, stands for loyalty over efficiency, secrecy over transparency, mutual care over competitiveness, collectivism over individualism, looseness over discipline, and emotional ties over merit. Neofamilism is thereby viewed as a source of all sorts of ills in Korean economy and society. With the challenges brought about by the financial crisis, Korean society, according to this trend, had to change or had already begun to change. The first trend foresees an arrival of a new society in which individualism will become a new norm, in turn requiring and generating relationships based on short-term trust rather than permanency. Neofamilism, according to this view, will not have a place in an information age that was rapidly coming to Korean society. One of the concerns that this trend illuminates is the need for a base of trust that would replace neofamilism once that base is lost to individualism and market principles.

Within this narrative of disappearing and weakening neofamilism are different views on the nature of how neofamilism's decline is occurring. While overall structural challenges to the Korean economic system are commonly highlighted as key factors for changes to neofamilism, some question how and where such changes will be initiated. One view acknowledges weakening dependence on neofamilial ties and maintains that this weakening will lead to a disappearance of the ties altogether; the primary concern here pertains to Korean politics, which is considered to be the main culprit for leading Korean society to neofamilism. The background of this view is that Korean politics has been entrenched with regionalism, and this sets the tone for society at large in terms of the prevalent practice of neofamilism. Unless a conscious effort extending to broader society is made to end neofamilial practices within Korean politics, neofamilism may persist. At the micro level, this view considers the owners of private enterprise to play a critical role by substituting neofamilism in company operations, particularly through a new pattern of recruitment based on merit.

The second perspective holds to the continuity of neofamilism, broadly contending that neofamilism will persist because it forms the emotional backbone of Korean society. However, such cultural determinism does not preclude possible changes to neofamilism. First, this view acknowledges objective changes occurring in the external economic environment, as well as the need for change. But it focuses more on social psychological tendencies as a source for neofamilism's continuity. For example, it contends that growing insecurity due to changes in the economic environment will drive people to depend more on personal ties for safety and security. This view predicts that neofamilial ties will still be needed for seeking jobs and financing and getting access to people and institutions. It also presents a differentiated view that blood ties strengthen or weaken, depending on circumstances, and the same goes for school ties and regional ties, but all three ties are generally viewed as enduring, despite external shocks to the Korean economy.

Like the first view, the second also sees politics and company leadership as initiators of change at macro and micro levels. Both views also acknowledge that Korean society is facing a fundamentally different international economic environment since the financial crisis. Where the two views diverge is on whether change is sought in the context of continuity or discontinuity of neofamilism. This difference notwithstanding, both views agree that change is not spontaneous and is based on social consensus through political process at the macro level. What is also important to note is that the institutional and social backgrounds for neofamilism have changed considerably since the period of state-led industrialization. The critical question then is whether and if so how neofamilism operates under different institutional, social, and political environments, which is the subject of chapter 7.

NEOFAMILISM: PERSONAL STORIES

While neofamilial practices are pervasive in Korean society, individuals experience the level and scope of neofamilial ties and practice neofamilism in different ways. The following interviews with the selected individuals, based on differences in their family, educational, and social economic status, demonstrate how neofamilial ties affected their paths in life in terms of the types of jobs and the roles and functions that they played.[9]

The Case of CEO Mr. C

Mr. C was born in the southeastern region of Korea and graduated from a prestigious high school, subsequently entering the School of Engineering at SNU.[10] After completing his military service as a naval officer, he entered the MCI through a special employment process. By recommendation from the director of the General Affairs Department of the ministry, he went on to work under the chief secretary for economic affairs at the Blue House (the president's office and residence of Korea). After the chief secretary was appointed minister of finance, Mr. C moved to the ministry with him as one of his secretaries. When the minister stepped down, Mr. C moved to company D, the chairman of which was close to the minister, and Mr. C shared high school ties with the chairman, who was senior to Mr. C. He served in different capacities at the group: branch head of the group in San Francisco, head manager of steel and metal parts, managing director and vice president for planning and coordination, and CEO of the entire company.

He acknowledged that at company D there were many of his high school alumni (nearly 30%–40%), including the founding president, and that he relied on his high school ties when contacting the ministries and the Blue House. He said it was inevitable to rely on the ties as there was no officially sanctioned lobbying. According to him, regionalism is not limited to Korea or to the present time; it is in fact ubiquitous all over the world and has persisted throughout Korean history. He noted that different regimes favored people who shared the same regional background with the president. He further mentioned that during Korea's industrialization, having a connecting link with the state was necessary for business. He also recollected that the business sector was inferior to the state in terms of personnel management and planning and thus had to emulate the state. On the matter of labor relations, however, each enterprise adopted its own method in dealing with labor because the state did not suggest any institutional examples to follow. Workers' conditions varied in terms of the size of the enterprise and type of industry. Regarding the different roles of the state, he contrasted Korea with the United States as follows: the government's industrial policies in Korea during the industrialization period was such that it further encouraged those who were doing well, which is quite different from the case of the United States, where the government role was more about maintaining a level playing field.

Regarding the scope of human and social relationships, he said that the bulk of his human contact during the heyday of industrialization in the 1970s was with those within the company (around 60%), while 20% was with high school friends outside the company. Regional ties were weak for him as he had left his hometown early in his life. He was little involved in NGOs or civic organizations.

The Case of Labor Organizer Mr. L

Mr. L was born in the countryside in C province in 1946.[11] He finished his high school education in his hometown. After finishing military service at an early age, he left his hometown and got a technical job at S cement factory in K province in 1968 through an open, competitive recruitment process. He worked there for three years and learned technical skills in the cement industry under a graduate of SNU engineering school. Then he applied for a job at K cement industry in J province. He was put in charge of a part of building the new cement industry there and worked hard. Production started in 1973, and he had a good relationship with the owner of the company until 1976, when he initiated organizing a labor union in the company. He explained the reason for organizing the union as follows: the working conditions were horrible, with long working hours from seven o'clock in the morning until eight in the evening. Monthly salaries were frequently not paid on time, with payments being deferred for up to two months, and 400% of salary as bonuses, which workers were supposed to receive, were unpaid. More seriously, the company did not treat workers as human beings; workers were treated as servants and were only sustained to barely survive. Management thought that workers did not have much choice other than to work at the company. The workers were mostly from the local areas adjacent to the company and from J province. There was a total of about 500 workers.

Mr. L was not a local person. He had had experience with a strong union at the previous company where he worked. He attributed the poor treatment of workers to the lack of a union. But the owner was wary of Mr. L's unionization efforts, even making frequent death threats to Mr. L. Management keenly monitored the workers to prevent them from joining the union. But

Mr. L persuaded the owner that the company would not collapse even with a labor union. Utilizing contacts in the government, the company tried to delay issuing the permit to unionize, but ultimately the permit was issued in January 1977 after more than seven months of delay. Mr. L said the company's attitude to the workers changed for the better after the new labor union was formed; management stopped calling workers names and treating them like servants He had to yield the chairmanship of the labor union to a person close to the company for three years, and only in 1979 did Mr. L became the leader after a close election victory.

Even after the union was established, management and the owner continued to pressure workers to withdraw from the union; at one point only four members were left, but eventually membership recovered. He recollected enduring the times and the struggle for justice. He also said the main sources of his success were in his honesty, establishing trust by keeping promises, and punctuality. While not scared, he confessed how lonely he sometimes was under the tough situation. Other than the support of his nuclear family, particularly his wife, he had no one who shared school, regional, or blood ties in his effort to create the union within the hostile environment.

The Case of Successful SMI Entrepreneur Mr. H

Mr. H was born in Ch'ungnam Province, in central South Korea.[12] He finished high school near his hometown and went to Seoul for college. He graduated from H university, majoring in industrial management. He planned his future business while performing his military service in the air force. The list of business ventures that he considered was quite long, including instant rice cakes, peanuts wrapped in squid, paper cups, and leather clothing. While manufacturing leather clothes, Mr. H met a businessman in helmet manufacturing and became a supplier of a helmet component. He came to know the helmet manufacturer through the businessman and took over the business from him. Mr. H recalls having to borrow from relatives and friends to take over the company. His business began to grow as he started exporting cloth helmet linings to Japan.

He also recollected his dealings with state officials. They were always lukewarm if not negative regarding his efforts to build new factories and gave various excuses. Every time he contacted them, he served them meals and gave money. In the worst case, it took him 10 years to solve one problem through a state agency. All the banks and agencies were like that, except for one SMI promotion corporation and the Korean Trade Association. Applying for bank loans involved reciprocation of some sort; sometimes bank clerks would outline personal demands in exchange for loans to be approved. He said he did not try using school or regional ties to get access to connections at banks and state agencies.

Regarding recruitment, Mr. H said there were many from his own province. He used high school and regional ties, and those recruited on these bases in turn brought in additional people based on the same connections. He said workers recruited from these sources are usually stable and stay longer. He said that the company adopted open recruitment by advertising in a major newspaper, which had the effect of reducing the proportion of employees from his own province, but nevertheless applicants from his own province still turned out to be recruited more often. He admitted that regional background is an important criterion even when recruitment is done openly. As to the question of what constituted the most important tie in Korean society, he mentioned blood ties without hesitation and added that his younger brother and brother-in-law had been helping him in important capacities. He said he does not trust people until he tests them out for three months.

As for Korean society in general, he remarked that somehow, he had a strong feeling that Korean society was dominated by SNU graduates and people from the southeastern region. Nevertheless, overall, he regarded school ties as not too negative. He said employees who were hired based on school and regional ties usually did not suddenly leave the company. He also said that the obsession with getting into top universities in Korea was not as negative as it is commonly made out to be in some parts of Korean society. On the contrary, he was of the opinion that it was natural that top university graduates receive better treatment for their hard work. He also shared that he found top university graduates to usually be better employees.

The Case of Unionist Mr. K

Mr. K was born in 1945 as the eldest son among four children.[13] He did not receive formal education and was self-taught. He joined a steel company in 1974 through an open competition. Officially, the recruitment was for regular salaried workers, but it actually served to recruit technicians. The monthly salary was 15,400 won, with 3,000 won spent for room and board. After on-the-job training, high school graduates were put into cold-rolled steel production for the first time in Korea. During the 1970s, a job training office was established, and workers took certification exams after one year of training.

The number of workers at the company ranged between 1,000 and 2,600, and workers were recruited nationwide. The salary was comparatively better than most at that time. Despite the higher compensation, bank workers, teachers, and bureaucrats who would sometimes apply would often withdraw after finding out it was a technician position. A union was organized in 1968, which Mr. K joined, and the union turned radical and continued to be so until 1990. Mr. K, a moderate labor union organizer, fought against the union's radical members, who launched frequent strikes and physical confrontations. Based on his struggles against the increasingly radicalized company union, he was elected as union leader in 1990. According to Mr. K, most of the workers felt lukewarm about the radical union; they were satisfied with the company's treatment and felt relieved that they could afford to support their families. Mr. K's view was that workers' class consciousness was not strong because their reference was to Korea's impoverished conditions of the past and also because they understood different and better results could be gained from negotiation than from struggle via militant actions.

Mr. K's approach to the management of the company was not to rely solely on struggle but acknowledged the need for negotiating with management. His view was that during the 1960s, workers were treated inhumanely, with low wages and long hours of work in the midst of poverty, and the Korean Confederation of Trade Unions (KCTU) (a radical union) took advantage of workers' cumulated inhumane treatments with the advent of the democratization movement from the 1980s onward. KCTU was against severe discipline and penalties imposed on workers and exploited rank-and-file anger. Convinced that workers were not supportive of radical unions, Mr. K instead worked to improve the welfare of workers almost by himself as a collaborationist union organizer. He concentrated on building a welfare house for workers, sharing profits, and gains in labor productivity. He also was instrumental in establishing a symbiotic model between workers and management.

There were hometown associations, school alumni associations, clan organizations, and retiree meetings in the company. The management tried to use them to deal with labor issues. Such informal organizations were also inevitably used when electing the head of unions. Mr. K, as union organizer and later leader of his company labor union, admitted that 80% to 90% of his personal life revolved around neofamilial organizations. He even pointed out that even within his own province, regionalism could still be observed among counties. He retired from the company in 2003.

In conclusion, the four personal stories illustrate variations in life paths and strategies depending on the individual's level of education and school, blood, and regional ties. The case of the labor organizer Mr. L contrasts with the case of the CEO at company D. The former, with little education and resources for mobilizing regional and blood ties, struggled against oppressive factory management not only for himself (although his approach was collaborationist) but also for other workers. The CEO, however, used connections through school ties and was able to navigate the world without serious challenges. The case of the SMI entrepreneur is a good example of combining the use of regional ties, blood ties, and effort in order to succeed. Mr. H had to struggle to deal with bankers and bureaucrats but ultimately created his own advantage despite their arbitrariness, without holding a grudge against society as a whole. The case of unionist Mr. K is almost opposite that of Mr. L's in that while both were engaged in unionization, Mr. K was in a regional environment where he felt comfortable drawing upon regional ties.

Together, the survey results and individual cases show how the top leadership's choice of personnel and the state's role as holder of various incentives gave rise to the ubiquity of neofamilial practice in Korean society at both business and personal levels. The overwhelming presence of neofamilism is well reflected in the general perception of the masses, but the extent of its use and strategies as to how to combine the ties varied, depending on individual backgrounds and personal choices for survival.

The 1997 Financial Crisis

CHAPTER 7

The 1997 financial crisis is frequently called the "IMF Crisis" in Korea, in reference to the severe shortage of foreign exchange reserves that drove the country to the brink of default and a subsequent bailout by the International Monetary Fund (IMF) Standby Credit Facility and other international financial support. The background and causes of the crisis have been hotly debated, and the implementation of the reform measures has been closely analyzed.[1] Social and institutional consequences at both micro and macro levels have also drawn much attention.[2] What has received less attention are the implications of the crisis for well-entrenched neofamilism. In terms of the impact on neofamilism, the two institutions that were most affected by the crisis are the family and the chaebols.

SOCIAL AND INSTITUTIONAL IMPACT

The 1997 financial crisis brought upon Korean society a collective psychological shock, made particularly acute as people had become accustomed to continuous economic growth and had not experienced economic downturn. The crisis was viewed as a national disgrace, a humiliation so severe that it was likened to a second annexation by international capital. The crisis also served as a sobering reminder of capitalism's vicissitudes. Korean economic development was externally dependent but pre-crisis had recorded mostly positive results by successfully utilizing international markets. At the societal level, the crisis marked the moment at which many Koreans experienced the vicious cycle of capitalism for the first time.

The string of business collapses also cast a light on the ambivalence that many Koreans had long felt toward chaebols. On one hand, chaebols were viewed as the primary beneficiaries of the state yet were exploitative of workers and did not pay back to society; on the other, it was grudgingly acknowledged that the Korean economy could not survive without them. It was also inconceivable to most Koreans that the chaebols would ever collapse, particularly given the longstanding state support that the chaebols received. The myth of "too big to fail" was quite pervasive throughout Korean society. Under such circumstances, the news of multiple chaebol collapses introduced yet another kind of shock that shattered once firmly rooted assumptions about society and economy.

In addition to the defaults of chaebols, the bankruptcies of SMEs—many of which had been dependent on chaebols but were also squeezed financially due to the credit crunch—further worried average Koreans as these events led to unemployment and declining national economic growth. For example, 123 bankruptcies were recorded in December 1997 and 151 cases in January 1998. Overall GNP growth plummeted from 6.8% in 1996 to 5.0% in 1997 and dropped to -6.7% in 1998.[3]

Factory closures, cancellations of investment projects, layoffs, and wage cuts ensued. The scrambling to meet debt payments coming due created a wave of secondary disintermediation and a severe credit crunch. Rising interest rates and the falling won against the dollar added further hardship.[4] GNP per capita in dollar terms fell by more than half, dampening the sense of pride that many had felt when their annual income surpassed the 10,000-dollar mark pre-crisis.[5] Given such overall economic decline, unemployment immediately affected many households. The Korean economy enjoyed near-full employment in 1996 and even 1997, with 2.0% and 2.6% unemployment rates, respectively. In 1998, right after the financial crisis, the unemployment rate jumped to 6.8%.[6] Also striking was a sudden increase in irregular workers (both temporary and daily workers) after the outbreak of the financial crisis. Right after the financial crisis, the proportion of temporary and daily workers grew from 45.9% in 1997 to 47.0% in 1998 and to 52.4% in 2000, exceeding the proportion of regular workers (47.5%).[7]

The impact of the financial crisis was much more palpable at the individual family level. The following analysis is telling of the various troubles and difficulties that families underwent. According to a national survey in Korea, when people were asked the following question, "During the economic crisis, did you or your family experience the following life events, such as decrease in property, income decline, unemployment, family disbanding (divorce, separation, leaving home), bankruptcy or credit delinquency, deterioration of health, or depression or death wish?" It is reported that 48.3% mentioned income decline, 36.4% decrease in property, 19.2% unemployment, 11.7% bankruptcy or credit delinquency, 16.5% deterioration of health, and 9.3% depression or death wish. Those who have never experienced negative life events amounted to about 40%, with the remaining 60% of people having experienced at least one misfortune in their own life or that of family members.[8]

The impact of income loss, however, was not evenly distributed. The first quintile of the population by income level experienced a 14.9% loss of income, the second quintile by 8.8%, the third by 6.9%, and the fourth by 5.5%, while the last quintile actually gained by 2.3%. The results indicate that income loss was most drastic among middle- and lower-income families due to unemployment, income reduction, and falling real estate values. Among households with a monthly income below 700,000 won who were surveyed, 56.1% reported that they felt seriously threatened by unemployment and bankruptcy in 1998, more than double that of December 1997 (25%).[9] However, upper-income brackets were able to gain income, attributable to higher interest rates. High interest rates and sudden drops in real estate prices gave rise to the collapse of the middle class. According to one survey, about 80% responded that their incomes fell on average by 20% to 40%.[10]

A survey from 2003 showed that for several years after the financial crisis, a considerable number of Korean people felt that they had fallen below their previous socioeconomic stratum. Compared to surveys from 1994, this indicates an expansion of a sense of relative deprivation. In the years of these two surveys, the proportion of those who considered themselves middle class fell by 18% percent, while self-identification as lower-middle and lower class increased by 14.7% and 1.5%, respectively.[11] Yet when questioned whether they believed their socioeconomic status would improve if they worked hard, 45.8% said yes in 1994 compared to 33.1% in 2003, decreasing by 11.3%. On the question of whether they think their socioeconomic status might fall, the proportion of respondents indicating yes increased by 17.8%, from 11.5% in 1994 to 29.3% in 2003.[12]

Such a negative impact at the macrostructural level was duly reflected in family life at the micro level. The loss of jobs of household heads also changed family dynamics. After the financial crisis, female unemployment rates became increasingly volatile, although lower than those of male workers.

However, the situation was quite different at the micro level. For example, a wife would be forced to find a job for a household in which the husband had lost his job. According to one study, more than 30% of full-time housewives attempted to get a job, and the proportion was much higher at 43.3% for those below a monthly income of one million won. The same study shows that among those surveyed, 53.7% of the wives were working, and 24.5% among them were already working even before the crisis; 10.6% were reemployed and 17.6% started working after the crisis. Among those newly employed after the crisis, 76.5% were newly reemployed or in cases where the husband had lost his job, whereas only 33.6% of wives whose husbands were employed sought jobs.[13] It goes without saying that job loss of the head of the household also affected the family's lifestyle. First, the level of consumption visibly changed. The reduction in consumption was most visible in clothing and footwear purchase, from -.6.8% from the previous year in 1997 to -26% in 1998, while crucial expenditures such as education were also cut.[14]

Many households also saw a dramatic shift in the roles between husband and wife. Wives were increasingly becoming the breadwinner as income contribution from the husband declined or disappeared, reflected in the husband staying home or roaming about the city. While this situation tended to cause a high level of stress among family members, some families were able to better adjust to the situation, as the following two examples show:

> During the financial crisis, I lost my house and company due to the bankruptcy of the small business that I ran. I tried to get a new job and failed, and instead my wife started insurance sales. Fortunately, my wife's income was quite good, and we were able to take our children back home from my in-laws. Now my wife is largely responsible for the family finances, and her voice is heard considerably more than before on decisions like the children's education, the house, and furniture. It is quite different from the times when I made most decisions, but I feel less burdened with responsibility for the family. Sometimes, I feel free and thus am satisfied with the new reality. (Mr. P, 38 years old)[15]

> I felt a deep sense of guilt due to the fact that as household head I did not play my role well and thus caused pain to my children. I blamed myself for the fact that my daughter could not complete high school.

I felt deep guilt toward my parents and brothers as I could not do enough even though I am the eldest son. I lost self-confidence and felt I was alone in the world. I seriously doubted whether I deserved to live in the world. (Early 40s, high school graduate; his business of exporting leather fabric)[16]

The intense financial burdens on families due to the unemployment of husbands and increasing tension from the role reversal in which wives began to work raised stress levels and negatively impacted marital relations. Such strained marital relations caused an unusual increase in divorces right after the financial crisis. Throughout the 1990s, the divorce rate was steady at around 1% until 1996. It is only after the 1997 financial crisis that the divorce rate nearly doubled to 2.0% in 1997 and reached 2.5% in 1998.[17] Compared to the previous decades, the economic difficulties brought on by the 1997 financial crisis so deeply affected well-established middle-class lifestyles and assets to the extent that the level of stress on families reached unprecedented levels.

How can the ultimate impact of these negative factors on family solidarity—which is closely related to the practice of neofamilism based on blood ties—be assessed? There are different analyses that indicate varying degrees of family breakdown. According to one view, family members united to overcome the crisis through mutual cooperation, practicing the Korean tradition of supporting family members in trouble. Households experiencing unemployment of the household head were found to have frequent dialogues between husband and wife, and levels of domestic violence and family disintegration went down. Generally, families expected more support from other family members than from the state. In times of crisis, it was found that kin members such as sisters and brothers were more relied upon than neighbors.[18] A report finding showed that among those surveyed, 13.4% got their support from in-law parents, parents, other relatives, and friends.[19]

A differing view suggests that although family solidarity and community is emphasized right after the start of a family crisis, the negative impact deepens as the situation shows little sign of improvement or gets worse. Family members console one another right after the household head experiences job loss and pretend to maintain a warm relationship, but this stage lasts about one month. Family members tend to avoid one another, and conflicts come to the surface. Family life becomes unstable as the family undergoes structural change and family relationships are restructured.[20] Under such circumstances, it is highly likely that people seldom receive support from relatives or friends, and relationships with siblings and friends also break down.[21]

It seems the two views reflect different cases and situations rather than contradict each other. As the second view indicates, the two views are sequential, in that at the beginning families are willing to support one another, but they gradually become exhausted providing continuous support.[22] A survey finding quoted in the previous chapter corroborates this dual aspect of family support: some respondents mentioned receiving family support, whereas others reported enduring suffering due to losses incurred by rendering support to family members (see chapter 6). On the question of whether Korean society will continue to rely on neofamilial ties, 64% responded it would continue one way or another, including familial ties. Overall, while the financial crisis appears to have weakened conceptions of the Korean family as well as familism among average Koreans, both will continue to persist.

CHAEBOL REFORMS AND NEOFAMILISM

Extensive measures were introduced as checks on the previously uncurbed managerial decision-making of chaebol owners. The measures can be grouped into three categories in terms of the degree of impact on neofamilism: direct impact, indirect impact, and background impact. Some measures, such as outside director reform, directly impact neofamilism by altering personnel policies. Other measures are more indirect in the sense that they contribute to changes in the way managerial decisions are made and procedures executed, in turn affecting the selection of people close to chaebol owners. For instance, the prohibition of crossholdings or mutual debt guarantees changes the way financial decisions are made by chaebol owners, in turn impacting the range of chaebol subsidiaries, where people with neofamilial ties are commonly put in charge. Another good example is financial reform. Under state-directed economic development, access to state resources through neofamilial connections was essential for chaebols' survival. Requiring chaebols to lower their debt level to 200% significantly affects their dependence upon the state for financing, which has the effect of reducing the need for neofamilial ties.[23] Another set of reform measures encompass broader institutional changes, while not directly impacting neofamilial practice at chaebols, and may set the background as well as serve as a catalyst for changes to neofamilism. One example is society-wide change as a result of labor relations reform, requiring compliance from all companies. To illustrate the impact of the chaebol reform measures on neofamilism, the outside director reform, inheritance regulation, financial reforms, and labor reforms will be analyzed in detail.

Outside Director System

Prior to the financial crisis, the duties and functions of boards of directors, such as making corporate decisions and overseeing the implementation of decisions, were not properly executed as stipulated in commercial codes. The reality was that many boards were composed of a senior managing director and managing director, who are under the command of the CEO, frequently along with family members and friends of the owners. Directors of the board thus were not in a position to oversee the activities of the CEO and were instead essentially reduced to subservient agents who received orders from the CEO. Filled with company executives, family members, and friends, many boards were effectively rubber stamps for the group chairman.

In addition, stockholder meetings and internal audits did not function well. There was no effective way to check arbitrary decisions, embezzlement, or breaches of duty of the chairman. The checking of internal directors had almost ceased to function prior to the financial crisis.[24] Thus, in the wake of the economic crisis, there were increasing calls to appoint outside directors. The outside director system was introduced to activate the functions of the board of directors. Outsider directors were to effectively oversee business decision-making and performance of internal directors. Beyond serving as a check on the CEO and internal directors, outsider directors are to solicit different opinions of various stakeholders, including the rights of minority holders, and to provide professional knowledge and experience to top management.[25]

According to laws pertaining to stock exchanges, appointing outside directors is mandatory for listed companies. The number of outside directors should be one-quarter of all directors, and at least one outside director should be appointed (1998). For companies exceeding two trillion won in assets, one-half of all directors must be outside directors, with a minimum of three directors

(2001). In 2000 and 2001, companies were to establish a committee responsible for recommending candidates for outside directors, and rights to recommend outside directors were extended to 1% of stockholders. Later, companies exceeding two trillion won in assets were required to have outside directors as one-third of their boards (2004). Most companies complied with the laws in electing and appointing outside directors. By June 30, 1999, the total number of outsider directors was 1,251; out of 722 listed companies, 647 companies elected outside directors (89.6%), averaging 1.73 per company.[26] In March 2001, 633 out of 699 listed companies elected and appointed outside directors, reaching an election ratio of 99.69%. The total number of outside directors was 1,469, averaging 2.32 per company.[27]

Due in large part to the mode of selecting outside directors after the reforms (CEO-recommended candidates proposed at stockholder meetings for approval), it is likely that those connected to the CEO through shared interests or neofamilial ties are ultimately elected. According to one study, the proportion of outside directors whose autonomy was suspect, due to direct or indirect relationship to the CEO, ranged between 32% and 37% from 2006 to 2010, and declined from 22% to 28% between 2012 and 2018. Among the outside directors, those who shared school ties (the same department of the same university) with CEOs or internal directors was 17.53% in 2006, 15.34% in 2010, and 7.29% in 2018, indicating that the proportion of outside directors with ties, including school ties, has gradually decreased since the financial crisis.[28] However, considering the possibility that most former high-ranking members of chaebol companies and former government officials could be related to the CEO through high school ties, regional ties, or both, the actual figures may be higher than the finding.

There are several studies supporting this kind of surmise. One analyzed the differences in investment behavior of CEOs, depending on the structure of the board of directors. CEOs of companies with boards composed of directors with high school and regional ties tended to overinvest in new projects and draw debt. The study concludes that in the presence of existing social ties between CEOs and outside directors, the official capacities of outside directors tended to be constrained.[29] The following story, which occurred some years after the outside director system was adopted, reveals the difficulty of achieving real change:

That outsider directors are merely rubber stamps is not new. It is meaningless to classify publicized decisions of the board of directors in terms of yes or no as there is little opposition. It is not easy to expect that totally unconnected persons are invited as outside directors. Companies seldom select outside directors who can oversee companies well, and big financial groups are no exception. They are run by people who belong in the same "league." There is a saying in the Korean financial world that friends and alums are acceptable as outside directors as long as they do not work at the company. The practice of outside directors recommending candidates for other outside directors is still alive. . . . One former outside director of a bank remarked that although the rule says the outside director recommendation committee is supposed to recommend candidates for outside directors, more often than not the ones elected are those whom the government or company executives want elected.[30]

In 2013, it is known that outside directors of major banks never cast a negative vote. There are 24 outside directors in Shinhan Bank, Kookmin Bank, Hana Bank, and Woori Bank. There were 224 matters on the agenda for which there were 5,376 instances of voting, but there was never a single nay vote.[31] The trend is the same at the top 10 chaebols. According to the CEO Score survey of the activities of 1,872 outside directors of 92 listed associated companies of the top 10 chaebols, "there were 4,626 meetings and 37,635 votes, among which only 38 votes were cast nay, while 97.7% of votes were cast yes. The main reason that outside directors do not voice opposition is because they have a personal relationship with the CEO. That is, there is intrinsic limitation in their voting due to school, regional, and other human ties."[32]

Such a poor track record of outside directors is confirmed by the general perception among business managers. According to one survey, the majority of respondents (22 out of 26) held the view that the role of outside directors was perfunctory or substantially limited at best. They found no changes in the corporate decision-making process as a result of outside board members participating. What was noteworthy is that the role and influence of outside directors was especially limited in companies directly controlled by owners. Those respondents who recognized changes incurred by the outside board member system also acknowledged that despite its growing significance, its influence in major decision-making was limited at best.[33]

Chaebol Succession (Inheritance)

Based on the increasing social criticisms that wealth and company management should not be inherited, so as to establish transparent and accountable governance, and to break up family-oriented management structures, the banning of irregular inheritance and bestowals is a major issue. In 1997, an aggregated tax on financing income and capital gains tax on equity were revived. In 1999, the law was revised to tighten up the taxes on inheritances and bestowals.[34]

Korean chaebols are notorious for attempting to realize family succession by passing on ownership and management power to the children (usually the eldest son) of the controlling family.[35] Family succession efforts commonly entail such tactics as illegal transfers of stock, internal transactions whereby the parent firm supports subsidiaries by showering them with business, thus violating fair competition, and disrupting fair trading in the market. Furthermore, management succession to unqualified children of the chaebol owner could negatively impact business performance, ultimately affecting not only company performance but also the national economy. Laws and regulations have been revised to punish illegal transfers between chaebol subsidiaries, but internal transactions with the intent to lay the foundation for family succession have not disappeared.

Family succession is not possible if stock is not concentrated in the hands of chaebol owners. Since they cannot maintain control without mutual and circular investment among subsidiaries, such ownership structure is essential in family succession of stock and control over management. Thus, family succession effectively incentivizes retaining an irregular ownership structure and closely aligns with broader sociocultural norms and the perception of business ownership. In Korean family tradition, the first son normally inherits all family assets, and it is this cultural norm that has strongly influenced succession practices of chaebol owners. If the first son cannot inherit, legal disputes usually arise among possible alternatives. The perception held by chaebol owners that their businesses belong to their families is also closely related to family succession. In their understanding of business, any sense of public-spiritedness or concern toward all company stakeholders is almost entirely lacking; from this conception emerges a near obsession to achieve family succession at all costs. This has brought about family feuds and raised questions about the legality of their actions. It is fair to say that with few exceptions, Korean chaebol owners have systematically continued the practice of family succession.

According to Korea's Fair Trade Commission, 18 of the top 40 chaebol groups have had disputes over succession of some kind among family members of the owners. Most cases were of primogeniture, while disputes among family members ensued otherwise. These sorts of struggles could be observed at major groups including Samsung, Lotte, Hanwha, and Doosan, taking various forms such as contention over legitimacy of succession, disputes over the scale of ownership, and struggle over positions.[36]

Another phenomenon that is relevant to neofamilism is the bestowal of stock to family members, extending to the third generation of chaebol owners. As a relatively new phenomenon, the practice arose amid intensifying regulation of chaebol owners and adopts early inheritance before the inclusive and comprehensive inheritance law was introduced. According to *CEO Score Daily*, 93 children of the top 30 chaebol families were found to have inherited significant amount in stock of both listed and unlisted companies, amounting to a total of 1.7 trillion won. Among them were one four-year-old child and eight children of eight years old. Additionally, 30% were under the age of 19.[37] What the issues and controversies surrounding chaebol succession indicate is not only the problems that chaebols have been causing to Korean society but also the robust survival of neofamilism, despite the disruptive impact of the financial crisis. In sum, chaebols still remain a major source, perhaps even the nucleus, of neofamilism in Korean society.

Financial Reforms

The pre-1997 financial sector was extremely underdeveloped with the state's extensive intervention, and moral hazard problems were pervasive. In the wake of the financial crisis, various institutional reform measures were taken. In the context of neofamilial practices, the financial reforms reduced the extent of state intervention in business, reflected in personnel decisions at financial institutions, allocation of financial resources, and supervisory functions.

Prior to the crisis, it was common for the state to be deeply involved in appointing the heads of state-controlled and commercial banks. This practice had serious implications for neofamilism, given chaebols' heavy dependence on state policy financing, as securing access to banks is essential to their survival. Likewise, state allocation of financial resources (so-called *kwanch'i kŭmyung*, or state-directed lending) was critical to meet the financial needs of chaebols. Chaebols were keenly interested in who was in charge of this function. Any changes to state involvement in personnel decisions at financial institutions and allocation of credits were bound to influence chaebols' strategies for mobilizing neofamilial resources. As for changes in supervisory functions over financial institutions, had the functions been properly performed following the regulations, the need for mobilizing neofamilial ties would have definitely been reduced.

The critical question is how objectively personnel policies at supervisory institutions like the Financial Services Commission were handled by the state. Amid persistent rumors and scandals regarding state intervention in personnel decisions, there is a widely held perception that the state has not ceased to exert influence in financial institutions.[38] Although it may appear weakened because of the privatization of banks, the state still retains robust influence over financial institutions. One finding shows that the government's influence on personnel issues in particular was in fact reinforced, although a subtle change had occurred in the ways in which the influence was delivered, from a direct to indirect form of intervention.[39]

On the question of the extent to which the state and politicians intervened in financial institutions' lending policies, the majority responded that they did not notice any substantial changes before and after the crisis.[40] Only seven out of 23 responding business managers thought that the level of influence or intervention was reduced considerably or moderately, while the majority held the view that state-controlled practices continued. Some noted similar observations as in commercial banks, saying that a subtle change had occurred in the ways in which the influence was delivered, from a direct to indirect form of intervention, such as those found in personnel issues.[41]

All in all, there is still room for neofamilial practice in interactions between the state and financial institutions through personnel issues. From the perspective of chaebols, there is no longer a strong need for state support in financing, particularly after debt levels were reduced to the 200% mark; thus, overall dependence on the state has decreased, although total autonomy from the state remains unrealistic.[42]

Labor Reform and Implications for Neofamilism

The financial crisis brought about a sea change in labor relations in Korea. Prior to the crisis, unionization and wage hikes were in full swing with democratization, and workers could expect lifetime employment, despite limitations on political activities.[43] The impact of the crisis on labor was serious and far-reaching and can be understood in political, economic, and social terms.

The breakout of the financial crisis considerably dampened the labor movement. Under the state-mediated compromise, tradeoffs were reached between the state and labor: labor organizers gained basic political rights with enhanced latitude to engage in union organizing and political activity, while business secured labor flexibility.[44] Under the changed circumstances against labor, workers began to adjust to the whims of the market. The labor union movement grudgingly accepted fragmentation and gradually learned the rules of bargaining within institutional boundaries.[45]

Labor faced a much grimmer situation in economic areas, with workers constantly exposed to threats of unemployment. The introduction of neoliberal policies and institutions into the financial and corporate sectors inevitably upended the employment status of many workers in the form of layoffs, wage cuts, and limited working hours. Lifelong employment was no longer guaranteed and workplace seniority was challenged for the first time. In short, labor markets became significantly more precarious in terms of wages and employment status.

A more serious impact on workers was the breakdown of bases for social solidarity. The lifelong employment system and the seniority principle were disrupted if not destroyed. Company loyalty, closely related to lifelong employment, began to erode. Most important, workers were divided into regular and irregular categories, with serious implications for neofamilism. The regular workers who are well protected with pensions and social insurance were able to continue to maintain solidarity based on neofamilism, whereas the irregular workers were legally deprived of solidarity based on neofamilial ties.

The "paternalistic human resources management" prior to the crisis adopted a more humanistic approach to workers that emphasized a reciprocal relationship rather than a one-way, top-down one. Both paternalistic human resources management and authoritarian human resources management are based on patriarchism, but whereas the latter is characterized as unilateral and arbitrary, the former is reciprocal and cooperative.[46] As such, workers' well-being, sharing of managerial information based on mutual understanding and communication, and improved compensation and working conditions were considered. Under the paternalistic management system, voluntary cooperation with management was expected of workers.

The financial crisis directly challenged the paternalistic practice of labor relations with the introduction of liberal economic measures such as labor flexibility and regular-irregular worker distinction. The balance of power once again shifted toward management and the state. The state and management began to review the age-old *yŏn'gong* (seniority) system, which compensates workers based on age and job tenure. New measures based on merit were introduced to replace the practice of the seniority principle.[47]

It is quite clear that the structural change in terms of the regular-irregular divide among workers struck a serious blow to the underlying sense of solidarity among workers, particularly based on regionalism and beyond. Yet the actual implementation of a neoliberal wage system demonstrates there has not been a complete break from the past. The implications for neofamilism are mixed: presumably there remains a strong basis for leveraging regionalism and familism among union-protected regular workers to their advantage, while irregular workers are scrambling for regular positions, still trying to leverage any available connections from neofamilism.

CHAEBOL DYNAMICS AND NEOFAMILISM

How much have chaebols changed since the financial crisis? The trend in degree of economic concentration in chaebols shows that in terms of value, the weight of the top 30 chaebols in GDP has clearly been increasing, even after the financial crisis. The portion of the top 30 chaebols' total sales in GDP in 1979 was 60.6%, peaking at 120.9% in 1990 and holding at 96.7% in 2010.[48] A similar trend can be found since 2010. Chaebols' portion of GDP has been growing, albeit with some fluctuation. With the year 2000 as a baseline, chaebols continued to grow up to the 1997 financial crisis, but showed a dramatic decline between 1998 and 2002. From 2002, chaebols began a path of recovery up to 2012, almost doubling from 2002. Although chaebols' proportion of GDP has began to decline since 2012, the decline is not as significant as that of the post-crisis years, and the trend of economic concentration in chaebols has continued.

Other indicators of economic concentration in chaebols are their assets as a proportion of national assets and their proportion of industrial sales. The proportion of assets shows an increasing trend for chaebols as a whole, regardless of their size, from 5.09% in 2008 to 7.31% in 2016. A similar trend occurred during the same period among the top 30 chaebols under chairman ownership, increasing from 4.41% to 5.52%.[49] Chaebols' share of sales in manufacturing and mining industries was 36.8% (total sales) and 31.9% (value-added) in 1987, 38.1% (total) and 33.6% (value-added) in 1993, and 40% (total) and 38.2% (value-added) in 1997. Throughout the 2000s, chaebols' proportion of total industrial sales declined from 49% in 2000 to 39% in 2016 but did not fall below the levels of the 1980s.[50]

The abuse of inside transactions, which was regarded as one serious problem of chaebols, clearly has not disappeared; in fact, the practice is alive and well even after more than two decades since the financial crisis. What is significant in terms of neofamilism is that inside transactions remain an important mechanism for helping family-owned subsidiaries and tie closely to family succession. With chaebols' intensifying effort to diversify their business vertically and horizontally, the ratio of internal transaction of the top 30 chaebols in 1989 was 23.73%, while that of the top five was even higher, at 29.63%. In 1993, the ratio of internal transactions of the top 30 chaebols was 21% in terms of purchases and 17% for sales.[51]

In the first decade of the 21st century, a similar trend continued (see table 14). From 2011 to 2015, the ratio of internal transactions ranged between 24% and 27% for purchases and between 24% and 26% for sales. What is notable is that as the regulation of internal transactions increased, more internal transactions were conducted at unlisted companies rather than at listed ones. Such a propensity toward unlisted companies was clearly demonstrated in 2011, when 93.8% of the 211 companies with inside transaction ratios above 70% were unlisted companies. None of the 79 companies with inside transaction ratios of 100% were listed companies. The main reason for conducting inside transactions through unlisted companies is that such entities are not as scrutinized as listed ones.[52] Unlisted companies also tend to serve as a channel for chaebol succession.

The change in the number of subsidiaries has been regarded as an indicator of chaebol expansion. Chaebols have been particularly criticized for indiscriminately expanding into new areas without considering the integrative

TABLE 14. Debt ratio trends of chaebols (in percentages)

SCALE OF CHAEBOLS	1995	1996	1997	1998	1999	2000
Top 5	297.6	344.2	472.9	235.1	148.7	162
Top 6–30	435.1	460.8	616.8	497.1	498.5	186
Top 30	347.5	386.5	512.8	379.8	218.7	171.2

Source: Fair Trade Commission website, cited in Jang-Sup Shin and Ha-Joon Chang, *Restructuring Korea Inc.,* 265.

effect upon their current business scope. This so-called octopus-like expansion also frequently impinges upon SMIs. Internal transactions usually accompany a chaebol's entry into a new business and may also involve the intent to execute an illicit succession strategy.[53] The number of subsidiaries has indeed grown steadily. In 1987, there were a total of 509 subsidiaries for the top 32 chaebols, averaging 20.8 subsidiaries per chaebol. In 1996, one year prior to the financial crisis, there were 669 subsidiaries among the top 30 chaebols, an average of 22.3 per chaebol. One year after the crisis in 1999, the total number of subsidiaries increased to 686, resulting in an average of 19.6 per chaebol.[54] In 2002, the total number of subsidiaries for the top 30 chaebols with owners was 607; 772 in 2007; 1,082 in 2011; and 1,256 in 2017. There were several years that showed decreases; for example, total subsidiary count changed by -5.86% from 1,212 in 2013 to 1,141 in 2014 and by -4.19% from 684 in 2004 to 656 in 2005. However, the number of subsidiaries of chaebol groups has grown since the financial crisis.[55]

Up until the financial crisis, Korean chaebols were notorious for their high debt-to-capital ratios, which had been increasing. As table 14 shows, the ratio for the five largest chaebols was 297.6% in 1995, increasing to 344.2% in 1996 and to 472.9% in 1997. The trend was the same for the top 30 chaebols, as the ratio was 347.5% in 1996, 386.5% in 1996, and 512.8% in 1997. Table 15 shows the ratio was close to or above 1,000% for some individual companies. Hanwha, for example, recorded 1,214.7%, Kumho 944%, and Hanjin 907.7% in 1998. Such high debt ratios were attributed to an octopus-style expansion strategy of diversifying business into areas that were not related to their core business in order to gain market share. In the wake of the financial crisis, the government ordered chaebols to reduce the debt ratio to 200% by 2000.

TABLE 15. Indebtedness of the top 30 chaebols, 1998

RANK	CHAEBOL	NO. OF SUBSIDIES	TOTAL ASSETS	DEBT/EQUITY RATIO
1	Hyundai	62	73,520	578.6
2	Samsung	61	64,536	370.9
3	Daewoo	37	52,994	471.9
4	LG	52	52,773	505.7
5	SK	45	29,267	467.9
6	Hanjin	25	19,457	907.7
7	Ssangyong	22	15,645	399.6
8	Hanwha	31	12,469	1,214.7
9	Kumho	32	10,361	944.0
10	Dong-Ah	22	9,054	359.8
11	Lotte	28	8,862	216.4
12	Halla	18	8,562	Negative capital
13	Daelim	21	7,001	513.5
14	Doosan	23	6,586	590.2
15	Hansol	19	6,268	399.9
16	Hyosung	21	5,249	465.0
17	Kohao	13	5,193	472.1
18	Kolon	25	4,894	433.4
19	Dong Kuk Steel Mill	17	4,865	323.8
20	Dong-bu	34	4,339	338.3
21	Anam	15	4,339	1,498.5
22	Jinro	15	4,258	Negative capital
23	Tong Yang	23	3,885	404.3
24	Haitai	15	3,747	1,501.2
25	Shinho	29	3,060	676.7
26	Daesan2	20	2,847	647.8
27	New Core	18	2,831	1,784.1
28	Keo Pyung	19	2,831	438.1
29	Kang Won Ind.	27	2,665	375.0
30	Saehan	16	2,659	419.3
	Total	804	435,318	518.9

Source: Adapted from "Heavy Borrowing Backfires," *Business Korea* 15, no. 5 (May 1998): 25.

Thus, the debt ratio decreased considerably to 162% for the top five chaebols and to 171.2% for the top 30 chaebols in 2000.

The high levels of debt had serious implications for neofamilial practices in that most debt financing previously came from government-controlled commercial banks and financial institutions, the domestic commercial paper market, and foreign banks. For example, bank and non-bank financial institutions provided 55% of financing for the top five chaebols in 1997.[56] Thus, chaebols relied heavily on neofamilial ties to gain access to financing institutions. It was most likely the case that the borrowed capital was invested to increase their affiliated companies, which were usually owned and managed by people related to chaebol owners. Considerably reduced debt ratios meant that chaebols no longer depended on the state for capital, which in turn lessened the need for mobilizing neofamilial ties to access capital.

Overall, there have been significant improvements in financial structure and profitability of chaebols and relatively little progress in governance and chairman-driven management, which has essentially remained intact. This can be seen in the expanded proportion of chaebols in the national economy.[57] From a neofamilial perspective, most institutional reforms related to chaebols are incomplete and uneven. Although the reduced debt-to-capital ratios of many chaebols considerably reduced their dependence upon the state, there are unmistakable signs of neofamilism persisting in the outside director system, illegal means of inheritance, inchoate shareholder rights practices, and misuse of internal transactions. The financial reforms brought about drastic changes in ownership, management, and lending styles. However, the state still wields considerable influence over personnel matters at financial institutions.

Labor had to bear the brunt of abrupt changes. The bifurcation of the workforce into regular and irregular workers was a big blow to worker solidarity. The disruption of lifetime employment and introduction of the merit-based wage system undermined neofamilial bases among workers, such as regionalism. However, this does not mean that neofamilism has disappeared completely in the labor sector. As recent examples of illicit hiring practices in labor unions demonstrate, familial ties took on new meaning by prioritizing the family members of union leaders.[58]

Korean families were seriously impacted by the financial crisis in terms of unemployment, credit crisis, and role reversal between spouses, which contributed to the disruption and disintegration of families in Korean society. Changes in lending practices put an end to personal debt guarantees, which were prevalent prior to the financial crisis, ushering in individualizing tendencies among family members. In these ways, the financial crisis left an indelible impact on Korean families. Yet it also seems that family ties became much more important in surviving a new era of uncertain and volatile employment. Among lower-class families, cooperation among family members has become indispensable for survival. For upper-class families, family ties have become essential for enjoying access to better employment and educational opportunities.[59]

For over two decades, the institutional reforms and psychological impact of the 1997 financial crisis severely tested the resilience of neofamilism in Korea. It is certainly true that there have been some changes within neofamilial practices in hiring, compensation, and access to information. Chaebols, the primary neofamilial stronghold, remain unchanged in terms of various facets of governance structure and operations. The state, also an important source of neofamilism, has changed significantly in terms of its planning capacity, intervention in financial institutions, and thus its relations with chaebols. At the same time, the state assumed new functions in social welfare and has maintained considerable influence over personnel policies at financial institutions. In the labor sector and among Korean families, neofamilial practice is thriving and successfully coping in a market-based, competitive employment environment. Thus, neofamilism has proven to be resilient in Korean society's new context before and after the financial crisis. However, a distinction should be clearly made between different types of neofamilism in terms of how and where it is practiced. As it emerged in the 1960s, neofamilism occurred in the context of state-led industrialization, while post-1997 neofamilism persists in the context of marketization in the aftermath of the 1997 financial crisis. If the former is labeled as type I, the latter can be called type II. The old form (type I), which developed under state-led late industrialization, survives in the new context of market-based competition (type II), representing an ongoing and tenuous co-existence of the two forms.

Conclusion

An apparent institutional irony has arisen from late industrialization: the quicker the rate at which late industrialization is pursued, the more likely it is that traditional institutions and values will be introduced into the process. Such irony is primarily attributed to notions of inferiority and urgency that stem from a sense of backwardness felt by leading elites in late-industrializing nations. Society and institutions undergo serious changes in the course of these efforts to overcome backwardness. Neofamilism is a social consequence of South Korea's late industrialization. It encompasses a socially meaningful unit that defines identity, survival strategies, and modes of institutional operation. Analysis of the byproducts of Korea's late industrialization through the lens of neofamilism shows that industrialization does not beget universal consequences.

To overcome a crude class-reductionist approach, the concept of class in late industrialization has evolved among social scientists to accommodate factors such as sociocultural milieu and political and international environments, in which industrialization and social changes occur. However, despite focusing on heterodox factors that would mitigate a crude class-reductionist approach, such revisionist works have been unable to articulate an alternative to class. In this study of neofamilism, social changes are approached to see how distinct outcomes from late industrialization give rise to possible alternatives. Thus, neofamilism coexists, overrides, and contends with the conventional concept of class to explain resulting phenomena of social change.

Further contextualization of industrialization began with a renewed interest in political economy and the subsequent "varieties of capitalism" approach, yet a significant gap remains between political economy and social change in the study of late industrialization. The findings of this book narrow this gap by proposing a way to understand the social implications of state-led economic policies. One of the findings is that state-society relations can be differentiated into four key types. By framing the case of South Korea within a "state-leading-society model," the impact of neofamilial structures on civil society and democratization becomes readily apparent. Accordingly, the acontextual approach that is currently popular in the literature on civil society is open to criticism; identifying civil society in relation to democratization requires a close examination of society at a macro level. In Korea's case, the neofamilial base of Korean society has hampered the development of civil society. Similarly, the social implications of state actions merited close attention, along with delineating the exact ways in which the state introduced traditional institutions and values into society and how neofamilism emerged from this deliberate effort.

In turn, neofamilism raises critical questions in understanding democracy and democratic consolidation. In the case of South Korea, neofamilism is shown to be a major cause of regionalism in voting, inability to attain democratic consolidation, and highly polarized party politics. Although South Korea's democratization satisfies the minimal definition of democratic consolidation in that there is no group in Korea opposed to democracy, the country's democracy is far from consolidated; highly polarized party politics render issues-based debate and compromise nearly impossible. This study has provided a well-grounded elucidation of prospects for Korean democratic consolidation, which has heretofore not been based on solid sociological analysis.[1] Furthermore, disaggregate and dynamic approaches to understanding the state made it possible to explore how a strong state gradually hollows out and how both the state and business ultimately weaken, expanding the patterns of state-society dynamics beyond the state-versus-society model.

This book demonstrates how traditional institutions are introduced into the process of late industrialization and their impacts on interactions between the state, business, and society. Studies of tradition have progressed little since the paradigm of modernization was heavily criticized in the mid-1970s and political economy began to focus on the roles of institutions and policies to explain the success of late industrialization. Tradition has mainly been approached in the contexts of management, of particular industrial sectors, or considered wholly external to industrialization. Tradition has been reconceptualized as an integral part of industrialization, as something that is enabled through deliberate state mediation.

Since each case of late industrialization differs in terms of the timing of industrialization as well as international and domestic contexts, it is not possible to expect the social consequences of each case to be similar. What these cases do share is a common framework for analysis, including criteria such as the types of elites involved, the context in which they come to recognize the sense of backwardness, and the traditional institutions and values on which they rely. For South Korea, the social and institutional legacies of its colonial history, the breakdown of the traditional ruling elite, and the international environment shaped by the Cold War contrast with the case of Japan, which possessed strong continuity of elites, traditional institutions, and values within an international environment largely characterized by imperialism. In the latter, elites achieved consensus to make judicious and conscious efforts to reinvent traditional institutions such as *ie*. South Korean elites were neither as united nor conscious about how to reinvent traditional institutions and values; due to Korea's colonial past, there was a lack of consensus on what constitutes Korean tradition and which values needed to be reinvented.

Despite differences in contextual conditions, what late industrialization cases have in common is that the facilitating factors of late industrialization form the seeds for institutional and social problems while late industrialization attains a certain level of success. Put differently, social and institutional problems are embedded in the dynamics of late industrialization, and it becomes difficult to pinpoint the sources of problems that emerge thereafter. This illustrates the difficulty of describing history in developmental terms or stages; the success and the problems start at the same time. In Japan, the seeds for the elites' subtle but tight grip on the masses had been sown much earlier than the 1930s, when militarism became visible. Similarly, the beginning of South Korea's industrialization set the stage for rampant regionalism, which seriously began to affect democratization later on.

Methodologically, implications for social changes in late industrialization can be derived from analyzing interactions between the state, business, and society; talent recruitment patterns of the state, the sense of backwardness, perceptions of tradition, and the status of traditional social structures are critical to such analysis. As these factors are historically and contextually determined, social changes of late industrialization are impossible to generalize. In this respect, our analysis has implications for other late industrialization cases in terms of how to approach the process and consequences of late industrialization.

Last, comparative studies of late industrialization, rather than domestic analysis alone, reveal possibilities for typologies of social changes in late industrialization. Comparative analysis of cases of late industrialization is possible by using the same variables. Another area of inquiry is the international environment in which a given case of late industrialization occurs. The international environment influences late industrialization strategies and policies, and in turn the consequences of late industrialization affect the international perspectives of late-industrializing countries. It is an intriguing question how differing circumstances of international order affect patterns of economic development in Japan, South Korea, and China: Japan's late industrialization was launched in the heyday of classical imperialism: for South Korea, the Cold War was an important factor in determining industrialization strategies; China has been industrializing in the context of globalization. A strong demand for international recognition also tends to accompany successful late industrialization. Thus, the international environment in which late industrialization occurs determines the differing ways in which such desire for recognition manifests, requiring serious analyses for the future.[2]

Several new developments raise the question of whether neofamilism is receding in Korea, with globalization being the most important driver. The crumbling of the state-based economic developmental model due to external economic pressures—though largely of Korea's own creation—was a bitter pill to swallow for Korean society. Most relevant was the undermining of the roles and functions of the state. As many argue, the state has not completely lost; in fact, the state picked up new functions in the aftermath of the 1997 financial crisis, including social welfare.[3]

However, the state lost the powers of economic planning and policy that it had employed during Korea's developmental period; no longer could state resources be allocated in favor of certain regions. The loss of these state powers marked an important turning point for the persistence of regionalism, which had originated from the perception and reality that the southeastern region was favored during state-led industrialization. The change was not instant but set the background for change.

Democratization brought about regime changes through elections, which in turn also drastically altered perceptions of the state. Region-based voting patterns persisted; the regional base of regimes shifted from the southeastern region to the southwestern region of Korea. The composition of elites began to shift accordingly, as did which regions became favorable in terms of recruitment. The most serious blow to regionalism was the dramatic impeachment of the conservative president Park Geun-hye in 2016–17. Its implications for regionalism are unmistakable, as her political stronghold was in the southeastern region. The successive political defeats for the conservative party in a series of political elections (2017 presidential election, 2018 local election, and 2020 general election) meant the striking shift in perception that it was the beginning of the end of the southeastern region's dominance in Korean politics. Southeast regionalism can historically be characterized as "winning regionalism" for its residents in that they have directly and indirectly benefited from state actions during the developmental era. However, regionalism in the southwestern region could be called "defensive regionalism" as it was formed in reaction to southeast regionalism and based on the perception and experiences that the southwestern region was discriminated against by the state. As such, the breakdown of southeast regionalism was a catalyst for southwest regionalism.

The adoption and expansion of social welfare played an important role in changing mass perception of the state. Korea has been known to be parsimonious in terms of welfare provision, with state adoption of new social welfare measures implemented only at the outbreak of the financial crisis in 1997. Although the scope of social welfare and the scale of benefits are still not extensive, the proportion of social welfare as part of the national budget has been growing.[4] The significance of social welfare in shifting neofamilism is that it is primarily based on individual and household conditions and not regional background. Thus, social welfare measures are important in changing the perception that the state favors certain regions. The impact of the adoption of social welfare on a more extensive scale also impacted family dynamics; it reduced the burden of the family to take care of parents medically and otherwise and also affected family solidarity.

Globalization also brought about significant changes in economic institutions. Chaebols became less dependent upon the state as the Korean government required them to reduce their debt ratios to 200% in the aftermath of the 1997 financial crisis. Corporate governance structure and business operations have gone through unprecedented changes, with increased outside influences and greater transparency. For example, the abrupt introduction of international standards in the financial sector considerably altered the strategies to access financial resources for both individuals and businesses. Influence from the state or a patron has become less meaningful, and a new system of insuring guarantees have largely replaced individual mutual guarantees. Lending is based more on a risk assessment of individual capacity to pay off debt. These changes undermined the neofamilial bases of family, school, and region.

With the weakening of neofamilial ties, the frequency of resorting to legal means for conflict resolution has grown unprecedentedly. By the early 2000s, this litigiousness had resulted in Korea becoming known as "a society of excessive suing." While population growth remained stable in the 1980s compared to that of 1910 to 2005, lawsuits per capita rose from two cases per 1,000 people between 1910 and 1980 to 25 cases per 1,000 people by 2005, more than a tenfold increase.[5]

Another statistic also confirms this increase in litigation cases. Between 1997 and 2007, the population grew by 6.4%, compared to an increase of 28.3% in litigation cases. The total number of legal dispute cases received was 3,125 per 10,000 people in 1997 and reached 3,846 per 10,000 people in 2006. Notably, civil cases showed the largest increase over criminal or family cases; civil cases nearly doubled from 139 per 1,000 people to 260, while criminal cases grew from 38 to 46 per 1,000 people. Such a contrast indicates that social conflicts more often were brought to court for resolution. This suggests that the practice of resolving conflicts through human relations based on neofamilial ties had weakened.[6]

Another legal development with a potentially serious impact on neofamilial practice is the legislative passage of the Act on the Ban of Illegal Solicitation and Bribery (also known as the Kim Young-ran Law), intended to prevent corruption. Under the act, public officials can face criminal charges for accepting a bribe worth more than one million won.[7] Beyond this specific measure, a broad movement to change traditional authority relations will also seriously impact relationships based on neofamilial ties. A law restricting workweeks to 52 hours affects workplace relations between employers and employees. Furthermore, protests against abuse and bullying by those in positions of power (*kapchil hyŏngsang*) have also been evolving spontaneously and will impact neofamilial practices by affecting hierarchical relations in Korean society. Ever-expanding campaigns for gender equality and anti-sexual harassment and abuse accelerate changes in human relations and further challenge the social order observed under neofamilism.

The booming popularity of social media is a relatively new but a pervasive phenomenon in South Korea. One survey reported that 47.7% used social networking services in 2019, up from 16.8% in 2011. Active participation in social media may play a role in overcoming narrow neofamilial social bases. Along these lines, the series of massive candlelight protests coordinated through social media that culminated in the successful impeachment of President Park Geun-hye is interpreted as a sign of a stronger civil society.[8]

While there are certainly signs that neofamilism is weakening in Korean society, there are also indications that suggest otherwise. For example, the media frequently reports malfeasance in neofamilial hiring practices across the entire spectrum of society.[9] Labor unions have employed illicit methods to give priority to family members in hiring new workers and reclassifying them as regular workers.[10] Several financial institutions were reported for recruiting based on neofamilial influence. University professors have been known to give better grades to their own children in classes. In a 2020 scandal involving the minister of justice, he and his wife were convicted of having forged citations for their daughter, a high school student, and fraudulently attributing first authorship to their child for a scientific journal article in order to improve prospects for college admissions.[11]

All of these cases speak volumes about the persistence of neofamilism in a new environment and demonstrate that the institutional backgrounds for neofamilism have changed. In the original form of neofamilism, the state was the main institution in charge of economic incentives, and thus access to such incentives was crucial. However, since the introduction of market principles in the economy and the increasing importance of laws and regulations, neofamilial practice is primarily employed to reduce uncertainty caused by market operations. The continuity of neofamilial practice to avoid the open competition accompanying the shift in institutional contexts can be characterized as type II neofamilism, distinct from the original form of neofamilism (type I). Perhaps for this reason, a survey from 2015 of people in their 20s to 40s on the prospects of neofamilism's persistence showed a similar response to a 2006 survey of people in their 60s and beyond.[12]

The conflicting evidence on the persistence of neofamilism speaks to the transitional nature of Korean society: even under market conditions, neofamilism is alive and well despite counterfactors such as globalization, the weakening of the conservative party, and the welfare system. A closer look at the sources of change is necessary to understand why neofamilism persists. To start, institutional reforms in the aftermath of the financial crisis were initially adopted with little resistance. As time progressed, embedded institutions began to show resistance, resulting in uneven change and intersectoral gaps in finance, labor relations, and corporate governance systems.[13] This situation gave rise to clashes between institutions and eventually the ascendance of embedded institutions, exemplified by the system of having outside board members on the board of directors and succession patterns in chaebols. Economic institutions are currently in the process of searching for a market system with a distinctly Korean flavor, an equilibrium between Korean embeddedness and hurried importation of IMF-prescribed institutions.

In politics, the impeachment of President Park Geun-hye and political defeat of the conservative Saenuri Party marked an important change in regionalism in Korean politics. Political regionalism has not disappeared completely, as clearly indicated in the results of the April 2020 general election. Korean politics has long been suffering from the disconnect between political parties and the general population. Regionalism underpins this disjuncture: political parties have relied on regionalism for elections and have been unresponsive to the general public. Korean society is in a confusing situation in which the political parties and general public continues to lack connection while regionalism lingers.

Similar observations can be made about civil society. As mentioned in chapter 5, civil society has grown remarkably with the unfolding of democratization, but the increase in sheer numbers does not mean the flourishing of civic-mindedness; the bulk of the increase in civil organizations was based on neofamilism. One study found that 50% of participation in civic organizations occurred in those based on school, blood, and regional ties, with the rest in leisure and religious organizations (10% and 15%, respectively). The participation in civil organizations, interest groups, and political organizations had previously been less than 10% (9.8% in 1999, 5.5% in 2003, and 7.1% in 2006).[14]

High participation rates in neofamilial organizations illustrate the neofamilial ethos and perspective. The neofamilial ethos is characterized by exclusivity, a sense of closed boundaries, intolerance to outsiders, and most importantly a poorly developed conception of a society beyond a narrowly defined small community. Thus, neofamilism can explain the lack of sufficient analytical attention to public space in much literature on Korean civil society and civic organizations. Under such circumstances, civic organizations without citizens can be easily transformed into self-serving politicized advocacy groups with a narrow base for compromise. Neofamilism thus explains the gap between a rather active political democracy and weak social democracy. Such poorly developed social democracy leaves room for regional political parties to further weaken political institutionalization in the Huntingtonian sense.

The emergence of multiple, disconnected civic organizations in Korea is quite analogous to Weimar society in Germany. Weimar society was notorious for its proliferating civic organizations that lacked both horizontal and vertical linkages.[15] Germans resided in their social organizations to deal with anxiety and uncertainty. These numerous civic organizations were not linked to political parties, which were highly fragmented and weakly developed.

Neofamilism appears to be both persisting and declining, depending on where one looks; Korean people and society seek comfort in neofamilial settings amid present uncertainty from the ongoing development of market principles in the economy and the seemingly irreconcilable contrast between the formal legal system and a highly volatile political party system. At the same time, a highly globalized economy, signs of breakdown of regionalism, and burgeoning changes in authority relations seemingly challenge neofamilism's endurance.

Overall, Korean society is largely in a state of split, schizophrenic flux, observed for example in cycles of reactive surges against national crisis followed by a return to normalcy. Candlelight demonstrations illustrate this phenomenon. This particular form of protest has occurred in times of crisis— such as the protests against the importation of beef tainted with mad cow disease, which resulted in the ousting of a president who was found to have abused and mismanaged state power—and could be considered a strong sign of healthy civil society. However, Korean society, after massive response to the national crisis caused by state mismanagement and the initial positive results of the management of the COVID-19 pandemic, devolved back to the original practice of lack of compromise and civility. This atavistic dynamic between two extreme positions can be regarded as reflecting anxiety shared by Korean people, a psychological vacuum formed by the lack of an identity base and set of survival strategies to replace weakening neofamilial ties. Critical situations on a national scale tend to induce the collective expression of this anxiety, while amplifying the fact that there are few other outlets to channel these thoughts and feelings. Thus, vitriolic, hostile expressions on social media should not be viewed as indicative of a highly activated or mature civil society, as most of them betray that they are not ready for discourse or compromise.[16]

Korean society and politics have undergone a prolonged transition: progressives and conservatives are in search of an alternative to regionalism but have yet to find one, and meanwhile they are losing support from the general population. It seems there may be a middle ground emerging in Korean politics. The process will be one in which imported democracy from the West transforms into a democracy infused with Korean tradition.[17] Similarly, Korean economic institutions and operations will continue to incorporate Korean embeddedness. Korean society is finding ways to build institutions, whether democratic or capitalist, that are socially compatible and culturally legitimate. The Western democracy imported from and imposed by the United States in the mid-20th century coexisted with Korean-style late industrialization, which was implemented with non-democratic elements. The challenge now is to overcome non-democratic legacies embedded in Korean society during industrialization and to strike a balance between individualism and collectivism. Only when Korea reaches such milestones will neofamilism cease to persist.

Notes

INTRODUCTION

1. Yi Munung, *Kongŏphwa kwajŏng*.
2. Chungang Sŏn'gŏ Kwalli Wiwŏnhoe [National Election Commission], https://www.nec.go.kr/portal/main.do.
3. Based on the author's survey results, as discussed in chapter 6.
4. Yi Chŏngjin, "Chŏngdang yŏnhap," 119.
5. Hyŏndae Sahoe Yŏn'guso, *Kungmin ŭisik kujo yŏn'gu*, 90.
6. Kim Chibŏm et al., *Han'guk chonghap sahoe chosa* (2011 survey).
7. Pak Hŭi, *Han'guk taegiŏp*, 221.
8. Mr. K, a unionist; see chapter 6.
9. John H. Goldthorpe, "Theories of Industrial Society"; and Clark Kerr, *Future of Industrial Societies*.
10. Leroy P. Jones and Il Sakong, *Government, Business, and Entrepreneurship*; Alice Amsden, *Asia's Next Giant*; Byung-Nak Song, *Rise of the Korean Economy*; and Meredith Woo-Cumings, "Introduction."
11. Peter Evans, *Embedded Autonomy*.
12. Peter B. Evans, Dietrich Rueschemeyer, and Theda Skocpol, *Bringing the State Back In*.
13. Val Burris, "Late Industrialization"; Yow-Suen Sen and Hagen Koo, "Proletarianization"; Kenji Hashimoto, "Class Structure"; and Hong-Zen Wang, "Class Structures"; Sin Kwangyŏng, *Kyegŭp kwa nodong undong*; Song Hogŭn, *Yŏllin sijang, tach'in chŏngch'i*; and Kim Hogi, *Hyŏndae chabonjŭi*.
14. Chalmers Johnson and E. B. Keehn, "Disaster in the Making"; and Chalmers Johnson, "Preconception vs. Observation."
15. Herbert Blumer differentiated five different responses of tradition to industrialization: rejective, disjunctive, assimilative, supportive, and disruptive. Herbert Blumer, *Industrialization*, 189ff. This book focuses on assimilative and supportive aspects of the responses of tradition to industrialization.
16. Yasusuke Murakami, "Ie Society" (1984); and Ralf Dahrendorf, *Society and Democracy*.
17. Kenneth Jowitt, "Soviet Neotraditionalism"; and Andrew G. Walder, *Communist Neo-Traditionalism*.

18. Daniel Harrison Kulp II, *Country Life*; Ch'oe Chaesŏk, *Han'gugin ŭi sahoe-jŏk sŏnggyŏk*; Pak Yŏngsin, *Yŏksa wa sahoe pyŏndong*; and Ok Sŏnhwa, "Hyŏndae Han'gugin." Kulp defined familism as follows: "Familism is a social system wherein all behavior, all standards, ideals, attitudes and values arise from, center in, or aim at the welfare of those bound together by the blood nexus fundamentally. The family is therein the basis of reference, the criterion for all judgments. Whatever is good for the family, however that good is conceived, is approved, and developed; whatever is inimical to the interests of the family, however they are formulated, is taboo and prohibited" (xxix).

19. J. P. Nettl and Roland Robertson, *International Systems*.

20. Byron K. Marshall, *Capitalism and Nationalism*.

21. Joseph Stalin, *Problems of Leninism*, 588-89.

22. Pak Chŏnghŭi, *Pak Chŏnghŭi sŏnjip*, 2:165-91.

23. Inoue Tomoichi, an influential Home Ministry bureaucrat, openly worried that Japan was falling behind the other powers, as measured by several indices of national strength. Not only were the Japanese people working far fewer hours than Western counterparts, even their hens appeared to be less than diligent—laying a mere 40 eggs per year, compared to 70 in Germany. The key to "managing a nation," concluded Inoue, was "making a people who work harder." Sheldon Garon, *Molding Japanese Minds*, 9.

24. Joseph Stalin, *Problems of Leninism*, 593-94; Holland Hunter, "First Soviet Five-Year Plan," 245; and Byron K. Marshall, *Capitalism and Nationalism*, 29. Park Chung Hee's opening ceremony of the seventh national assembly session, July 10, 1967 (Year Beginning Speech, 1966, 1. 18): "To us one year is merely a moment of the perpetuity and really a short time, but what we can achieve and how we achieve for one year will have a decisive impact on the process of the modernization of fatherland." For more on Park Chung Hee, see chapter 3.

25. Robert E. Cole, "Theory of Institutionalization," 52.

26. David L. Hoffmann, *Peasant Metropolis*, chap. 2.

27. Roger L. Janelli and Dawnhee Yim Janelli, *Ancestor Worship*; and Seung-Kyung Kim, *Class Struggle*.

28. Yasusuke Murakami, "Ie Society" (1984); and Stephen Vlastos, *Mirror of Modernity*. On the ambivalence of post-colonial leaders on their tradition, see Mary Matossian, "Ideologies."

29. Reinhard Bendix, *Nation-Building and Citizenship*, 416.

30. Theda Skocpol, "Bringing the State Back In," 21.

31. Ralf Dahrendorf, *Society and Democracy*; Hagen Koo, *Korean Workers*; and William W. Lockwood, *Economic Development of Japan*.

32. Bernard S. Silberman, *Cages of Reason*.
33. W. Dean Kinzley, *Industrial Harmony*; Koji Taira, "Factory Legislation"; Robert E. Cole, "Theory of Institutionalization"; and Robert J. Smith, *Japanese Society*.
34. Reinhard Bendix, *Nation-Building and Citizenship*, 395.
35. Reinhard Bendix, *Nation-Building and Citizenship*, 394.
36. The social structure of a country's "transitional phase" should, therefore, be a primary focus of analysis rather than be dismissed as a survival of the past. Reinhard Bendix, *Nation-Building and Citizenship*, 410.
37. "If one wants to give the social structure of Imperial Germany a name, it would be the paradoxical one of an industrial-feudal society." Ralf Dahrendorf, *Society and Democracy*, 58.

1. THE SOCIOLOGY OF LATE INDUSTRIALIZATION

1. Herbert Blumer, *Industrialization*, 3.
2. Gabriel A. Almond and G. Bingham Powell Jr., *Comparative Politics*; Walt W. Rostow, *Stages of Economic Growth*; Clark Kerr, *Future of Industrial Societies*; and John H. Goldthorpe, "Theories of Industrial Society."
3. Peter A. Hall, "Dilemmas," 137; and Arif Dirlik, "Rethinking Colonialism," 444.
4. The clear sign for admission to the end of universalism was Samuel Huntington's remark that the United States is a unique case. Samuel P. Huntington, "West Unique," 28–46.
5. An exception to this trend is literature on world-system theory and the dependency school. However, insofar as social changes are considered, they were viewed as the reflection of economic realities. Immanuel Wallerstein, *Capitalist World-Economy*; and Immanuel Wallerstein, *Politics of the World-Economy*.
6. The second reason history matters is that actors or agents can learn from experience. Historical institutionalists understand that behavior, attitudes, and strategic choices take place inside particular social, political, economic, and even cultural contexts. Sven Steinmo, "Institutionalism," 183.
7. Wolfgang Streeck, "Taking Capitalism Seriously."
8. Peter Evans, "Development as Institutional Change."
9. Jeremy Boissevain, "Place of Non-Groups," 544–46. *Non-group* refers either to individual or to the process of transition from individual level to group level. See also Eric R. Wolf, "Kinship, Friendship."
10. Mustafa Emirbayer, "Manifesto."

11. Examples are the non-group approach proposed in social anthropology; second society and neotraditionalism in approaching socialist societies; and, finally, a proposition that a new paradigm is needed to understand post-socialist societies, focusing not on change from a traditional to modern society but where transition from socialist modern to capitalist modern society occurs. Liping Sun, "Societal Transition."

12. John H. Goldthorpe, "Employment, Class, and Mobility."

13. John Walton, "Theory and Research."

14. Marx said in *Capital*: "Ironically, it is not a question of the higher or lower degree of development of the social antagonisms that result from the natural laws of capitalist production. It is a question of these laws themselves, of these tendencies working with iron necessity towards inevitable results. The country that is more developed industrially only shows, to the less developed, the image of its own future." Reinhard Bendix, *Nation-Building and Citizenship*, 383. On Marx's thought on India, see Ashutosh Kumar, "Marx and Engels." On the limitations of rational-choice theory in capturing distinctiveness and subtleties in area studies, see Chalmers Johnson and E. B. Keehn, "Disaster in the Making."

15. Ralph Miliband, *State in Capitalist Society*; Nicos Poulantzas, "Problem of the Capitalist State"; Guillermo A. O'Donnell, *Modernization*; and Bob Jessop, *Capitalist State*.

16. Theda Skocpol, "Critical Review"; Theda Skocpol, *States and Social Revolutions*; Peter Evans, *Dependent Development*; Peter B. Evans, Dietrich Rueschemeyer, and Theda Skocpol, *Bringing the State Back In*; and Fred Block, *Revising State Theory*.

17. Scholars in the so-called varieties of capitalism school, for instance, also tried to understand the "institutional similarities and differences among the developed economies" as a "response to the economic problems"; see Peter A. Hall and David Soskice, *Varieties of Capitalism*.

18. Chalmers Johnson, *MITI*.

19. Bruce Cumings, "Legacy"; Thomas B. Gold, *State and Society*; Alice H. Amsden, *Asia's Next Giant*; Robert Wade, *Governing the Market*; Ziya Öniş, "Logic"; and Jung-en Woo, *Race to the Swift*.

20. Peter B. Evans, *Dependent Development*; and Peter Evans, "Class, State, and Dependence."

21. The embedded autonomy framework by Peter Evans was first proposed by Karl Polanyi, who questioned the myth of the free market and argued that markets are socially embedded. Peter Evans, *Embedded Autonomy*; and Karl Polanyi, *Great*

Transformation. The direction of focus is from society to market or economics rather than from economics to society, which is the focus of this book.

22. In this respect, the present study takes quite the opposite approach from that of economic sociology, which posits that society was incorporated to the extent that it helps to explain economic change.

23. Neil J. Smelser and Richard Swedberg, "Sociological Perspective"; and Richard Swedberg, "Economic and Sociological Approaches."

24. Peter A. Hall, "Dilemmas," 137.

25. Sin Kwangyŏng, *Kyegŭp*; Sŏng Hogŭn, *Yŏllin sijang*; and Kim Hogi, *Hyŏndae chabonjŭi*.

26. Jan Pakulski and Malcolm Waters, "Social Class."

27. E. P. Thompson, *English Working Class*, 11; Ronald Aminzade, *Class, Politics*; Richard Biernacki, *Fabrication of Labor*; Craig Calhoun, *Question of Class Struggle*; Gareth Stedman Jones, *Languages of Class*; William H. Sewell Jr., *Work and Revolution*; and D. Lockwood, "Sources of Variation."

28. Michael Mann, "Sources of Variation."

29. Michael Mann, "Sources of Variation."

30. Neville Kirk, "History."

31. David Camfield, "Re-orienting Class Analysis," 427.

32. James Wickham, "Social Fascism"; and Michael Mann, "Sources of Variation."

33. This refers to the repressed and underprivileged elements of the populace as a whole, without any clear structural configuration. Hagen Koo, *Korean Workers*.

34. Max Weber's focus on the intervention of status and power in the market is a good starting point to think about different patterns of social change, due to different weights of state and market in industrialization. Also, his consideration of status brings back the persistence of traditional institutions and values in approaching social change under state-led industrialization. In short, the critical question regarding social change in late industrialization is how to consider the strong role of the state and traditional institutions and values. Max Weber, "Status Groups and Classes," 302-5.

35. Edward Shils, *Tradition*, 12.

36. Daniel Lerner, *Passing of Traditional Society*.

37. Olivia Harris, "Temporalities of Tradition," 7.

38. Eric R. Wolf, "Kinship"; Edward Shils, *Tradition*; and Ruth Benedict, *Chrysanthemum and the Sword*.

39. Edward Shils, *Tradition*, 15.

40. "Tradition is the living faith of the dead, traditionalism is the dead faith of the living." Jaroslav Pelikan, *Vindication*, 8.
41. Mayfair Mei-Hui Yang, *Gifts, Favors, and Banquets*.
42. Karl W. Deutsch, "Social Mobilization."
43. Reinhard Bendix, *Nation-Building and Citizenship*, 372.
44. S. N. Eisenstadt, "Multiple Modernities"; and Yu Yingshi, *Chinese History*, 372.
45. Reinhard Bendix, *Nation-Building and Citizenship*, 411.
46. "Modernity can be seen as a process of radical creation out of the past, rather than the outcome of the functional differentiation, rationalization, conformity to the Western social institution, or indeed to modernization." Jeremy Smith, "Japan's Modernity," 102.
47. Chee Meow Seah, *Asian Values*; Geert Hofstede and Michael Harris Bond, "Confucius Connection"; Kuan Yew Lee, "Asian Values"; Francis Fukuyama, "Asian Values"; and David S. Landes, *Wealth and Poverty*.
48. Masahiko Aoki, *Comparative Institutional Analysis*; Chalmers Johnson, *MITI*; and Wolfgang Streeck and Kozo Yamamura, *Origins of Nonliberal Capitalism*.
49. W. Dean Kinzley, *Industrial Harmony*; Koji Taira, "Factory Legislation"; Robert E. Cole, "Theory of Institutionalization"; Robert J. Smith, *Japanese Society*; and Stephen Vlastos, *Mirror of Modernity*.
50. On socialist cases of interactions between modernization and tradition, see Kenneth Jowitt, "Soviet Neotraditionalism"; and Andrew G. Walder, *Communist Neo-Traditionalism*.
51. J. P. Nettl and Roland Robertson, *International Systems*; and S. N. Eisenstadt, "Multiple Modernities."
52. Ibrahim Kaya, *Social Theory*.
53. Yun-Shik Chang, "Personalist Ethic," 124.
54. Norman Jacobs, *Korean Road to Modernization*.
55. Gregory Henderson, *Korea*.
56. Pak Yŏngsin, *Yŏksa wa sahoe pyŏndong*; Pak Hŭi, "Han'guk taegiŏp"; Kim Manhŭm, "Chŏngch'i kyunyŏl"; Kim Yonghak, "Ellit'ŭ ch'ungwŏn"; Yu Sŏkch'un and Sim Chaebŏm, "Han'guk sahoe pyŏnhyŏk"; and Yun-Shik Chang, "Personalist Ethic."
57. Yi Munung, *Kongŏphwa kwajŏng*; and Ch'oe Chaesŏk, *Han'gugin*.
58. Clark W. Sorensen, *Over the Mountains*; Roger L. Janelli, *Making Capitalism*; and Seung-Kyung Kim, *Class Struggle*.
59. Cho Hyŏng, "Han'guk ŭi tosi pigongsik"; and Hŏ Sŏngnyŏl, "Tosi muhŏga."

60. In this regard, Dore's remarks a generation ago are quite apt and relevant to this study: "The predominance of this kind of personalistic dependency may be ascribed to cultural and personality characteristics. . . . But it can also be attributed to the structural characteristics of society. . . . The situation is clearly different from that in the societies which nurtured bourgeois liberalism." Ronald P. Dore, "South Korean Development," 299–300, 301.

61. Thorstein Veblen, *Imperial Germany*; and Reinhard Bendix, "Preconditions of Development."

62. Alexander Gerschenkron, *Economic Backwardness*.

63. Joseph A. Schumpeter, *Imperialism*.

64. Reinhard Bendix, *Nation-Building and Citizenship*, 395.

65. Reinhard Bendix, *Nation-Building and Citizenship*, 394.

66. Ralf Dahrendorf, *Society and Democracy*, 33–37.

67. Ralf Dahrendorf, *Society and Democracy*, 44.

68. Lysbeth Walker Muncy, *Junker*.

69. Yasusuke Murakami, "Ie Society" (1985); and Steven Rosefielde, "Stalinism." On Korea, see chapter 2.

70. Max Weber, cited in Richard Swedberg, "Afterword," 379.

71. Ralf Dahrendorf, *Society and Democracy*, 44.

72. Max Weber, *Economy and Society*, 1:302–5.

2. THE COLONIAL ORIGINS OF NEOFAMILISM

1. Sin Yongha, *Ilche singminji kŭndaehwanon*; Yang Chihye, "Chŏnsi ch'ejegi"; and Kim Kyŏngil, *Ilje ha nodong undongsa*.

2. Sin Yongha, *Ilche singminji kŭndaehwanon*, 35.

3. Hŏ Suyŏl, *Kaebal ŏmnŭn kaebal*.

4. An Pyŏngjik, "Singminji Chosŏn ŭi koyong kujo"; An Pyŏngjik, "Han'guk kŭnhyŏndaesa"; Dennis L. McNamara, *Colonial Origins*; Carter J. Eckert, *Offspring of Empire*; Cho Sŏkkon, "Sut'allon kwa kŭndaehwaron"; Chŏng T'aehŏn, "Sut'allon ŭi songnyuhwa"; and Sin Yongha, "Singminji kŭndaehwaron."

5. That the development-exploitation debate has intensified in proportion to Korean achievement of extraordinarily high and rapid economic growth (in effect, raising the political stakes) again suggests that a political agenda has been interposed between data and theory.

6. Pae Sŭngjun, "Chosŏn kongŏphwa"; An Pyŏngjik, "Singminji Chosŏn ŭi koyong kujo"; and Yang Chihye, "Ilbon Chilso Piryo Chusik Hoesa."

7. A critical remark on colonial studies made in another context is also relevant to the Korean case: "Modernity was never itself the object of a non-teleological

criticism. This is what the post-colonial present demands. Rather than the anti-colonial problems of overthrowing colonialism (or the West) what is important for this present is a critical interrogation of the practices, modalities, and projects through which modernity inserted itself into and altered the lives of the colonized." David Scott, "Colonialism," 523.

8. For a critical discussion of this problem in political science and area studies, see Chalmers Johnson and E. B. Keehn, "Disaster in the Making"; and Chalmers Johnson, "Preconception vs. Observation."

9. Bruce Cumings, "Origins and Development."

10. Michael Robinson, "Broadcasting"; and Kim Tongno, "Singmin sidae ŭi kŭndaejŏk sut'al."

11. Gi-Wook Shin and Michael Robinson, *Colonial Modernity*, introduction and chap. 3.

12. Soon-Won Park, "Colonial Industrial Growth, 131.

13. Georges Balandier, "Colonial Situation," 51.

14. Georges Balandier, "Colonial Situation," 54.

15. Of course, Balandier's main concern was the way ethnic groups or tribes were treated in the African context, as if they were a part of a social whole without considering the colonial situation. His inter-ethnic premise of the colonial situation can be extrapolated more generally to issues between different sectors, such as political, social, and economic sectors. I thank Clark Sorensen for reminding me of this point.

16. P. Mercier, "Problems of Social Stratification," 341.

17. D. M. P. McCarthy explores how colonial bureaucrats' interest in control hindered market development in Tanganyika (Tanzania). D. M. P. McCarthy, *Colonial Bureaucracy*.

18. Georges Balandier, "Colonial Situation," 28.

19. For the case of American Indians, see Thomas R. Berger, *Long and Terrible Shadow*.

20. Peter P. Ekeh, *Colonialism and Social Structure*, 17.

21. Fanny Colonna, "Educating Conformity," 362.

22. Ekeh suggested three forms of institutions in a colonial society as an example of the fragmentation of colonial society (indigenous institutions, migrated institutions, and emergent social institutions). Peter P. Ekeh, *Colonialism and Social Structure*, 15.

23. Landlords were not easily able to transform themselves into capitalists because of the colonial power's interest in control in the rural areas. Bruce Cumings, "Legacy," 492.

24. "Secondary adjustments, namely, practices that do not directly challenge staff but allow inmates to obtain forbidden satisfactions or to obtain permitted

ones by forbidden means. These practices are variously referred to as the angles, knowing the ropes, conniving, gimmicks, deals or ins. Such adaptations apparently reach their finest flower in prisons, but of course other total institutions are overrun with them, too. Secondary adjustments provide the inmate with important evidence that he is still his own man, with some control of his environment; sometimes a secondary adjustment becomes a kind of lodgment for the self." Erving Goffman, *Asylums*, 55.

25. Fanny Colonna, "Educating Conformity," 354.

26. Fanny Colonna, "Educating Conformity," 358.

27. Fanny Colonna, "Educating Conformity," 362.

28. Chŏng Chaech'ŏl, *Ilje ŭi tae Han'guk singminji kyoyuk*, chap. 6.

29. Andrew J. Grajdanzev, *Modern Korea*, 265.

30. Gregory Henderson, *Korea*, 89. Korea was referred to as *Chōsen* in Japanese during the colonial rule.

31. An analysis of the school records of Kyŏnggi High School reveals that as colonial rule progressed, a more sophisticated list of items to check student behaviors was developed. For instance, in 1918 there were nine items—personality, behavior, strength, weakness, hobbies, facial look, uniform, language, and punishment—and by 1930 there were 11—character, willpower, behavior, language, skills, strength, weakness, special features, hobbies, punishment/reward, and student activity. Ha Yong-Chool, "Analysis of School Registrars."

32. Han Uhŭi, "Pot'ong hakkyo," 63.

33. Han Uhŭi, "Pot'ong hakkyo," 65.

34. Han Uhŭi, "Pot'ong hakkyo," 65. In 1915, only 17.7% of school-aged children in the urban areas and 2.6% of those in rural areas entered primary schools, and in 1926, it changed to 33.8% and 16.2%, respectively. Han Uhŭi, "Pot'ong hakkyo," 67.

35. Gregory Henderson, *Korea*, 90.

36. Many Japanese officials referred to this phenomenon of educational credentialism. Zenshō Eisuke, *Suigen gun ichi*, 110; and Chōsen Sōtokufu, *Chōsenjin no shisō to seikaku*.

37. Andrew J. Grajdanzev, *Modern Korea*, 266.

38. Annual Government General's Office Statistical Reports, respective years, cited in Hashitani Hiroshi, "1930-40nyŏndae Chosŏn sahoe," 398.

39. Tongnip Undongsa P'yŏnch'an Wiwŏnhoe, *Tongnip undongsa 9*, 300.

40. Chŏng Sehyŏn, *Hangil haksaeng*; Kim Sŏngsik, *Iljeha Han'guk haksaeng*; and Cho Tonggŏl, "Han'guk kŭndae haksaeng undong."

41. Cho Tonggŏl, "Han'guk kŭndae haksaeng undong," 326-27.

42. Chōsen Sōtokufu, Keimukyoku, *Dōmei kyūkō*, 6-7, 43-46.

43. Chōsen Sōtokufu, Keimukyoku, *Dōmei kyūkō*, 52-53.

44. Tongnip Undongsa P'yŏnch'an Wiwŏnhoe, *Tongnip undongsa 9*, 696.

45. The numbers were recounted based on data in Cho Tonggŏl, "Han'guk kŭndae haksaeng undong," 326–91.

46. Cho Tonggŏl, "Han'guk kŭndae haksaeng undong," 458–60.

47. Pak Kyŏngsik, *Ilbon chegukchuŭi*, 544–53. For similar patterns in other cases, see Cho Tonggŏl, "Han'guk kŭndae haksaeng undong," 450; and Kyŏngsang-buktosa P'yŏnch'an Wiwŏnhoe, *Kyŏngsang-buktosa*, 1:460.

48. Pak Kyŏngsik, *Ilbon chegukchuŭi*, 314.

49. Gregory Henderson, *Korea*, 111.

50. Social networks were formed through school ties to protect their interests; Sollin high school graduates, many of whom became employees of the Korean Shokusan Bank, looked after one another in terms of promotion and transfer, reflecting limited social trust basis for all leading elite groups in a dynamic environment. For the landlord case, see Hong Sŏngch'an, *Han'guk kŭndae nongch'on*, 350–61.

51. Andrew J. Grajdanzev, *Modern Korea*, 84.

52. In this regard, an article in *Tong-A Ilbo* (April 12, 1927) is revealing: "Industrial development draws rural people to cities. Rural youth's dream is to leave the villages to enjoy cultural activities in cities. What of the Korean situation? There is no pull of rural youth from industrial sectors, but land is being taken away from peasants and exploitation of landlords is becoming more severe and threatening the lives of peasants." Quoted in Kim Yŏnggŭn, "1920nyŏndae nodongja," 147.

53. Sin Yongha, *Han'guk kŭndae sahoesa yŏn'gu*; Chu Ponggyu, *Ilcheha nongŏp kyŏngjes*; and Ch'a Kibyŏk, *Ilche ŭi Han'guk singmin t'ongch'i*.

54. *Untouchables* refers to official slaves, *kisaeng* (female entertainer at a bar), and butchers, for example.

55. Kim Yŏngmo, "Ilje sidae taejiju," 110–11.

56. Zenshō Eisuke, *Kōryō-gun*, 196.

57. Practically all the official publications on rural conditions used these categories. For examples, see notes 67 and 68.

58. Ha Yong-Chool, "Analysis of School Registrars."

59. Zenshō Eisuke, "Chōsen ni okeru dōzoku buraku no kōzō," 20.

60. Zenshō Eisuke, "Chōsen ni okeru dōzoku buraku no kōzō."

61. Keikido Naimufu, *Keikido nōson shakai jijyŏ*, 26, 27, 29.

62. Keikido Naimufu, *Keikido nōson shakai jijyŏ*, 28.

63. Hong Sŏngch'an, *Han'guk kŭndae nongch'on*, 359.

64. Inaba Iwakichi, "Chōsen no bunka mondai," 80–81. He further observed that there are no extended families without *yangban*.

65. For colonial authorities choosing landowners, see Hong Sŏngch'an, *Han'guk kŭndae nongch'on*, 359.

66. Yasuda Mikita, "Chōsen ni okeru kazoku," 9-10.
67. Nomura Chōtaro, "Chōsen kazoku," 21.
68. Suzuki Eitarō, "Chōsen no nōson," 7, cited in Hashitani Hiroshi, "1930-40nyŏndae," 409.
69. Zenshō Eisuke, *Chōsen no shuraku zenhen*, 593.
70. Mun Sojŏng, "Iljeha Han'guk nongch'on," 18.
71. Ha Sangrak, "Ilche sidaeŭi sahoe pojang," 27-31.
72. O Chŏng, "Chōsen no shinzoku kankei," 103.
73. Zenshō Eisuke, *Chōsen no shuraku zenhen*, 110.
74. Ki Chŏn, "Chugŭl saram," 2-3.
75. Andrew J. Grajdanzev, *Modern Korea*, 187.
76. Essential elements include a household head with strong authority and loosely blood-based kin structure.
77. Kawashima Takeyoshi, *Kazoku oyobi kazokuhō*, 205-55; and Patrick Beillevaire, "Family," 242-43.
78. Kang Inch'ŏl, "Han'guk chŏnjaeng kwa sahoe insik."
79. Kim Tongch'un, "1950nyŏndae Han'guk," 206.
80. Kim Tongch'un, "1950nyŏndae Han'guk," 199.
81. Kim Tongch'un, "1950nyŏndae Han'guk," 200.
82. On the confused family law system at the end of the colonial rule, see Yang Hyŏna, "Han'guk ŭi hoju chedo"; Hong Yanghŭi, "Singminji sigi ch'injok kwansŭp"; Sungyun Lim, *Rules of the House*; and Kwŏn Hŭijŏng, "Singminji sidae Han'guk kajok." On how the adoption of the *myŏn* as a new administrative unit dissolved voluntary basis of the village-based self-help institution (*tonggey*), see Yun Haedong, *Chibae wa chach'i*. On the failed attempt to change Korean tradition, see the case of the attempt to abolish local bazaars in colonial Korea: Hŏ Yŏngnan, *Ilje sigi changsi yŏn'gu*. And on the partial success of the colonial reform, the enforcement of lunar calendar system, and local bazaars, see Hŏ Yŏngnan, *Ilje sigi changsi yŏn'gu*, part 2.
83. In this context Bendix's comment is quite apt: "Another limitation becomes apparent when one applies these concepts to colonial and post-colonial societies. Can any colonial society be said to have the characteristics of 'tradition'? Does it have universally accepted norms? And since the prevailing norms surely do not apply to the subject population, in what sense can one in fact speak of one society? To contrast the past and present social structure one should take account of at least two traditions: the native tradition and the tradition of a dual society created by the colonizing country." Reinhard Bendix, *Nation-Building and Citizenship*, 403.
84. James Mahoney, "Path Dependence."

3. THE STATE AND TRADITION

1. On the early life of Park Chung Hee, see Carter J. Eckert, *Park Chung Hee*.
2. Han'guk Kunsa Hyŏngmyŏngsa P'yŏnch'anwiwŏnhoe p'yŏn, *Han'guk kunsa hyŏngmyŏngsa*, 3.
3. Pak Chŏnghŭi, *Kukka wa hyŏngmyŏng kwa na*, 29-30. For another example of Park's negative view of Korean history, see Pak Chŏnghŭi, *Minjok ŭi chŏryŏk*, 252.
4. Pak Chŏnghŭi, *Chungdan*, 271.
5. Pak Chŏnghŭi, *Choguk ŭi kŭndaehwa*, 6. For another example, see Pak Chŏnghŭi, *Minjok ŭi chŏryŏk*, 252.
6. Pak Chŏnghŭi, *Country, the Revolution and I*, 252.
7. Pak Chŏnghŭi, *Choguk ŭi kŭndaehwa*, 158.
8. Park also points out the relative backwardness vis-à-vis Japan (Pak Chŏnghŭi, *Pak Chŏnghŭi sŏnjip*, 5:386) and North Korea (Pak Chŏnghŭi, *Pak Chŏnghŭi sŏnjip*, 1:16).
9. Pak Chŏnghŭi, *Pak Chŏnghŭi sŏnjip*, 3:119.
10. Pak Chŏnghŭi, *Pak Chŏnghŭi sŏnjip*, 1:2.
11. Sin Hangsu, "Pak Chŏnghŭi chŏnggwŏn"; and Kim Tongno, "Pak Chŏnghŭi sidae."
12. Mary Matossian, "Ideologies."
13. Pak Chŏnghŭi, *Chungdan*, 269.
14. Pak Chŏnghŭi, annual New Year message, January 18, 1966, cited in Chŏng Chaegyŏng, *Pak Chŏnghŭi*, 2:487.
15. Opening Ceremony of the 7th National Assembly session, July 10, 1967, cited in Chŏng Chaegyŏng, *Pak Chŏnghŭi*, 2:486. A similar statement was made: "To us one year is merely a moment of the perpetuity and really a short time, but what we can achieve and how we achieve for one year will have a decisive impact on the process of the modernization of fatherland." Pak Chŏnghŭi, annual New Year message, January 18, 1966, cited in Chŏng Chaegyŏng, *Pak Chŏnghŭi*, 2:487.
16. T'onggyech'ŏng, *T'onggyero pon Han'guk*, 313.
17. T'onggyech'ŏng, *T'onggyero pon Han'guk*, 136-37.
18. Yi Taegŭn, "Han'guk chŏnjaeng," 306-7.
19. Kim Taehwan, "1950nyŏndae Han'guk," 181.
20. Tanimura Takeo, "Haebang hu chabon hyŏngsŏng," 312-31.
21. Edward S. Mason et al., *Economic and Social Modernization*, 13.
22. Pak Chongch'ŏl, "Suip taech'e wŏnjo."
23. Leroy P. Jones and Il Sakong, *Government*, 94-97.
24. His sense of urgency to overcome backwardness manifested in his preoccupation with the scale of business, such as production capacity. For example, in

1966, given the domestic market for ethylene, an international consultant recommended producing 30,000 tons, but considering the capacity for export in the future, 60,000 tons was considered; Park raised it to 100,000 tons. O Wŏnch'ŏl, "Sanŏp chŏnllyak kundan sa," September 24, 1992.

25. Ha Yongch'ul, *Hubal sanŏphwa*, 119.

26. Pak Chunghun, Minister of Industry and Commerce under Park Chung Hee, interview with *Han'guk Kyŏngje Sinmun* [*Korea Economic Daily*], October 12, 1992.

27. The first and perhaps most important difference between the Rhee and Park regimes was the degree of leadership commitment to growth. Rhee was an independence leader who devoted his attention to politics and national integration while largely ignoring economics. Park's orientation could not be more different, with economic growth having priority second only to national and personal political survival. Since only the higher goals are seen as being furthered by growth, economic affairs have been enshrined as the dominant operational system objective. Leroy P. Jones and Il Sakong, *Government*, 290.

28. For details on the history and contents of Korea's economic plans and the state's role in economic development and transition to export promotion strategy, see Leroy P. Jones and Il Sakong, *Government*; and Alice H. Amsden, *Asia's Next Giant*.

29. Different interpretations exist for the reason to shift to the export promotion strategy under the Park Chung Hee regime. On the domestic origin of the policy shift, see Kimiya Tadasi, *Pak Chŏnghŭi*. On the US influence, see Yi Pyŏngjŏn, "Naengjŏn pundan ch'eje"; on the domestic response to US influence, see Stephan Haggard, *Pathways*. For comparisons of ISI and export-led industrialization (ELI) strategies, see Gary Gereffi and Donald L. Wyman, *Manufacturing Miracles*; and Stephan Haggard, *Pathways*.

30. A contrast in economic opportunities between import substitution and export promotion can be seen in the increase of manufacturing firms from 15,204 in 1960 to 25,726 in 1977, while the number of workers employed in those manufacturing firms increased from 275,254 to 1,918,981 during the same period. Eui Hang Shin and Seung Kwon Chin, "Social Affinity," 8.

31. Anne O. Krueger, "Political Economy."

32. Kim Chusin, the second interview, December 18, 1999.

33. Leroy P. Jones and Il Sakong, *Government*, 254.

34. O Wŏnch'ŏl, *Chunghwahak kongŏphwa*, 179, cited in Ha Yongch'ul, *Hubal sanŏphwa*, 128.

35. Mr. O, interview by the author, April 18, 2001, in Ha Yongch'ul, *Hubal sanŏphwa*, 139.

36. Wontack Hong, *Trade, Distortions*, 82–83; and Youngil Lim, *Government Policy*, 18.

37. Youngil Lim, *Government Policy*, 24.

38. *Chosŏn Ilbo* [Chosŏn daily], March 29, 1963, 4; and *Chosŏn Ilbo* [Chosŏn daily], November 27, 1962, 1.

39. O Wŏnchŏl, "Sanŏp chŏnllyak kundan sa," September 30, 1992, 3, cited in Ha Yongch'ul, *Hubal sanŏphwa*, 137–38.

40. Leroy P. Jones and Il Sakong, *Government*, chap. 4.

41. O Wŏnch'ŏl called this method "impact policy." The main ideas behind this approach were that if the state selects and nurtures strategic industries, (1) the level of all industries will be one step further elevated; (2) the effect will reach the entire economy; (3) investment efficiency will improve; and (4) time for industrialization will be shortened. In Ha Yongch'ul, *Hubal sanŏphwa*, 107.

42. Mr. K, interview by the author, January 26, 2015, discussed in chapter 6.

43. Ha Yongch'ul, *Hubal sanŏphwa*, 129.

44. Song Hyorim, *Kakkaisŏ pon Pak Chŏnghŭi*, 102.

45. O Wŏnch'ŏl, *Han'gukhyŏng kyŏngje kŏnsŏl*, 3:343, cited in Ha Yongch'ul, *Hubal sanŏphwa*, 130.

46. Kim Chusin, the second interview, December 18, 1999.

47. O Wŏnchŏl, "Sanŏp chŏnllyak kundan sa," September 24, 1992, cited in Ha Yongch'ul, *Hubal sanŏphwa*, 120.

48. O Wŏnch'ŏl, "Sanŏp chŏnllyak kundan sa," September 24, 1992, cited in Ha Yongch'ul, *Hubal sanŏphwa*, 120.

49. One example for President Park's urgency was well reflected in the following case. He ordered a comprehensive overhaul of export policies based on resolving differences and coordination among ministries involved in exports, but the report should be done within 10 days. Office of the President, "Such'ul ch'okchin'gwa sin sijang kaech'ŏk" [Export promotion and market expansion], in *Taet'ongnyŏng ŭimyŏng jisi* [Based on president's order], document no. 91-1, tae 1-1, no. 48, December 5, 1964.

50. His sense of urgency manifested itself in several different ways. It was clearly seen in his frequent visits to industrial sites for personal inspection. For example, for the 22 months between his inauguration and October 1965, he recorded 43 local visits over 109 days. This means he spent 1.15 days per week for field visits, and by 1977 the number of visits reached 183. Song Hyorim, *Kakkaisŏ pon Pak Chŏnghŭi*, 102.

51. In another example, on April 10, 1973, regarding the compensation issues for industrial zones, President Park ordered the final decisions to be ready right away, and the report was done in four days. Office of the President, "Kakha chisi sahang chung chunghwahakkongŏppunya sujŏng (pujŏnji)" [Revision of president's instructions on heavy-chemical industry sector], in *Taet'ongnyŏng ŭimyŏng jisi* [Based on president's order], document no. 91-1, tae 2-2, no. 214, April 14, 1973.

52. O Wŏnch'ŏl, interview by the author, April 18, 2001, in Ha Yongch'ul, *Hubal sanŏphwa*, 165.

53. Businessman L interview, April 22, 2002, in Ha Yongch'ul, *Hubal sanŏphwa*, 165.

54. O Wŏnch'ŏl, personal communication with the author, April 13, 2001.

55. Pragmatism refers to the tendency to easily make changes to accommodate the need to realize set goals. It is natural that pragmatism becomes frequent due to the sense of urgency and under strong pressure to realize unrealistically high economic targets. The background of pragmatism in decision-making and implementation is that any means can be mobilized to achieve goals. Here it highlights the situation where due to the lack of experience of the state and business, decisions are made hurriedly and frequently change. See Leroy P. Jones and Il Sakong, *Government*, 60-61.

56. Leroy P. Jones and Il Sakong, *Government*, 63.

57. T. Seo, personal communication with the author, May 29, 2001.

58. Mr. S, interview by the author, October 6, 1999, in Ha Yongch'ul, *Hubal sanŏphwa*, 173.

59. O Wŏnch'ŏl, *Han'gukhyŏng kyŏngje kŏnsŏl*, 7:524-27.

60. Ha Yongch'ul, *Hubal sanŏphwa*, 139.

61. Ha Yongch'ul, *Hubal sanŏphwa*, 189.

62. Han Chŏnghwa, "Han'guk taegiŏp," 423.

63. For Park Chung Hee's reliance on the military, see Suk-Choon Cho, "Bureaucracy," 73; and Se-Jin Kim, *Politics of Military Revolution*, 161-66.

64. On the details regarding the increasing regional bias toward the southeast, see Ha Yongch'ul, *Hubal sanŏphwa*, chap. 4. The southeast population was 19% of the whole population. Kim Manhŭm, *Han'guk ŭi chŏngch'i kyunyŏl*, 81.

65. Son Chongho, "Han'guk kogŭp kongmuwŏn," 11.

66. Ha Taegwŏn, "Han'guk insa haengjŏng,"108.

67. Pak Tongsŏ, *Han'guk kwallyo chedo*; Yu Hun, "Han'guk kogŭp kongmuwŏn"; No Chŏnghyŏn, "Han'guk kwallyo"; Yang Sŏngch'ŏl, *Han'guk chŏngburon*; Son Chongho, "Han'guk kogŭp kongmuwŏn"; and Kim Manhŭm, "Han'guk ŭi chŏngch'i kyunyŏl." On the provincial origins of high-ranking officials, see Ha Taegwŏn, "Han'guk insa haengjŏng," 108.

68. The southeastern region includes North and South Kyŏngsang Provinces, and southwestern region includes North and South Chŏlla Provinces. Park Chung Hee was from the southeastern region (North Kyŏngsang Province).

69. Chŏng Chŏnggil, *Taet'ongnyŏng ŭi kyŏngje ridŏsip*.

70. Mr. L, former official of the MCI, interview by the author, April 15, 2000, in Ha Yongch'ul, *Hubal sanŏphwa*, 105.

71. On the data sources, Yong-Chool Ha and Myung-Koo Kang, "Creating a Capable Bureaucracy," 83-91. On the trend of the number of SNU graduates, see Yong-Chool Ha and Myung-Koo Kang, "Creating a Capable Bureaucracy," 91.

72. Examples of company-specific incentives are clearly seen in Article 46 of the Enforcement Decree of Trade Law. The article was revised 11 times from 1967 to 1979; most of the revisions were aimed at permitting particular companies or nstitutions to import certain goods. Ha Yongch'ul, *Hubal sanŏphwa*, 177-78.

73. Pak Pyŏngyun, "Chunghwahak," 59.

74. Pak Pyŏngyun, "Chunghwahak," 62-67.

75. Kong Chŏngja, "Han'guk taegiŏpka," 202-3.

76. *Chosŏn Ilbo* [Chosŏn daily], July 19, 1980.

77. Y. Yi, personal communication with the author, in Ha Yongch'ul, *Hubal sanŏphwa*, 143.

78. Pak Hŭi, "Han'guk taegiŏp," 127. It is not merely coincidental that this pattern was similar to that within the government. Ch'oe Tonggyu, *Sŏngjang sidae*, 318.

79. Pak Pyŏngyun, "Chunghwahak," 59.

80. Pak Pyŏngyun, "Chunghwahak," 84.

81. Hong Wan'gi, interview by the author, November 24, 1999, in Ha Yongch'ul, *Hubal sanŏphwa*, 88.

82. Nam Ch'unho, "Inongmin ŭi chigŏp idong."

83. Roger L. Janelli, *Making Capitalism*, 136; Robert F. Spencer, *Yŏgong*; and Seung-Kyung Kim, *Class Struggle*. Regionalism was pervasive among workers on a daily basis: for example, when a watch went missing in a female dormitory of a factory in the Changwon-Masan industrial complex, a female worker from the southeastern region immediately suspected that one from the southwestern region stole it. Seung-Kyung Kim, *Class Struggle*, 24.

84. Mr. L, interview by the author, April 7, 2002, in Ha Yongch'ul, *Hubal sanŏphwa*, 167.

85. Mr. P, interview by the author, August 10, 2001, in Ha Yongch'ul, *Hubal sanŏphwa*, 168.

86. Mr. L, interview by the author, April 7, 2002, in Ha Yongch'ul, *Hubal sanŏphwa*, 180.

87. Mr. L, interview by the author, April 10, 2000, in Ha Yongch'ul, *Hubal sanŏphwa*, 182.

88. Mr. H, interview by the author, November 17, 1999, in Ha Yongch'ul, *Hubal sanŏphwa*, 184.

89. Mr. O, interview by the author, April 18, 2001, in Ha Yongch'ul, *Hubal sanŏphwa*, 185.

90. Privatism is defined here as attitude and behavior in both private and public spheres, based on exclusivity against people outside neofamilial connections. This sense is different from that used by Jürgen Habermas, who tends to focus on individuals' political indifference by retreat from politics and turning to (nuclear) family, career, and consumption in an advanced capitalist context. Jürgen Habermas, *Legitimation Crisis*, 75. However, privatism in the context of civil society in Korea is analogous to what Kerstin Jacobsson calls civic privatism in Poland. She differentiates the privatism of Habermas from civil privatism as follows: "I use civic privatism to connote an attitude of active individuals to their engagement in civil society and thus based on a civic/citizen identity. What I am arguing in this study of animal rights/welfare activists in Poland is that the ethos of the private sphere is readily brought into their civil society engagement." Kerstin Jacobsson, "Rethinking Civic Privatism," 85.

91. Louis Wirth, "Urbanism," 36–42.

92. Kim Manhŭm, "Chŏngch'i kyunyŏl."

93. Leroy P. Jones and Il Sakong, *Government*, 266.

94. Sŏ Chaejin, *Han'guk ŭi chabonga kyegŭp*, 124.

95. Hong Changp'yo, "Han'guk esŏ ŭi hach'ŏng," 111.

96. Hong Wan'gi, personal communication with the author, November 24, 1999, in Ha Yongch'ul, in *Hubal sanŏphwa*, 188.

97. Han Iksu, CEO, Hanil Precision Machinery, interview by the author, July 16, 2015.

98. Nodongch'ŏng, *Han'guk nodong t'onggye yŏn'gam*, 52–59.

99. Kap Hwan Oh and Hae-Young Lee, "Urbanism in Korea," 234.

100. Once any group is organized based on school, regional, blood, and other ties, it easily turns into one beyond the original purpose of the group. Pak Chŏnghŭi, *Choguk ŭi kŭndaehwa*, 16.

101. Ŭn Chŏngt'ae, "Pak Chŏnghŭi sidae"; Kim Tongno, "Simin undong"; and Ch'oe Yŏnsik, "Pakchŏnghŭi ŭi minjok."

102. Pak Chŏnghŭi, *Pak Chŏnghŭi sŏnjip*, 1:102–14. However, he never failed to mention negative aspects of tradition, such as lack of sincerity and carrying through, the *yangban* system, hierarchy orientation, clannishness, regionalism, and school ties. Chŏng Chaegyŏng, *Pak Chŏnghŭi*, 2:485.

103. There were some exceptions, such as the New Ritual Ordinance, which tried to change wasteful practices of marital ceremony and ancestral worship. See Ko Wŏn, "Pak Chŏnghŭi." The New Village Movement was named as such in 1969 as a village modernization campaign, which was extended to urban areas and factories in 1975. The National Charter of Education in 1968 promoted Korean tradition: mutual aid and patriotism are highlighted. The Second Economy Campaign was

first propounded in the New Year's address of Park Chung Hee in 1968, and the gist of it is that spiritual change should follow material progress. See Pak T'aegyun, "1960nyŏndae."

104. The Yusin (Reform) regime was established after Park abolished the old constitution and adopted the new one, by which the president was to be elected indirectly and which significantly restricted individual and press freedom, in October 1972.

105. Kim Tongno, "Pak Chŏnghŭi sidae."

106. For details on the changes that the *yangban* class, the ruling class, had gone through during the colonial period, see chapter 2.

107. Mr. W, a former high-ranking bureaucrat who was quite close to President Park Chung Hee, interview by the author, August 18, 2015, in Seoul.

108. Yong-Chool Ha, "Myth of the Breakdown."

109. Kim Sŏnyŏp, "Han'guk taedosi chumin," 211; and Kim Manhŭm, "Chiyŏk kyunyŏl."

4. HOLLOWING OUT BUREAUCRACY

1. In a different context from the developmental state, Joel S. Migdal proposed to study the state in terms of process and interaction with non-state actors. See Joel S. Migdal, *Strong Societies*, chap. 1.

2. On the importance of considering time in social sciences, see Paul Pierson, *Politics in Time*; Margaret Levi, *Of Rule and Revenue*; and Barbara Geddes, *Politician's Dilemma*.

3. On the dynamics of the strong and the weak, see Erving Goffman, *Asylums*; James C. Scott, *Weapons of the Weak*; and Susie Scott, "Revisiting the Total Institution."

4. Bruce G. Carruthers, "When Is the State Autonomous?"; and George Steinmetz, "Myth and the Reality."

5. Evelyn B. Davidheiser, "Strong States, Weak States."

6. David C. Cole and Yung Chul Park, *Financial Development*; Barry Eichengreen, "Government"; Joseph H. Stern et al., *Industrialization*; and, for partial exception, Byung-Sun Choi, *Economic Policymaking*.

7. Eric A. Nordlinger, *On the Autonomy*.

8. On taking the state as abstract entity, see introduction, n. 1.

9. Kate Crowley et al., *Reconsidering Policy*, 55–74.

10. S. N. Eisenstadt, "Bureaucracy." Thus, it becomes difficult to apply a Weberian template, based primarily on Western experiences, to the cases of late industrialization. Late industrialization differs from market-based industrialization in terms of mode of industrialization, state status, and the number and nature of

social and economic institutions outside of the state. The dynamics of the state is defined through interactions with such internal and external institutions. As such, a new conceptual framework is necessary to understand the dynamics of the state under late industrialization. See Marshall W. Meyer and M. Craig Brown, "Process of Bureaucratization," 364–65; and Arthur L. Stinchcombe, "Social Structure and Organizations," 142–93.

11. Mr. L, a former official of MCI, interview by the author, April 15, 2000, in Ha Yongch'ul, *Hubal sanŏphwa*, 107:

> Q: Were there informal groups within the MCI?
> A: Naturally, school seniors and juniors grouped themselves.
> Q: Were they organized by regional background?
> A: Not to the same degree, but those from Taegu (southeastern region) were seen flocking toward themselves, while those from Ch'ungch'ŏng did not do so.
> Q: How about those from the southwestern region?
> A: Yes, they did. However, they could not do so openly. Those from the southeastern region naturally gathered among themselves because there were many from the region.

12. Mr. S, a former official of MCI, interview by the author, October 20, 1999, in Ha Yongch'ul, *Hubal sanŏphwa*, 107:

> Q: When do you think such informal groups organized within the ministry? Did those from the southeastern region organize themselves first, or did those from other regions start first?
> A: It was the opposite. That is, under similar conditions, those from the southeastern region were doing better in taking certain posts and advancing in promotions, and thus those from the southwestern region felt threatened.

13. Mr. C, a former official of MCI, interview by the author, March 23, 2001, in Ha Yongch'ul, *Hubal sanŏphwa*, 108:

> Q: Was there an effort to promote internal solidarity among bureaucrats from the same region?
> A: It was the case with bureaucrats from the southeastern region and they were watchful over those from the southwestern region. Whenever those from the southwestern region had meetings among themselves, those from the southeastern region asked the following question: Did you have a meeting for unity? As such those from the southwestern region had difficulty organizing themselves.

Q: How frequently did members from the southwestern region gather?

A: They did once in a while, but due to scrutiny from southeastern region members it was difficult to have frequent meetings.

Q: Then such informal groups affected personnel policies?

A: Yes, I am quite sure. Those from the southeastern region took care of personnel issues all by themselves.

Q: Is it true that southeastern region members were put into positions of high visibility and thus they get could get promoted quicker?

A: Yes, that was the case. Even when the same positions are given to both groups, the difference was those from the southeastern region got recognition, and that made a lot of difference.

14. Mr. S, a former official of MCI, interview by the author, May 17, 2009, in Ha Yongch'ul, *Hubal sanŏphwa*, 109:

Q: When you made decisions and implemented them, did you utilize school and regional ties?

A: I could not help using them.

Q: How was outside influence?

A: Issuing permits after briberies is not good for business. Monetary dealings should not be involved in decision-making and implementation. However, it was quite natural that favors were rendered if there were shared school ties like Seoul National University (SNU) or ministry officials and businesspeople shared similar professional areas.

15. In addition to school and regional ties, shared military service was sometimes a source of solidarity.

16. Refer to the section "Family-School-Regional Nexus in the Business Sector" in chapter 3.

17. *Chosŏn Ilbo* [Chosŏn daily], March 22, 1973, 2.

18. *Chosŏn Ilbo* [Chosŏn daily], June 3, 1976, 2.

19. *Chosŏn Ilbo* [Chosŏn daily], June 2, 1978, 2; and *Chosŏn Ilbo* [Chosŏn daily], September 23, 1978, 2.

20. Ha Yongch'ul, *Hubal sanŏphwa*, 185.

21. Mr. O, interview by the author, April 25, 2001, in Ha Yongch'ul, *Hubal sanŏphwa*, 114.

22. *Chosŏn Ilbo* [Chosŏn daily], January 15, 1970, 1.

23. An Haegyun, *Han'guk haengjŏng ch'ejeron*, 264–69.

24. Kim Hŭng Ki, *Yŏngyok ŭi Han'guk kyŏngje*, 265.

25. "We staked our life on the job, there was no one who knew anything, and thus it was like wandering around the virgin forest. In such a situation nobody could have strong conviction about what he did. We did our best and left the rest in god's hands . . . we simply sowed seeds and planted trees and hoped for the best." Mr. O, former MCI official, interview by the author, April 25, 2001, in Ha Yongch'ul, *Hubal sanŏphwa*, 126–27.

26. The wild horse phenomenon manifested in three primary ways. First, business would contact the president or higher levels of bureaucracy to scrap the government plans; second, the government selects a final beneficiary among different companies based on the plan; third, business shares its profits with politicians. The first form tended to occur most frequently, whereas the last was least damaging to state interests. The wild horse phenomenon seriously undermined bureaucratic stability and was essentially the result of business learning how to manipulate the state through the top leader, thereby undercutting regular decision-making processes and ignoring relevant regulations. Ha Yongch'ul, *Hubal sanŏphwa*, 148.

27. In 1965, President Park issued a directive to eliminate inter-ministerial differences in rules and regulations related to export, in which ministries were urged to reach a broad consensus for a new comprehensive list of measures, including export promoting finance, interest rates, inspection, and measures for resource mobilization in implementing the rules and regulations. He never failed to mention that it should take no more than 10 days. Ha Yongch'ul, *Hubal sanŏphwa*, 157.

28. Ha Yongch'ul, *Hubal sanŏphwa*, 163.

29. Ha Yongch'ul, *Hubal sanŏphwa*, 160–61. The sense of urgency was equally felt in the financing sector. For example, Park urged banks to prioritize the development of machinery industries even by deemphasizing their main business of financing and pressuring them to pay more attention to the completion of major state-led industrial projects. Ha Yongch'ul, *Hubal sanŏphwa*, 127.

30. O Wŏnch'ŏl, "Sanŏp chŏnllyak kundan sa," in Ha Yongch'ul, *Hubal sanŏphwa*, 126.

31. To meet export targets, President Park and ministers on down had to exhort business for export through close contact. Minister Chang, for example, checked export records daily and called owners of chaebols into his office to encourage exports. Every appeal made by business was reported to the Expanded Export Promotion Conference for resolution. President Park spared no effort in supporting the ministry. Ha Yongch'ul, *Hubal sanŏphwa*, 166.

32. Businessmen and bureaucrats had to work together even on Sundays in the Mobile Ministry, a temporary arrangement established in 1971 whereby the ministry's officials were present where factories and business quarters were located to expedite

issuing permits and other supportive measures. In 1976, export exhorters were dispatched to different companies to urge on exports. Out of such constant contact emerged the phenomenon of "mingling" between the state and business, which in turn gave rise to changes in the way business perceived the state. Ha Yongch'ul, *Hubal sanŏphwa*, 167.

33. Ha Yongch'ul, *Hubal sanŏphwa*, 169.
34. S. N. Eisenstadt, "Bureaucracy," 305–6.
35. S. N. Eisenstadt, "Bureaucracy," 318.
36. Ha Yongch'ul, "Hanil kwallyoje pigyo."
37. In contrast, Japan was able to maintain symbiotic relations between state and business with a clear boundary, and in the Soviet Union, social and economic interests were absorbed into the state (absorption model). Jan Pakulski, "Bureaucracy."
38. *Pokchibudong* can be roughly translated as "buck passer" but more specifically refers to a situation in which bureaucrats do not take initiative to avoid risk and are solely interested in protecting their positions and interests.
39. On the hollowing out of one sector of state bureaucracy spilling into another, see Ha Yongch'ul, "Pogŏn chŏngch'aek," 33–68. The author's research deals with how what happened to Korean economic bureaucracies affected non-economic bureaucracy. Its basic argument is that when economic bureaucracies become involved in the state's priority tasks of economic development, the ethos and modes of bureaucratic operation affect non-economic bureaucracy, such as the Ministry of Health and Social Affairs. The study analyzes how the autonomy of the ministry was lost in managing the conflict between oriental herbal medicine and Western medicine. The non-economic bureaucracy's loss of autonomy is called the secondary hollowing out.
40. Stephan Haggard and Chung-In Moon, "Institutions and Economic Policy."
41. Eun Mee Kim, *Big Business, Strong State*; and Eun Mee Kim, "Crisis of the Developmental State."
42. Hyun-Chin Lim and Jin-Ho Jang, "Between Neoliberalism and Democracy."
43. *Sky Daily*, February 14, 2012.
44. There were more than 38 incentive measures to promote export. Wontack Hong, *Trade, Distortions*, 82–83.
45. In this regard, the view that the state succumbed to becoming hostage to and "captured" by business stops short of dealing with specific business strategies and defining the nature of state-business relations. Although the hostage argument explains the limited capacity of the state due to its dependence of business for economic success, it does not explain the respective and mutual statuses of the state and business. Sagong Yŏngho, "Kabujangjŏk haengjŏng," 116–17.

46. Kenneth Jowitt, *Leninist Response.*
47. Paul Shankman, "Phases of Dependency."
48. Sanggongbu, *Sanggong Chŏngch'aek Simnyŏnsa,* 282. On the significance of the export promotion meetings, see Yung Whee Rhee, Bruce Ross-Larson, and Garry Pursell, *Korea's Competitive Edge,* chaps. 2 and 3.
49. There were many cases of collusion between business and officials at the MCI to obtain preferential interests for exporters. The ministry was heavily criticized as being an agent for chaebols in securing preferential treatments. *Chosŏn Ilbo* [Chosŏn daily], May 22, 1966.
50. From the latter part of the 1960s, business became overly sensitive in demonstrating export records. *Chosŏn Ilbo* [Chosŏn daily], February 20, 1969, 3.
51. *Chosŏn Ilbo* [Chosŏn daily], May 31, 1972, 1, 4; and *Chosŏn Ilbo* [Chosŏn daily], October 24, 1971, 2.
52. Yu Inhak, *Han'guk chaebŏl ŭi haebu,* 70–71.
53. *Chosŏn Ilbo* [Chosŏn daily], November 21, 1974, 2.
54. *Chosŏn Ilbo* [Chosŏn daily], October 15, 1975, 2.
55. *Sindonga,* "Kwŏndu Chwadam: Mainŏsŭ sŏngjang," 109.
56. Kyŏngje Kihoegwŏn, *1973nyŏn kyŏngje paeksŏ,* 36.
57. On the example for the Economic Planning Board to reorganize nonperforming projects, due to chaebols' appeals to political circles, see Kim Hŭng Ki, *Yŏngyok ŭi Han'guk kyŏngje,* 228–31.
58. Joseph H. Stern et al., *Industrialization,* 41.
59. Kyŏngje Kihoegwŏn, *Uri kyŏngje ŭi changgi chŏnmang.*
60. Yi Chŏng, "Ulsan Chosŏnso 1," 68.
61. Pak Pyŏngyun, *Chaebŏl kwa chŏngch'i,* 198–99.
62. Pak Yunu, "6 konghwaguk," 490.
63. Yi Manhŭi, "Han'guk ŭi sanŏp chŏngch'aek," 87. Chaebols demanded many benefits in return for streamlining their business, such as financial assistance, compensation for investment made, and monopolistic or oligopolistic status in the market. For example, Hyundai Yanghaeng demanded compensation for reducing debt, capital reassessment, and takeovers of technology and construction contracts. Yi Manhŭi, "Han'guk ŭi sanŏp chŏngch'aek," 98.
64. Hyundai Yanghaeng was established in 1962 by Chŏng Inyŏng. It later became Hanguk Heavy Industry in 1980 and ultimately Doosan Heavy Industries in 2000. On its taking over assets while excluding debt, see Kyŏngje Kihoegwŏn, *Kyŏngje Kihoegwŏn 30nyŏnsa,* 216–17.
65. Sŏul Taehakkyo Haengjŏng Taehagwŏn, *Chŏngch'aek chiphaeng sarye,* 105–6.
66. Pak Wŏnbae, "Chaegye pihwa," 467–68.
67. Yu Yongŭil, "P'asan chikchŏn," 439; and Yi Changgyu, *Kyŏngje nŭn tangsin.*

68. Yu Inhak, *Han'guk chaebŏl ŭi haebu*, 139.

69. *Policy funds*, or policy finance, refers to loans, insurance, and/or guarantees the state provides to facilitate industrial development. Policy funds are distributed by state-supported special banks, such as Korea Development Bank, Export-Import Bank, and Small-Medium Industry Bank.

70. Ch'oe Pyŏngsŏn, "Chŏngch'i kyŏngje ch'eje," 266.

71. Ha Yongch'ul, *Hubal sanŏphwa*, 226; and Hwang Chongsŏng, "Minjuhwa," 256-57.

72. *Chosŏn Ilbo* [Chosŏn daily], June 24, 1990, 6.

73. Ha Yongch'ul, *Hubal sanŏphwa*, 226.

74. Pressure from the political circles for favoritism was suspected regarding the blitzkrieg-like decision having ignored conventional procedure, such as holding public hearings. *Han'guk Kyŏngje Sinmun* [Korea economic daily], July 5, 1992, 3.

75. R. A. W. Rhodes, "Hollowing Out"; H. Brinton H. Milward and Keith G. Provan, "Hollow State"; and Ian Holliday, "British State Hollowing Out?" The structure of state-business relations in Korea is quite different from that of Japan in that the role of Korea's top leader is visible and its bureaucracy is not as stable as Japan's, due to external penetration and influence from the top leader. In addition, due to the stronger sense of urgency in Korea compared to Japan, the state interfered in business far more arbitrarily than it did in Japan. Thus, the concept of reciprocal consent is not likely to apply to Korea's state-business relations. On the reciprocal consent in understanding state-business relations in Japan, see Richard J. Samuels, *Japanese State*. Also, it seems that the state's decision on deselection in Korea is more unpredictable than in Japan, due to the higher possibility of penetration by business in state bureaucracy compared to Japan. On MITI's selection and deselection of industries, see Saadia M. Pekkanen, *Picking Winners?*

76. One example is that between 1980 and 1983, more than 1.1 trillion won was poured into industrial restructuring through the Bank of Industrial Development. Sŏn Haktae, "Han'guk ŭi chunggongŏp, 160.

77. Eun Mee Kim, *Big Business, Strong State*, 194.

78. Yi Sŏngt'ae, "Han'guk sahoe chibaeja," 264-65.

79. K, former minister, Ministry of Finance and chief secretary to president, interview by the author, May 15, 2003.

80. Ha Yongch'ul, "Pogŏn chŏngch'aek."

81. There were roughly three patterns of implementation: cases strictly following laws and regulations, cases in which laws and regulations were ambiguously interpreted and applied, and arbitrary and illegal cases. Where contacts between bureaucrats and business were not institutionalized and thus bureaucrats could

contact business on a personal basis, chances for arbitrary decision and implementation were quite high.

5. CIVIL SOCIETY AND DEMOCRATIZATION

1. This literature can be roughly classified into three groups: political thought approach or intellectual historical studies, ideal-typical research, and historical-case studies. On examples of political thought or intellectual historical approaches, see Adam Ferguson, *History of Civil Society*; Francis Hutcheson, *Nature and Conduct*; Adam Smith, *Moral and Political Philosophy*; John Keane, *Civil Society*; Becker, *Emergence of Civil Society*; and Adam B. Seligman, *Idea of Civil Society*. For an ideal-typical approach, see Jürgen Habermas, *Structural Transformation*. On historical-regional approaches, see Naomi Chazan, "Africa's Democratic Challenge"; Isabel V. Hull, *Sexuality*; Nancy Bermeo and Philip G. Nord, *Civil Society*; Theda Skocpol and Morris P. Fiorina, *Civic Engagement*; Marc Morjé Howard, *Weakness of Civil Society*; Sheri Berman, "Civil Society"; Doh C. Shin, *Mass Politics*; Richard Price, *British Society*; and Frank J. Schwartz and Susan J. Pharr, *State of Civil Society*.

2. Edward Shils, "Virtue of Civil Society," 9.

3. Marvin B. Becker, *Emergence of Civil Society*.

4. Adam B. Seligman, *Idea of Civil Society*, 168–69.

5. On the abuse of the concept of civil society, Seligman says, "I would hazard the guess that the use of the term civil society instead of democracy in Eastern Europe to describe the above organizational features of social life is to be explained less by any additional analytic weight carried by the idea of civil society than simply by the fact that civil society as a term was neutral and uncorrupted by forty years of State propaganda, whereas the term democracy . . . was heavily tainted by the past." Adam B. Seligman, *Idea of Civil Society*, 204.

6. Axel Honneth, "Conceptions of 'Civil Society,'" 19.

7. On too much emphasis on elites, Marc Morjé Howard says, "Analysis has tended to focus too much on elites and institutions rather than on society and ordinary citizens. They have therefore been too quick in overlooking or dismissing the relative societal similarities among post-communist societies in the regions." Marc Morjé Howard, *Weakness of Civil Society*, 146.

8. Cited in Sheri Berman, "Civil Society," 407. See Marc Morjé Howard, *Weakness of Civil Society*, 152, on the lesser importance of the number of organizations as a sign of civil society.

9. Luis Roniger, "Civil Society," 68.

10. Frank Trentmann, *Paradoxes*, 7.

11. Cited in Piotr Sztompka, "Mistrusting Civility," 193.

12. Civil society has been found in the economy and in the polity, in the area between the family and the state or the individual and the state, in non-state institutions that organize and educate citizens for political participation, and even as an expression of the whole civilizing mission of modern society. Krishan Kumar, "Civil Society," 383.

13. Sun Hyuk Kim classifies Korean literature on civil society in terms of whether civil society is treated as an independent or dependent variable. Works that treat civil society as a dependent variable are further organized into three subcategories: works on conceptual and perception issues related to civil society, those focusing on historical aspects, and empirical works on attributes and changes of civil groups. The following works belong to the first subcategory: Pae Tongin, "Simin sahoe ŭi kaenyŏm"; Yang Sŭngt'ae, "Konggongsŏng"; and Sin Kwangyŏng, "Simin sahoe kaenyŏm." On the second, see Ko Sŏngguk, "Han'guk simin sahoe." On the third, see Pak Myŏnggyu, "Han'guk ŭi simin sahoe"; and Sunhyuk Kim, "Discussions of Civil Society."

14. On the impacts of democratic movements on civil society, see Chŏng T'aesŏk, "Simin sahoe wa NGO"; and Yu P'almu and Kim Hogi, *Simin sahoe wa siminundong*. On the impacts of civil society on democracy, see Sunhyuk Kim, *Politics of Democratization*; Cho Hiyŏn, *Han'guk ŭi minjujuŭi*; Yun Sangch'ŏl, *1980nyŏndae Han'guk*; and An Pyŏngjun et al., *Kukka, simin sahoe, chŏngch'i minjuhwa*.

15. Han Wansang, "Han'guk esŏ simin sahoe"; Ch'oe Changjip, *Han'guk minjujuŭi iron*; Mun Pyŏngju, "Han'guk minjujuŭi"; Son Hoch'ŏl, "Kukka-simin sahoeron"; Kim Sŏngguk, "Han'guk ŭi simin sahoe"; and Kim Sŏngguk, "Sinsahoe undong ŭi ironjŏk kiban."

16. Yu P'almu, "Han'guk simin sahoe."

17. Pak Hyŏngjun, "Simin sahoe iron."

18. Kim Sŏngguk, "Han'guk ŭi simin sahoe."

19. Yu P'almu and Kim Hogi, *Simin saho wa siminundong*, 256.

20. Kim Sŏngguk, "Han'guk ŭi simin sahoe."

21. Pae Tongin, "Simin sahoe ŭi kaenyŏm."

22. Son Hoch'ŏl, "Kukka-simin sahoeron," 25–30.

23. Ch'oe Changjip, *Han'guk minjujuŭi iron*.

24. As for a rare example that discusses nationalism in relation to civil society, see Pak Myŏnggyu, "Han'guk ŭi simin sahoe."

25. John Garrard, *Democratisation in Britain*, 101. In the British case of the state-versus-society model, it was more negative in terms of society's shying away from the state, whereas in France it was more positive in society's opposition to

the state. On the weak presence of the state in the development of civil society, see Richard Price, *British Society*, chap. 6.

26. On the growth of voluntary organizations, see R. J. Morris, *Class, Sect and Party*.

27. John Garrard, *Democratisation in Britain*, 107.

28. It is known that British and French colonial rule had divergent impacts on African societies. However, this thesis is rejected among most African scholars. The following analysis is based on the literature that rejects divergent impact of British and French rule. On the various approaches to the colonial impact on Africa, see Kathryn Firmin-Sellers, "Institutions," 253-72.

29. Joel S. Migdal, *Strong Societies*, chaps. 1 and 2; and Peter M. Lewis, "Political Transition," 46.

30. Naomi Chazan, "Africa's Democratic Challenge," 285.

31. Naomi Chazan, "Africa's Democratic Challenge," 285.

32. Naomi Chazan, "Africa's Democratic Challenge," 286.

33. Peter M. Lewis, "Political Transition," 40.

34. Naomi Chazan, "Africa's Democratic Challenge," 286.

35. Joseph Berliner, *Factory and Manager*, 160-206; and Jan Pakulski, "Bureaucracy."

36. Alena V. Ledeneva, *Russia's Economy*.

37. Wlodzimierz Wesolowski, "Nature of Social Ties," 120-21.

38. With the exception of the smaller Jacobin clubs in the 1790s, German bodies were distinguished by their apolitical view of civil society: they saw their mission as complementing their states by improving the local infrastructure and gathering information to assist official knowledge and not as opposing or eliminating government. Administrators played a disproportionate role in German clubs, and confidence in enlightened reform absolutism remained high. Frank Trentmann, *Paradoxes*, 15.

39. Daniel A. McMillan, "Energy," 188.

40. Ralf Dahrendorf, *Society and Democracy*, 58.

41. Sheri Berman, "Civil Society," 425.

42. Sheri Berman, "Civil Society," 426.

43. W. Dean Kinzley, *Industrial Harmony*.

44. Sheldon Garon, *Molding Japanese Minds*, 20.

45. Sheri Berman, "Civil Society," 414.

46. John A. Hall, "Nature of Civil Society," 39. On the counterargument that the state plays a positive role in civil society formation, see Theda Skocpol and Morris P. Fiorina, *Civic Engagement*.

47. Kim Manhŭm, "Chŏngch'i kyunyŏl," 225-29.

48. Modular citizens are those "who are members of groups but not too strongly attached to any one group; a sense of moral obligation that forces individuals to

honor their commitments willingly, not because of social pressure; cultural homogeneity within a given nation-state, involving the elimination of 'semi-private and local' languages and idioms; and rationality, including 'the non-conflation of issues, the separating-out of the social strands.'" Charles Kurzman, review of *Conditions of Liberty*, 345.

49. Sunhyuk Kim, *Politics of Democratization*.

50. On the details of the tense situation, see Sunhyuk Kim, *Politics of Democratization*, 86–93. Specific sectoral and regional representations were as follows: by sector, 253 Catholic priests, 270 Protestant pastors, 160 women's movement leaders, 308 from the Council for the Promotion of Democracy Movement, 171 peasant activists, 39 labor activists, 18 urban poor activists, 43 publishers and journalists, 43 authors and writers, 66 artists, 55 educators, 12 youth movement leaders, and 44 lawyers; and by region, 11 from Kyŏnggi Province, 73 from Kangwŏn Province, 29 from Ch'ungnam Province, 54 from Ch'ungbuk Province, 40 from Chŏnnam Province, 56 from the city of Pusan, and 89 from Kyŏngbuk Province. Sunhyuk Kim, *Politics of Democratization*, 92. Specific names of organizations are the Seoul Labor Movement Coalition (Sonoryon), the Korean Council for Labor Welfare, the Protestant Peasant Association (Kinong), and the Catholic Peasant Association (Kanong).

51. Sunhyuk Kim, *Politics of Democratization*, 139.

52. Kim Sŏngsu, "Minjuhwa kwajŏng," 135; and Yi Kapyun and Mun Yongjik, "Han'guk ŭi minjuhwa," 229.

53. Han Sangjin, "Minjung sahoehak," 126.

54. Doh C. Shin, *Mass Politics*, 252–53.

55. Doh C. Shin, *Mass Politics*, 252.

56. Doh C. Shin, *Mass Politics*, 252.

57. David I. Steinberg, "Civil Society," 157.

58. Kim Wŏn, *Ich'yŏjin kŏt*, 90.

59. Doh C. Shin, *Mass Politics*, 205.

60. Three-fifths (60%) of the Korean population are primordialists, whose public life is still confined within the boundaries of interpersonal or religious ties. They represent nearly five times as many as extra-primordialists (13%), who are active beyond those boundaries. Doh C. Shin, *Mass Politics*, 109.

61. Doh C. Shin, *Mass Politics*, 205.

62. Doh C. Shin, *Mass Politics*, 108.

63. Kang Sanguk, "NGO ŭi sŏngjang," 17–18.

64. Doh C. Shin, *Mass Politics*, 22.

65. Sŏng Hogŭn, "Sinsahoe undong," 1.

66. The financial sources of the Coalition for Environmental Protection are as follows: about 50% member contribution and donations, 23% from various projects,

21.7% from profit-making activities, and 4.1% from educational projects. Yu Sŏkch'un, *Han'guk ŭi simin sahoe*, 11.

67. *Han'guk Ilbo* [Hanguk daily], "Toel kŏri man choch'a taninŭn," 26.

68. Hong Ilp'yo, "Ije tasi wit'aeroun mohŏm," 15-16.

69. *Han'gyŏre*, "Nodong·sahoe tanch'e," 20; *Han'gyŏre*, "Int'ŏbyu," 18; *Han'gyŏre*, "'Ch'amyŏhanŭn simin,'" 6; *Han'guk Ilbo* [Hanguk daily], "Simin p'awŏ," 19; and *Han'guk Ilbo* [Hanguk daily], "Sinnyŏn t'ŭkchip," 34.

70. Yang Kiho, "Han'guk simin tanch'e," 73-75; *Han'guk Ilbo* [Hanguk daily], "Iisyuwa hyŏnjang/simindanch'e," 17.

71. Yu Sŏkch'un and Kim Yongmin, "Han'guk simin tanch'e"; and Kim Tongno, "Simin undong." On another example for civic activists entering politics, see *Chosŏn Ilbo* [Chosŏn daily], "Undonggwŏn pyŏnhyŏk," 22.

72. *Han'gyŏre*, "Undonggwŏn," 20; *Han'gyŏre*, "Ttajyŏbŏpsida," 9; *Chosŏn Ilbo* [Chosŏn daily], "Undonggwŏn pyŏnhyŏk," 22; *Han'gyŏre*, "Simin tanch'e," 26; and *Han'guk Ilbo* [Hanguk daily], "Todŏksŏng siryŏn," 7, 13.

73. *Han'guk Ilbo* [Hanguk daily], "Isyuwa hyŏnjang," 17; Yi Yonghwan, "Simin innŭn simin tanch'e," 28; and Yu Sŏkch'un, *Han'guk ŭi simin sahoe*, 55-56.

74. Sunhyuk Kim, *Politics of Democratization*, 97.

75. Hagen Koo, *Korean Workers*, 118. The activist's name was Bang Yongsŏk, the president of the Wonpoong Textile union. Students, according to him, were apt to engage in a kind of "political adventurism" at the risk of destroying unions.

76. Yu Simin, interview. Also, according to other data, as of February 2003, 43 (16%) of the 273 members of the National Assembly were arrested for their political activities (anti-regime opposition), and when labor activists and anti-poverty movement activists are added, 70 members of the National Assembly had experiences in political struggles in the past. *Chosŏn Ilbo* [Chosŏn daily], "Undonggwŏn pyŏnhyŏk."

77. Generation 386 refers to the cohort who were in their thirties (3), entered college in the 1980s (8), and were born in the 1960s (6).

78. Whang Seongjoon, "8onyŏndae undonggwŏn."

79. On the gap that arises between masses and political activists, Yi Sinhaeing's remarks are suggestive: "intellectual movements by college students and religious leaders do not reflect the whole picture of Korean society. They reflect some sectors of the society which are receptive to the movements. Therefore, it is my view that civic and social movements do not represent our whole society or are the manifestation of legitimacy of the whole society." Yi Sinhaeing, "Han'guk simin sahoe," 42.

80. Chŏng Sunmi, *Han'guk haengjŏng kaehyŏk*. For examples, revelations of political scandals such as the expensive dress lobby scandal, Lee Yongho gate,

Jung Hyunjoon gate, Chin Seunghyun gate, Yoon Taeshik gate, Choi Kyuson gate, the military service evasion scandal, and the special allotment of apartment scandal.

81. Calculated based on Kim Hyŏnu, *Han'guk chŏngdang*.

82. Max Weber, *Social and Economic Organization*, 329–41. The dynamics of Korea's strong state has been treated elsewhere; see Ha Yongch'ul, *Hubal sanŏphwa*.

83. Yi Pyŏnggon, "Han'guk sahoe," 215.

84. Some examples are the inability to decide on a nuclear waste site, the second mobile communication system development decisions, decisions on the entry of Samsung Motors, conflict between herbal medicine specialists and pharmacists, and chaos surrounding the separation between prescription and dispensation of drugs. Thus, the weakened role of the state further exacerbated the politicization process of civic organizations. See Ha Yongch'ul, "Pogŏn chŏngch'aek"; and Ha Yongch'ul, *Hubal sanŏphwa*.

6. DAILY PRACTICE OF NEOFAMILISM

1. Survey questions were prepared by the author and the survey was conducted by Han'guk Risŏch'i (Korea Research) in Seoul, Korea, on April 9, 2015. The size of the sample ($N = 106$) is not large enough to be representative of the entire Korean society, but as it was selected based on particular age brackets (those in their 60s and 70s, as they were active during the peak of industrialization), region, education, and gender, it secured a high level of typicality about Korean society. See John Gerring, *Social Science Methodology*, 96–97; and Malcolm Williams, *Making Sense*. As Layna Mosely points out, although it isn't representative in the statistical sense, the sample is diverse and informative on the variables that matter to the present analysis. Layna Mosley, *Interview Research*. In addition to the 2015 survey, surveys on 44 people were randomly done by the author over a period of three years, from 2004 to 2007. The goal was not to secure systematic patterns of neofamilial attitudes and behaviors, but to identify various behavioral manifestations of neofamilism in daily life for the purpose of illustration.

2. Among 36 who said the ties were not that relevant, either co-workers (38.8%) without the ties or neighbors (33.3%) were mentioned as the important source of social interactions. In terms of limits of neofamilial ties, the results from 44 randomly selected people indicate that 37% could ask for help only from those who are directly connected through neofamilial ties, while 56% felt they could do so with the acquaintances of the directly connected. See Ha Yongch'ul, *Hubal sanŏphwa*. On the range of trust in the case of Italy, see Jeremy Boissevain, "Place of Non-Groups."

3. See note 1. The survey question asks, "To what extent do you think familial ties, school ties, and regional ties affected economic behaviors during the 1960s and 1970s?"

4. Q11: "Do you think the rapid democratization since 1987 has changed human relations based on blood, regional, and school ties?" Q12: "What do you think of the degree of conflicts among different economic strata during the democratization?"

5. The following statements are from the random surveys and the 2015 survey, as introduced in note 1.

6. On the top leader's focus on export goals, see Ha Yongch'ul, *Hubal sanŏp-hwa*, 156–57.

7. Quotations are from the surveys of 44 people.

8. Quotations are from the surveys of 44 people.

9. The author conducted in-depth interviews in 1999 and 2015 with 10 people of different professions; out of the 10 cases, four are selected here, reflecting different career patterns, to demonstrate the relationship between career development and neofamilial ties.

10. Interview by the author, January 8, 2015.

11. Interview by the author, October 31, 2015.

12. Interview by the author, November 24, 1999.

13. Interview by the author, January 26, 2015.

7. THE 1997 FINANCIAL CRISIS

1. Donald Kirk, *Korean Crisis*; Robert F. Emery, *Korean Economic Reform*; Brian Bridges, *Korea after the Crash*; Robert Wade, "Gestalt Shift"; Ha-Joon Chang, "Korea"; Stephan Haggard, *Political Economy*; and Kyu-Sung Lee, *Korean Financial Crisis*.

2. Jiho Jang, "Economic Crisis"; Tran Van Hoa, *Social Impact*; and Song Puyong, "IMF ch'eje."

3. The interest rate was raised in order to stabilize the won. The overnight call rate rose from 12.15% on December 1, 1997, to 31.32% on December 31, 1997. Young Baek Choi, "On Financial Crisis," 487.

4. *Sŏul Kyŏngje Sinmun* [*Seoul Economic Daily*], October 21, 1998.

5. Kyu-Sung Lee, *Korean Financial Crisis*, 26.

6. Jiho Jang, "Economic Crisis," 54. Note the percentage change over the same month of last year, cited in Jiho Jang, "Economic Crisis," 55.

7. National Statistical Office, in Jiho Jang, "Economic Crisis," 56.

8. Nam Ŭnyŏng, "Oehwan wigi," 73.

9. Paek China, "Kyŏngje wigi," 32.
10. Paek China, "Kyŏngje wigi," 32.
11. Mun Hyŏngjin, "Oehwan wigi ihu," 93.
12. Mun Hyŏngjin, "Oehwan wigi ihu," 98–99.
13. Im Insuk, *Sirŏp kwa kajok*, cited in Paek China, "Kyŏngje wigi," 37.
14. Jiho Jang, "Economic Crisis," 59.
15. Paek Chin, "Kyŏngje wigi," 38.
16. Ham Inhŭi, "Sahoe kyŏngjejŏk wigi," 553.
17. Yi Chuhong, "Han'guk sahoe ŭi ihonyul," 116.
18. Chŏng Chinsung, "Kyŏngje wigi," 109.
19. Chŏng Chinsung, "Kyŏngje wigi," 109.
20. Kim Ŭnmi and Yi Sŏni, "Kosirŏp sidae ŭi kajok"; An Pyŏngch'ŏl, "Sirŏp kwa kajok"; Chang Hyekyŏng and Kim Yŏngnan, "IMF wa kajok munje"; and Paek China, "Kyŏngje wigi."
21. Chŏng Chinsung, "Kyŏngje wigi," 109.
22. Ham Inhŭi, "Sahoe kyŏngjejŏk wigi," 538.
23. The reduction of debt ratios was part of the agreement between President Kim Dae Jung and the chaebols on January 13, 1998.
24. Yang Tongsŏk, "Saoe isa chedo," 253; and Peter M. Beck, "Revitalizing Korea's Chaebol," 1028.
25. Yang Tongsŏk, "Saoe isa chedo," 254; and Yang Chongmin, "Net'ŭwŏk'ŭ punsŏk."
26. Yi Kisu, "Saoe isa chedo ŭi kanghwa," 77.
27. Yang Tongsŏk, "Saoe isa chedo," 264.
28. Yi Sujŏng, "Saoe isa ŭi tongnipsŏng," 10–20; and Yi Kisu, "Saoe isa chedo ŭi kanghwa," 79.
29. Son Hyŏk and Chŏng Chaegyŏng, "Saoe isa nŭn ch'oego"; and Sŏ Chŏngil, Yi Kyŏnghwan, and Yun Sungnam, "Sin'gyu isa immyŏng."
30. *Mŏni Tudei*, "Kyŏngyŏngjin e kildŭryŏjin isahoe."
31. *Herŏldŭ Kyŏngje* [Herald economy], April 21, 2014.
32. Kim Hyŏngŏn, "Sahoe isanimdŭl, annyŏng hasimnikka?," 1.
33. Ha Yongch'ul, "Oehwan wigi," 216; and Joongi Kim, "Next Stage," 17. One study observes that companies adopted the outside director system and elected even greater numbers of outside directors than required by law, while outside directors still do not perform their functions properly. The authors argue that this is an indication that companies do not comply with the original intentions of the outside director system; instead, they changed the system to meet their purpose. Yi Kyŏngmuk and O Chonghyang, "Saoe isa ŭi ch'ogwa," 1229.
34. Kim Chin, *Sangsokse mit chŭngyŏse*.

35. Song Kich'ŏl, "Taegiŏp ŭi kyŏngyŏngja."
36. *Pusan Ilbo* [Pusan daily], August 21, 2015.
37. *CEO Sŭkoŏdeili* [*CEO Score Daily*], November 30, 2001.
38. Ha Yongch'ul, "Oehwan wigi," 214.
39. Ha Yongch'ul, "Oehwan wigi," 213. Indirect intervention involves going through a formal procedure, such as holding a personnel committee meeting, but a subtle message on the regime's preference is conveyed to the committee.
40. The pervasive perception that the state influence over financial institutions on personnel and lending policies persists is in contrast to the government view that Korean financial institutions are autonomous in the two areas. Kim Jong Chang, chairman, Korean Financial Supervisory Board, interview by the author, July 8, 2008.
41. Ha Yongch'ul, "Oehwan wigi," 213.
42. An interesting and important change in lending practice at the micro level was the renewal and expansion of the bank credit review system. For business, a basic information system regarding the nature of business and its prospects was established to review requests for loans. For individuals, a new credit scoring system was introduced to evaluate individuals' loan limit. In the past, whether the loans were made out for personal use or for businesses, the judgment of the person in charge carried weight, but since the financial crisis, credit is determined by the system rather than by personal judgment. Credit reviews prior to the crisis frequently varied from one branch of the bank to another. This would have serious consequences for neofamilism in that prior to the crisis, companies or individuals could go to another branch or bank officials in the event that they could not get satisfactory decisions on their loan applications. That is, they could mobilize neofamilial ties before applying for loans or when they were rejected for prior loan applications. Banking was also more individualized: after the crisis, banks no longer approached individual credit within the context of the entire family but treated each member on his or her own. Lee Young Jin, Shinhan Bank, interview by the author, July 15, 2008.
43. Cho Sŏngjae, "Chojik kwa pun'gyu," 19.
44. Note that the basic political rights for organizers pertained to enhanced latitude to engage in union organizing, political activity, and so on; thus, it was good for labor organizers, whereas average workers suffered from the economic crisis, such as greater vulnerability to layoffs.
45. Yi Chongsŏn, "IMF kyŏngje wigi," 198–99.
46. Hyo-Soo Lee, "Paternalistic Human Resource Practices," 841.
47. Hyo-Soo Lee, "Paternalistic Human Resource Practices," 842.
48. *Sky Daily*, "Taegiŏp punsŏk."

49. Wi P'yŏngnyang, "Chaebŏl ro ŭi kyŏngje chipchung," 12.
50. Wi P'yŏngnyang, "Chaebŏl ro ŭi kyŏngje chipchung," 13.
51. Han'gyŏre, "30tae chaebŏl naebu kŏrae."
52. Yŏnhap News, "Chuyo chaebŏlgŭrup."
53. Yi Chaehyŏng, "Tae-chung-so kiŏp," 4.
54. Sin Kwangsik, Chaebol kaehyok, 44.
55. Wi P'yŏngnyang, "Chaebŏl ro ŭi kyŏngje chipchung," 19.
56. Peter M. Beck, "Revitalizing Korea's Chaebol," 1021.
57. Ch'oe Chŏngp'yo, "Oehwan wigi chikhu," 62–63.
58. Yŏnhap News, "Sŏul Kyot'onggongsa." Seoul City Transportation Corporation changed the status of 1,285 employees who were on indefinite contract to regular worker status. It turned out that 108 out of 1,285 had family ties to current employees of the corporation, including sons and daughters (31), brothers and sisters (22), uncles (15), and spouses (12).
59. Sŏul Kyŏngje Sinmun [Seoul economic daily], January 13, 2019.

CONCLUSION

1. David Beetham, "Conditions."
2. J. David Singer and Melvin Small, "Composition and Status Ordering"; Benjamin de Carvalho and Iver B. Neumann, Small State Status Seeking; and Jonathan Renshon, Fighting for Status.
3. Hyeong-Ki Kwon, "Asian Financial Crisis"; Hyun-Chin Lim and Jin-Ho Jang, "Between Neoliberalism and Democracy"; Kyung Mi Kim, Korean Developmental State; Robert Wade, "Globalization"; and Linda Weiss, "Developmental States."
4. The proportion of social welfare in GDP has shown considerable growth for the past 20 years: 6.4% in 2005, 8.4% in 2008, 10.5% in 2015, and 15.6% in 2020. And the budgetary weight of social welfare in the national budget also has changed: 24.2% in 2005, 25.2% in 2006, 25.9% in 2007, 26.2% in 2009, 27.7% in 2010, 29.9% in 2014, and 33.7% in 2018. Hangyŏre, "Pokchi·Kyoyuk·Kukpang"; Chamyŏyŏndae, "2019nyŏn pogŏnbokchi"; and KOSIS [Korean Statistical Information Service], "Sahoebokchi jich'ul" [Social welfare expenditure], February 28, 2022, https://kosis.kr/index/index.do.
5. Kim Tuyŏl, Kyŏngje sŏngjang.
6. T'onggyech'ŏng, Han'guk sahoe t'onghyang 2008, 294–95.
7. For many Koreans, the name Kim Young-ran did not hold special meaning until it became associated with a new controversial law. Initiated by former judge Kim Young-ran, the so-called Kim Young-ran Law—a severe, far-reaching

anti-corruption law—took effect on September 28, 2016. Under the law's terms, a public official or even schoolteacher could face criminal charges for accepting a bribe worth more than one million won. The public reaction is mixed. Some welcome the law as a catalyst to eradicate corruption. Others question the impartiality of the law. Critics believe that the broad scope of the law enables authorities to abuse it. This is because of the possibility for arbitrary application of the law, due to the seemingly fine line between bribes and simple favors. It is yet to be seen whether the enactment of the law will be the starting point toward a more transparent society or will exacerbate litigiousness and contentiousness.

8. *Chosŏn Ilbo* [Chosŏn daily], January 27, 2020.

9. See *Han'gyŏre*, April 11, 2018, on various kinds of illegal practice of hiring in the government. The report says there were 2,311 cases of violations in hiring in various public agencies between 2013 and 2017.

10. *Chungang Ilbo* [Chungang daily], September 10, 2019.

11. *Chosŏn Ilbo* [Chosŏn daily], December 23, 2020.

12. See chapter 7.

13. As analyzed in chapter 7, chaebol reforms advanced more in the field of finance but were slow to change in terms of corporate governance, which reflects tenacity in regard to neofamilism.

14. Sŏng Hogŭn, "Kongnonjang"; see Jennifer S. Oh, "Strong State."

15. Sheri Berman, "Civil Society," 414.

16. Sŏng Hogŭn, "Kongnonjang"; and Tracii Ryan et al., "How Social Are Social Media?"

17. On the social, cultural, and institutional consequences of the compressed modernity of South Korea, see Kyung-Sup Chang, *Logic of Compressed Modernity*.

Bibliography

Alavi, Hamza. "The State in Post-colonial Societies: Pakistan and Bangladesh." In *Politics and State in the Third World*, edited by Harry Goulbourne. Hong Kong: Macmillan, 1983.
Alexander, Jeffrey C., ed. *Real Civil Societies: Dilemmas of Institutionalization*. London: Sage Publications, 1998.
Almond, Gabriel A., and G. Bingham Powell Jr. *Comparative Politics: A Developmental Approach*. Boston: Little, Brown, 1966.
Aminzade, Ronald. *Class, Politics, and Early Industrial Capitalism: A Study of Mid-Nineteenth-Century Toulouse, France*. Albany: State University of New York Press, 1981.
Amsden, Alice H. *Asia's Next Giant: South Korea and Late Industrialization*. New York: Oxford University Press, 1989.
An Haegyun. *Han'guk haengjŏng ch'ejeron* [Korean administrative system]. Seoul: Seoul National University Press, 1986.
An Pyŏngch'ŏl. "Sirŏp kwa kajok: sirŏp ŭi yŏnghyang, maegae yoin, taeŭng chŏllyak ŭl chungsim ŭro" [Unemployment and family: Impact of unemployment, intervening factors, and coping strategies]. *Minjok kwa munhwa* [Nation and culture], no. 7 (1998): 203-17.
An Pyŏngjik. "Han'guk kŭnhyŏndaesa yŏn'gu ŭi saeroun paerŏdaim" [A new paradigm in the study of Korean modern and contemporary history]. *Ch'angjak kwa pip'yŏng* [Creative writing and criticism] 98 (Winter 1997): 39-58.
———. "Singminji Chosŏn ŭi koyong kujo e kwanhan yŏn'gu" [A study of employment structure in the colonial Korea]. In *Kŭndae Chosŏn ŭi kyŏngje kujo* [The economic structure of modern Korea]. Seoul: Pibong, 1989.
An Pyŏngjun et al. *Kukka, simin sahoe, chŏngch'i minjuhwa* [State, civil society, and political democratization]. Seoul: Hanul, 1995.
An Pyŏngyŏng. "Han'guk ŭi haengjŏng hyŏnsang kwa haengjŏnghak yŏn'gu ŭi chuch'esŏng" [Administrative behaviors in Korea and how to study their distinctiveness]. *Han'guk chŏngch'ihak hoebo* [Journal of Korean political science] 13 (December 1979): 49-66.

Aoki, Masahiko. *Toward a Comparative Institutional Analysis*. Cambridge, MA: MIT Press, 2001.
Argyriades, Demetrios. "From Bureaucracy to Debureaucratization?" *Public Organization Review* 10, no. 3 (2010): 275-97.
Armstrong, Charles K., ed. *Korean Society: Civil Society, Democracy and the State*. London: Routledge, 2002.
Avineri, Shlomo. "Marx and Modernization." *Review of Politics* 31, no. 2 (April 1969): 172-88.
Balandier, Georges. "The Colonial Situation: A Theoretical Approach." In *Social Change: The Colonial Situation*, edited by Immanuel Wallerstein. New York: John Wiley and Sons, 1966.
———. *The Sociology of Black Africa: Social Dynamics in Central Africa*. Translated by Douglas Garman. New York: Praeger, 1970.
Barr, Michael D. "Lee Kuan Yew and the 'Asian Values' Debate." *Asian Studies Review* 24, no. 3 (September 2000): 309-34.
Beck, Peter M. "Revitalizing Korea's Chaebol." *Asian Survey* 38, no. 11 (November 1998): 1018-35.
Becker, Marvin B. *The Emergence of Civil Society in the Eighteenth Century: A Privileged Moment in the History of England, Scotland, and France*. Bloomington: Indiana University Press, 1994.
Beetham, David. "Conditions for Democratic Consolidation." *Review of African Political Economy* 21, no. 60 (June 1994): 157-72.
Beillevaire, Patrick. "The Family: Instrument and Model of the Japanese Nation." In *A History of the Family*, edited by André Burguière, Christiane Klapisch-Zuber, Martine Segalen, and Françoise Zonabend, translated by Sarah Hanbury Tenison, Rosemary Morris, and Andrew Wilson. Cambridge, MA: Harvard University Press, 1996.
Bendix, Reinhard. *Nation-Building and Citizenship: Studies of Our Changing Social Order*. New York: Wiley, 1964.
———. "Preconditions of Development: A Comparison of Japan and Germany." In *Aspects of Social Change in Modern Japan*, edited by R. P. Dore. Princeton, NJ: Princeton University Press, 1967.
Benedict, Ruth. *The Chrysanthemum and the Sword: Patterns of Japanese Culture*. Boston: Houghton Mifflin, 1946.
Berger, Thomas R. *A Long and Terrible Shadow: White Values, Native Rights in the Americas, 1492-1992*. Vancouver: Douglas and McIntyre; Seattle: University of Washington Press, 1991.
Berliner, Joseph. *Factory and Manager in the USSR*. Cambridge, MA: Harvard University Press, 1957.

Berman, Sheri. "Civil Society and the Collapse of the Weimar Republic." *World Politics* 49, no. 3 (April 1997): 401–29.
———. "Modernization in Historical Perspective: The Case of Imperial Germany." *World Politics* 53, no. 3 (April 2001): 431–62.
Bermeo, Nancy, and Philip G. Nord, eds. *Civil Society before Democracy*. Lanham, MD: Rowman and Littlefield, 2000.
Biernacki, Richard. *The Fabrication of Labor: Germany and Britain, 1640–1914*. Berkeley: University of California Press, 1995.
Block, Fred. *Revising State Theory: Essays in Politics and Postindustrialism*. Philadelphia: Temple University Press, 1987.
Blumer, Herbert. *Industrialization as an Agent of Social Change: A Critical Analysis*. Edited by David R. Maines and Thomas J. Morrione. New York: Aldine de Gruyter, 1990.
Boissevain, Jeremy. *Friends of Friends: Networks, Manipulators and Coalitions*. Oxford: Blackwell, 1974.
———. "The Place of Non-Groups in the Social Sciences." *Man* 3, no. 4 (December 1968): 542–56.
Bridges, Brian. *Korea after the Crash: The Politics of Economic Recovery*. London: Routledge, 2001.
Burris, Val. "Late Industrialization and Class Formation in East Asia." *Research in Political Economy* 13 (1992): 245–83.
Business Korea. "Heavy Borrowing Backfires." 15, no. 5 (May 1998).
Calhoun, Craig. *The Question of Class Struggle: Social Foundations of Popular Radicalism during the Industrial Revolution*. Chicago: University of Chicago Press, 1982.
Callon, Scott. *Divided Sun: MITI and the Breakdown of Japanese High-Tech Industrial Policy, 1975–1993*. Stanford, CA: Stanford University Press, 1995.
Camfield, David. "Re-orienting Class Analysis: Working Classes as Historical Formations." *Science & Society* 68, no. 4 (2004/2005): 421–46.
Campos, Jose Edgardo, and Hilton L. Root. *The Key to the Asian Miracle: Making Shared Growth Credible*. Washington, DC: Brookings Institution, 1996.
Carruthers, Bruce G. "When Is the State Autonomous? Culture, Organization Theory, and the Political Sociology of the State." *Sociological Theory* 12, no. 1 (March 1994): 19–44.
Ch'a Kibyŏk, ed. *Ilche ŭi Han'guk singmin t'ongch'i* [Japanese colonial rule in Korea]. Seoul: Ch'ŏngunsa, 1985.
Chamyŏyŏndae [Solidarity for Participation]. "2019 nyŏn pogŏnbokchi punya yesan(an) punsŏk" [An analysis of the 2019 social welfare budget (draft)]. November 7, 2018.

Chang, Ha-Joon. "Korea: The Misunderstood Crisis." *World Development* 26, no. 8 (1998): 1555-61.

Chang Hyekyŏng and Kim Yŏngnan. "IMF wa kajok munje: sirŏp e ttarŭn kajok saenghwal kwa kajok anjŏngsŏng" [IMF and family problems: Family life and stability under unemployment]. *Han'guk sahoe* [Korean society], no. 2 (1999): 81-116.

Chang, Kyung-Sup. *The Logic of Compressed Modernity*. Cambridge, UK: Polity Press, 2022.

Chang, Sea-Jin. *Financial Crisis and Transformation of Korean Business Groups: The Rise and Fall of Chaebols*. Cambridge: Cambridge University Press, 2003.

Chang, Yunshik, ed. *Korea: A Decade of Development*. Seoul: Seoul National University Press, 1980.

Chang, Yun-Shik. "The Personalist Ethic and the Market in Korea." *Comparative Studies in Society and History* 33, no. 1 (January 1991): 106-29.

Chazan, Naomi. "Africa's Democratic Challenge." *World Policy Journal* 9, no. 2 (Spring 1992): 279-307.

Chen, Ling. "Preferences, Institutions and Politics: Re-Interrogating the Theoretical Lessons of Developmental Economies." *New Political Economy* 13, no. 1 (March 2008): 89-102.

Chibber, Vivek. "Building a Developmental State: The Korean Case Reconsidered." *Politics & Society* 27, no. 3 (1999): 309-46.

——. "Bureaucratic Rationality and the Developmental State." *American Journal of Sociology* 107, no. 4 (January 2002): 951-89.

Chin Tŏkkyu. "Kwallyo wa kun" [Bureaucracy and the military]. *Sahoe chŏngch'aek kwa chŏngch'aek yŏn'gu* [Social sciences and policy studies] 6, no. 3 (1984): 17-25.

Chin Tŏkkyu et al. *1950nyŏndae ŭi insik* [Understanding of the 1950s]. Seoul: Hangilsa, 1981.

Cho, Hee-Yeon, and Eun Mee Kim. "State Autonomy and Its Social Conditions for Economic Development in South Korea and Taiwan." In *The Four Asian Tigers: Economic Development and the Global Political Economy*, edited by Eun Mee Kim. San Diego: Academic Press, 1998.

Cho Hiyŏn. *Han'guk ŭi minjujuŭi wa sahoe undong: pip'an silch'ŏn tamnon ŭi pogwŏn kwa chaegusŏng ŭl wihayŏ* [Korean democracy and social movements: For the reconstruction of reformulation of the discourse, criticism, practice]. Seoul: Dang Dae, 1998.

Cho Hyŏng. "Han'guk ŭi tosi pigongsik pumun kŭlloja e kwanhan yŏn'gu" [A study of workers in urban informal sectors in Korea]. *Han'guk munhwa yŏn'guwŏn* [Korean Institute of Cultural Studies, research proceedings] 41 (1982): 99-131.

Cho Kapche. "Kŭndaehwa hyŏngmyŏngga Pak Chŏnghŭi: nŏk tal nŭjŭn t'ŭlchong" [Park Chung Hee, a revolutionary for modernization: Four months late scoop]. *Wŏlgan Chosŏn* [Chosŏn monthly], February 2000.

Cho Sŏkjun et al. *Han'guk haengjŏng ŭi yŏksajŏk punsŏk, 1968-1984* [A historical analysis of Korean public administration]. Seoul: Seoul National University Press, 1987.

Cho Sŏkkon. "Sut'allon kwa kŭndaehwaron ŭl nŏmŏsŏ: singminji sidae ŭi chaeinsik" [Beyond exploitation and modernization: A reinterpretation of Japanese colonial rule in Korea]. *Ch'angjak kwa pip'yŏng* [Creation and criticism] 96 (Summer 1997): 355-70.

Cho Sŏngjae. "Chojik kwa pun'gyu t'onggye ro pon nosa kwan'gye 20 nyŏn" [Twenty years' labor management: Statistics and analysis]. *Nodong ribyu* [Labor review] 30 (June 2007): 3-29.

Cho Sŏnil. "T'alkwallyoje nolli ŭi pip'anjŏk koch'al: kwallyoje nolli wa ŭi kyŏrhap kanŭngsŏng ŭl chungsim ŭro" [A critical review of the debureaucratization thesis: With a focus on search for compatibility with bureaucratic system]. *Han'guk haengjŏng hakpo* [Korean journal of public administration] 23, no. 2 (1989): 635-52.

Cho, Suk-Choon. "The Bureaucracy." In *Korean Politics in Transition*, edited by Edward Reynolds Wright. Seattle: University of Washington Press, 1975.

Cho Tonggŏl. "Han'guk kŭndae haksaeng undong chojik ŭi sŏnggyŏk pyŏnhwa" [Organizational changes in student movements in modern Korea]. In *Han'guk kŭndae minjok undongsa yŏn'gu* [A history of modern nationalistic movement in Korea], edited by Han'guk Yŏksa Yŏn'guhoe. Seoul: Ilchogak, 1993.

Ch'oe Chaesŏk. *Han'gugin ŭi sahoejŏk sŏnggyŏk* [Social characteristics of Korean people]. Seoul: Kaemunsa, 1977.

Ch'oe Changjip, ed. *Han'guk chabonjuŭi wa kukka* [Capitalism and the state in Korea]. Seoul: Hanul, 1985.

——. *Han'guk hyŏndae chŏngch'i ŭi kujo wa pyŏnhwa* [The structure and change of Korean modern politics]. Seoul: Kkach'i, 1989.

——. *Han'guk minjujuŭi iron* [The theory of Korean democracy]. Seoul: Hangilsa, 1993.

——. *Han'guk ŭi nodong undong kwa kukka* [Labor movement and the state in Korea]. Seoul: Yŏrŭmsa, 1988.

——. *Minjuhwa ihu ŭi minjujuŭi* [Democracy after democratization]. Seoul: Nanam, 2005.

Ch'oe Chŏngp'yo. "Oehwan wigi chikhu ŭi chaebŏl yŏn'gu wa kŭ sŏngkwa e taehan yŏn'gu" [Evaluation of the studies of chaebols after the financial crisis]. *Sanŏp chojik yŏn'gu* [Study of industrial organization] 17, no. 1 (2009): 46-66.

Ch'oe Naktong. "Kŭmyungdan" [Financial corps]. In *Han'guk ŭi kyŏngje kwallyo* [Korean economic bureaucrats], edited by Son Kwangsik. Seoul: Tarakwon, 1979.

Ch'oe Pyŏngsŏn. *Chŏngbu kyujeron* [Political economy of regulation and deregulation]. Seoul: Pommunsa, 1992.

———. "Chŏngch'i kyŏngje ch'eje ŭi chŏnhwan kwa kukka nŭngnyŏk: kyŏngje chayuhwa wa minjuhwa rŭl chungsim ŭro" [The transformation of political conomic system and the state capacity: With a focus on economic liberalization and democratization]. *Han'guk chŏngch'i hakpo* [Korean political science review] 23, no. 2 (1990): 27-49.

Ch'oe Tonggyu. *Sŏngjang sidae ŭi chŏngbu: Han'gang ŭi kijŏk ikkŭn kwallyo chojik ŭi yŏkhal* [The government of growth age: The role of bureaucracy in the Han River miracle]. Seoul: Han'guk Kyŏngje Sinmunsa, 1991.

Ch'oe Yŏnsik. "Pak Chŏnghŭi ŭi minjok ch'angjo wa tongwŏndoen kungmin t'onghap" [Park Chung Hee's invention of nation and mobilized national integration]. *Han'guk chongch'i oegyosa nonch'ong* [Journal of Korea political and diplomatic history] 26, no. 2 (2007): 43-73.

Choi, Byung-Sun. *Economic Policymaking in Korea: Institutional Analysis of Economic Policy Changes in the 1970s and 1980s*. Seoul: Chomyung Press, 1991.

———. "Financial Policy and Big Business in Korea: The Perils of Financial Regulation." In *The Politics of Finance in Developing Countries*, edited by Stephan Haggard, Chung H. Lee, and Sylvia Maxfield. Ithaca, NY: Cornell University Press, 1993.

Choi, Young Baek. "On Financial Crisis in Korea." *Korea Observer* 34, no. 3 (Autumn 1998): 485-509.

Chŏng Chaech'ŏl. *Ilche ŭi tae Han'guk singminji kyoyuk chŏngch'aeksa* [Japan's colonial educational policies toward Korea]. Seoul: Ilchisa, 1985.

Chŏng Chaegyŏng. *Pak Chŏnghŭi Taet'ongnyŏng chŏn'gi* [Biography of Park Chung Hee]. Seoul: Tongsŏch'ulpansa, 1995.

Chŏng Chinsung. "Kyŏngje wigi wa kajok saenghwal" [Economic crisis and family life]. *Han'guk inguhak* [Korea journal of population studies] 24, no. 1 (2006): 91-121.

Chŏng Chŏnggil. *Taet'ongnyŏng ŭi kyŏngje ridŏsip: Pak Chŏnghŭi, Chŏn Tuwahn, Ro T'aeu chŏngbu ŭi kyongje chŏngch'aek kwalli* [President's economic leadership: Park Chung Hee, Chun Doo-whan, Rho Tae-woo regimes' economic policy management]. Seoul: Han'guk Kyŏngje Sinmunsa, 1994.

Ch'ong Mu Chŏ [Ministry of General Affairs, Republic of Korea]. *Gazettes*, various years.

Chŏng Sehyŏn. *Hangil haksaeng minjok undongsa yŏn'gu* [A study of anti-Japanese student movements]. Seoul: Ilchisa, 1975.

Chŏng Sunmi. *Han'guk haengjŏng kaehyŏk: chŏngch'i kwŏllyŏk kwa kwallyoje ŭi kwan'gye* [Administrative reforms in Korea: The relationship between political power and bureaucrats]. Pusan: Pusan University Press, 1999.

———. "Simin tanch'e ŭi chayuljŏk pup'ae ch'ŏkkyŏl undong i kongjikcha yulli e mich'in yŏnghyang" [The impact of the anti-corruption campaigns of civil organizations on the ethics of bureaucrats]. *Kungmin yulli yŏn'gu* [Studies of national ethics] 52 (2003): 155–68.

Chŏng T'aehŏn. "Sut'allon ŭi songnyuhwa sok e sarajin singminji" [Vulgar exploitation theory and the disappearance of real nature of colonialism]. *Ch'angjak kwa pip'yŏng* [Critical writing and criticism] 97 (Fall 1997): 344–57.

Chŏng T'aesŏk. "Simin sahoe wa NGO e kwanhan ch'oegŭn nonŭi ŭi pip'anjŏk kŏmt'o" [A critical review on recent discussion of civil society and NGOs]. *Kyŏngje wa sahoe* [Economy and society] 68 (2005): 161–88.

Chŏng Yongdŏk. "Miguk haengjŏnghak ŭi mugukkasŏng i Han'guk ŭi haengjŏnghak paljŏn e mich'in yŏnghyang" [The impact of the statelessness in American public administration on the development of public administration in Korea]. *Hangejŏng nonch'ong* [Journal of public administration] 34, no. 1 (1996): 1033–49.

———. "Uri nara kyuje chŏngch'aek ŭi p'yŏngga (8-3 kin'gŭp kyŏngje choch'i) ŭi kyŏngu rŭl chungsim ŭro" [An evaluation of Korea's regulation policy: The case of August 3 emergency measure]. *Han'guk haengjŏng hakpo* [Korean journal of public administration] 17 (1983): 89–117.

Chŏn'guk Kyŏngjein Yŏnhaphoe [Korean Federation of Industries]. *Chŏn'gyŏngnyŏn 40nyŏnsa (Sang)* [The 40 years of the Korean Federation of Industries]. Vol. 1. Seoul: Chŏn'guk Kyŏngjein Yŏnhaphoe, 2001.

———. *Han'guk kyŏngje chongch'aek 40nyŏnsa* [The 40 years' history of the Korean economic policy]. Seoul: Chŏnguk kyŏngjein yŏnhaphoe, 1986.

Chōsen Sōtokufu [Chōsen Government General's Office]. *Chōsenjin no shisō to seikaku* [The ideological orientations and character of Korean people]. March 1913.

———. *Chōsenjin no shisō to seikaku* [The ideological orientations and character of Korean people]. *Chōsa shiryō* [Data series] 20 (1927).

———. *Seikatsu jōtai chōsa: Suigen gun ich* [A survey of living conditions (in Japanese)]. *SuwonGun* [County] 28, no. 1 (1929).

Chōsen Sōtokufu [Chōsen Government General's Office], Gakumukyoku [Bureau of Education]. *Chōsen shogakkō ichiran, Shōwa jūyonnen* [Prospectus of schools in Korea]. Keijō: Chōsen Sōtokufu, 1937.

Chōsen Sōtokufu [Chōsen Government General's Office], Keimukyoku [Police Division]. *Chōsen ni okeru dōmei kyūkō no kōsatsu* [A survey of student strikes in Korea]. Keijō: Chōsen Sōtokufu, 1929.

Chosŏn Ilbo [Chosŏn daily]. "Undonggwŏn pyŏnhyŏk seryŏk ŭi yakchin/ chŏngch'igwŏn, simin tanch'e e nŭn nuga inna?" [The emergence of the political activists and progressive groups/Who are in political circles and civic organizations?]. Special report series, February 20, 2003, 22.

———. "Undonggwŏn pyŏnhyŏk seryŏk ŭi yakchin/chŏngch'igwŏn, simin tanch'e e nŭn nuga inna?" [The emergence of political activists and progressive groups/ Who are in political circles and civic organizations?]. Special report series, March 2, 2003, 22.

Chu Ponggyu. *Ilcheha nongŏp kyŏngjes* [A history of agricultural economy under the colonial rule]. Seoul: Seoul Taehakkyo Ch'ulp'anbu, 1995.

Cole, David C., and Princeton N. Lyman. *Korean Development: The Interplay of Politics and Economics*. Cambridge, MA: Harvard University Press, 1971.

Cole, David C., and Yung Chul Park. *Financial Development in Korea, 1945-1978*. Cambridge, MA: Council on East Asian Studies, Harvard University, 1983.

Cole, Robert E. "The Theory of Institutionalization: Permanent Employment and Tradition in Japan." *Economic Development and Cultural Change* 20, no. 1 (October 1971): 47-70.

Coleman, James S. *Foundations of Social Theory*. Cambridge, MA: Belknap Press of Harvard University Press, 1990.

Colonna, Fanny. "Educating Conformity in French Colonial Algeria." Translated by Barbara Harshav. In *Tensions of Empire: Colonial Cultures in a Bourgeois World*, edited by Frederick Cooper and Ann Laura Stoler. Berkeley: University of California Press, 1997.

Crowley, Kate, Jenny Stewart, Adrian Kay, and Brian W. Head. *Reconsidering Policy: Complexity, Governance and the State*. Bristol, UK: Policy Press, 2020.

Cumings, Bruce. "The Legacy of Japanese Colonialism in Korea." In *The Japanese Colonial Empire, 1895-1945*, edited by Ramon H. Meyers and Mark R. Peattie. Princeton, NJ: Princeton University Press, 1984.

———. "The Origins and Development of the Northeast Asian Political Economy: Industrial Sectors, Product Cycles, and Political Consequences." In *The Political Economy of the New Asian Industrialism*, edited by Frederic C. Deyo. Ithaca, NY: Cornell University Press, 1987.

Dahrendorf, Ralf. *Society and Democracy in Germany*. Garden City, NY: Doubleday, 1967.

Davidheiser, Evelyn B. "Strong States, Weak States: The Role of the State in Revolution." *Comparative Politics* 24, no. 4 (July 1992): 463-75.

de Carvalho, Benjamin, and Iver B. Neumann, eds. *Small State Status Seeking: Norway's Quest for International Standing*. London: Routledge, 2015.

Deutsch, Karl W. "Social Mobilization and Political Development." *American Political Science Review* 55, no. 3 (September 1961): 493-514.

Deyo, Frederic C., ed. *The Political Economy of the New Asian Industrialism*. Ithaca, NY: Cornell University Press, 1987.

Dirlik, Arif. "Rethinking Colonialism: Globalization, Postcolonialism, and the Nation." *Interventions* 4, no. 3 (2002): 428-48.

Dore, Ronald P. "The Late Development Effect." In *Modernization in South-East Asia*, edited by Hans-Dieter Evers. Singapore: Oxford University Press, 1973.

———. "South Korean Development in Wider Perspective." In *Korea: A Decade of Development*, edited by Yunshik Chang. Seoul: Seoul National University Press, 1980.

Easter, Gerald M. "Personal Networks and Postrevolutionary State Building: Soviet Russia Reexamined." *World Politics* 48, no. 4 (July 1996): 551-78.

———. *Reconstructing the State: Personal Networks and Elite Identity in Soviet Russia*. Cambridge: Cambridge University Press, 2000.

Eckert, Carter J. *Offspring of Empire: The Koch'ang Kims and the Colonial Origins of Korean Capitalism, 1876-1945*. Seattle: University of Washington Press, 1991.

———. *Park Chung Hee and Modern Korea: The Roots of Militarism, 1866-1945*. Cambridge, MA: Harvard University Press, 2016.

Eichengreen, Barry. "Government, Business and Finance in Korean Industrial Development." *International Economic Journal* 26, no. 3 (2012): 357-77.

Eisenstadt, S. N. "Bureaucracy, Bureaucratization, and Debureaucratization." *Administrative Science Quarterly* 4, no. 3 (1959): 302-20.

———. "Multiple Modernities." *Daedalus* 129, no. 1 (Winter 2000): 1-29.

———. "Political Struggle in Bureaucratic Societies." *World Politics* 9, no. 1 (1956): 15-36.

———. "Problems of Emerging Bureaucracies in Developing Areas and New States." In *Industrialization and Society*, edited by Bert F. Hoselitz and Wilbert E. Moore. Paris: UNESCO-Mouton, 1970.

Ekeh, Peter P. *Colonialism and Social Structure: An Inaugural Lecture Delivered at the University of Ibadan on Thursday, 5 June 1980*. Ibadan, Nigeria: University of Ibadan, 1983.

Emery, Robert F. *Korean Economic Reform: Before and since the 1997 Crisis*. Aldershot, UK: Ashgate, 2001.

Emirbayer, Mustafa. "Manifesto for a Relational Sociology." *American Journal of Sociology* 103, no. 2 (1997): 281-317.

Evans, Peter, "Class, State, and Dependence in East Asia: Lessons for Latin Americanists." In *The Political Economy of the New Asian Industrialism*, edited by Frederic C. Deyo. Ithaca, NY: Cornell University Press, 1987.

———. *Dependent Development: The Alliance of Multinational, State, and Local Capital in Brazil*. Princeton, NJ: Princeton University Press, 1979.

———. "Development as Institutional Change: The Pitfalls of Monocropping and the Potentials of Deliberation." *Studies in Comparative International Development* 38, no. 4 (2004): 30-52.

———. *Embedded Autonomy: States and Industrial Transformation*. Princeton, NJ: Princeton University Press, 1995.

Evans, Peter B., Dietrich Rueschemeyer, and Theda Skocpol, eds. *Bringing the State Back In*. Cambridge: Cambridge University Press, 1985.

Ferguson, Adam. *An Essay on the History of Civil Society*. Edited by Fania Oz-Salzberger. Cambridge: Cambridge University Press, 1995.

Firmin-Sellers, Kathryn. "Institutions, Context, and Outcomes: Explaining French and British Rule in West Africa." *Comparative Politics* 32, no. 3 (April 2000): 253-72.

Foster, George M. "Peasant Society and the Image of Limited Good." *American Anthropologist* 67, no. 2 (April 1965): 293-315.

Friedrich, Carl J. *Tradition and Authority*. New York: Praeger, 1972.

Fukuyama, Francis. "Asian Values and the Asian Crisis." *Commentary* 105, no. 2 (1998): 23-27.

———. *Trust: The Social Virtues and the Creation of Prosperity*. New York: Free Press, 1995.

Garon, Sheldon. *Molding Japanese Minds: The State in Everyday Life*. Princeton, NJ: Princeton University Press, 1997.

Garrard, John. *Democratisation in Britain: Elites, Civil Society and Reform since 1800*. Basingstoke, UK: Palgrave, 2002.

Geddes, Barbara. *Politician's Dilemma: Building State Capacity in Latin America*. Berkeley: University of California Press, 1994.

Gereffi, Gary, and Donald L. Wyman, eds. *Manufacturing Miracles: Paths of Industrialization in Latin America and East Asia*. Princeton, NJ: Princeton University Press, 1990.

Gerring, John. *Case Study Research: Principles and Practices*. New York: Cambridge University Press, 2007.

———. *Social Science Methodology: A Unified Framework*. 2nd ed. Cambridge: Cambridge University Press, 2011.

Gerschenkron, Alexander. *Economic Backwardness in Historical Perspective: A Book of Essays*. Cambridge, MA: Belknap Press of Harvard University Press, 1962.

Goffman, Erving. *Asylums: Essays on the Social Situation of Mental Patients and Other Inmates.* Garden City, NY: Anchor Books, 1961.
Gold, Thomas B. *State and Society in the Taiwan Miracle.* New York: M. E. Sharpe, 1986.
Goldthorpe, John H. "Employment, Class, and Mobility: A Critique of Liberal and Marxist Theories of Long-Term Change." In *Social Change and Modernity,* edited by Hans Haferkamp and Neil J. Smelser, 123-47. Berkeley: University of California Press, 1992.
——. "Theories of Industrial Society: Reflections on the Recrudescence of Historicism and the Future of Futurology." In "Reflections on Durkheim," special issue, *European Journal of Sociology / Archives Européennes de Sociologie / Europäisches Archiv für Soziologie* 12, no. 2 (1971): 263-88.
Graham, Edward M. *Reforming Korea's Industrial Conglomerates.* Washington, DC: Institute for International Economics, 2003.
Grajdanzev, Andrew J. *Modern Korea.* 1944; New York: Octagon Books, 1978.
Ha Sangrak. "Ilche sidaeŭi sahoe pojang" [Social security in the colonial Korea]. *Ŭiryopohŏm* [Medical insurance] 66 (February 1984): 27-31.
Ha Taegwŏn. "Han'guk insa haengjŏng ŭi pyŏnch'ŏn: kach'i galdŭngjŏk kwanjŏmesŏ ŭi koch'al" [Changes in personnel policy in Korea: From the perspective of value conflicts]. *Han'guk haengjŏng hakpo* [Korean public administration review] 24, no. 1 (1990): 89-116.
Ha Yong-Chool. "Analysis of School Registrars Preliminary Summary." Unpublished research memorandum, 1997.
——. "Colonial Rule and Social Change: The Paradox of Colonial Control." In *Colonial Rule and Social Change in Korea, 1910-1945.* Seattle: University of Washington Press, 2013.
——. "Late Industrialization, the State, and Social Changes: The Emergence of Neofamilism in South Korea." *Comparative Political Studies* 40, no. 4 (April 2007): 363-82.
——. "The Myth of the Breakdown of Tradition and Korean Social Science: A Search for Indigenization." *Korean Social Science Journal* 35, no. 1 (2008): 97-122.
Ha, Yong-Chool, and Myung-Koo Kang. "Creating a Capable Bureaucracy with Loyalists: The Internal Dynamics of the South Korean Developmental State, 1948-1979." *Comparative Political Studies* 44, no. 1 (2011): 78-108.
Ha, Yong-Chool, and Wang Hwi Lee. "The Politics of Economic Reform in South Korea: Crony Capitalism after Ten Years." *Asian Survey* 47, no. 6 (November/December 2007): 894-914.

Ha, Yong-Chool, Wang-Hwi Lee, and Sunil Kim. "Hybrid Capitalism? Institutional Scanning after the Economic Crisis in South Korea." Unpublished paper, 2018.

Ha Yongch'ul. "Hanil kwallyoje pigyo: iIbon Kwallyoje ŭi tTŭksŏng ŭl Chungsim ŭro" [A comparative study of Korean and Japanese bureaucracy: With a focus on the characteristics of Japanese bureaucracy]. *Yangyŏng haksul yŏn'gu nonmunjip* [Yangyoung collection of research papers] 2 (1994).

———. *Hubal sanŏphwa wa kukka ŭi tonghak: t'al kwallyohwa was kangsŏng kukka ŭi kongdonghwa* [Late industrialization and the dynamics of the state: Debureaucratization and the hollowing out of the strong state]. Seoul: Sŏul Taehakkyo Ch'ulp'anbu, 2006.

———. "Oehwan wigi ihu chŏngsil chabonjuŭi ŭi chedojŏk kiban: yebijŏk koch'al" [Continuity and change in the institutional foundations of Korean crony capitalism: A preliminary assessment]. *Han'guk chŏngch'i yŏn'gu* [Journal of Korean politics] 21, no. 3 (2012): 207–48.

———. "Pogŏn chŏngch'aek kyŏljŏng kwajŏng esŏ kukka ŭi yŏkhal: 1993nyŏn hanyak chojegwŏn punjaeng ŭl chungsimŭro" [The role of the state in health policy-making: The case of the 1993 Korean herbal pharmacy disputes]. *Han'guk chŏngch'i yŏn'gu* [Journal of Korean politics] 14, no. 2 (2005): 33–68.

Habermas, Jürgen. *Legitimation Crisis*. Translated by Thomas McCarthy. Boston: Beacon Press, 1973.

———. *The Structural Transformation of the Public Sphere: An Inquiry into a Category of Bourgeois Society*. Translated by Thomas Burger. Cambridge, MA: MIT Press, 1989.

Haengjŏng Chach'ibu Haengjŏng Kwalliguk p'yŏn [Bureau of Administrative Management, Ministry of the Interior], ed. *Chŏngbu chojik pyŏnch'ŏnsa (ha)* [History of changes in government organizations, vol. 2]. Seoul: Ministry of the Interior, 1998.

Haggard, Stephan. *Pathways from the Periphery: The Politics of Growth in the Newly Industrializing Countries*. Ithaca, NY: Cornell University Press, 1990.

———. *The Political Economy of the Asian Financial Crisis*. Washington, DC: Institute for International Economics, 2000.

Haggard, Stephan, and Chung-In Moon. "Institutions and Economic Policy: Theory and a Korean Case Study." *World Politics* 42, no. 2 (January 1990): 210–37.

Hall, John A. "The Nature of Civil Society." *Society* 35 (May–June 1988): 32–41.

Hall, Peter A. "The Dilemmas of Contemporary Social Science." *boundary 2* 34, no. 3 (Fall 2007): 121–41.

Hall, Peter A., and David Soskice, eds. *Varieties of Capitalism: The Institutional Foundations of Comparative Advantage*. Oxford: Oxford University Press, 2001.

Ham Inhŭi. "Sahoe kyŏngjejŏk wigi was chungsanch'ŭng kajok ŭi 'p'umwi harak'" [Socioeconomic crisis and the "fall from grace" of the middle-class family in Korea]. *Han'gukhak yŏn'gu* [Journal of Korean studies] 43, no. 12 (2012): 531-69.

Han Chŏnghwa. "Han'guk taegiŏp ŭi kŏsi kyŏngyŏng mit' kiŏp chŏllyak t'ŭksŏng" [The characteristics of macro management and business strategies of Korean chaebols]. In *Han'guk taegiŏp ŭi kyŏngyŏng t'ŭksŏng: o daegŭrup ŭi chuyo kiŏp yŏn'gu* [Management styles of Korean chaebols: A study of the five biggest chaebols], edited by Sin Yugŭn et al. Seoul: Segyŏngsa, 1995.

Han Sangjin. "Minjung sahoehak ŭi iron kujo wa chaengjŏm: pangbŏmnonjŏk nonŭi" [The theoretical structure and major issues of "mass sociology": A methodological discussion (in Korean)]. *Sahoe kwahak kwa chŏngch'aek yŏn'gu* [Social sciences and policy studies] 8, no. 1 (1986): 99-130.

Han Uhŭi. "Pot'ong hakkyo e taehan chŏhang kwa kyoyungnyŏl" [Resistance to and educational zeal for colonial primary schools]. *Kyoyuk iron* [Educational theory] 6 (1991): 63-77.

Han Wansang. "Han'guk esŏ simin sahoe, kukka kŭrigo kyegŭp: kwayŏn simin undong ŭn kaeryangjuŭijŏk sŏnt'aek in'ga" [Civil society, the state, and class: Are civic movements a non-radical choice?]. In *Han'guk ŭi kukka wa simin sahoe* [State and civil society in Korea], edited by Korean Association of Sociology and Korean Association of Political Science. Seoul: Hanul, 1992.

Han'guk Chŏngch'i Munje Yŏn'guso [Institute of Korean Politics]. *Pak Chŏnghŭi sidae ŭi kyŏngje pihwa* [Untold stories on economy under Park Chung Hee]. Seoul: Tonggwang, 1987.

Han'guk Chŏngch'ihakhoe p'yŏn [Korean Political Science Association], ed. *Hyŏndae Han'guk chŏngch'i wa kukka* [The contemporary Korean politics and the state]. Seoul: Pŏmmunsa, 1986.

Han'guk chonghap sahoe chosa. 2011 survey, a part of the questions on Procedural Justice. KGSS, Research Center, Sunggyungwan University, 2003-2012.

Han'guk Chŏngsin Munhwa Yŏn'guwŏn p'yŏn [Korean Institute for Korean Studies], ed. "Haengjŏng munhwa ŭi hyŏngsŏng kwa sŏnggyŏk" [The formation and nature of Korean administrative culture]. *Han'guk ŭi sahoewa munhwa* [Korean society and culture] 17. Seoul: Han'guk Chŏngsin Munhwa Yŏn'guwŏn, 1991.

Han'guk Ilbo [Hanguk daily], ed. *Chaegye hoego* [Reflections on business world]. Vol. 8. Seoul: Han'guk Ilbosa, 1981.

——. "Ch'amyŏhanŭn simin' 'sahoejŏk chiwŏn' chŏlsil" [In desperate need for social support for participating citizens]. January 19, 1999.

——. "Iisyuwa hyŏnjang/simin tanch'e" [Issues and reality: Pros and cons on the political participation of civic organizations]. Special report. September 23, 2003, 17.

262 Bibliography

——. "Simin p'awŏ, inki chisangjuŭi kwansim kkŭlgi" [Growing civil power and popularity-seeking trends]. April 3, 1997, 19.
——. "Simin tanch'e(3) mudyŏjin pip'an kallal, hoegil moksori" [Lackluster civic voice with lack of diversity]. Special report series, June 11, 2001, 26 (30th edition).
——. "Sinnyŏn t'ŭkchip/simin ŭi him ŭro segye rŭl pakkuja" [Change the world by civic power]. January 1, 2001, 34.
——. "Todŏksŏng siryŏn: simindanch'ehyŏpŭihoe, Kang Mun'gyu Kongdong Taep'yo (han'gugint'ŏbyu)" [Morality on trial: Interview with Mr. Kang Mungyu, co-representative of the Association of Civic Organizations]. March 26, 1997, 7, 13, 24.
——. "Toel kŏri man choch'a taninŭn inki chisangjuŭi." [Civic organizations that pursue only popular activities]. June 21, 2001, 26.
Han'guk Kunsa Hyŏngmyŏngsa P'yŏnch'anwiwŏnhoe p'yŏn [The Editorial Committee for the History of Korean Military Revolution]. *Han'guk kunsa hyŏngmyŏngsa*. Vol. 1. Seoul: Kukka Chaegŏn Ch'oego Hoeŭi, 1963.
Han'guk Kyŏngje Sinmun Kyŏngjebu p'yŏn [The economic department of Korean Economic Daily], ed. *Han'guk ŭi kyŏngje kwallyo* [Economic bureaucrats of South Korea]. Seoul: Han'guk Kyŏngje Sinmun [Korea Economic Daily], 1994.
Han'guk Muhyŏk Hyŏphoe [Korea Trade Association]. *Muyŏk kwan'gye pŏpkyujip* [Collection of laws on trade]. Seoul: Han'guk Muhyŏkhyŏphoe, 1991.
Han'guk sahoe t'onghyang 2008 [Korean social trends 2008]. Seoul: T'onggyech'ŏng, 2008.
Han'guk Sahoesa Yŏn'guhoe [Study group of Korean social history]. *Han'guk sahoe ŭi sinbun kyegŭp kwa sahoe pyŏndong* [Status, class, and social change in Korea]. Seoul: Munhak kwa Chisongsa, 1987.
Han'gyŏre. "'Ch'amyŏhanŭn simin' 'sahoejŏk chiwŏn' chŏlsil" [In desperate need for citizen participation and social support]. January 19, 1999, 6.
——. "Int'ŏbyu 18myŏn: chŏngnyŏn t'oeim aptun Kang Mun'gyU YMCA samu ch'ongjang" [Interview with Mr. Kang, Moongyu, a retiring secretary general of Korean YMCA]. December 26, 1995, 18.
——. "Nodong·sahoe tanch'e wa yŏndae 'tolp'agu" [Labor and social organizations and their coalitions as a breakthrough]. May 17, 1996, 22.
——. "Pokchi·Kyoyuk·Kukpang Yesan Pijung 2008nyŏn 50% tolp'a" [The budgetary proportion of social welfare, education, and national defense broke 50% level in 2008]. October 2, 2006.
——. "Simin tanch'e" [Civic organizations]. June 11, 2001, 26.
——. "Simin tanch'e naebu suri chung" [Civic organizations are undergoing internal repair]. Special report series on life and women, March 28, 1997, p. 11.

———. "30tae chaebŏl naebu kŏrae/maeip 21% maech'ul 17%/kongjŏng kŏraewi" [Internal tradings of 30 chaebols]. April 7, 1993.

———. "T'tajyŏbŏpsida/386 sedae chŏngch'i seryŏkhwa" [Let's discuss the issue of the politicization of Generation 386]. September 29, 1999, 40 (fourth edition).

———. "Undonggwŏn twihŭndŭn chŏngch'i seryŏkhwa nonjaeng" [Debates on the politicization of civic movement]. September 25, 1995, 20.

Haptong yŏngam [Haptong yearbooks]. *Haptong inmyŏngrok* [Haptong who's who]. Seoul: Haptong T'ongsinsa [Haptong News Agency], various years.

Harris, Olivia. "The Temporalities of Tradition: Reflections on a Changing Anthropology." In *Grasping the Changing World: Anthropological Concepts in the Postmodern Era*, edited by Václav Hubinger. London: Routledge, 1996.

Hashimoto, Kenji. "Class Structure in Contemporary Japan." Translated by Jackie Miyasaka. *International Journal of Sociology* 30, no. 1 (2000): 37-64.

Hashitani Hiroshi. "1930-40nyŏndae Chosŏn sahoe ŭi t'ŭkchire taehayŏ" [On the nature of Korean society in the 1930s and 1940s]. In *Han'guk kŭndae sahoe kyŏngjesa ŭi che munje* [Questions on social and economic history in modern Korea], edited by Yi Haeju and Ch'oe Sŏn'gil. Pusan: Pusan Taehakkyo Ch'ulp'anbu, 1995.

Henderson, Gregory. *Korea: The Politics of the Vortex*. Cambridge, MA: Harvard University Press, 1968.

Hŏ Sŏngnyŏl. "Tosi muhŏga chŏngch'akchi ŭi koyonggujo e taehan il koch'al" [A study of the employment structure in illegal settlements]. *Han'guk sahoehagyŏn'gu* [Study of Korean sociology] 6, no. 1 (1982): 173-208.

Hŏ Suyŏl. *Kaebal ŏmnŭn kaebal: ilje ha Chosŏn kyŏngje kaebal ŭi hyŏnsang kwa ponjil* [Development without development: The true nature of Korean economic development under the colonial rule]. Seoul: Ŭnhaeng Namu, 2011.

Hŏ Yŏngnan. *Ilje sigi changsi yŏn'gu: 5-ilchang ŭi pyŏndong kwa chiyŏk chumin* [A study of bazaar reforms under the colonial rule: Changes in changes in periodic bazaar opening and local residents]. Seoul: Yŏksa Pip'yŏngsa, 2009.

Hoffmann, David L. *Peasant Metropolis: Social Identities in Moscow, 1929-1941*. Ithaca, NY: Cornell University Press, 1994.

Hofstede, Geert, and Michael Harris Bond. "The Confucius Connection: From Cultural Roots to Economic Growth." *Organizational Dynamics* 16, no. 4 (1988): 5-21.

Holliday, Ian. "Is the British State Hollowing Out?" *Political Quarterly* 71, no. 2 (April 2000): 167-76.

Hong Changp'yo. "Han'guk esŏ ŭi hach'ŏng yeyŏrhwae kwanhan yŏn'gu" [(A) study on the subcontract system in Korea]. PhD diss., Seoul National University, 1993.

Hong Ilp'yo. "Ije tasi wit'aeroun mohŏm ŭi kiro e sŏn Han'guk simin undong" [Korean civic movements on the tight rope]. *Kyŏngje wa sahoe* [Economy and society] 45, no. 3 (2000): 114-33.

Hong Sŏngch'an. *Han'guk kŭndae nongch'on sahoe ŭi pyŏndong kwa chijuch'ŭng—20segi chŏnban'gi Chŏnnam Hwaun-gun Tongbuk-myŏn ildae ŭi sarye* [The dynamics in modern Korean rural society and landlord class: The case of Tongbuk-myon in Hwasun County in the first part of the 20th century]. Seoul: Chisik Sanŏpsa, 1992.

Hong, Wontack. *Trade, Distortions and Employment Growth in Korea*. Seoul: Korea Development Institute, 1979.

Hong Yanghŭi. "Singminji sigi ch'injok kwansŭp ŭi ch'angch'ul kwa ilbon minbŏp" [Inventing customs of domestic relations and the application of japanese civil law under Japanese colonialism]. *Han'gukhak* [Korean studies quarterly] 28, no. 3 (2005): 121-45.

Honneth, Axel. "Conceptions of 'Civil Society.'" *Radical Philosophy* (Summer 1993): 19-22.

Howard, Marc Morjé. *The Weakness of Civil Society in Post-Communist Europe*. Cambridge: Cambridge University Press, 2003.

Hull, Isabel V. *Sexuality, State, and Civil Society in Germany, 1700-1815*. Ithaca, NY: Cornell University Press, 1996.

Hunter, Holland. "The Overambitious First Soviet Five-Year Plan." *Slavic Review* 32, no. 2 (June 1973): 237-57.

Huntington, Samuel P. "The West Unique, Not Universal." *Foreign Affairs* 75, no. 6 (November/December 1996): 28-46.

Hutcheson, Francis. *An Essay on the Nature and Conduct of the Passions and Affections: With Illustrations on the Moral Sense*. Gainesville, FL: Scholars' Facsimiles & Reprints, 1969.

Hwang Chongsŏng. "Minjuhwa, kukka, kŭrigo kiŏp: chŏngbo t'ongsin sanŏp sarye." [Democratization, the state, and business: The case of the information and communication industry]. In *Minjuhwa sidae ŭi chŏngbu wa kiŏp*, edited by Mun Chŏngin, 241-65. Seoul: Orŭm, 1998.

Hwang, Kelley K. "South Korea's Bureaucracy and the Informal Politics of Economic Development." *Asian Survey* 36, no. 3 (March 1996): 306-19.

Hyŏndae Sahoe Yŏn'guso. *Kungmin ŭisik kujo yŏn'gu* [A study of the attitudinal structure of Korean people]. Seoul: Hyŏndae Sahoe Yŏn'guso, 1982.

Ikegami, Eiko. *The Taming of the Samurai: Honorific Individualism and the Making of Modern Japan*. Cambridge, MA: Harvard University Press, 1995.

Ikenberry, G. John. "The Irony of State Strength: Comparative Responses to the Oil Shocks in the 1970s." *International Organization* 40, no. 1 (Winter 1986): 105-37.

Im Chongguk. "Che 1 Konghwaguk kwa ch'inil elitŭ" [The First Republic and pro-Japanese elites]. In *Haebang chŏnhu sa ŭi insik* [Understanding of the history of Liberation]. Seoul: Hangilsa, 1985.

Im Insuk. *Sirŏp kwa kajok puranjŏngsŏng: Seoul-Han'guk yŏsŏnghakhoe kongdong simpojiŏm, 1999* [Unemployment and family insecurity: The collection of papers for the Seoul City-Korean Association of Women's Studies, 1999].

Inaba Iwakichi. "Chōsen no bunka mondai" [Cultural issues in Korea]. *Tōa keizai kenkyū* [East Asian economic studies] 6 (1922).

Inglehart, Ronald. *Modernization and Postmodernization: Cultural, Economic, and Political Change in 43 Societies*. Princeton, NJ: Princeton University Press, 1997.

Inglehart, Ronald, and Wayne E. Baker. "Modernization, Cultural Change, and the Persistence of Traditional Values." *American Sociological Review* 65, no. 1 (February 2000): 19-51.

Inglehart, Ronald, and Christian Welzel. "How Development Leads to Democracy: What We Know About Modernization." *Foreign Affairs* 88, no. 2 (March/April 2009): 33-48.

Jacobs, Norman. *The Korean Road to Modernization and Development*. Urbana: University of Illinois Press, 1985.

Jacobsson, Kerstin. "Rethinking Civic Privatism in a Postsocialist Context: Individualism and Personalization in Polish Civil Society Organizations." In *Civil Society Revisited: Lessons from Poland*, edited by Kerstin Jacobsson and Elżbieta Korolczuk. New York: Berghahn Books, 2017.

Janelli, Roger L. *Making Capitalism: The Social and Cultural Construction of a South Korean Conglomerate*. Stanford, CA: Stanford University Press, 1993.

Janelli, Roger L., and Dawnhee Yim Janelli. *Ancestor Worship and Korean Society*. Stanford, CA: Stanford University Press, 1982.

Jang, Jiho. "Economic Crisis and Its Consequences." *Social Indicators Research* 62/63 (April 2003): 51-70.

Jessop, Bob. *The Capitalist State*. New York: New York University Press, 1982.

Johnson, Chalmers. *MITI and the Japanese Miracle: The Growth of Industrial Policy, 1925-1975*. Stanford, CA: Stanford University Press, 1982.

———. "Preconception vs. Observation, or the Contributions of Rational Choice Theory and Area Studies to Contemporary Political Science." *PS: Political Science and Politics* 30, no. 2 (1997): 170-74.

Johnson, Chalmers, and E. B. Keehn. "A Disaster in the Making: Rational Choice and Asian Studies." *National Interest* 36 (Summer 1994): 14-22.

Jones, Gareth Stedman. *Languages of Class: Studies in English Working Class History 1832-1982*. Cambridge: Cambridge University Press, 1983.

Jones, Leroy P. *Public Enterprise and Economic Development: The Korean Case.* Seoul: Korea Development Institute, 1976.

Jones, Leroy P., and Il Sakong. *Government, Business, and Entrepreneurship in Economic Development: The Korean Case.* Cambridge, MA: Council on East Asian Studies, Harvard University, 1980.

Jowitt, Kenneth. *The Leninist Response to National Dependency.* Berkeley: Institute of International Studies, University of California, 1978.

——. "Soviet Neotraditionalism: The Political Corruption of a Leninist Regime." *Soviet Studies* 35, no. 3 (July 1983): 275-97.

Kanaya, Nobuko. "Civil Society and Social Capital in Japan: A Study Regarding Neighborhood Associations and Social Trust." *Komyuniti seisaku* [Community policy] 6, no. 6 (July 2008): 124-42.

Kang, David C. *Crony Capitalism: Corruption and Development in South Korea and the Philippines.* Cambridge: Cambridge University Press, 2002.

Kang Inch'ŏl. "Han'guk chŏnjaeng kwa sahoe insik mit munhwa ŭi pyŏnhwa" [The Korean War and changes in social consciousness and culture]. In *Han'guk chŏngjaeng kwa sahoe kujo ŭi pyŏnhwa* [The Korean War and changes in the social structure], edited by Han'guk Chŏngsin Munhwa Yŏn'guwŏn [The Academy of Korean Studies]. Seoul: Paeksan, 1999.

Kang, Myung Hun. *The Korean Business Conglomerate: Chaebol Then and Now.* Berkeley: Institute of East Asian Studies, 1996.

Kang Sanguk. "NGO ŭi sŏngjang kwa injŏk chawŏn ŭi t'ŭksŏng e kwanhan yŏn'gu" [A study of the growth of NGO and the background of their members]. *Han'guk haengjŏng yŏn'gu* [Korean journal of public administration] 11, no. 3 (Autumn 2002): 17-18.

Katzenstein, Peter J., ed. *Between Power and Plenty: Foreign Economic Policies of Advanced Industrial States.* Madison: University of Wisconsin Press, 1978.

Kawashima Takeyoshi. *Kazoku oyobi kazokuhō* [Family and family law: Family law, collections of Kawashima], vol. 10. Tokyo: Iwanami Shoten, 1983-1986.

Kaya, Ibrahim. *Social Theory and Later Modernities: The Turkish Experience.* Liverpool: Liverpool University Press, 2004.

Keane, John, ed. *Civil Society and the State: New European Perspectives.* London: Verso, 1988.

Keikido Naimufu. *Keijido nōson shakai jijyō* [The state of Kyonggi Province'sagricultural society]. Seoul: Keikido Naimufu, 1927.

Kerr, Clark. *The Future of Industrial Societies: Convergence or Continuing Diversity?* Cambridge, MA: Harvard University Press, 1983.

Ki Chŏn, "Chugŭl saram ŭi saenghwal kwa sal saram ŭi saenghwal" [Life for those who want to live and life for those who want to die]. *Gaebyok* [Daybreak], March 1925, 2-3.

Kim Chayŏng and Kang Sŭngmuk. "Kajokpŏp kaejŏng kwa taehaksaeng ŭi ch'injok mit sŏng kwa pon e taehan yŏn'gu" [A study on revision of family law and changes in university students' perception about surname and family clan]. *Chŏnbuk taehakkyo pŏphak yŏn'gu* [Chonbuk law review] 34 (December 2011): 169-92.

Kim Chibŏm, Kang Chŏngha, Kim Sŏkho, Kim Ch'anghwan, Pak Wŏnho, Yi Yunsŏk, Ch'oe Sŭlgi, and Ki Sori. *Han'guk chonghap sahoe chosa* [Korean general social survey]. Seoul: Sŏnggyun'gwan Taehakkyo Sŏbeirisŏch'i sent'ŏ, 2003-2012.

Kim Chin. *Chŏngwadae Pisŏsil 1: Yuksŏng ŭro tŭrŏbon Pak Chŏnghŭi sidae ŭi chŏngch'i kwŏllyŏk pisa* [The Blue House secretariat 1: The oral testimonies of the untold stories of political power during Park Chung Hee era]. Seoul: Chung Ang Daily, 1992.

———. *Sangsokse mit chŭngyŏse kwase chedo hamnihwa pangan* [Rational measures for inheritance and gift taxes]. Seoul: Han'guk Chose Yŏn'guwŏn [Korean Institute for Taxes], 2008.

Kim Chŏngnyŏm. *Han'guk kyŏngje chŏngch'aek 30onyŏnsa: Kim Chŏngnyŏm hegorok* [Thirty years of Korean economic policy: Memoir of Kim Joeng Nyom]. Seoul: Chungang Daily, 1990.

Kim Chongyŏng. "Kŭmyung silmyŏng kŏrae e kwanhan chŏngch'aek kyŏlchŏng kwajŏng punsŏk: chŏngbu, kiŏp, sahoe undong ŭi yŏkhak kwan'gyer rŭl chungsim ŭro" [An analysis of the decision-making process on real name system in finance: With a focus on interactions among the government, business, and social movements]. PhD diss., Korea University, 1996.

Kim, Euiyoung. "The Limits of NGO Government Relations in South Korea." *Asian Survey* 49, no. 5 (September/October 2009): 873-94.

Kim, Eun Mee. *Big Business, Strong State: Collusion and Conflict in South Korean Development, 1960-1990*. Albany: State University of New York Press, 1997.

———. "Crisis of the Developmental State in South Korea." *Asian Perspective* 23, no. 2 (1999): 35-55.

Kim Haedong. "Kwallyo haengt'ae wa kajokchuŭi" [Bureaucratic behaviors and familism]. *Han'guk haengjŏng hakpo* [Korean public administration review] 12, no. 12 (1978): 95-111.

Kim Hogi. *Hyŏndae chabonjuŭi wa Han'guk sahoe* [Modern capitalism and Korean society]. Seoul: Sahoe Pipyongsa, 1995.

Kim Hojŏng. "Han'guk haejŏng munhwa wa kwallyo haengt'ae e mich'inŭn ŏnghyang" [The impact of administrative culture on bureaucratic behaviors in Korea]. *Sahoe chosa yŏn'gu* [Journal of social research] 4, no. 1 (1985): 1-27.

———."Han'guk kwallyo haengt'ae ŭi kyŏlchŏng yoin: pokchi pudong ŭi wŏnin" [The determinants of Korean bureaucrats' behaviors]. *Han'guk haengjŏng hakpo* [Korean public administrative review] 28, no. 4 (1994): 21-49.

———. "Han'guk ŭi chŏnt'ongjŏk haejŏng munhwa wa kwallyo haengt'ae e kwanhan yŏn'gu: Kyŏnghŏmjŏk yŏn'gu rŭl wihan chunbi tangye" [A study of the relationship between administrative culture and bureaucratic behaviors in Korea: A preparatory step toward empirical studies]. *Pusandae sahoe kahak nonch'ong* [Pusan University journal of social sciences] 6 (1984): 131-48.

Kim Hŭng Ki, ed. *Yŏngyok ŭi Han'guk kyŏngje: Pisa Kyŏngje Kihoegwŏn 33nyŏn* [Ups and downs of Korean economy: Hidden history of 33 years of the Economic Planning Board]. Seoul: Maeil Economic Daily, 1999.

Kim Hyŏngŏn. "Tesk'ŭ k'allŏm: Sahoe isanimdŭl, annyŏng hasimnikka?" [Desk column: Outside directors, are you all right?]. *Herŏldŭ Kyŏngje* [Herald economy], May 7, 2014.

Kim Hyŏnu. *Han'guk chŏngdang tonghap undongsa* [A history of mergers of political parties in South Korea]. Seoul: Eulyoo, 2000.

Kim Ipsam. "Kim Ipsam hoegorok: sijang kwa kiŏpka chŏngsin" [Memoir of Kim Ip Sam: market economy and entrepreneurship]. *Han'guk Kyŏngje Sinmun* [*Korea Economic Daily*], March 1998-August 2000.

Kim, Joongi. "The Next Stage of Reforms: Korean Corporate Governance in the Post-Asian Financial Crisis Era." *Asian Journal of Comparative Law* 1 (2006): 1-23.

Kim, Kwang Suk, and Michael Roemer. *Growth and Structural Transformation*. Cambridge, MA: Council on East Asian Studies, Harvard University, 1979.

Kim Kwangmo. *Han'guk ŭi sanŏp paljŏn kwa chunghwahak kongŏphwa chŏngch'aek* [South Korea's economic development and heavy chemical industrial policies]. Seoul: Chigumunhwasa, 1988.

———. "Pak Chŏnghŭi ŭi kyŏngje paljŏn chŏngch'aek kwa kwallyŏ" [Park Chung Hee's economic development and bureaucrats]. In *Hyŏndaesa rŭl ŏttŏ'ke pol kŏt inga IV* [How to approach modern history, vol. 4]. Seoul: Tonga Ilbo, 1990.

Kim, Kwang-Ok. "Structural Changes in Villages and the Nature of Political Structure." In *Collection of the Papers in Honor of the Retirement of Professor Kim Wonryong*, no. 2, 723-47. Seoul: Ilchi-Sa, 1987.

Kim Kyŏngil. *Ilje ha nodong undongsa* [History of labor movement under the Japanese colonial rule]. Seoul: Ch'angjak kwa Pip'yŏng, 1992.

Kim, Kyung Mi. *The Korean Developmental State*. Singapore: Palgrave Macmillan, 2020.

Kim Manhŭm. "Chiyŏk kyunyŏl ŭi chŏngdang ch'eje wa sŏn'gŏ chedo kaep'yŏn: kaep'yŏn nollan kwa saeroun taean" [Regional cleavage and electoral system: New direction of institutional reforms]. *Han'guk chongch'iyŏn'gu* [Journal of Korean politics] 20, no. 1 (2011): 236-57.

———. "Chŏngch'i kyunyŏl, chŏngdang chŏngch'i kŭrigo chiyŏkchuŭi." *Han'guk chŏngch'i hakpo* [Korean political science review] 28, no. 2 (1995): 215-37.

———. "Han'guk ŭi chŏngch'i kyunyŏl e kwanhan yŏn'gu: chiyŏk kyunyŏl ŭi chŏngch'i kwajŏng e taehan kujojŏk chŏpkŭn" [A study of Korean political schism: A structural approach to regionalism]. PhD diss., Seoul National University, 1991.

Kim Migyŏng. "Han'guk e issŏsŏ chŏngbu-kiŏp kwan'gye ŭi yuhyŏng mit pyŏnhwa punsŏk: pandoch'e sanŏp ŭl chungsim ŭro" [Patterns and changes in state-business relations in South Korea: The case of semi-conductor industry]. PhD diss., Sungkyungwan University, 1995.

Kim Myŏngsu. "Kukka ŭi chayulsŏng kwa kaeimnyŏk: Han'guk ŭi chunghwahak kongŏphwa kyehoek ŭl chungsim ŭro" [State autonomy and intervention: The case of heavy chemical industry development plan]. *Hanyangdae sahoegwahak nonch'ong* [The journal of social science studies] 7 (1988): 283-302.

Kim Pyŏngguk. "Kukka kujo wa kukka nŭngnyŏk: Han'guk kwa meksik'o ŭi taeoe pulgyunhyŏng kwalli chŏngch'aek ŭi pigyo" [State structure and state capability: A comparative study of trade imbalance in South Korea and Mexico]. *Han'guk kwa kukje chŏngch'i* [Korea and world politics] 4, no. 1 (1988): 55-95.

Kim Pyŏngwŏn. "Han'guk haengjŏngbu nae ŭi kwallyo chŏngch'i: hwangyŏng chŏngch'aek e kwanhan kaebalbuchŏ wa pojŏnbuchŏ ŭi kwan'gye punsŏk" [Bureaucratic politics in Korea's administration: An analysis of the relationship between development and preservation ministries]. *Han'guk haengjŏng hakpo* [Korean public administration review] 27, no. 1 (1993): 171-94.

Kim, Se-Jin. *The Politics of Military Revolution in Korea*. Chapel Hill: University of North Carolina Press, 1971.

Kim, Seung-Kyung. *Class Struggle or Family Struggle? The Lives of Women Factory Workers in South Korea*. Cambridge: Cambridge University Press, 1997.

Kim Sŏkjun. "Chŏnhwan'gi ŭi Han'guk haengjŏng ŭi saeroun paerŏdaim mosaek: kukkaron ŭl t'onghan munjejegi" [Search for a new paradigm in transitional Korean public administration: Raising questions based on state theories]. *Han'guk haengjŏng hakpo* [Korean public administration review] 22, no. 2 (1988): 431-59.

Kim Sŏngguk. "Han'guk chabonjuŭi paljŏn kwa simin sahoe" [The development of capitalism in Korea and civil society]. In *Han'guk sahoehakhoe and Han'guk chŏngch'i hakhoe* [Korean Association of Sociology and Korean Association of Political Science], edited by Han'guk ŭi Kukka wa Simin Sahoe. Seoul: Hanul, 1992.

———. "Han'guk ŭi simin sahoe wa sinsahoe undong" [Civil society and new society movement in Korea]. In *Simin sahoe wa siminundong 2* [Civil society and civic movements, vol. 2], edited by Yu P'almu and Kim Jeonghoon. Seoul: Hanul, 2001.

———. "Sinsahoe undong ŭi ironjŏk kiban: simin sahoeron kwa kwallyŏnhayŏ" [A theoretical foundation of new society movement: In relation to civil society]. In *Sinsahoe undon gŭi sahoehak: segyejŏk ch'use wa Han'guk* [Sociology of new society movement: World trends and Korea], edited by Kwon Taewhan, Lim Hyunjin, and Song Hogeun. Seoul: Seoul National University Press, 2001.

Kim Sŏngjin, ed. "Chadongch'a 5 sa ŭi robi ch'anggu: Han'guk Chadongch'a Hyŏphoe" [Windows of lobbying for the five automobile companies: Korean automobile association]. *Opsŏbŏ* [Observer], August 1992, 340-49.

———. *Pak Chŏnghŭi sidae: kŭ kŏt ŭn uri ege muŏt iŏttŏnga* [Park Chung Hee era: What was it to us?]. Seoul: Chosŏn Ilbo, 1994.

Kim Sŏngsik. *Iljeha Han'guk haksaeng tongnip undongsa* [A history of Korean student independence movements]. Seoul: Chŏngŭmsa, 1974.

Kim Sŏngsu. "Minjuhwa kwajŏng esŏ Han'guk chungsanch'ŭng ŭi yŏkhwal: minjuhwa undong ch'amyŏ tonggi e taehan punsŏk" [South Korea's democratization and the role of Korean middle class]. *Kukche chŏngch'i nonch'ong* [Korean journal of international relations] 43, no. 1 (2003): 135-62.

Kim Sŏnyŏp. "Han'guk taedosi chumin ŭi kaeinjŏk yŏnjulmang e kwanhan kyŏnghŏmjŏk yŏn'gu" [An empirical study on the personal network of residents of large cities in Korea]. PhD diss., Korea University, 1991.

Kim, Sunhyuk. "Discussions of Civil Society and Their Implications for Public Administration." Paper presented at the joint summer convention of Korean Association of Public Administration and Korean Association of Public Policy, 2003.

———. *The Politics of Democratization in Korea: The Role of Civil Society*. Pittsburgh, PA: University of Pittsburgh Press, 2000.

Kim T'aehwan. "Hubal sijanghwa e issŏsŏ kiŏp chiptan hyŏngsŏng e taehan chŏngch'i iron" [A political theory on the formation of business group in the marketization of late industrialization]. *Han'guk chŏngchi hakpo* [Korean political science review] 35, no. 2 (2001): 367-88.

Kim Taehwan. "1950nyŏndae Han'guk kyŏngje ŭi yon'gu: kongŏp ŭl chungsim ŭro" [Korean economy in the 1950s: Industrial sector]. In *1950nyŏndae ŭi insik* [Understanding of the 1950s], edited by Chin Tŏkkyu et al., 157-251. Seoul: Hangilsa, 1981.

Kim Tongch'un. "1950nyŏndae Han'guk nongch'on esŏ kajok kwa kukka" [Family and state in the 1950s of South Korea]. In *1950nyŏndae nambukhan ŭi sŏnt'aek kwa kuljŏl* [Choices and deviations in the 1950s of South and North Korea], edited by Yŏksa Munje Yŏn'guso [Institute for Historical Studies]. Seoul: Yŏksabipyongsa, 1998.

Kim Tongno. "Pak Chŏnghŭi sidae chŏnt'ong ŭi chaech'angjo wa t'ongch'i cheje ui hwangnip" [The reinvention of tradition and the consolidation of the governing system under Park Chung Hee regime]. *Tongbang hakchi* [Journal of oriental studies] 150, no. 6 (June 2010): 319-53.

———. "Simin undong ŭi chŏngch'i ch'amyŏ rŭl t'onghae pon simin undong ŭi sŏngjang kwa han'gye" [Overpoliticization of civil society and its declining social significance]. *Hyŏnsang kwa insik* [Phenomenon and epistemology] 37, no. 3 (2013): 58-85.

———. "Singmin sidae ŭi kŭndaejŏk sut'al kwa sut'al ŭl t'onghan kŭndaehwa" [Modernization through modern expropriation in the colonial era]. *Ch'angjak kwa pipy'ŏng* [Creation and criticism] 3 (1998): 112-32.

Kim Tuyŏl. *Kyŏngje sŏngjang ŭl wihan sabŏpchŏk kiban mosaek: minsa sosong ŭi hyŏnhwang wa chŏngch'aek kwaje* [Search consolidation of civil law foundation and economic growth: The status of civic cases and policy agenda]. Seoul: Korea Development Institute, 2007.

Kim Ŭngnyŏl. "Hyŏllyŏn chungsimjŏk chiptanjuŭi" [Collectivism based on consanguineous groups]. *Han'gukhak yŏn'gu* [Journal of Korean studies] 2 (December 1989): 159-82.

Kim Ŭnmi and Yi Sŏni. "Kosirŏp sidae ŭi kajok sŭt'ŭresŭ" [High unemployment era and stress on family]. *Human Ecology Research (Journal of the Korean Home Economics Association)* 36, no. 4 (1998): 251.

Kim Wŏn. *Ich'yŏjin kŏt e taehayŏ* [Memories of things lost]. Seoul: Imaejin, 2011.

Kim Yŏnggŭn. "1920nyŏndae nodongja ŭi chonjae hyŏngt'ae e kawanhan yŏn'gu" [A study of the existence of labor in Korea during the 1920s]. In *Iljehu Han'guk ŭi sahoe kyegŭp kwa sahoe pyŏndong* [Social class and social changes in Korea under Japanese colonial rule]. Study Group of Korean Social History. Seoul: Munhak kwa Chisong, 1988.

Kim Yŏngha. "Han'guk kwŏnwijuŭi hyŏngsŏng paegyŏng yŏn'gu" [A study of the emergence of authoritarianism in South Korea]. *Han'guk haengjŏngsa hakchi* [Journal of Association for Korean Public Administration History] 2 (1993): 141-59.

Kim Yonghak. "Ellit'ŭ ch'ungwŏn e issŏsŏ ŭi chiyŏk kyŏkch'a" [Regional differences in elite recruitment: Micro motives and macro consequences]. In *Han'guk ŭi chiyŏkchuŭi wa chiyŏk kaldŭng* [Regionalism and regional conflicts in South Korea], edited by Korean Association of Sociology. Seoul: Seongwon, 1990.

———. "Han'guk sahoe ŭi hagyŏn: sahoejŏk chabon ŭi ch'angch'ul esŏ injŏk chabon ŭi yŏkhwal" [School ties in Korean society: The role of human capital in creating social capital]. *Han'guk Sahoehakhoe* [Korean Sociological Association] (June 2003): 53-68.

———. "Kwallyo ch'ungwŏn ŭi chiyŏkchŏk kyŏch'a ŭi misijŏk tonggi wa kŏsijŏk kyŏlgwa" [Micro motives of bureaucratic recruitment and macro consequences]. In *Han'guk ŭi chiyŏkchuŭi wa chiyŏk kaldŭng* [Regionalism and regional conflicts in South Korea], edited by Han'guk Sahoehakhoe p'yŏn [Korean Sociological Association]. Seoul: Sŏngwŏnsa, 1990.

Kim Yongho. "Chŏn Tuhwan chŏnggwŏn ŭi pusil kiŏp chŏngni hŭngmak" [The hidden stories behind the restructuring of non-performing companies under Chun Du Whan regime]. *Ent'ŏpraiz* [Enterprise], no. 46 (July 1988).

Kim Yonghwan. *Hoegorok: Imja, chane ga saryŏnggwan aninga* [Kim Yong Hwan memoir: Are you not a commander?]. Seoul: Maeil Kyŏngje Sinmunsa, 2002.

Kim Yŏngmo. "Ilje sidae taejiju ŭi sahoejŏk paegyŏng kwa idong" [Social backgrounds of big landlords and their social mobility under the colonial rule]. *Asea yŏn'gu* [The journal of Asiatic studies] 14, no. 2 (1971): 107-25.

Kim Yonguk. "Kwallyo haengt'ae wa hakbŏl" [Bureaucratic behaviors and school ties]. *Han'guk haengchŏng hakpo* [Korean public administration review] 12 (December 1978): 128-37.

Kimiya Tadasi. *Pak Chŏnghŭi chŏngbu ŭi sŏnt'aek* [The Park government's choice]. Seoul: Humanitas, 2008.

Kinzley, W. Dean. *Industrial Harmony in Modern Japan: The Invention of a Tradition*. London: Routledge, 1991.

Kirk, Donald. *Korean Crisis: Unraveling of the Miracle in the IMF Era*. New York: St. Martin's Press, 2000.

———. *Korean Dynasty: Hyundai and Chung Ju Yung*. Armonk: M. E. Sharpe, 1994.

Kirk, Neville. "History, Language, Ideas and Post-Modernism: A Materialist View." *Social History* 19, no. 2 (May 1994): 221-40.

Ko Sŏngguk. "Han'guk simin sahoe ŭi hyŏngsŏng kwa paljŏn" [Formation and development of civil society in Korea]. *Asia munhwa* [Asian culture] 10 (1994): 181-203.

Ko Wŏn. "Pak Chŏnghŭi chŏnggwon sigi kajŏng ŭirye chunch'ik kwa kŭndaehwa ŭi pyŏnyong e kwanhan yŏn'gu" [Development, acculturation, and modernization in South Korea during the Park Chung Hee regime with a focus on simplified family ritual standards]. *Tamron* 9, no. 3 (2006): 191-223.

Kohli, Atul. "Where Do High Growth Political Economies Come From? The Japanese Lineage of Korea's 'Developmental State.'" *World Development* 22, no. 9 (1994): 1269-93.

Kong Che-uk, Park Hyŏnjun, Pae Ugin, Sŏ Kwanmo, and Yi Chinkyŏng. *Sahoe kgyegŭmron* [Theories of social class]. Seoul: Hangilsa, 1989.

Kong Chŏngja. "Han'guk taegiŏpka ŭi kajok honmaek e kwanhan yŏn'gu" [A study of marriage networks of Korean chaebols]. PhD diss., Sociology Department of Ewha Women's University, 1989.

Koo, Hagen. *Korean Workers: The Culture and Politics of Class Formation*. Ithaca, NY: Cornell University Press, 2001.

———, ed. *State and Society in Contemporary Korea*. Ithaca, NY: Cornell University Press, 1993.

Krueger, Anne O. "The Political Economy of the Rent-Seeking Society." *American Economic Review* 64, no. 3 (June 1974): 291-303.

Kuk Minho. "Chŏngbu wa kiŏp: 1980nyŏndae ch'o kyŏngje chayulhwa choch'i ihu ŭi pyŏnhwa wa kŭ han'gyejŏm" [Government and business: Changes and limits since the liberalization measures in the beginning of the 1980s]. *Han'guk Sahoehakhoe* [Korean Sociological Association] 22 (Summer 1988): 1155-81.

Kulp, Daniel Harrison, II. *Country Life in South China: The Sociology of Familism*. New York: Teachers College, Columbia University, 1925.

Kumar, Ashutosh. "Marx and Engels on India." *Indian Journal of Political Science* 53, no. 4 (October-December 1992): 493-504.

Kumar, Krishan. "Civil Society: An Inquiry into the Usefulness of an Historical Term." *British Journal of Sociology* 44, no. 3 (September 1993): 375-95.

Kuromiya, Hiroaki. *Stalin's Industrial Revolution: Politics and Workers, 1928-1932*. Cambridge: Cambridge University Press, 1988.

Kurzman, Charles. Review of *Conditions of Liberty: Civil Society and Its Rivals*, by Ernest Gellner. *Social Forces* 74, no. 1 (September 1995): 344-47.

Kwŏn Hŭijŏng. "Singminji sidae Han'guk kajok ui pyŏnhwa: 1920nyŏndae ihon sosong kwa ihon sarye rŭr chungsimŭro" [Changes in Korean families during the colonial era: The case of divorce cases in the 1920s]. *Pigyo munhwa yon'gu* [Comparative cultural studies] 11, no. 2 (2005): 35-62.

Kwon, Hyeong-Ki. "Asian Financial Crisis and Transformation of Korean Capitalism." In *Changes by Competition: The Evolution of the South Korean Developmental State*. Oxford: Oxford University Press, 2021.

Kyŏngje Kihoegwŏn [Economic Planning Board]. *Kyŏngje Kihoegwŏn 30nyŏnsa: Kaebal yŏndae ŭi chŏngch'aek* [The 30-year history of the Economic Planning Board: Economic policies during the years of development]. Seoul: Miraesa, 1994.

———. *1973nyŏn kyŏngje paeksŏ* [Economic white paper, 1973]. Seoul: Kyŏngje Kihoegwŏn, 1974.

———. *1972nyŏn kyŏngje paeksŏ* [Economic white paper, 1972]. Seoul: Kyŏngje Kihoegwŏn, 1973.

———. *Uri kyŏngje ŭi changgi chŏnmang 1972-1981* [The long-term forecast of our economy, 1972-1981]. Seoul: Kyŏngje Kihoegwŏn, 1973.

Kyŏngsang-buktosa P'yŏnch'an Wiwŏnhoe [The Editorial Committee for the History of Kyŏngsang-bukto]. *Kyŏngsang-buktosa* [The history of North Kyŏngsang Province]. 3 vols. Taegu: Kyŏngsangbuktosa P'yŏnch'an Wiwŏnhoe, 1983.

Landes, David S. *The Wealth and Poverty of Nations: Why Some Are So Rich and Some So Poor*. New York: Norton, 1998.

Ledeneva, Alena V. *Russia's Economy of Favours*: Blat, *Networking and Informal Exchange*. Cambridge: Cambridge University Press, 1998.

Lee, Hahn-Been. "Developmentalist Time and Leadership in Developing Countries." CAG Occasional Paper. Bloomington, IN: Comparative Administrative Group, 1965.

Lee, Hyo-Soo. "Paternalistic Human Resource Practices: Their Emergence and Characteristics." *Journal of Economic Issues* 35, no. 4 (December 2001): 841–69.

Lee, Kuan Yew. "Asian Values and the Crisis." Interview by Terry McCarthy. *Time International* 150, no. 29 (March 16, 1998).

Lee, Kyu-Sung. *Korean Financial Crisis of 1997: Onset, Turnaround, and Thereafter*. Washington, DC: World Bank, 2011.

Lee, Young Youn, and Hyun-Hoon Lee. "Korea: Financial Crisis, Structural Reform and Social Consequences." In *The Social Impact of the Asia Crisis*, edited by Tran Van Hoa, 57–84. New York: Palgrave, 2000.

Lerner, Daniel. *The Passing of Traditional Society: Modernizing the Middle East*. New York: Free Press, 1958.

Levi, Margaret. *Of Rule and Revenue*. Berkeley: University of California Press, 1988.

Lewis, Peter M. "Political Transition and the Dilemma of Civil Society in Africa." *Journal of International Affairs* 46, no. 1 (Summer 1992): 31–54.

Lim, Hyun-Chin, and Joon Han. "The Social and Political Impact of Economic Crisis in South Korea: A Comparative Note." *Asian Journal of Social Science* 31, no. 2 (2003): 198–220.

Lim, Hyun-Chin, and Jin-Ho Jang. "Between Neoliberalism and Democracy: The Transformation of the Developmental State in South Korea." *Development and Society* 35, no. 1 (June 2006): 1–28.

Lim, Sungyun. *Rules of the House: Family Law and Domestic Disputes in Colonial Korea*. Oakland: University of California Press, 2019.

Lim, Youngil. *Government Policy and Private Enterprise: Korean Experience in Industrialization*. Berkeley: Institute of East Asian Studies, University of California, 1981.

Lindblom, Charles E., and Edward J. Woodhouse. *The Policy-Making Process*. 3rd ed. Englewood Cliffs, NJ: Prentice Hall, 1992.

Lockwood, D. "Sources of Variation in Working Class Images of Society." *The Sociological Review* 14, no. 3 (1966): 249–67.

Lockwood, William W. *The Economic Development of Japan: Growth and Structural Change, 1868-1938*. Princeton, NJ: Princeton University Press, 1954.

Mahoney, James. "Path Dependence in Historical Sociology." *Theory and Society* 29, no. 4 (August 2000): 507-48.
Mann, Michael. "Sources of Variation in Working-Class Movements in Twentieth-Century Europe." *New Left Review* 212 (1995): 14-54.
Marshall, Byron K. *Capitalism and Nationalism in Prewar Japan: The Ideology of the Business Elite, 1868-1941.* Stanford, CA: Stanford University Press, 1967.
Marx, Karl, and Friedrich Engels. *The Marx-Engels Reader.* Edited by Robert C. Tucker. New York: Norton, 1972.
Mason, Edward S., Mahn Je Kim, Dwight H. Perkins, Kwang Suk Kim, and David C. Cole. *The Economic and Social Modernization of the Republic of Korea.* Cambridge, MA: Harvard University Asia Center, 1981.
Masuda Shūsaku. "Chōsen ni okeru buraku chūshin jinbutsu ni tsukiteno ichi kōsatsu" [An observation of major village figures in Korea]. *Chōsen* 257 (November 1936): 86-110.
Mathias, Peter. *The First Industrial Nation: An Economic History of Britain 1700-1914.* 1969; New York: Routledge, 2001.
Matossian, Mary. "Ideologies of Delayed Industrialization: Some Tensions and Ambiguities." *Economic Development and Cultural Change* 6, no. 3 (1958): 217-28.
McCarthy, D. M. P. *Colonial Bureaucracy and Creating Underdevelopment: Tanganyika, 1919-1940.* Ames: Iowa State University Press, 1982.
McMillan, Daniel A. "Energy, Willpower, and Harmony: On the Problematic Relationship between State and Civil Society in Nineteenth-Century Germany." In *Paradoxes of Civil Society: New Perspectives on Modern German and British History,* edited by Frank Trentmann. New York: Berghahn Books, 2000.
McNamara, Dennis L. *The Colonial Origins of Korean Enterprise, 1910-1945.* Cambridge: Cambridge University Press, 1990.
Mercier, P. "Problems of Social Stratification in West Africa." In *Social Change: The Colonial Situation,* edited by Immanuel Wallerstein. New York: John Wiley and Sons, 1966.
Meyer, Marshall W. "Debureaucratization?" *Social Science Quarterly* 60, no. 1 (1979): 25-34.
Meyer, Marshall W., and M. Craig Brown. "The Process of Bureaucratization." *American Journal of Sociology* 83, no. 2 (September 1977): 364-85.
Migdal, Joel S. "Introduction: Developing a State-in-Society Perspective." In *State Power and Social Forces: Domination and Transformation in the Third World,* edited by Joel S. Migdal, Atul Kohli, and Vivienne Shue. Cambridge: Cambridge University Press, 1994.

———. *State in Society: Studying How States and Societies Transform and Constitute One Another.* Cambridge: Cambridge University Press, 2001.

———. *Strong Societies and Weak States: State-Society Relations and State Capabilities in the Third World.* Princeton, NJ: Princeton University Press, 1988.

Miliband, Ralph. *The State in Capitalist Society.* London: Weidenfeld & Nicolson, 1969.

Milward, H. Brinton, and Keith G. Provan. "The Hollow State: Private Provision of Public Services." In *Public Policy for Democracy*, edited by Helen Ingram and Steven Rathgeb Smith. Washington, DC: Brookings Institution, 1993.

Ministry of Commerce and Industry. See Sanggongbu.

Mŏni Tudei [Money today]. "Kyŏngyŏngjin e kildŭryŏjin isahoe" [Tamed board of directors]. September 23, 2014.

Morris, R. J. *Class, Sect and Party: The Making of the British Middle Class: Leeds, 1820–1850.* Manchester, UK: Manchester University Press, 1990.

Mosley, Layna, ed. *Interview Research in Political Science.* Ithaca, NY: Cornell University Press, 2013.

Mun Chŏngin, ed. *Minjuhwa sidae ŭi chŏngbu wa kiŏp* [State and business under democratization]. Seoul: Orŭm, 1998.

Mun Hyŏngjin. "Oehwan wigi ihu Han'guk sahoe pyŏndong yangsang e taehayŏ" [A study for changed aspects after currency crisis in Korean society]. *Kukche chiyŏk yŏn'gu* [Journal of international area studies] 11, no. 1 (2007): 83–102.

Mun Pyŏngju. "Han'guk minjujuŭi roŭi ihaeng kwa konggohwa, 1979–1994: kukka-chŏngch'isahoe-siminsahoe ŭi kwan'gye mit naebu tonghag ŭl chungsim ŭro" [The transition and consolidation of Korean democracy, 1979–1994: With a focus on the relationship and dynamics among the state, political society, and civil society]. PhD diss., Kongguk University, 1996.

Mun Sojŏng. "Iljeha Han'guk nongch'on kajok e kwanhan yŏn'gu" [Study of rural family under colonial rule]. In *Iljeha Han'guk ŭi sahoe kyegŭp kwa sahoe pyŏndong* [Social class and social changes in Korea under Japanese colonial rule], edited by Han'guk Sahoe Yŏn'guhoe [Study Group for Korean Society]. Seoul: Munhak kwa Chisŏng, 1988.

Mun Sŏngnam. "Chiyŏk sahoe ŭi yŏn'gojuŭi" [A study of regional cronyism]. In *Haksul palp'yo nonmunjip* [Collection of research papers], no. 1. Chŏnju: Institute of Social Sciences, Chonnam National University, 1998.

Muncy, Lysbeth Walker. *The Junker in the Prussian Administration under William II, 1888–1914.* Providence, RI: Brown University Press, 1944.

Murakami Yasusuke. "Ie Society as a Pattern of Civilization." *Journal of Japanese Studies* 10, no. 2 (1984): 279–363.

———. "Ie Society as a Pattern of Civilization: Response to Criticism." *Journal of Japanese Studies* 11, no. 2 (Summer 1985): 401-21.
Na Chungsik. "Han'guk chungang chaejŏng kigu pyŏnch'ŏn ŭi yŏksajŏk punsŏk: Pak Chŏnghŭi, Kim Yŏngsam, Kim Taejung chŏngbu ŭi chaemu haengjŏng chojik kaep'yŏn e kwanhan sarye pusŏk ŭl chungsim ŭro" [A historical analysis of changes in the finance organizations of Korean government: The cases of the reorganizations of the finance organizations under Park Chung Hee, Kim Young Sam, and Kim Dae Jung administrations]. *Han'guk haengjŏng nonjip* [Korean public administration research] 11, no. 3 (1999).
Nakamura, Robert, and Frank Smallwood. *The Politics of Policy Implementation.* New York: St. Martin's Press, 1980.
Nam Ch'unho. "Inongmin ŭi chigŏp idong ŭl t'onghaesŏ pon Han'guk sahoe ŭi kyegŭp kucho ŭi pyŏnhwa" [Changes in Korean social structure based on occupational mobility of rural emigrants]. *Sahoe wa yŏksa* [Society and history] 14 (1988): 84-119.
Nam Ŭnyŏng. "Oehwan wigi ihu sahoejŏk wihŏm kwa chugwanjŏk kyech'ŭng isik" [Social risks and subjective consciousness of social strata after the financial crisis]. *Han'guk Sahoehakhoe nonmumjip* [Collection of papers of the Korean Sociological Association] 20, no. 12 (2012): 67-80.
Nettl, J. P. "The State as a Conceptual Variable." *World Politics* 20, no. 4 (July 1968): 559-92.
Nettl, J. P., and Roland Robertson. *International Systems and the Modernization of Societies: The Formation of National Goals and Attitudes.* New York: Basic Books, 1968.
No Chŏnghyŏn. "Han'guk kwallyo ellit'ŭ ŭi kach'i ch'egye wa sŏngbun e kwanhan chosa yŏn'gu" [An analysis of the value system and backgrounds of Korean bureaucratic elites]. *Yŏnsedae haengjŏng nonch'ong* [Yonsei journal of public administration] 6, (1980): 5-53.
Nodongch'ŏng [Office of Labor Affairs]. *Han'guk nodong t'onggye yŏn'gam* Yearbook of labor statistics of South Korea]. Seoul: Sŏul Nodongch'ŏng, 1977.
Nomura Chōtaro. "Chōsen kazoku seido no suii" [Trends in Korean family system]. *Chōsen* 296 (January 1940): 17-37.
Nordlinger, Eric A. *On the Autonomy of the Democratic State.* Cambridge, MA: Harvard University Press, 1981.
———. "The Return to the State: Critiques." *American Political Science Review* 82, no. 3 (September 1988): 875-901.
O Chŏng. "Chōsen no shinzoku kankei" [Family relation in Korea]. *Chōsen* (December 1927): 77-105.

O Wŏnch'ŏl. *Chunghwahak kongŏphwa wa 8onyŏndae ŭi miraesang: uri nara ŭi paljŏn yuhyŏng ŭl chungsim ŭro* [Heavy chemical industrialization and the future blueprint of the 1980s: With a focus on the developmental pattern of South Korea]. Seoul: Chunghwa Kongŏphwa Ch'ujin Wiwŏnhoe, Kihoektan [Planning Corps, the Planning Committee for Heavy and Chemical Industrialization], 1973.

——. *Han'gukhyŏng kyŏngje kŏnsŏl: enjiniŏring ŏproh'i* [Korean-style economic development: An engineering approach]. 5 vols. Seoul: Kia Economic Institute, 1995-96.

——. *Han'gukhyŏng kyŏngje kŏnsŏl* [Korean-style economic development]. Vol. 6, *Enŏji chŏngch'aek kwa chungdong chinch'ul* [Energy policy and advance to Middle East]. Seoul: Kia Economic Institute, 1997.

——. *Han'gukhyŏng kyŏngje kŏnsŏl* [Korean-style economic development]. Vol. 7, *Naega chŏnjaeng ŭl hajanŭn kŏt to aniji annŭnya* [I am not even proposing to launch a war]. Seoul: Institute of Korean Style Economic Development, 1999.

——. "Sanŏp chŏnllyak kundan sa" [A history of industrial corps]. *Han'guk Kyŏngje Sinmun* [*Korea Economic Daily*], September 17, 1992; September 24, 1992; September 30, 1992; March 18, 1993; October 25, 1993; July 1992-April 1994.

O'Donnell, Guillermo A. *Modernization and Bureaucratic-Authoritarianism: Studies in South American Politics*. Berkeley: Institute of International Studies, University of California, 1973.

Oh, Jennifer S. "Strong State and Strong Civil Society in Contemporary South Korea: Challenges to Democratic Governance." *Asian Survey* 52, no. 3 (May/June 2012): 528-49.

Oh, Kap-Hwan, and Hae-Young Lee. "Urbanism in Korea: A New Way of Life?" In *Korea: A Decade of Development*, edited by Yunshik Chang. Seoul: Seoul National University Press, 1980.

Ok Sŏnhwa. "Hyŏndae Han'gugin ŭi kajokchuŭi kach'igwan e taehan yŏn'gu" [A study of Korean perceptions of familism]. Master's thesis, Seoul National University, 1989.

Okimoto, Daniel I. *Between MITI and the Market: Japanese Industrial Policy for High Technology*. Stanford, CA: Stanford University Press, 1989.

Olson, Mancur. *The Rise and Decline of Nations: Economic Growth, Stagflation, and Social Rigidities*. New Haven, CT: Yale University Press, 1982.

Öniş, Ziya. "The Logic of the Developmental State." *Comparative Politics* 24, no. 1 (October 1991): 109-26.

Pae Pyŏnghyu. "Kiŏpkye ŭi chagŭm kyŏngjaeng" [Fight over capital in Korean business world]. *Sindonga [New Donga]*, June 1979.

———. "Taeu kŭrup ŭn kŏnjae han'ga?" [Is Daewoo Group safe?]. *Sindonga* [New Donga], March 1981.
Pae Sŭngjun. "Chosŏn kongŏphwa esŏ singminji kongŏp ŭro: singminji sigi kongŏp yŏn'gu ŭi hŭrŭm kwa kwaje" [From Chosŏn industrialization to colonial industry: A critical review in the study of the industry in the colonial period]. *Yŏksa yŏn'gu* 35, no. 12 (2018): 359–87.
Pae Tongin. "Simin sahoe ŭi kaenyŏm: sasangsajŏk chŏpkŭn" [Concept of civil society: A political thought approach]. In *Han'guk ŭi kukka wa simin sahoe* [Korean state and civil society], edited by Korean Association of Political Science and Korean Association of Sociology. Seoul: Hanul, 1992.
Paek China. "Kyŏngje wigi e ttarŭn kajok saenghwal ŭi pyŏnhwa wa kajokchuŭi" [Changes in family life and familism under the economic crisis]. *Sahoe paljŏn yŏn'gu* [Journal of social development studies], no. 7 (2001): 27–50.
Paek Wangi. "Han'guk ŭi haengjŏng munhwa: ŭisikjuŭi rŭl chungsim ŭro" [The Korean administration culture: From the perspective of formalism]. *Han'guk haengjŏng hakpo* [Korean public administration review] 12 (1978): 112–27.
Pak Changwang. "Taet'ongnyŏng ŭi ridŏsip i ch'ejesŏng wa e mich'in yŏnghyang e kwanhan yŏn'gu: che 3, 4, 5, Konghwaguk ŭl chungsim ŭro" [The analysis of the impact of the president's leadership on the outcome of the system: The cases of the Fourth, Fifth, and Sixth Republics]. PhD diss., Konkuk University, 1993.
Pak Chongch'ŏl. "Han'guk kwa Taeman ŭi such'ul sanŏphwa chŏngch'aek kwa kukka ŭi yŏkhal" [Export promotion policies in South Korea and Taiwan and the role of the state]. *Han'guk kwa kukje chŏngchi* [Korea and world politics] 4, no. 2 (1988): 163–95.
———. "Suip taech'e wŏnjo ŭi chŏngch'i kwajŏng" [Import substitution aids and political process]. In *Hyŏndae Han'guk chŏngch'iron* [Modern Korean politics], edited by Han Paeho. Seoul: Nanam, 1990.
Pak Chŏnghŭi. *Charip e ŭi ŭiji: Pak Chŏnghŭi Taet'ongnyŏng ŏrok* [Will to be independent: Collections of speeches by President Park Chung Hee]. Edited by Sim Yungt'aek. Seoul: Hollym, 1972.
———. *Choguk ŭi kŭndaehwa* [Modernization of fatherland]. Seoul: Tong A Ch'ulp'ansa, 1965.
———. *Chungdan hanŭn cha nŭn sŭngnihaji mothanda* [He who stops does not win]. Edited by Sin Pŏmsik. Seoul: Hollym, 1968.
———. [Park Chung Hee] *The Country, the Revolution and I*. 2nd ed. Seoul: Hollym, 1970. English translation of *Kukka wa hyŏngmyŏng kwa na*.
———. *Kukka wa hyŏngmyŏng kwa na*. Seoul: Chiguch'on, 1963.
———. *Minjok ŭi chŏryŏk* [The nation's potential]. Seoul: Kwangmyŏng Ch'ulp'ansa, 1971.

―――. *Pak Chŏnghŭi sŏnjip* [Selected writings of Park Chung Hee]. Vol. 1, *Kilŭl ch'ajasŏ* [In search for the road]; vol. 2, *Na ŭi sarang, na ŭi choguk* [My love, my fatherland]; vol. 3, *Unmyŏngŭl nŏmŏ* [Beyond our fate]; vol. 5, *Urinŭn chŏnjinhago itta* [We are marching forward]. Edited by Sin Pŏmsik. Seoul: Chimungak, 1968-69.

―――. *Pak Chŏnghŭi Taet'ongnyŏng yŏnsŏl munjip* [Collection of President Park Chung Hee's speeches]. Vol. 3. Seoul: Chimungak, 1969.

―――. *Uri minjok ŭi nagal kil* [Our nation's path]. Seoul: Tong A Publishing Co., 1962.

Pak Chŏno. "Han'guk esŏ ŭi ch'ŏngch'ijŏk p'i-immyŏngja wa kowijik ŏkwallyo ŭi chŏngch'aek sŏnghyang kwa sangho kwan'gye" [Differences in policy orientations and the relationship between political appointees and career bureaucrats in South Korea]. *Han'guk haengjŏng hakpo* [Korean public administration-review] 27, no. 4 (1993): 1121-238.

―――. "Han'guk haengjŏng munhwa yŏn'gu ŭi panghyang kwa kwaje" [Directions and issues in the study of Korean administrative culture]. *Han'guk haengjŏng hakpo* 26, no. 1 (1992): 19-38.

Pak Chŏno and Pak Kyŏnghyo. *Han'guk kwallyoje ŭi ihae* [Understanding of Korean bureaucracy]. Seoul: Pommunsa, 2001.

Pak Ch'unghun. *Idang hoegorok* [Memoir of Idang]. Seoul: Pakyŏngsa, 1988.

Pak Hŭi. "Han'guk taegiŏp ŭi chojik kwalli wa nosa kwan'gye e kwanhan yŏn'gu: kajokjuŭi ŭi yŏnghyang ŭl chungsim uro" [A study of organization management in Korean chaebols and labor relations: With focus on impacts on familism (in Korean)]. PhD diss., Yonsei University, 1993.

Pak Hyŏngjun. "Simin sahoe iron ŭi chaegusŏng kwa pip'anjŏk chaegusŏng" [Restoration of civil society theories and its critical reformulation]. In *Siminsahoe iron kwa minjujuŭi* [Theories of civil society and democracy]. Seoul: Ŭiam, 1992.

Pak Kwangju. "Kukkaron ŭl t'onghan Han'guk chongch'i ŭi parŏdaiim mosaek: ch'oegŭn ŭi yŏn'gu tonghyang kwa kŭ pansŏng" [Search for a paradigm for Korean Politics through state theories: The current research trends and reflection]. *Hyŏnsang kwa insik* [Phenomenon and epistemology] 9, no. 2 (1985): 30-78.

Pak Kyŏngsik, ed. *Chosŏn munje charyo ch'ongsŏ* [Collection of colonial document series]. Vol. 8. Tokyo: Asia Mondai Kenkyūsho, 1983.

―――. *Ilbon chegukchuŭi ŭi Han'guk chibae* [Japanese imperial domination of Korea]. Seoul: Ch'ŏnga Ch'ulp'ansa, 1986.

Pak Myŏnggyu. "Han'guk ŭi simin sahoe wa minjokchuŭi" [Korean civil society and nationalism]. *Ch'ŏrhak kwa hyŏnsil* [Philosophy and reality], no. 6 (1998): 70-84.

Pak Myŏngsu. "Han'guk kwallyoje ŭi kaehyŏk: t'algwallyohwa rŭl wihan siron" [Administrative reform and democratization of bureaucracy]. *Kukka Chŏngch'aek yŏn'gu* [Chung-Ang public administrative review] 12 (1998): 125-38.

Pak Pyŏngyŏng. "Han'guk chŏngbu-kiŏp kwangye ui tayangsŏng kwa kŭ kyŏljŏng yoin: 1980nyŏndae sŏmyu, chadongch'a, pandoch'e sanŏp ŭl chungsim ŭro" [Diverse state-business relations and its determinants: The cases of textile, auto, and semi-conductor industries in the 1980s]. PhD diss., Yŏnsei University, 1999.

Pak Pyŏngyun. *Chaebŏl kwa chŏngch'i: Han'guk chaebŏl sŏngjangsa* [Chaebols and politics: The story behind development of chaebols in Korea]. Seoul: Han'guk Yangsŏ, 1982.

———. "Chunghwahak kongŏpkye ŭi naemak" [Untold stories of heavy chemical industries]. *Sindonga*, May 1980.

Pak T'aegyun. "1960nyŏndae chungban anbo wigi wa che 2 kyŏngjeron" [The security crisis of the mid-1960s and the second economy treatise]. *Yŏksa wa pip'yŏng* 8 (2005): 250-76.

Pak Tongsŏ. *Han'guk haengjŏng ŭi paljŏn* [The development of Korean public administration]. Seoul: Pŏmmunsa, 1980.

———. *Han'guk haengjŏng ŭi yŏn'gu* [A study of Korean public administration]. Seoul: Bommunsa, 1994.

———. *Han'guk kwallyo chedo ŭi yŏksajŏk chŏngae* [The historical development of Korean bureaucracy]. Seoul: Han'guk Yŏn'gu Tosŏgwan, 1961.

Pak Tongsŏ and Yi Kŭn Ju. *Han'guk haengjŏng munhwa ŭi sun-ginŭngsŏng* [The functionality of Korean public administrative culture]. Seoul: Han'guk Haengjŏng Yŏn'guwŏn, 2000.

Pak Ŭngyŏng. "Chosŏn chongdokpu kwallyo ŭi hyŏngsŏng kwa kyegisŏng" [The formation and development of Chosun Governor's General]. *Haengjŏngsa yŏn'gu* [Journal of administrative history] 3 (1996): 165-83.

———. *Iljeha chosŏnin kwallyo yŏn'gu* [Study of Korean bureaucrats under Japanese colonial rule]. Seoul: Hangminsa, 1999.

Pak Wŏnbae. "Chaegye pihwa: sin-gunbu ŭi 1980nyŏn chunghwahak t'uja chojŏng—Kim Ujung moryak ch'in Chŏng Chuyong ŭi norimsu" [Secret stories in the business: The investment adjustment of the new military group in 1980—Chung Joo Yong's hidden tactics against Kim Woo Joong]. *Opsŏbŏ* [Observer], December 1991, 458-71.

Pak Yŏngsin. *Yŏksa wa sahoe pyŏndong* [History and social change]. Seoul: Minyŏngsa/Han'guk Sahoehak Yŏn'guso, 1987.

Pak Yunu. "6 konghwaguk ŭi tae chaebŏl tŭkhye ŏpchong chŏnmunhwa: sinario nya chwajŏldoen kaehyŏk inya" [The industry specialization policies of big chaebols under the Sixth Republic: Scenarios or the aborted reforms]. *Opsŏbŏ* [Observer], May 1991, 214-41.

——. "Taep'yojŏk pusil kiŏp hŭkcha chŏnhwan ŭi imyŏn" [The hidden stories of turn to surplus of major non-performing companies]. *Opsŏbŏ* [Observer], December 1991, 488-525.

Pakulski, Jan. "Bureaucracy and the Soviet System." *Studies in Comparative Communism* 19, no. 1 (Spring 1986): 3-24.

——. "Legitimacy and Mass Compliance: Reflections on Max Weber and Soviet-Type Societies." *British Journal of Political Science* 16, no. 1 (January 1986): 35-56.

Pakulski, Jan, and Malcolm Waters. "The Reshaping and Dissolution of Social Class in Advanced Society." *Theory and Society* 25, no. 5 (October 1996): 667-91.

Park, Chung Hee. See Pak Chŏnghŭi.

Park, Soon-Won. "Colonial Industrial Growth and the Emergence of the Korean Working Class." In *Colonial Modernity in Korea*, edited by Gi-Wook Shin and Michael Robinson. Cambridge, MA: Harvard University Asia Center, 1999.

Pekkanen, Robert. *Japan's Dual Civil Society: Members without Advocates*. Stanford, CA: Stanford University Press, 2006.

Pekkanen, Saadia M. *Picking Winners? From Technology Catch-up to the Space Race in Japan*. Stanford, CA: Stanford University Press, 2003.

Pelikan, Jaroslav. *The Vindication of Tradition*. New Haven, CT: Yale University Press, 1984.

Peterson, Steven A. "Privatism and Politics: A Research Note." *Western Political Quarterly* 37, no. 3 (September 1984): 483-89.

Pierson, Paul. *Politics in Time: History, Institutions, and Social Analysis*. Princeton, NJ: Princeton University Press, 2004.

Polanyi, Karl. *The Great Transformation: The Political and Economic Origins of Our Time*. 2nd ed. Boston: Beacon Press, 2001.

Poulantzas, Nicos. "The Problem of the Capitalist State." *New Left Review* 58, no. 6 (1969): 67-78.

Pressman, Jeffrey L., and Aaron Wildavsky. *Implementation*. 3rd ed. Berkeley: University of California Press, 1984.

Price, Richard. *British Society, 1680-1880: Dynamism, Containment and Change*. Cambridge: Cambridge University Press, 1999.

Putnam, Robert D. *Making Democracy Work: Civic Traditions in Modern Italy*. Princeton, NJ: Princeton University Press, 1993.

Qi, Xiaoying. "*Guanxi*, Social Capital Theory and Beyond: Toward a Globalized Social Science." *British Journal of Sociology* 64, no. 2 (2013): 308-24.

Renshon, Jonathan. *Fighting for Status: Hierarchy and Conflict in World Politics.* Princeton, NJ: Princeton University Press, 2017.

Rhee, Yung Whee, Bruce Ross-Larson, and Garry Pursell. *Korea's Competitive Edge: Managing the Entry into World Markets.* Baltimore: Johns Hopkins University Press for the World Bank, 1984.

Rhodes, R. A. W. "The Hollowing Out of the State: The Changing Nature of the Public Service in Britain." *Political Quarterly* 65, no. 2 (April 1994): 138–51.

Robinson, Michael. "Broadcasting, Cultural Hegemony, and Colonial Modernity in Korea, 1924–1945." In *Colonial Modernity in Korea,* edited by Gi-Wook Shin and Michael Robinson. Cambridge, MA: Harvard University Asia Center, 1999.

Roniger, Luis. "Civil Society, Patronage, and Democracy." In *Real Civil Societies: Dilemmas of Institutionalization,* edited by Jeffrey C. Alexander. London: Sage Publications, 1998.

Rosefielde, Steven. "Stalinism in Post-Communist Perspective: New Evidence on Killings, Forced Labour and Economic Growth in the 1930s." *Europe-Asia Studies* 48, no. 6 (September 1996): 959–87.

Rostow, Walt W. *The Stages of Economic Growth.* New York: Cambridge University Press, 1960.

Ryan, Tracii, Kelly A. Allen, DeLeon L. Gray, and Dennis M. McInerney. "How Social Are Social Media? A Review of Online Social Behaviour and Connectedness." *Journal of Relationships Research* 8 (2017): 1–8.

Saada, Emmanuelle. "Transatlantic Perspectives on the *Colonial Situation.*" In "Regards croisés: Transatlantic Perspectives on the Colonial Situation," special issue, *French Politics, Culture & Society* 20, no. 2 (Summer 2002): 1–3.

Sagong Yŏngho. "Kabujangjŏk haengjŏng munhwa wa kyuje kwallyo ŭi p'ohoek e kwanhan yŏn'gu" [Paternalistic administrative culture and the capture of regulatory bureaucrats]. PhD diss., Seoul National University, 1998.

———. "Kabujangjŏk haengjŏng munhwa sok esŏ ŭi kyuje kigwan mit kwallyo ŭi p'ohoek hyŏnsang" [The phenomenon of regulatory bureaucrats' capture in paternalistic administrative culture]. *Han'guk haengjŏng hakpo* [Korean public administration review] 32, no. 2 (1998): 113–29.

Samuels, Richard J. *The Business of the Japanese State: Energy Markets in Comparative and Historical Perspective.* Ithaca, NY: Cornell University Press, 1987.

———. "The Industrial Destructuring of the Japanese Aluminum Industry." *Pacific Affairs* 56, no. 3 (Autumn 1983): 495–509.

Sanggongbu [Ministry of Commerce and Industry]. *Muyŏk chinhŭng 40yŏn: kŭ kwajŏng kwa chŏngch'aek* [Forty years of export promotion: The process and policies]. Seoul: MCI, 1988.

———. *Sanggong Chŏngch'aek Simnyŏnsa* [Ten-year history of Ministry of Commerce and Industry]. Seoul: MCI, 1969.
———. *T'oejikcha insa charyo* [Personnel dossiers for retirees]. Seoul: MCI, 1948-1979.
Savage, Mike, and Andrew Miles. *The Remaking of the British Working Class, 1840-1940*. New York: Routledge, 1994.
Schlesinger, Arthur, Jr. "On the Inscrutability of History." *Encounter* 27 (November 1966): 10-17.
Schneider, Ben Ross. "The Career Connection: A Comparative Analysis of Bureaucratic Preferences and Insulation." *Comparative Politics* 25, no. 3 (April 1993): 331-50.
Schumpeter, Joseph A. *Imperialism and Social Classes*. New York: Augustus M. Kelley, 1951.
Schwartz, Frank J., and Susan J. Pharr, eds. *The State of Civil Society in Japan*. Cambridge: Cambridge University Press, 2003.
Scott, David. "Colonialism." *International Social Science Journal* 49, no. 154 (December 1997): 517-26.
Scott, James C. *Weapons of the Weak: Everyday Forms of Peasant Resistance*. New Haven, CT: Yale University Press, 1985.
Scott, Susie. "Revisiting the Total Institution: Performative Regulation in the Reinventive Institution." *Sociology* 44, no. 2 (April 2010): 213-31.
Seah, Chee Meow. *Asian Values and Modernization*. Singapore: Singapore University Press, 1977.
Seligman, Adam B. *The Idea of Civil Society*. New York: Free Press, 1992.
Selznick, Philip. *Leadership in Administration: A Sociological Interpretation*. 1957; Berkeley: University of California Press, 1984.
Sen, Yow-Suen, and Hagen Koo. "Industrial Transformation and Proletarianization in Taiwan." *Critical Sociology* 19, no. 1 (1992): 45-67.
Sewell, William H., Jr. *Work and Revolution in France: The Language of Labor from the Old Regime to 1848*. Cambridge: Cambridge University Press, 1980.
Shankman, Paul. "Phases of Dependency in Western Samoa." *Practicing Anthropology* 12, no. 1 (1990): 12-13.
Sharma, Shalendra D. *The Asian Financial Crisis: Crisis, Reform and Recovery*. Manchester, UK: Manchester University Press, 2003.
Shils, Edward. "Tradition." *Comparative Studies in Society and History* 13, no. 2 (April 1971): 122-59.
———. *Tradition*. Chicago: University of Chicago Press, 1981.
———. "The Virtue of Civil Society." *Government and Opposition* 26, no. 1 (1991): 3-20. The text for a *Government and Opposition* lecture delivered at the Athenaeum Club on January 22, 1991.

Shin, Doh C. *Mass Politics and Culture in Democratizing Korea*. Cambridge: Cambridge University Press, 1999.

Shin, Eui Hang, and Seung Kwon Chin. "Social Affinity among Top Managerial Executives of Large Corporations in Korea." *Sociological Forum* 4, no. 1 (March 1989): 3-26.

Shin, Gi-Wook, and Michael Robinson, eds. *Colonial Modernity in Korea*. Cambridge: Harvard University Asia Center, 1999.

Shin, Jang-Sup, and Ha-Joon Chang. *Restructuring Korea Inc.: Financial Crisis, Corporate Reform, and Institutional Transition*. London: Taylor & Francis Group, 2003.

Silberman, Bernard S. *Cages of Reason: The Rise of the Rational State in France, Japan, the United States, and Great Britain*. Chicago: University of Chicago Press, 1993.

Sin Changsŏp and Chang Hajun. "Han'guk kŭmyung wigi ihu kiŏp kujo chojŏng e kwanhan pip'anjeok p'yŏngga" [A critical evaluation of business restructuring in South Korea since the financial crisis]. *Han'guk kyŏngje ŭi punsŏk* [Analysis of Korean economy] 9, no. 3 (2003): 255-304.

Sin Giuk. "Singminji chosŏn yŏn'gu tonghyang" [Trends in the studies of the colonial Korea]. *Han'guksa simin kangjwa* [Citizens' forum on Korean history] 20, no. 2 (1997): 43-57.

Sin Hangsu. "Pak Chŏnghŭi chŏnggwŏn ki chŏnt'ong sasang e taehan insik p'yŏnhwa wa kungmin yulli kyŏyuk" [Changes in the perceptions of traditional thoughts during the Park Chung Hee regime and national ethics education]. *Sach'ong* 102 (2021): 81-118.

Sin Higwŏn. "Chŏngbu wa chaebŏl kan ŭi chŏllyakchŏk sangho chagyong e kwanhan yŏn'gu: chaebŏl kyuje rŭl chungsim ŭro" [A study of strategic interactions between the state and chaebols: The case of the deregulation of chaebols]. PhD diss., Seoul National University, 1994.

Sin Hyŏnmin. "Samsŏng sŭngyongch'a: Ch'ŏngwadae kŏneksyŏn silch'e" [Samsŏng car: Connection with the Blue House]. *Sindonga*, November 1993.

Sin Kwangsik. *Chaebŏl kaehyok ŭi chŏngch'aek kwaje wa panghyang* [Policy issues and direction for chaebol reforms]. Seoul: Korea Institute for Development, 2000.

Sin Kwangyŏng. *Kyegŭp kwa nodong undong ŭi sahaehak* [Class and sociology of labor movement]. Seoul: Nanam, 1994.

———. "Simin sahoe kaenyŏm kwa simin sahoe hyŏngsŏng" [The concept of civil society and the formation of civil society]. In *Simin sahoe wa siminundong 2* [Civil society and civic movements, vol. 2], edited by Yu P'almu and Kim Jeonghoon. Seoul: Hanul, 2001.

Sin Yongha. *Chosŏn toji chosa saŏp yŏn'gu* [A study of the Cadastral survey in Kore]. Seoul: Chisik Sanŏpsa, 1982.

———. *Han'guk kŭndae sahoesa yŏn'gu* [A study of social history of modern Korea]. Seoul: Ilchisa, 1987.

———. *Ilche singminji kŭndaehwanon pip'an* [A critique of the colonial modernity]. Seoul: Munhak kwa Chisŏngsa, 1998.

———. "Singminji kŭndaehwaron chaejŏngnip e taehan pip'an" [A critique of the reformulation of colonial modernity]. *Ch'angjak kwa pip'yŏng* [Creation and critique] 25, no. 4 (Winter 1997): 8-38.

Sindonga [New Donga]. "Kwŏndu Chwadam: Mainŏsŭ sŏngjang: Han'guk kyŏngje ŭi chindan" [Opening discussion: Diagnosis of South Korea's negative growth economy]. July 1980.

Sindonga P'yŏnjipbu [Editors of *Sindonga*]. "8.3 kingŭp choch'i ŭi paegyŏng kwa p'amun" [The background and impact of the August 3 emergency measures]. *Sindonga*, September 1972.

Singer, J. David, and Melvin Small. "The Composition and Status Ordering of the International System: 1815-1940." *World Politics* 18, no. 2 (1966): 236-82.

Skocpol, Theda. "Bringing the State Back In: Strategies of Analysis and Current Research." In *Bringing the State Back In*, edited by Peter B. Evans, Dietrich Rueschemeyer, and Theda Skocpol. New York: Cambridge University Press, 1985.

———. "A Critical Review of Barrington Moore's Social Origins of Dictatorship and Democracy." *Politics and Society* 4, no. 1 (1973): 1-34.

———. *States and Social Revolutions: A Comparative Analysis of France, Russia, and China*. Cambridge: Cambridge University Press, 1979.

Skocpol, Theda, and Morris P. Fiorina, eds. *Civic Engagement in American Democracy*. Washington, DC: Brookings Institution Press, 1999.

Sky Daily. "Taegiŏp punsŏk, maenyŏn chasan kŭpp'aengch'ang chisokhae 10nyŏnjŏn taebi 896cho chŭngga" [An analysis of chaebols: A rapid annual increase of 896 trillion won in property since 10 years ago]. February 14, 2012.

Smelser, Neil J., and Richard Swedberg. "The Sociological Perspective on the Economy." In *The Handbook of Economic Sociology*, edited by Neil J. Smelser and Richard Swedberg. Princeton, NJ: Princeton University Press, 1994.

Smith, Adam. *Moral and Political Philosophy*. Edited by Herbert W. Schneider. New York: Hafner, 1948.

Smith, Jeremy. "Japan's Modernity and New Critiques of the Sociology of Modernization." *Thesis Eleven* 51, no. 1 (November 1997): 91-105.

Smith, Robert J. *Japanese Society: Tradition, Self and the Social Order*. New York: Cambridge University Press, 1983.

Sŏ Chaejin. *Han'guk ŭi chabonga kyegŭp* [Capitalist class in Korea]. Seoul: Nanam, 1991.
Sŏ Chŏngil, Yi Kyŏnghwan, and Yun Sungnam. "Sin'gyu isa immyŏng e taehan yŏn'gu: saoe isa chedo toip e taehan ch'oego kyŏngyŏngja ŭi tikŏpŭlling haengwi rŭl chungsim ŭro" [A study of the appointments of outside directors: Introduction of outside directors and decoupling of CEOs]. *Chojik kwa insa kwalli yŏn'gu* [Organization and personnel management studies] 2, no. 2 (2015): 103-29.
Son Chongho. "Han'guk kogŭp kongmuwŏn ŭi ch'ulsin paegyŏng mit kach'i ŭisik e kwanhan yŏn'gu" [Personal backgrounds of high-ranking bureaucrats and their value consciousness in South Korea]. *Kyŏnggi taehak nonmunjip* [Collections of research papers, Kyŏnggi University] 20 (1987): 157-92.
Sŏn Haktae. "Han'guk ŭi chunggongŏp chŏngch'aek kwajŏng e nat'anan kukka chayulsŏng" [State autonomy in Korea's decision-making on the heavy chemical industry]. PhD diss., Seoul National University, 1991.
Son Hoch'ŏl. "Kukka-simin sahoeron: Han'guk chŏngch'i ŭi sae taean in'ga?" [Is state-civil society concept a new alternative to the understanding of Korean politics?]. In *Simin sahoe wa siminundong 2* [Civil society and civic movements, vol. 2], edited by Yu P'almu and Kim Jeonghoon. Seoul: Hanul, 2001.
Son Hyŏk and Chŏng Chaegyŏng. "Saoe isa nŭn ch'oego kyŏngyŏnggja ŭi kamsija inga ttonŭn chijija inga? Saoe isa wa ch'oego kyŏngyŏngja ŭi sahoejŏk kwan'gye ka kwaing t'ujae mich'inŭn yŏnghyang" [Are outside directors overseers or supporters for CEOs? An analysis of the impact of social connections between outside directors and CEOs on overinvestment]. *Hoegyehak yŏn'gu* [Korean accounting review] 40, no. 5 (2015): 327-66.
Son Kwangsik, ed. *Han'guk ŭi kyŏngje kwallyo* [Economic bureaucrats in Korea]. Seoul: Tarakwŏn, 1979.
Song, Byung-Nak. *The Rise of the Korean Economy*. New York: Oxford University Press, 2003.
Sŏng Hogŭn. "Kongnonjang ŭi yŏksajŏk hyŏngsŏng kwajong: wae uri inga?" [Historical formation of public sphere: Why are we the problem?]. *Han'guk ŏnllonhakhoe symposium mit semina* [Symposium and seminar, Korean Association of Communication Studies] (May 2011): 27-48.
———. "Sinsahoe undong ch'amyŏja punsŏk: nuga, wae, ŏttŏk'e ch'amyŏhanŭnga?" [The analysis of participants in the new social movements in Korea: Who participates, how, and why?]. *Han'guk sahoe kwahak* 20, no. 3 (1998): 45-74.
———. *Yŏllin sijang, tach'in chŏngch'i* [Open market, closed politics]. Seoul: Nanam, 1994.
Song Hyegyŏng. "Che 1 Konghwaguk insa haengjŏng e kwanhan yŏn'gu: kogŭp kwallyo ŭi sahoejŏk paegyŏng mit ch'ungwŏn ŭl chungsim ŭro" [A study of the

personnel administration of the First Republic: Social backgrounds of the high-ranking bureaucrats and their recruitment]. PhD diss., Yŏnsei University, 1998.

Song Hyorim. *Kakkaisŏ pon Pak Chŏnghŭi Taet'ongnyŏng* [President Park Chung Hee from a close distance]. Seoul: Hwimun Ch'ulpansa, 1977.

Song Kich'ŏl. "Han'guk taegiŏp ŭi kyŏngyŏngja e kwanhan yŏn'gu: tŭk'i kŭ ŭi sŭnggye rŭl chungsim ŭro" [A study of managers of Korean large business groups: Cases of successions]. *Kyŏngyŏng nonch'ong* (Koryŏ Taehakkyo Kyŏngyŏng Taehak [The Business School of Korea University]) 34 (1991): 1-41.

Song Puyong. "IMF ch'ejeha ŭi sirŏp taech'aek: chiyŏk kyŏngje hwalsŏnghwa rŭl wihan hyŏnhwang punsŏk mit taean" [Unemployment measures under the financial crisis: The analysis of the current situation and policies to improve regional economy]. Kyŏngnam Yŏn'guwŏn, *Chŏngch'aek pokŏsŭ chŏngch'aek chamun* [Policy focus, policy advice], no. 7 (1998): 1-31.

Sorensen, Clark W. *Over the Mountains Are Mountains: Korean Peasant Households and Their Adaptations to Rapid Industrialization.* Seattle: University of Washington Press, 1988.

Sŏul Sanggong Hoeŭiso [Seoul Chamber of Commerce]. *Han'guk kyŏngje 20 nyŏnŭi hoego wa chŏnmang* [Reflection of the 20 years of Korean economy]. Seoul: Chamber of Commerce, 1982.

Sŏul Taehakkyo Haengjŏng Taehagwŏn [Graduate School of Public Administration, Seoul National University]. *Chŏngch'aek chiphaeng sarye (II)* [The collection of policy implementation cases, vol. 2]. Seoul: Seoul Taehakkyo Haengjŏng Taehagwŏn [Graduate School of Public Administration, Seoul National University], 1983.

Sŏul Taehakkyo Haengjŏng Taehagwŏn Chosa Yŏn'gusil [Research Office, Graduate School of Public Administration, Seoul National University]. *Ch'oego kwalli* [Top management]. Seoul: Research Office, Graduate School of Public Administration, Seoul National University, 1965.

Sŏul Taehakkyo sahoehak yŏnguhoe [Sociology study group of Seoul National University]. *Sahoe kyech'ŭngnon* [Social stratification]. Seoul: Tasan, 1991.

Spencer, Robert F. *Yŏgong: Factory Girl.* Seoul: Royal Asiatic Society, Korea Branch, 1988.

Stalin, Joseph. *Problems of Leninism.* Moscow: Foreign Languages Publishing House, 1945.

Steinberg, David I. "Civil Society and Human Rights in Korea: On Contemporary and Classical Orthodoxy and Ideology." *Korea Journal* 37, no. 3 (Autumn 1997): 144-65.

Steinmetz, George. "The Myth and the Reality of an Autonomous State: Industrialists, Junkers, and Social Policy in Imperial Germany." *Comparative Social Research* 12 (December 1990): 239-93.
Steinmo, Sven. "Institutionalism." In *International Encyclopedia of the Social and Behavioral Sciences*, 2nd ed., edited by James D. Wright. Amsterdam: Elsevier Science, 2015.
Stepan, Alfred. *The State and Society: Peru in Comparative Perspective*. Princeton, NJ: Princeton University Press, 1978.
Stern, Joseph H., Ji-hong Kim, Dwight H. Perkins, and Jung-ho Yoo. *Industrialization and the State: The Korean Heavy and Chemical Industry Drive*. Cambridge, MA: Harvard Institute for International Development, 1995.
Stinchcombe, Arthur L. "Social Structure and Organizations." In *Handbook of Organizations*, edited by James G. March. Chicago: Rand McNally, 1965.
Streeck, Wolfgang. "Taking Capitalism Seriously: Towards an Institutionalist Approach to Contemporary Political Economy." *Socio-Economic Review* 9, no. 1 (2011): 137-67.
Streeck, Wolfgang, and Kozo Yamamura, eds. *The Origins of Nonliberal Capitalism: Germany and Japan in Comparison*. Ithaca, NY: Cornell University Press, 2001.
Suleiman, Ezra N. "State Structures and Clientelism: The French State versus the 'Notaires.'" *British Journal of Political Science* 17, no. 3 (July 1987): 257-79.
Sun, Liping. "Societal Transition: New Issues in the Field of the Sociology of Development." *Modern China* 34, no. 1 (January 2008): 88-113.
Suzuki Eitarō. "Chōsen no nōson shakai shūdan nit tsuite" [On rural social organization in Korea]. *Chōsa geppō* [Research monthly], September 1943, 7.
Swedberg, Richard. "Afterword: The Role of the Market in Max Weber's Work." *Theory and Society* 29, no. 3 (June 2000): 373-84.
——. "Economic and Sociological Approaches to Markets." In *Principles of Economic Sociology*, edited by Richard Swedberg. Princeton, NJ: Princeton University Press, 2003.
Sztompka, Piotr. "Mistrusting Civility: Predicament of a Post-Communist Society." In *Real Civil Society: Dilemmas of Institutionalization*, edited by Jeffrey C. Alexander. London: Sage Publications, 1998.
Taehan Muyŏk Chinhŭng Kongsa [Korea Trade-Investment Promotion Agency]. *KOTRA 40onyŏn: mahŭnsal KOTRA such'ul-t'uja iyagi* [Forty years of KOTRA: Stories of export and investment]. Seoul: KOTRA, 2002.
Taet'ongnyŏng Pisŏsil [The Secretariat for the President]. "Sanggong kwangye, munsŏ pŏnho" [Documents on Ministry of Commerce and Industry], 5647-5980, 1964-1977.

———. "Ŭimyŏng chisi, munsŏ pŏnho" [Documents based on President's order, document number], 1-239, 1964-1978.

Taet'ongnyŏng Pisŏsil p'yŏn [Presidential Secretary Office], ed. *Pak Chŏnghŭi Taet'ongnyŏng yŏnsŏlmunjip* [Collection of President Park Chung Hee's speeches], vols. 1, 2. Seoul: Taet'ongnyŏng Pisŏsil, 1965.

Taira, Koji. "Factory Legislation and Management Modernization during Japan's Industrialization, 1886-1916." *Business History Review* 44, no. 1 (Spring 1970): 84-109.

Tanimura Takeo. "Haebang hu chabon hyŏngsŏng kwa paljŏn" [Capital formation and development]. In *1950nyŏndae ŭi insik* [Understanding of the 1950s], edited by Chin Tŏkkyu et al., 312-31. Seoul: Hangilsa, 1981.

Thompson, E. P. *The Making of the English Working Class.* 1963; New York: Vintage Books, 1966.

Tonga Ilbo [Tonga daily], *Tonga yŏngam* [Tonga yearbook], and *Tonga inmyŏngrok* [Tonga who's who]. Various years.

T'onggyech'ŏng [Statistics Korea]. *Han'guk sahoe t'onghyang 2008* [Korean social trends 2008]. Seoul: Institute for Statistics Development, 2008.

———. *T'onggyero pon Han'guk ŭi paljach'wi* [The path to development of Korea through statistics]. Seoul: T'onggyech'ŏng, 1995.

Tongnip Undongsa P'yŏnch'an Wiwŏnhoe [The Editorial Committee for Independence Movement]. *Tongnip undongsa 9: haksaeng tongnip undongsa* [History of independence movement, vol. 9: History of the student independence movement]. Seoul: Koryŏ Tosŏ, 1980.

Trentmann, Frank, ed. *Paradoxes of Civil Society: New Perspectives on Modern German and British History.* New York: Berghahn Books, 2000.

Ŭn Chŏngt'ae. "Pak Chŏnghŭi sidae sŏngyŏkhwa saŏp ŭi ch'ui wa sŏnggyŏk" [Sanctuarization projects under Park Chung Hee: Trends and characteristics]. *Yŏksa munje yŏn'gu* [Critical studies on modern Korean history] 15 (December 2005): 241-77.

Ungson, Gerardo R., Richard M. Steers, and Seung Ho Park. "Reappraising Korea: The Crisis, Aftermath, and Future Challenges." *MIR: Management International Review* 39, no. 4 (1999): 51-83.

Van Hoa, Tran. *The Social Impact of the Asia Crisis.* New York: Palgrave, 2000.

Veblen, Thorstein. *Imperial Germany and the Industrial Revolution.* New York: Macmillan, 1915..

Vlastos, Stephen, ed. *Mirror of Modernity: Invented Traditions of Modern Japan.* Berkeley: University of California Press, 1998.

Wade, Robert. "Gestalt Shift: From 'Miracle' to 'Cronyism' in the Asian Crisis." In *Institutions and Role of the State*, edited by Leonardo Burlamaqui, Ana Célia Castro, and Ha-Joon Chang. Cheltenham, UK: Edward Elgar, 2000.

———. "Globalization and Its Limits: Reports of the Death of the National Economy Are Greatly Exaggerated." In *National Diversity and Global Capitalism*, edited by Suzanne Berger and Ronald Dore. Ithaca, NY: Cornell University Press, 1996.
———. *Governing the Market: Economic Theory and the Role of Government in East Asian Industrialization*. Princeton, NJ: Princeton University Press, 1990.
Walder, Andrew G. *Communist Neo-Traditionalism: Work and Authority in Chinese Industry*. Berkeley: University of California Press, 1988.
Wallerstein, Immanuel. *The Capitalist World-Economy*. Cambridge: Cambridge University Press, 1979.
———. *The Politics of the World-Economy: The States, the Movements, and the Civilizations*. Cambridge: Cambridge University Press, 1984.
Walton, John. "Theory and Research on Industrialization." *Annual Review of Sociology* 13 (1987): 89-108.
Wang, Hong-Zen. "Class Structures and Social Mobility in Taiwan in the Initial Post-war Period." *China Journal*, no. 48 (July 2002): 55-85.
Weber, Max. *Economy and Society*. 2 vols. Edited by Guenther Roth and Claus Wittich. 1968; Berkeley: University of California Press, 1978.
———. *From Max Weber: Essays in Sociology*. Edited by H. H. Gerth and C. Wright Mills. 1948; London: Routledge & Kegan Paul, 1974.
———. "Status Groups and Classes." In *Economy and Society*, vol. 1, edited by Guenther Roth and Claus Wittich. 1968; Berkeley: University of California Press, 1978.
———. *The Theory of Social and Economic Organization*. Edited by Talcott Parsons. Translated by A. M. Henderson and Talcott Parsons. New York: Free Press, 1947.
Weiss, Linda. "Developmental States in Transition: Adapting, Dismantling, Innovating, Not 'Normalizing.'" *Pacific Review* 13, no. 1 (2000): 21-55.
Wesolowski, Wlodzimierz. "The Nature of Social Ties and the Future of Post-communist Society: Poland after Solidarity." In *Civil Society: Theory, History, Comparison*, edited by John A. Hall. Cambridge: Polity Press, 1995.
Whang Seongjoon. "8onyŏndae undonggwŏn ch'ulsin wŏlganjosŏn kijaga mannan hanch'ongnyŏnŭl pŏrin chŏnbuk taehaksaengdŭl." *Wŏlganjosŏn* [Monthly Chosum] 6 (2003): 200-216.
Wi P'yŏngnyang. "Chaebŏl ro ŭi kyŏngje chipchung: kŭ tongt'aejŏk pyŏnhwa wa chŏngch'aekchŏk sisajŏm" [Chaebols and economic concentration: Dynamic change and policy implications]. *Kyŏngjegaehyŏk ripotŭ* [Economic reform report], no. 2 (2018): 1-28.
Wi P'yŏngnyang and Kim Uch'an. "Kungnae chaebŏl kŭrup p'aengch'ang e kwanhan punsŏk kwa kŭ taeŭng pangan mosaek" [An analysis of the expansion of

chaebols and search for measures to control it]. *Kyŏngjegaehyŏk ripotŭ* [Economic reform report], no. 6 (2011): 1–36.

Wickham, James. "Social Fascism and the Division of the Working Class Movement: Workers and Political Parties in the Frankfurt Area 1929–1930." *Capital and Class* 3, no. 1 (1979): 1–34.

Wilks, Stephen, and Maurice Wright. *Comparative Government-Industry Relations: Western Europe, the United States, and Japan.* Oxford: Clarendon Press, 1987.

Williams, Malcolm. *Making Sense of Social Research.* London: Sage Publications, 2003.

Wirth, Louis. "Urbanism as a Way of Life." In *New Perspectives on the American Community*, edited by R. L. Warren and L. Lyng, 36–43. Homewood, IL: Dorsey Press, 1983.

Wolf, Eric R. "Kinship, Friendship, and Patron-Client Relations in Complex Societies." In *Social Anthropology of Complex Societies*, edited by Michael Banton, 1–22. New York: Routledge, 2004.

Woo, [Meredith] Jung-en. *Race to the Swift: State and Finance in Korean Industrialization.* New York: Columbia University Press, 1991.

Woo-Cumings, Meredith. "Introduction: Chalmers Johnson and the Politics of Nationalism and Development." In *The Developmental State*, edited by Meredith Woo-Cumings. Ithaca, NY: Cornell University Press, 1999.

———. "Slouching toward the Market: The Politics of Financial Liberalization in South Korea." In *Capital Ungoverned: Liberalizing Finance in Interventionist States*, by Michael Loriaux, Meredith Woo-Cumings, Kent E. Calder, Sylvia Maxfield, and Sofía A. Pérez. Ithaca, NY: Cornell University Press, 1997.

Yang Chihye. "Chŏnsi ch'ejegi Ilbon Chilso Hŭngnam piryo kongjang ŭi imgŭm kyujŏng kwa 'minjok munje'" [Wage and nationality at the Japanese Hŭngnam Nitrogen Fertilizer Company under the war mobilization system]. *Sahak yŏn'gu* [The review of Korean history] 127, no. 9 (2017): 441–85.

———. "Chŏnsi ch'ejegi Ilbon Chilso Piryo Chusik Hoesa ŭi singminji nosa kwan'gye" [The colonial labor relation of Nihon Chisso during the wartime regime—focusing on the employment structure of fertilizer factory in Hungnam]. *Han'guksa yŏn'gu* [The journal of Korean history] 175 (2016): 189–237.

Yang Chongmin. "Net'ŭwŏk'ŭ punsŏk ŭl t'onghae parabon Han'guk sahoe isa chedo ŭi chŏngch'ak kwajŏng: 1998–2007 chaebŏl ŭi kyeyŏlsa rŭl chungsim ŭro" [A network analysis of the development of Korea's outside director system: The cases of the subsidiaries of chaebols from 1998 to 2007]. *Han'guk sahoehakhoe sahoehak taehoe nonmunjip* (Hugi Sahoehak Taehoe) [The collection of papers for the Second Congress of Korean Association of Sociology] (December 2008): 176–214.

Yang Hyŏna. "Han'guk ŭi hoju chedo: singminji yusan sok e sumswinŭn kajok chedo" [The household head system in Korea: The family system alive as a legacy of the colonial rule]. *Yŏsŏng kwa sahoe* [Women and society] 10 (1995): 214-37.

Yang Kiho. "Han'guk simin tanch'e ŭi chŏngch'ijŏk kinŭng punsŏk: chamyŏ yŏndae rŭl chungsim ŭro" [An analysis of political functions of Korean civic organizations: A case of the coalition for political participation]. *21 Segijŏngch'ihakhoebo* [Journal of 21st-century politics] 10, no. 2 (2000): 73-75.

Yang, Mayfair Mei-Hui. *Gifts, Favors, and Banquets: The Art of Social Relationships in China*. The Wilder House Series in Politics, History and Culture. Ithaca, NY: Cornell University Press, 1994.

Yang Sŏngch'ŏl. *Han'guk chŏngburon: yŏktae chŏnggwŏn kowijik hangjŏng ellit'ŭ yŏn'gu, 1948-1993* [A study of Korean government: The recruitment of high-ranking administrative elites, 1948-1993]. Seoul: Pagyŏngsa, 1994.

Yang Sŭngt'ae. "Konggongsŏng kwa sangŏpsŏng ŭi sai esŏ: mujonjaejŏk chonjae ŭi chayujuŭijŏk simin sahoe kaenyŏm ŭi pip'anjŏk kŭkpok ŭl wihan yebijŏk yŏn'gu" [Between publicness and commerciality: A preliminary work to critically overcome civil society as a non-existential existence]. In *Han'guk ŭi kukka wa simin sahoe*, edited by Han'guk Chŏngch'i Hakhoe and Han'guk Sahoe Hakhoe [Korean Association of Political Science and Korean Association of Sociology]. Seoul: Hanul, 1992.

Yang Tongsŏk. "Saoe isa chedo ŭi unyŏng hyŏnhwang kwa hwalsŏnghwa pangan" [The status of the operations of the outside director system and search for improvement]. *Kiŏppŏb yŏn'gu* [Business law review] 8 (October 2001): 253-77.

Yasuda Mikita. "Chōsen ni okeru kazoku seido no hensen" [The development of the family system in Korea]. *Chōsen* 296 (January 1940): 7-16.

Yi Chaehyŏng. "Tae-chung-so kiŏp kwan'gye e taehan chŏngch'aek kwaje" [A study of big-small-medium industry relations]. *KDI FOCUS* 21 (2012): 1-8.

Yi Chaehyŏng and Park Pyŏnghyŏng. *Kiŏp chiptan naebu kŏrae ŭi p'yŏngga wa chŏngch'aek taeŭng* [Evaluations and internal trading and policy measures]. Seoul: Korea Development Institute, 2016.

Yi Changgyu. *Kyŏngje nŭn tangsin i taet'ongnyŏng iya: Chŏn Tuhwan sidae ŭi kyŏngje pisa* [On economic issues, you are president: Hidden economic stories of the Chun Tu Whan era]. Seoul: Chung-Ang Daily, 1991.

Yi Chŏng. "Kosŏngjang sidae ŭi pihwa" [Stories behind the high economic growth era]. "Ch'angwŏn kongdan 1" [Changwon Industrial Complex 1], *Chugan Maegyŏng* [Weekly Maegyong], no. 257, August 2, 1984; "Ch'angwŏn kongdan 2" [Changwon Industrial Complex 2], *Chugan Maegyŏng* [Weekly Maegyong], no. 258, August 9, 1984; "Ch'angwŏn kongdan 3" [Changwon Industrial Complex 3], *Chugan Maegyŏng* [Weekly Maegyong], no. 259, August 16, 1984;

"Ch'angwŏn kongdan 4" [Changwon Industrial Complex 4], *Chugan Maegyŏng* [Weekly Maegyong], no. 260, August 23, 1984; "Ch'angwŏn kongdan 5" [Changwon Industrial Complex 5], *Chugan Maegyŏng* [Weekly Maegyong], no. 261, August 30, 1984.

———. "Kosŏngjang sidae ŭi pihwa" [Stories behind the high economic growth era]. "Ulsan Chosŏnso 1" [Ulsan Shipyard 1], *Chugan Maegyŏng* [Weekly Maegyong], no. 251, June 21, 1984; "Ulsan Chosŏnso 2" [Ulsan Shipyard 2], *Chugan Maegyŏng* [Weekly Maegyong], no. 252, June 28, 1984.

Yi Chŏngjin. "Chŏngdang yŏnhap kwa chiyŏkchuŭi" [Political party coalition and regionalism]. *Han'guk kwa kukche chŏngch'i* [Korea and world politics] 41 (Fall 2003): 111–38.

Yi Chongsŏn. "IMF kyŏngje wigi wa Han'guk nosa kwangye ŭi pyŏnhwa" [The financial crisis and changes in labor relations in South Korea]. In *Han'guk sahoe* [Journal of social research] 14, no. 1 (2001): 173–203.

Yi Chuhong. "Han'guk sahoe ŭi ihonyul chŭngga e kwanhan yŏn'gu-1997 nyŏn ihu kujojŏk yoin ŭl chungsim ŭro" [A study of increase in divorce rates in South Korea with a focus on structural factors since 1997]. *Sahoe yŏn'gu* [Social studies] 1 (2003): 115–42.

Yi Hanbin, Pak Tongsŏ, Park Munok, Yuh un, No Yunghŭi, No Jŏnghyŏn, Tong Honguk, et al. *Han'guk haengjŏngŭi yŏksajŏk punsŏk, 1948–1967* [Historical analysis of Korean administration, 1968–1984]. Seoul: Han'guk Haengjŏng Munje Yŏn'guso, 1969.

Yi Kapyun and Mun Yongjik. "Han'guk ŭi minjuhwa: chŏn'gae kwajŏng kwa sŏnggyŏk" [Democratization in South Korea: Development and characteristics]. *Han'guk chŏngch'i hakpo* [Korean political science review] 29, no. 25 (1995): 217–32.

Yi Kisu. "Saoe isa chedo ŭi kanghwa rŭl tullŏssan chaengjŏm" [Debates on reinforcement of outside director system]. *Sangsabŏp yŏn'gu* 19, no. 3 (2001): 59–98.

Yi Kyŏngmuk and O Chonghyang. "Saoe isa ŭi ch'ogwa sŏnim e kwanhan chedoronjŏk koch'al" [An institutional approach to the over-election of outsider directors]. *Kyŏngyŏnghak yŏn'gu* [Business administration studies] 31, no. 5 (2002): 1229–54.

Yi Kyungwhan and Chŏng Il. "Saoe isa ŭi immyŏng e kwanhan yŏn'gu: sahoejŏk yŏngyŏ rŭl chungsim ŭro" [Research on the appointments and social ties of outside directors]. *Chŏllyak kyŏngyŏng yŏn'gu* [Journal of strategic management] 14, no. 3 (December 2011): 21–44.

Yi Manhŭi. "Han'guk ŭi sanŏp chŏngch'aek kyŏljŏng esŏ ŭi Kyŏngje Kihoegwŏn ŭi yŏkhal" [The role of the Economic Planning Board in Korea's industrial policy-making]. PhD diss., Yonsei University, 1992.

———. "Sanŏp chŏngch'aek kyŏljŏng esŏ ŭi Kyŏngje Kihoegwŏn yŏkhal ŭi han'gye: chungwhahak t'uja chojŏng ŭi kyŏnghŏm" [The role and limitations of the Economic Planning Board in industrial policy-making: Experiences of the heavy chemical industry]. *Hanse chŏngch'aek* [Hanse journal of economic policy-making] 5, no. 2 (1998): 73–76.

Yi Munung. *Kongŏphwa kwajŏng e issŏsŏ kŭlloja ŭi saenghwal mit chigŏp chŏgŭng e kwanhan yŏn'gu* [Adaptation of workers in the process of industrialization]. Research paper no. 86-4, Institute of Korean Studies (Seoul), 1986.

Yi Pyŏnggon. "Han'guk sahoe ŭi pujŏng pup'ae siltae mit taech'aek: kongmuwŏn ŭi Pujŏngbŏp ŭl chungsim ŭro" [Corruptions in Korean society and anti-corruption measures: The case of corruptions in public bureaucracy]. *Han'guk kongan haejŏnghak hoebo* 12 (2001): 205–37.

Yi Pyŏngjŏn. "Naengjŏn pundan ch'eje, kwŏnwijuŭi chŏnggwŏn, chabonjuŭi sanŏphwa" [The Cold War division system, the authoritarian regime, and the capitalist mode of industrialization]. *Tonghyang kwa chŏnmang* [Journal of Korean social trends and perspectives] 28 (1995): 64–96.

Yi Sinhaeing. "Han'guk simin sahoe undong ŭi tŭngjang, chŏngae kwajŏng, sŏnggyŏk: chisigin pumun undong ŭi seryŏkhwa" [The emergence, the development, and the character of the civic movement in Korea: The empowerment of the movement in the intellectual sector]. Paper read at the Conference on the Growth of the Civil Society and the Civic Movement, Seoul, Korea, May 9, 2000, 5–42.

Yi Sŏngt'ae. "Han'guk sahoe chibaeja chaebŏl ŭi ŭisik nŭngnyŏk yŏn'gu (I)" [A study of chaebols' conscious thinking capacity (I)]. *Opsŏbŏ* [Observer], May 1991, 252–65.

———. "Han'guk sahoe chibaeja chaebŏl ŭi ŭisik nŭngnyŏk yŏn'gu (II)" [A study of chaebols' conscious thinking capacity (II)]. *Opsŏbŏ* [Observer], June 1991, 476–95.

Yi Sujŏng. "Saoe isa ŭi tongnipsŏng punsŏk (2017–2018): taegyumo kiŏp chiptan sosok sangjang hoesa rŭl chungsim ŭro" [An analysis of the autonomy of outside directors, 2017–2018: Cases of listed companies under large business groups]. *Kyongje kaehyŏk* [Economic reforms], no. 7 (2018): 1–42.

Yi Taegŭn. "Han'guk chŏnjaeng ŭi sahoe kgyŏngjejŏk yŏnghyang" [The socioeconomic impact of the Korean War]. *Kukche chŏngch'i nonch'ong* [Korean journal of international politics] 30, no. 3 (1990): 300–319.

Yi T'aeuk. "Kyŏngjeryŏk chipchung kwa Han'guk kyŏngje paljŏn" [A review on the concentration of economic power in the course of Korea's economic development]. *Sijang kyŏngje* [Journal of market economy] 27, no. 1 (1998): 229–56.

Yi Yonghwan. "Simin innŭn simin tanch'e rŭl wihan unyŏng pangan" [A search for civic organizations with real citizen participation]. *Semyong nonch'ong* [Semyong collection of research papers] 8 (2000): 25–39.

Yŏnhap News. "Chuyo chaebŏlgŭrup naebugŏrae kyeyŏlsa hyŏnhwang" [Internal transactions among subsidiaries of major chaebol groups]. October 6, 2012.

———. "Sŏul Kyot'onggongsa ch'aeyongbiri ŭihok, ch'ŏljŏhan kamsa p'iryohada" [Suspicion of irregular hiring practices at the Seoul City Transportation Corporation: A thorough investigation is demanded]. October 17, 2018.

Young, Crawford. *The African Colonial State in Comparative Perspective*. New Haven, CT: Yale University Press, 1994.

Yu Hun. "Han'guk kogŭp kongmuwŏn ŭi sahoejŏk paegyŏng" [Social backgrounds of Korea's high-ranking bureaucrats]. *Haengjŏng nonch'ong* [Korean journal of public administration] 4, no. 2 (1966): 243–66.

Yu Inhak. *Han'guk chaebŏl ŭi haebu* [The anatomy of Korean chaebols]. Seoul: P'ulbit, 1991.

Yu P'almu. "Han'guk simin sahoe punsŏk ŭl wihan kaenyŏm t'ŭl" [A conceptual framework for the analysis of civil society in South Korea]. In *Simin sahoe wa siminundong 1* [Civil society and civic movements, vol. 1], edited by Yu P'almu and Kim Hogi. Seoul: Hanul, 1995.

Yu P'almu and Kim Hogi, eds. *Simin sahoe wa siminundong 1* [Civil society and civic movements, vol. 1]. Seoul: Hanul, 1995.

Yu Simin. Interview. *Sindonga* [New Donga], no. 20, December 1, 1991.

Yu Sŏkch'un, ed. *Han'guk ŭi simin sahoe, yŏn'go chiptan, sahoejaboni Korean* [Civil society, network groups, and social capital]. Seoul: Chayu Kiŏpwŏn, 2004.

Yu Sŏkch'un and Sim Chaebŏm. "Han'guk sahoe pyŏnhyŏk undong tugaji kiban" [Two bases in social reform movements in Korean society]. In *Han'guk ŭi chiyŏkchuŭi wa chiyŏk* [Regionalism and regional conflicts in Korea], edited by Han'guk sahoe hakhoe p'yŏn. Seoul: Sŏngwŏnsa, 1990.

Yu Sŏkch'un and Wang Hyesook. "Oewhan wigi nŭn palchŏn kukka rŭl pyŏnhwa sik'yŏnnŭga?" [Did the financial crisis change the developmental state?]. *Han'guk sahoehak* [Korean sociology] 41, no. 5 (2007): 64–97.

Yu Sŏkch'un and Kim Yongmin. "Han'guk simin tanch'e ŭi mokchŏk chŏnch'i: kyŏngsillyŏn kwa chamyŏ yŏndae rŭl chungsim ŭro" [Substitution of goals in civic organization in Korea: Coalition for economic justice and practice and coalition for political participation]. *Tonga yŏn'gu* [Tonga research] 12, no. 2 (2000): 5–38.

Yu Yingshi. *Chinese History and Culture*. Vol. 2, *Seventeenth Century through Twentieth Century*. New York: Columbia University Press, 2016.

Yu Yongŭil. "P'asan chikchŏn ŭi Taeu Chosŏn: kisa hoesaeng chakjŏn naemak" [Daewoo shipbuilding on the brink of bankruptcy: The inside stories of the rescue of Daewoo Company]. *Sindonga* [New Donga], January 1989.

Yun Haedong. *Chibae wa chach'i: singminji ch'ollak ŭi sam kungmyŏn kujo* [Domination and self-rule: Three aspects of colonial villages]. Seoul: Yŏksa wa Pip'yŏngsa, 2006.

Yun Sangch'ŏl. *1980nyŏndae Han'guk ŭi minjuhwa ihaeng kwajŏng* [Democratic transition in South Korea in the 1980s]. Seoul: Seoul National University Press, 1997.

Zenshō Eisuke. "Chōsen ni okeru dōzoku buraku no kōzō (1)-(3)" [Structure of clan villages in Korea (1)-(3)]. *Chōsa geppō* [Research monthly] (October-December 1940).

———. *Seikatsu jōtai chōsa: Kōryō-gun* [A survey of living conditions: The case of Kangnung-gun (county)]. *Chōsa shiryŏ* [Data series] 32, no. 3 (1931).

———. *Seikatsu jōtai chōsa: Suigen gun ichi* [A survey of living conditions: The case of Suwŏn-gun (county) part 1]. *Chōsa shiryŏ* [Data series] 28, no. 1 (1929).

———. *Seikatsu jōtai chōsa go: Chōsen no shuraku zenhen* [A survey of living conditions 5: Korean villages part 1]. *Chōsa shiryō* [Data series] 38 (1938).

Zysman, John, and Andrew Schwartz. "Reunifying Europe in an Emerging World Economy: Economic Heterogeneity, New Industrial Options, and Political Choices." *Journal of Common Market Studies* 36, no. 3 (September 1998): 405-29.

Index

absorption model, 234n37
accommodation/resistance axis, 37
Act on the Ban of Illegal Solicitation and Bribery (aka Kim Young-ran Law), 207
Africa, 29, 127, 135, 220n15, 239n28; postcolonial African society, 31; tribal and kinship ties, 31
agriculture, 41, 50, 53, 57, 66
Alexander, Jeffrey C., 129
Algeria, 35
Alliance for National Mobilization, 53
anti-authoritarian struggles, ix, 127, 133, 143, 145, 159
anti-communism, 18, 61
anti-democratic tendencies, 146
anti-dictatorial movements, 128
anti-Japanese resistance, 40, 44, 45, 52
anti-Korean-Japanese normalization, 149
area studies, 216n14, 220n8
Asia, 15, 20, 127, 129
"Asian values," 20
assimilation policy, 40
associations: alumni, 2, 152, 181; business, 148; civic, 148; hometown, 2, 181; primordial, 147
"attention-seeking" behaviors, 149
authoritarian human resources management, 195

authoritarian regime, 99, 130-31, 143, 147, 151
authority, 18, 34, 39-40, 54, 99, 153, 207, 210, 223n76; state, 22, 135, 157
autonomy, 38, 63; bureaucratic, 107, 110-12; of chaebols', 114, 194; of civil society, 129; embedded autonomy, 4, 217n21; financial, 148; individual or personal, 129, 138-39; ministry, 108, 234n39; national, 149; neofamilial ties and, 143; organizational, 110; outside directors', 190; relative autonomy of the state, 15-16, 24, 115; social, 130; of social organizations, 136, 140

backwardness: economic, 4; elites' perception or sense of, 6-7, 10, 100, 102, 104, 125, 152, 202, 204; ideologies for overcoming, 23; Korea's, 62-64, 67-68, 224n24; vis-à-vis Japan, 7, 63, 224n8
Balandier, Georges, 29-30, 220n15
Bendix, Reinhard, xiii, 8-10, 24, 223n83
Berman, Sheri, 138
blue-collar workers, 143
Blue House, 177
Blumer, Herbert, 213n15
bourgeoisie, 134; Korean, 144

bureaucracy, 37, 95, 112–13, 159; business penetration/influence on, 93, 105, 111, 118–19, 122, 126, 236n75; chaos, 113; goal-attainment orientation in, 111; graduates of universities in, 91; hollowed out, 104, 110–14, 119, 122, 142, 156, 234n39; informal groupings inside, 105, 111; Korean, xi, 27, 73, 79, 96, 103, 112–13, 233n26, 236n75; neofamilial recruitment in, 170; non-economic, 234n39; "politicization" of, 106, 125; promotion and transfer policies, 111; recruited by merit, 100; stability of, 104–5; weakened, 104, 110. *See also* debureaucratization; recruitment; "wild horse phenomenon"
bureaucratic organization, 90, 103, 111–12
boundaries with outside environment, 111–13
bureaucratic stability, 107, 111, 233n26
bureaucratization, 96, 101, 112–14. *See also* debureaucratization
bureaucrats: career, 81, 85–86, 89; in Chosun dynasty, 63; colonial, 220n17; competition among, 125–26; in consultative meetings, 71; corruption among, 157; dealings with business, 75–77, 108, 111, 117, 122, 125–26, 164–65, 181–82, 233n32, 236n81; evaluation of, 105–7, 125; high-ranking, 75, 81, 83, 91, 105; Korean, 77, 100, 102, 172, 234n38; in MCI, 70, 117; middle-level, 81; public perception of, 157; recruitment of, 10, 100; regional bias in promotion of, 88; role in developmental state, 104–5; role in industrialization, 24; role under President Park, 79, 92, 106; samurai-turned-bureaucrats, 24; solidarity among, 106, 231n13; and speed of implementation, 76, 108; vulnerability of, 117–19
bushi (samurai), 55

capitalism, 15, 27, 183; "varieties of," 14, 16, 20–21, 202, 216n17
Catholic Peasant Association (Kanong), 240n50
Central Intelligence Agency (KCIA), 109
chaebols: collapses and defaults, 183–84; consolidation, 123; debt levels, 188, 194; debt-to-capital ratios, 198–200, 206, 244n23; dependence on the state, 194; economic concentration in, 96, 114, 196–97; expansion of, 114; family succession and inheritance, 90, 192–93, 209; impact of 1997 financial crisis on, 183; inside ownership structure, 59, 90, 192; influence on the state, 121, 123–24; licensure of, 72; linkage with SMES, 96–97, 184; as microcosm of Korean society, xii; neofamilial ties and practices at, 97, 188–89; octopus-style expansion, 198; preponderance in the Korean economy, xi; reform measures, 188–89, 200; relation to civil society, 132–33; as source of neofamilism in Korean society, 193; special favors demanded by, 123, 235n49, 235n57, 235n63; state support of, 184, 233n31; subsidiaries, 197–98; ties with the state, 97, 201;

white-collar employees in, 91, 97. See also conglomerates; outside directors
Chang Myon regime, 61
Changwon National Industrial Complex, 109, 228n83
Chazan, Naomi, 135
China, 43, 51, 205
Chŏgudongmaeng (Red Friend Alliance), 46
Chŏng Chuyŏng, 79
Chōsen, 41-42, 221n30
Chosun dynasty, 63
Christianity, 30
Chun Du Hwan, 143
circles, ix-x, 118, 123, 152, 173, 235n57, 236n74
"civic movement without citizens," 147
civic organizations, 131, 137-38, 145, 148-50, 178, 209-10; politicization process, 242n84
civil codes, 53, 138
civil organizations, 128, 134, 137-41, 148-49, 209; German, 138, 239n38; Korean tendency toward politicization of, 149
civil service examination, xi, 85-88
civil society, 96, 101, 127-30, 134, 137-39, 237n5, 238n12, 239n46; autonomy in relation to the state, 139-40; bottom-up socioeconomic model, 139, 158; groups, 135, 140, 143-45, 149-56, 209, 237n8, 239n38; elite-oriented approach to, 128; formation of, 128, 136, 139-40, 147; impact of democratic movements on, 141, 143-47, 159, 203, 209, 238n14; Korean, 131-33, 137, 139, 142-53, 157-59, 203,

208-11, 229n90; Korean scholarship on, 130-33, 143-47, 210, 238n13, 238n24; top-down political model, 139; universalistic view of, 129, 132
clan, 229n102; organizations, 1, 3, 52-53, 56, 181; ties, 95; villages, 51-52
class, 4, 142, 202; analysis, 13, 16-17, 26, 171, 202; anti-class-forming factors, 18, 142; in colonial society, 32-33, 51; conflict, 1, 138; consciousness, 3, 17-18, 100, 171, 181; dominant, 10; formation, 17-18, 22, 25, 32; identity, 18, 22, 95-96, 134; in Korean industrialization, 100, 202; relations, 6, 31; ruling, 15, 42, 50, 58, 99, 230n106; social distance between, 166; as a social outcome, 26; social units other than, 3, 11, 14, 18, 23, 25, 202; tensions, 171; trans-class orientations, 145. See also middle class; ruling class; working class; yangban
clientelism, 5
Coalition for Environmental Protection, 240n66
cognitive dissonance, 146-47
Cold War, 157, 204-5
collaboration, 37, 181-82
collective mass consciousness, 145
collectivism, 10, 22, 24, 175, 211
collusion, 79, 92, 94, 105, 235n49
Colonial Functional Space (CFS) category, 34-35
colonialism, 29-30, 32, 34, 39, 45
colonial rule, 27-29, 153; clan villages under, 52-53; complexity of, 28-29; and control, 30, 32-40, 44, 46, 49, 58-59, 135; disequilibrium of, 31-32, 49, 58; education under, 35-36, 38-41,

colonial rule (*continued*)
45, 49, 58, 61; family system under, 53-54; inventing tradition under, 59; Japanese, xi, 27, 41-42, 44, 47, 52, 221nn30-31; justification of, 37; Korean capitalists under, 38; old social structure destroyed by, 100; paradox of, 47; Park Chung Hee and, 61, 98; resistance under, 37-38; situation, 29-32, 35, 38-39, 47, 55, 58, 220n15; social consequences under, 31, 58, 60; suppression of labor unions under, 57; traditional groups and classes under, 25; traditional institutions and values and, 39, 59; *yangban* and, 49-50
Colonial Social Space (CSS) category, 34, 36, 38-39, 49, 51
colonial society, 28-29, 31-32, 35, 220n22, 223n83; fragmentation of, 33, 220n22; Korean, 28, 43-44, 51
colonial space, 29-34, 36-37; accommodation/resistance axis, 37; arbitrariness of, 33; boundary blurring and fluidity, 32-33, 36; education system change, 49, 51; family system in, 51; structural categories of, 34, 36; student uprisings in, 44-47
Colonial Superstructural Space (CSUS) category, 34, 36-40, 49, 51, 220n7
commoners, 50-51, 57
communism, 7, 44; Communist Bloc, 13; communist system, 136
compressed modernity, 247n17
Confucian values, 18, 20
conglomerates, xi, 91, 96. *See also* chaebols
corporate governance, 206, 209, 247n13

corruption, 61, 65, 68-69, 105, 153, 157, 207, 247n7
coup d'état, 7, 61, 64, 80, 143
COVID-19 pandemic, 211
cronyism, 131,
crossholding, 188

Daewoo, 120-21; Heavy Industries, 121; Shipbuilding, 120
Dahrendorf, Ralf, 1, 24
debt payments, 184
debureaucratization, 104, 112, 114
decision-making: and implementation, 73, 77, 79, 102; in the MCI, 103, 105, 122, 232n1; neofamilial ties and, 163-64; political influence on, 156, 233n26; pragmatism in, 126, 227n55; president-centered, 68, 107-9, 111, 113, 119, 125; top-down style, 78, 108-9, 119, 148; within chaebols, 188-89, 191-92
Declaration of Democratic Reform, 143
democracy, Western, 211
democratic consolidation, 203
democratization: bottom-up model vs. elite-led, 128, 131, 139, 144, 153; and breakdown of the Cold War international system, 157; British, 134; and civil society, 128, 130, 132, 141, 144, 159, 203, 209; Council for the Promotion of Democracy Movement, 240n50; Council of Movement for People and Democracy, 144; Korean society views on, 145-46, 243n4; and labor relations, 195; movements, 128-30, 139, 144, 181; and neofamilism, 165, 203-4; relationship with socioeconomic changes, 130;

and the state, 133, 156, 205; and state-business relations, 114; and state-society relations, 158; student activists and, 152
dependency, 23, 27, 96, 112, 125, 143, 148, 219n60; bargaining, 122, 125; commanding, 112-13, 116, 119, 124-25; and development, x, 132; manipulative, 116, 119, 124; mutual, 111; school, 215n5; on the state by business, 108, 114-15, 123-24
depoliticization, 137
de Tocqueville, Alexis, 8
development, 11, 22, 33, 183; bank, 8, 236n69; capitalist, 13-14, 131; dependent, x, 132; colonial sources of, 27; "development without development," 27; economic, x, xii, 1-4, 16, 23, 39, 61, 64, 102, 131-32, 139, 145, 174, 205; enterprise-based approach to, 71-72, 77; -exploitation debate, 28-29, 49, 219n5; historical, 20, 127, 129; industrial, 4, 109, 222n52, 236n69; late, 10, 23 24, 72, 138; Japanese economic, 27; market, 220n17; neofamilism and, 98-100, 103-4; Park Chung Hee's prioritization of, 68, 80, 90, 126; plans, 70; postcolonial economic, 28, 59-61; state, x-xi, 2, 15-16, 102-4, 110, 114-15, 156, 188, 225n28, 230n1, 234n39; targeted, 71, 73-74, 79, 233n29; unilinear, 13
dictator, 79, 146
differentiation, 14-15, 31, 33, 51, 58, 149, 218n46
diffusion, 95, 97
discrimination, 27-28, 30-31, 35-36, 45
disequilibrium, 31-34, 49, 58
Domestic Security Law, 47

Doosan, 193, 199, 235n64
Dore, Ronald P., 219n60
dumping, 117

East Asian countries, 15-16, 20
Eastern Europe, 127, 129, 136, 156, 237n5
economy: Comprehensive Economic Stabilization Policies, 129; concentration of, 96, 196-97; determinism of, 13, 17; five-year plans, 65; growth of, 2, 7, 15, 90, 183-84, 219n5, 225n27; political, x, xii, 4, 14-16, 25-26, 202-3; sociology of, 217n22; state-led development of, 131; structuralism of, 17
Economic Planning Board (EPB), 121, 235n57
educational credentialism, 221n36
Educational Edict and Laws, 41
Eisenstadt, S. N., 112
Ekeh, Peter P., 35-37, 220n22
elections, 2, 96, 134, 142, 156, 161, 205-6, 209; national assembly, 2, 55-56, 142, 155; presidential, 2, 142, 154
electronics sector, 73-74, 118
elitism, 136, 152
Enforcement Decree of Trade Law, 228n72
England, 55, 66, 127, 140
ethos, 25, 128, 131, 159; of civil society, 133, 137, 140-41, 229n90; of industrial policy implementation, 77, 234n39; neofamilial structures and, 5, 95-96, 147, 210; of state-business relations, 115; under colonial rule, 38
Evans, Peter, 16, 217n21
Expanded Export Promotion Conference, 233n31

exploitation, 27, 30, 35-36, 39, 49, 222n52; dichotomy with development, 28-29, 219n5

export, 66, 97, 108-10, 115, 179, 187; export-first principle, 71, 110, 116; export-led industrialization (ELI), 225nn28-30, 235nn48; goals and targets, 66-67, 108-10, 126, 171, 225n24; incentive measures, 71-72; 113, 116-17, 234n44; MCI pressure on companies for, 92, 105-8, 116-17, 119, 233n31, 234n32; performance, 66, 76; president's involvement with, 73-77, 79, 90, 108, 125, 226n49, 233n27, 233n31; promotion, 5, 68-71; records, 69, 76, 106, 109-10, 233n31, 235n50; rules and regulations, 233n27; support policy, 69, 71-72, 92

familism, 2-3, 5, 18, 22, 53, 56, 59, 188, 196, 214n18

family, 5, 14, 206-8; breakdown with 1997 financial crisis, 183-88, 245n42; in chaebol ownership and management, 90-91, 105, 189, 192-93, 197; and civil society, 127, 131, 238n12; extended, 51, 53-54; Japanese system of, 55, 138; Korean system of, 36, 39, 50-51, 53-59, 188, 223n82; in labor sector, 200, 208; law system, 223n82; in neofamilial interactions, 168-70; nuclear, 56, 95, 179, 229n90; Park Chung Hee's views on, 63; solidarity, 53-54, 56, 187-88, 206; student groups as "family" organizations, 152; ties, 1-2, 39, 201, 246n58; as traditional institution, 19-20, 214n18

Fifth Republic, 143

filial piety, 99

finance: and bank credit review system, 245n42; crisis, 157, 159, 183-90, 201, 205-6; impact on chaebols, 196-200; institutions, 52, 167, 193-94, 200-201, 208-9, 245n40; and labor reforms, 195-96, 200; and neofamilial relations, 165-67, 173-76; sector, 8, 193, 207

Financial Services Commission, 194

First Republic, 81-82

fragmentation, 33, 136, 195, 220n22

France, 127, 129, 238n25

functionalism, x, 13

gender equality, 208

"Generation 386," 152, 241n77

Germany: as case of late industrialization, 23-25, 63, 100, 214n23; and civil organizations, 137-38, 140; Imperial Germany, 215n37; and traditional institutions and values, xii; Weimar society, 210

Gerschenkron, Alexander, 23

globalization, 173, 205-6, 209

GNP, 96; growth, 65, 184; per capita, 64, 184

Goffman, Erving, 38, 221n24

Grajdanzev, Andrew, 54

Great Britain, 129, 133-34, 137, 158

Greater East Asia Co-Prosperity Sphere, 34

groups: anti-authoritarian activists, 139, 143-45, 158; informal, 104, 110, 152, 231nn11-12, 232n13; interest, 148, 209; "non-groups," 14, 216n9; opposition, 24, 128, 133, 136, 141, 143, 146-47, 153, 158; people's movement, 144, 150-51; social, 31, 43, 100, 129, 138

Habermas, Jürgen, 229n90, 237n1
Hanguk Heavy Industry, 120, 235n64
Han'guk Nohyop (Korean Council for Labor Welfare, KCLW), 144
Hanjin, 198-99
Hankook Fertilizer Company, 109
Hanwha, 193, 198-99
"harnessing" strategy, 7, 99
heavy chemical industries, 2, 73, 107, 118, 120, 124; program, 118
Henderson, Gregory, 41-42, 47
historical institutionalism, 14
hollowed commanding, 122-24
Honneth, Axel, 128
household head, 185-87, 223n76
human resources, 75, 195
hyangyak, 98
Hyŏgudongmaeng (Revolutionary Friend Alliance), 46
Hyundai Construction Co., 118
Hyundai Heavy Industries, 2, 118, 120
Hyundai Yanghaeng, 120, 235nn63-64

identity: in civil society, 130, 229n90; class basis of, 134; through education, 42, 44; family as sources of, 51, 59; informal, 104; intra-bureaucracy, 104; Korean ethnic, 27, 33-34; multiple identities, 8, 17-18, 59; neofamilial, 95-97, 141-42, 167, 202, 211; primary tie-based sources of, 2, 5-6; secret organizations as sources of, 47; in state-business relationship, 75
ie (家), 21, 55, 138, 204
"IMF Crisis," 183
"impact policy," 226n41
impeachment, 206, 208-9
implementation: economic goals and strategies, 66, 68; in enterprise-based approach to development, 71-73, 77; of export targets, 92; impact of hollowed commanding on, 123; of industrialization tasks, 8; legal, 164; in the MCI, 102-5, 232n14; of post-crisis reform measures, 183, 189, 196; pragmatism and particularism in, 76-81, 116, 120, 126, 227n55, 236n81; president-centered decision-making and, 107-13, 125-26

import substitution strategy, 68; import-substituting industrialization (ISI), 69, 225n29

incentives, 4-5, 16, 35, 68, 79-80, 90, 134, 140; administrative, 71, 111; company-specific, 117, 228n72; merit-based, 113; state, 5, 71-72, 80, 90-91, 95, 111-13, 115, 117, 124, 143, 171, 182, 208

India, 216n14
indigenous institutions, 34, 220n22
indigenous people, 58
indirect intervention, 245n39
individualism, 22, 95, 97, 129, 134, 173, 175, 211
Industrial Complex Development Corporation, 109
industrialization, 4, 92, 201-5; business sector's bargaining power in, 121-23; under colonial rule, 29, 35, 49; company-specific policies of, 90, 125; cultural aspects in, 16; East Asian, 15-16, 20; and modernization, 20-24; neofamilism and, 6, 39, 156, 165, 167, 169-72, 176-78, 242n1; patterns of, 9-18; policies of, 11, 70, 123, 177; responses of tradition, 213n15; state-led, xii, 4-5, 9-11, 20, 23, 100, 103, 158, 176, 201, 205, 217n34, 226n41;

industrialization (*continued*)
spontaneous vs. state-led, 133, 158, 230n10, 217n34; and state-society relations, 137-39, 142-43, 153, 158; structural changes arising from, 165; top leader's urgent pursuit of, xi, 63-65, 68-69, 72, 79-81, 90; and tradition, 6, 24-26, 98, 100-101, 157, 211; and universal social consequences, x, 158; zones of, 226n51. *See also* late industrialization
industrialization, late, xi-xii, 2-11, 13, 18, 20-26, 67, 70, 98, 100-101, 104-5, 217n34; civil society and, 130, 132-33, 147; comparative studies of, 137, 140, 158, 205; concept of class in, 202; institutional imperatives of, 5, 81; political sociology of, 133; social implications of Korea's, 79-80, 171; South Korea's, xii, 1, 3, 6, 18, 26, 59, 79-80, 95-96, 132, 202, 211; state and business shared goals in, 112-13, 115-16, 119, 124; the state in, 25, 103, 231n10; traditional institutions in, 21, 202-5
inferiority, 4, 7, 10, 62, 68, 127, 202
informal practices, 136
information age, 175
information flows, 12
inheritance law, 193
institutions, 14, 21, 101, 183; and bureaucratic organization, 112; and change, x, 3, 7-9, 16, 31, 79, 90, 189; and civil society, 147; colonial-era, 28, 35, 37-38, 49, 220n22; economic, 23, 159, 206, 209, 211, 231n10; elites and, 237n7; embedded, 209; evolution of, x; financial, 167, 193-95, 200-201, 208; formal, 136; German political, 138; indigenous, 34, 220n22; and industrialization, 13, 16, 26; informal, 136; legal, 127; and management of social conflicts, 8-9; migrated, 35, 37, 220n22; monocropping, 14; patrimonial, 22; and neofamilial practices, 95, 142, 176; and politics, 158-59, 210; state, 128, 139; in state-business relations, 77, 93, 103; total, 38, 221n24; traditional, xii, 2-3, 5, 7, 9-11, 18-25, 38-39, 52, 58-59, 98-100, 137, 140, 156, 202-4, 217n34; Western, 159. *See also* non-state institutions
interest rates, preferential, 121
International Cooperation Administration (ICA), 65
international environment, 202, 204-5
International Monetary Fund (IMF) Standby Credit Facility, 183
intersystem spillover, 31
intervention: by business, 108; capricious, 76, 110, 140; colonial, 30; President Park's, 66, 73-74, 106, 108-11; state, 8, 15, 23, 25, 70, 102, 123, 140, 193-94, 201, 245n39
ironies, social and institutional, 3-4
irregular workers, 184, 195-96, 200

Jacobsson, Kerstin, 229n90
Japan, 100; assimilation of Korean people into, 34; education in, 40-41, 43; elites, 6-7; emulation of, xi; family system in, 54-55; hegemony of, 28, 34; history of, 25; Home Ministry, 214n23; industrialization, 15; Japanese Military Academy, 61; Korea falling behind, 63, 224n8; as late industrialization case, 137-40, 204-5, 234n37; lifetime employment institutions in, 21; Meiji Japan, 6-7,

55, 98–99; opposition to industrialization in, 24; personnel policy in, 113; role of tradition in late industrialization, xii, 21; seized Japanese-owned properties, 65; state-business relations in, 236n75; superiority of, 45; traditional institutions and values, 10, 21, 24, 55, 61, 138–40, 204
Japanese colonial rule, xi, 27, 30, 34, 40–47; authorities, 36, 40, 52–54, 221n36; exploitation-centered orthodoxy, 28; and ideology, 40, 43; opposition between exploitation and development, 27–29; orthodox and revisionist paradigms, 27–28, 49
Johnson, Chalmers, 15, 220n8
June Democratic Uprising, 143
Junkers, 24, 100, 138, 140

Kabo Reform, 50
kapchil hyŏngsang, 207
Kim Dae Jung, 2, 150–51, 154, 244n23
Kim Eun Mee, 123
Kim Sun Hyuk, 238n13
Kim Woo-choong, 121
Kim Young-ran Law, 207, 246n7
Kim Young-sam, 82, 150–51, 154
kisaeng, 222n54
Kŏje, 118
Korea, 11, 100–101; civil society in, 130–33, 156–59; Korean colonial society, 27–28, 41–43, 51–55; as late industrialization case, 4, 16, 18, 22–25; neo-familial ethos and structural features in, 5–6, 95–96, 201–11; 1997 financial crisis in, 183–84; pervasiveness of high school ties in, xi; as relatively backward, 62–68; state and business in, 112–14

Korea Environment Movement Coalition, 150
Korea Fair Trade Commission, 193, 198
Korea University, 89
Korean Automobile Industry Association, 121
Korean Confederation of Trade Unions (KCTU), 181
Korean Council for Labor Welfare, 144, 240n50
Korean Federation of Industrialists, 91
Korean Financial Supervisory Board, 245n40
Korean Peninsula, 27, 61, 157
Korean Shokusan Bank, 222n50
Korean Trade Association, 180
Korean War, 55–57, 62, 64, 100
Korea's Citizens' Coalition for Economic Justice (KCEJ), 148
ku, 53
Kulp, Daniel Harrison II, 214n18
Kumho, 198–99
Kumi, 61, 118
Kwangju: massacre of 1980, 147; student uprising of 1929, 44
Kwangyang, 118
kye, 52, 91, 98

labor, 53, 57, 98, 114, 144, 159, 172, 181, 200; activists, 151, 240n50, 241n76; bifurcation into regular and irregular workers, 196, 200; cheap (forced) Korean, 27; market, 172, 195; movements, ix, 55, 151, 195; suppression, 123
labor unions, ix, 3, 57, 134–35, 151, 178–79, 181–82, 200, 208, 241n75; leaders, 181, 200; organizers, 151, 178, 181–82, 195, 245n44. *See also* strikes

labor-capital relations, 138, 195
labor-management relations, ix, 3, 9, 21, 29, 98-99, 177, 189, 196, 209
land reform, 189, 195
land survey, 49
landlords, 49-53, 55, 57, 100, 220n23, 222n50; landlord-tenant disputes, 50, 222n52; landowners, 138, 222n65
Latin America, 16, 144
liberation, 38, 41, 57, 59, 63, 65, 131
lifetime employment, 21, 195, 200
litigiousness, 207, 247n7
loans: guarantees, 188, 201, 207; and guarantors, 164, 170
lobbying, 78, 80, 94, 121-22, 177
Lotte, 193, 199
loyalty, 8, 80, 85, 90, 99, 104, 126, 172, 175, 195; colonial, 40
lunar calendar system, 223n82

macrosociology, 14, 16
Manchuria, 53
Manchurian invasion, 46
Manchurian Military Academy, 61
manipulative dependency, 119
Mann, Michael, 17
March First Independence Movement, 42, 44
market: coexistence with the state, 8, 16; under colonial control, 38; within confines of institutions, 21; curb, 69; domestic, 65, 68-69, 74, 92, 110, 173, 225n24; export, 73; in import substitution strategy, 68; international, 69-70, 73-74, 80, 109-10, 115, 125, 173, 183; market-based economic relations, 25-26, 127, 134, 201, 220n17; market-based industrialization and development, xii, 15, 230n10; and non-market factors, 22, 24-25, 217n34; opportunities, 108; principles, 133-34, 175, 208-10; private loan, 118; as socially embedded, 217n21
marital relations, 187
Marxian paradigm/perspective, ix, 15
Marxists, 132
masses: attitudes toward democratization, 139, 146; in democratization, 131; dual aspect of Korean, 133, 146; influence of neofamilism on, 182; in June Democratic Uprising, 143; justification of military coup d'état to, 7; in Korean society, 22, 145-46; Park Chung Hee views on, 62-63; relation to political activists, 131, 133, 144-45, 147, 150, 152-53, 241n79; relationship with political elite groups, 129, 131, 144, 156. See also *minjung*
Mercier, P., 31
merit, xi, 80-81, 90, 126, 173, 175, 196; principle, 88, 111; system, 81, 126, 200; recruitment based on, xi, 9, 24, 88-89, 98, 100, 104-5, 110, 113, 176
middle class, ix, 50, 96, 101, 130, 138-40; Korean, 96-97, 131-32, 142, 145, 185, 187
Migdal, Joel S., 135, 230n1
militarism, 17, 204
military, 85-87; anti-military regime demonstrations, 147; coup d'état, 7, 61, 64, 68, 90, 143; force, 23; government, 120; order on SNU campus, 152; Park Chung Hee service in, 61; police, 45; postcolonial conscription into, 55; President Park politically dependent on, 80, 227n63;

rule, 61, 114, 120, 146; service, 168, 177–79, 232n15, 242n80
mimetic recruitment patterns, 90
Minch'ongyŏn (Youth Coalition for Democracy Movement, YCDM), 144
"mingling," 92, 105, 125–26, 234n32
Ministries, 77, 85, 87, 102, 104, 107–8, 177; coordination among, 109, 116, 226n49, 233n27; interorganization boundaries, 111; intra-ministerial instability, 110; personnel policies, 109. See also Mobile Ministry
Ministry of Commerce and Industry (MCI), x, 70–71, 84, 87, 92; meetings with business, 71, 116; recruitments, 104; weakened coordinating power, 116, 118
Ministry of Communication, 121
Ministry of Health and Social Affairs, 234n39
minjung, 131–32, 145; movement, 18
Mint'ongyŏn (People's Movement Coalition for Democracy and Reunification [PMCDR]), 144
"Miracle on the Han River," x
MITI (Ministry of International Trade and Industry [Japan]), 236n75
mobile communications industry, 121
Mobile Ministry, 233n32
modernity, 19–20, 57, 129, 218n46; civil society as symbol of, 158; colonial, 29, 35, 39, 49, 219–20n7; industrialization distinct from, xiii, 100; and tradition, 12–13
modernization, 10, 13–14, 29, 218n46; approach and perspective of, 19; Japanese, 55; in late industrialization, 24; New Village Movement and, 229n103; Park Chung Hee's views on, 63–64, 224n15; and tradition, 19–22, 218n50; theory/paradigm, xii, 3, 7, 13, 15, 19–21, 25–26, 203, 214n24; Western, 13, 20
modular citizens, 239n48
monosectoral analysis, 27–29, 49, 58
moral hazard, 110, 193
mutual debt guarantees, 188
mutual friendship societies, 44
myŏn (village administration unit), 49, 52–53, 223n82

Nakdong River, 118
National Assembly, 2, 93, 149–50, 155, 161, 241n76
National Charter of Education, 229n103
National Congress for Democracy and Reunification (NCDR), 144
national liberation, 38
National Movement Headquarters for Democratic Constitution (NMHDC), 144
nationalism, 18, 29, 40, 44, 98, 238n24; anticolonial, 32; historiography, 38; nationalistic facade, 158
nation-building, 7, 17,
"natives," 34
neofamilial ties, xi, 92, 95–97, 111, 142–43, 160–65, 168–77, 188, 242n2; and application of laws, 164, 171, 207; career development and, 176, 195, 243n9; and connections, 58, 95, 141, 188, 229n90; and economic behavior, 141, 161–66, 169–70, 190, 194–95, 200, 245n42; and embeddedness, 159; as information sources, 142, 163, 171; and political behavior, 161; at workplace, 160, 176, 200

neofamilism, x-xii, 59-60, 91, 100, 156, 171-72, 175-76; behavioral consequences of, 160; behavioral manifestations of, 242n1; and chaebol reforms, 188-89, 193, 197-200, 247n13; and civil society, 130, 133, 139, 141-43; definition, 1, 5-6, 12, 18, 23, 95-98; ethos of, 96, 210; and financial sector reforms, 193-94, 245n42; and hiring practices, 201, 208; and Korean developmental state, 103-4, 110; labor reforms and, 195-96; perceptional aspects of, 160; persistence of, 200-203, 205-6, 208-11; practices, 142-43, 147, 162-67, 169, 175-76, 187, 193, 200, 207; as sociocultural pattern of sociability, 57; as survival strategies, 133, 146, 167, 182-83, 211; type I/II, 208
neotraditionalism, xiii, 216n11; and personal relations, 23
network analysis, 5
networks: informal, 79, 141; neofamilial units and, 96, 142, 158, 171; patron-client, 135; social, 22, 222n50; traditional, 1, 22
New Guidance for Villages project, 53
New Ritual Ordinance, 229n103
New Village Movement, 99, 229n103
newly industrializing countries (NICS), 16, 20
Newspaper Law, 47
NGOs, 178
non-state actors, 9, 230n1
non-state institutions, 238n12
North Korea, 7, 157, 224n8

Onsan, 118
organizations: autonomous, 140; bureaucratic, 90, 103-4, 111-12; clan, 1-3, 52-53, 56, 181; of colonial superstructural space, 34; formed during democratization, 130, 144, 240n50; industrial, 9; informal, 96, 104, 126, 139, 181; mass, 147; neofamilial, 182, 209-10; primary, ix; secret, 44-49, 152; social, 134-36, 237n8; student, 43-44, 46, 48-49, 135, 150, 152; village, 53; voluntary organizations, 134, 139, 239n26; women's, 135; workers,' 38, 137. *See also* civic organizations; civil organizations
Orientalism, 20
orthodox interpretation. *See* Japanese colonial rule
outside directors, 188-91, 200, 244n33

Park Choong Hun, 106
Park Chung Hee, xi, 2, 6-7, 61, 98, 104, 143, 146, 214n24, 224n1, 225n29, 227n63, 227n68, 230n103, 230n107
Park Geun-hye, 206, 208-9
Parsonian paradigm, xi
particularism, 9, 11, 76-77, 126
party politics, 203
paternalism, 9, 18, 21
paternalistic human resources management, 195
path dependence, 14, 60, 114
patriarchism, 195
patrimonial institutions, 22
permits, 110, 232n14, 234n32
personal connections, 47, 65, 97, 100
personalistic dependency, 219n60
personnel policy, 104, 112-13, 126
petrochemical industries, 73-74, 120
pokchibudong, 113, 234n38
Poland, 136, 141, 152, 229n90
Police Law, 47

"political adventurism," 241n75
political parties, 134, 136-38, 141, 143, 150, 153, 156, 209-10; bourgeois, 138; opportunism of, 156
politicization of bureaucracy, 106, 125
politics, 1, 13; civil organizations in, 149; and civil society, 159, 229n90; in Japan, 24; Korean, 59, 63, 99, 151, 153-57, 174-76, 206, 209, 211, 225n27, 241n71; polarized party, 203; and scandals, 241n80
postcolonial world, 17
postmodern approach to tradition, 19
power: business sector's bargaining, 121, 125; equilibrium, 112; Korean bureaucracy's decision-making, xi, 105, 116, 118; lobbying, 78; in the market, 217n34; military, 114; neofamilial ties in attaining, 93; ownership and management, 192; Park Chung Hee's ascent to, 61, 63, 68, 80, 90; patriarchal, 51; political parties' securing, 156; protests against abuse by those in positions of, 207; state, 56, 96, 122, 131, 135, 141-43, 210. *See also* colonial power
pragmatism, 17, 76-77, 98, 116, 126, 227n55
primogeniture, 193
primordialists, 240n60
privatism, 95, 229n90; civic vs. civil, 229n90
production capacity, 74, 224n24
promotion, ix, 88-89, 96, 105-6, 111, 142, 167-68, 222n50, 231n12
Protestant Peasant Association (Kinong), 240n50
protests, candlelight, 208, 210
provincial origins, 83, 227n67

Public Order Maintenance Law, 47
public sphere, 135, 229n90
Publication Law, 47
Pyongmin Party, 151

rational-choice theory, 216n14
reciprocal consent, 236n75
recruitment: 5, 98, 100, 110; based on merit, 176; high school ties as source for, xi; increase of regionalism in, 80-81, 85, 100, 206; of leaders and activists in, 148; mimetic patterns of, xi, 9, 90; and neofamilial ties, 168, 170, 172; open, 178, 180; "parachute" style of, 105; patterns of MCIs, 102-5; of state officials, 8-11, 204; state's exam-based merit system of, 24, 88-91
regionalism, xi, 1-3, 22, 177, 182; breakdown of, 210; combining merit with, 88-90, 100, 104-5, 110-11, 126; "defensive," 206; and Korean civil society, 131-32, 159; in Korean elections, 96, 142, 153, 156, 203, 209; and Korean politics, 175, 204, 209, 211; as main source of social trust, 59; in MCIs recruitment, 80-83; Park Chung Hee's views on, 229n102; persistence of, 205; solidarity among workers, based on, 196, 200, 228n83; southeast, 206; southwest, 206; "winning," 206; within labor unions or labor-management relations, ix
religion, 17, 31, 36
resistance, 4, 11, 24, 34, 36-39, 42-43, 53, 113, 120, 209; anti-colonial, 40-41, 49, 55; student, 43-44
resistance/accommodation axis, 34, 36-39, 41; resisting accommodation, 37

resistant traditionalism, 38
"re-traditionalization," 55
"reverse teleology," 28
revisionist approach, 27-28
Rhee, Seung Man, 61, 68, 225n27
Roh Tae Woo, 121, 143, 154
Roniger, Luis, 129

Saenuri Party, 209
Samsung, 120-22, 193, 199, 242n84
samurai-turned-bureaucrats, 24
Sangnokhoe (Evergreen Group), 46-47
school ties, 1, 5; colonial education legacy of social relations based on, 49; as distinct feature of Korean society, 22; originating in colonial rule, xi, 39, 47, 222n50; pervasive informal organizations within MCI based on, 104, 232n14; postcolonial Korean elite behaviors based on, 59; regionalism and, xi; role in chaebols' corporate governance, 190; role in daily personal experiences, 160, 164, 168-69, 172-77, 180, 182, 243nn3-4; role in Park's personnel policies, 110-11, 229n102; recruitment of state officials, 80, 89, 91-95; as source of social trust, 59; state embedded in society through, 4
Schumpeter, Joseph, 9
Second Economy Campaign, 99, 229n103
Second Republic, 82
secondary adjustments, 220-21n24
secondary education, 41; vocational high school, 41, 94
Seligman, Adam, 127, 237n5
seniority system (*yŏn'gong*), 196

Seoul, 44, 57, 83, 85-89, 91, 148, 161, 164, 179, 242n1
Seoul Labor Movement Coalition (Sonoryon), 150, 240n50
Seoul National University (SNU), 88, 152, 232n14; graduates, 88-89, 91, 105, 180, 228n71; School of Engineering, 177-78
shareholder rights, 200
Shils, Edward, 18
Shin, Doh C., 146
shipbuilding industry, 2, 118, 120-21; Daewoo Shipbuilding, 120; Hyundai Yanghaeng, 120, 235n63; Hyundai's Ulsan shipyard construction, 119; Okp'o Shipbuilding, 121
Sinudongmaeng (New Friend Alliance), 46
sirhak, 98
Six-Point Revolutionary Pledge, 61
Skocpol, Theda, 8, 239n46
small to medium-sized enterprises (SMES), 73, 91, 96-97, 184
SMI promotion corporation, 180
social change: civil society and, 130, 132-34, 137-38, 140, 158; colonial, 28, 31, 57-58; neofamilism as explaining, 202; relationship between tradition and, 19, 21, 23; in state-led late industrialization, xii, 4, 6-8, 10, 14-18, 25-26, 68, 73, 80, 171, 204-5; Weber on different patterns of, 217n34; in world-system theory and dependency school, 215n5
social connections, 173
social consequences: of colonial rule, 28, 31-32, 37, 39, 44; of late industrialization, xii, 4, 10, 25, 101, 204; neofamilism as, 6; from traditional

social structure, 10; universal, x, 14–15, 132, 158
social democracy, 210
social media, 208, 211
social memory, 18
social mobility, 5, 58, 169, 171
social movements, 128–31, 143, 241n79
social psychological tendencies, 176
social solidarity, 58, 129, 195
social structure: in colonial space, 33, 223n83; of a country's "transitional phase," 215n36; government as integral part of, 8–11; of Imperial Germany, 215n37; in industrialization, 13, 24; neofamilism as distinct, 6; traditional, 10–11, 25, 55, 100, 204; in Western model of democratization, 131, 139–40
social welfare, 8, 52–53, 58, 138, 201, 205–6, 246n4
socialist system, 136
society: colonial, 27–35, 39, 42–44, 49–51, 220n22, 223n83; corruption in, 65, 69; cultural characteristics of Korean, 131–32; disruption and disintegration of families in Korean, 201; elites' position in, 6, 237n7; hierarchical relations in Korean, 207–8; high school education in, 44; industrial-feudal, 215n37; Korean, ix–xiii, 1–3, 139, 153, 156–57, 205, 207–11, 219n60, 242n1; neofamilism in Korean, 96–100, 142–43, 160–76, 180–84, 188, 193; as object of analysis in political economy, 16–17; political, 132, 151; political parties' linkage to, 136; postcolonial Korean, 55, 57–63; post-socialist, 216n11; relational approach to, 14; relationship between opposition groups and, 141, 147–49, 153, 241n79; second, 216n11; socialist, 136, 139, 216n11; state capacity to change, 8, 10–12; state embedded in, 4, 103, 124, 126, 217nn21–22; state open to, under export promotion, 69; statist or elitist tradition in, 137; strong, 135; structure and ethos of, 128; as a "totality of social relations," 17; traditional Korean, 22–23; under state-led industrialization, 4, 24; "web-like," 135; Weimar, 210. See also civic society; civil society; colonial society
sociology, 4, 13–14, 16, 133
solidarity: of common school experiences and locality under colonial rule, 47–49, 58; of land ownership and political influence, 56; among family, 56, 187, 206; within the MCI, 104, 106, 231n13; regional, 5; of neofamilial ties, 195–96; within secret ideological circles, 152; shared military service as a source of, 232n15; traditional networks of obligation and, 1; among workers, 18, 91, 200. See also social solidarity
Solidarity movement, 141, 152
Sorensen, Clark W., 220n15
southeast region, 85, 89, 206; provinces, 2, 104, 161, 227n68, 231nn11–13
southwest/southwestern region, 227n68, 228n83; affected by neofamilial ties on personal political decisions, 161; bias against, 85–87; as "defensive regionalism", 206; high-ranking managerial members of chaebol from, 91; informal groups in MCI from, 104, 231nn11–13; Kim

southwest/southwestern region (*continued*)
  Dae Jung share of vote from, 2; for regional base of regimes, 206; SNU graduates in MCI from, 89; under-representation of high-ranking bureaucrats from, 81, 83
Soviet Union, xii, 6, 11, 24, 113, 136, 234n37
special industrial zone, 2
speed of implementation, 76
Stalin, 6-7
state: as abstract entity, 103, 230n8; access to, 58-59, 65; autonomy, 10, 24, 115, 234n39; "bring the state back in," 4, 14-15; capacity, 8-12, 15, 124; "capture" by business, 233n26, 234n45; and civil, 132-33, 140, 148, 156-59, 238n12, 238n25, 239n46; disaggregate and dynamic/interactive approach, 103-4, 230n11; dominance, 131-32; East Asian states, 16; embeddedness, 4; expansion of social welfare, 206; incentives, 5, 71, 80, 90-91, 105, 111, 124, 171, 182, 208; incorporation of traditional institutions and values, 21, 203; industrialization led by the, xii, 4-5, 9-12, 23, 67, 70-73, 100, 176, 201; influence in financial institutions, 193-94, 200, 245n40; influence on class formation, 18; intervention, 23, 25, 70, 102, 193, 226n41; labor reforms mediated by the, 195-96; leading society model, 133, 137, 139-40, 143, 203; lending directed by the, 193-94; and market in industrialization, 217n34; micro-level internal changes, 103; mimesis of state by society, 126, 177; modes of recruitment, 9, 170; officials, 11, 24, 179; ownership, 49; power, 56, 96, 122, 131, 135, 141-43, 205, 210; pragmatism in decision-making, 227n55; role of the, xii, 3-4, 6, 8, 12, 15, 20, 113-14, 204-6, 225n28, 230n10, 234n37, 242n84; state-in-society model, 133-34, 143; over society model, 133, 136, 139; and society relations/dynamics, 25-26, 130, 133, 137, 139, 158, 203; strong, 27-28, 58, 102, 115, 124, 140, 144, 203, 242n82; versus society model, 131, 133, 139, 143-45, 203, 238n25; weak, 102-3, 115, 123-24, 135-36, 140. *See also* authority; developmental state
state-business relations, x-xii, 16, 102-5, 110-25; blurring of boundaries in, 79-80, 110, 236n75; dependence of business on the state, 65, 69, 71, 102; "enterprise-based" support, 77, 108; favors, 68-69, 123; goals of, 75; neo-familism in, 91-97, 103, 188; networks between state officials and business managers, 105; policy finance in, 236n69; President Park's influence on, 66-73, 108; pressure to export in, 110; state-business collusion, 68, 94; state-business "mingling," 105, 234n32. *See also* commanding dependency; dependency, bargaining; hollowed commanding; manipulative dependency
state-directed lending (*kwanch'i kŭmyung*), 194
static approaches/analyses, 14, 20, 22, 103, 115, 132
statist or elitist tradition, 137
status: based on hierarchy among opposition groups, 136; colonial-era

peasant, 54; in colonial functional space, 38; as component of neofamilism, 5; employment, 195; identity based on economic, 17, 100, 147, 166, 171; of the Japanese family, 55; role of neofamilism in chaebol white-collar workers', 97; socioeconomic, 177, 185; of traditional social elites, 24; Weber on status and power in the market, 217n34; *yangban* class, 50–52

Steinberg, David, 146

strategic industries, 226n41

strikes, 45–46, 181

student movements, 44, 47, 146, 149, 152

students-turned-workers, 151

Sunkyong Group, 121

Sunshine Policy, 157

Supreme Council for National Reconstruction, 61

surveillance, 34, 44, 46–47, 136

survival strategies, 95–96, 135, 141–42, 167, 202, 211

system boundaries, 33; blurred, 30–31

Tadohae, 100

Taiwan, xi, 15–16, 74

Tanzania, 220n17

tenant farmers, 50

Third World states, 63

Thompson, E. P., 17–18

ties: blood (familial), school, and regional, 1, 3, 5, 95–96, 142, 160, 166–67, 172–74; forms of organization, 2; high school, xi, 39, 47, 49, 59, 89, 91, 95, 104, 177, 190; kinship, 10, 24, 31; neighborhood, 22; primary, 5, 95; traditional, 22, 25. *See also* Africa:

tribal and kinship ties; clan; family; neofamilial ties; school ties

time, in social sciences, 17–19, 230n2

Tomoichi, Inoue, 214n23

tonggey, 223n82

"too big to fail" myth, 184

top leader: attitude toward traditional values and institutions, 10; close relationship with state bureaucracy and business, 73; export promotion as most important concern of, 107, 243n6; highly centralized decision-making by, 107, 111, 125, 233n26; implementation style of, 78, 126, 171–72, 182; in Korea's industrialization, 59; role in developmental state in Korea, 102, 104, 236n75

top-down decision-making and implementation, 78, 119

total institutions, 38, 221n24

trading companies, 116–17

tradition: as basis for path dependence in historical institutionalism, 14; Blumer on different responses of tradition to industrialization, 213n15; definitions of, 18–21, 24–26, 203–4; of education as shortcut to governmental positions, 42; of hiring bureaucrats through examinations, 81; invented, 59, 98–99; invention of, 7–9, 21; Japanese, 55, 138, 140; Korean family, 192; in late industrialization, 1, 3, 15, 98, 100, 132, 171; of mutual cooperation among family members, 187; new social units as amalgams of modernity and, 12; persistence of, 6; positive role for, xii, 13, 98, 211; reinventing, 10, 19, 138, 157, 204; socialist cases of, 218n50; strong statist or

tradition (*continued*)
  elitist, 137, 152; as symbols of resistance and control, 38-39, 52-53, 223n83; through the backdoor, 7, 98; use to explain economic institutions and development, 16, 26. *See also* "harnessing" strategy
traditional institutions and values: interactions with colonial rule, 39, 59, 223n82; introduced and reinforced through mediation of the state, 2-3, 7, 21; persistence of, 217n34; as playing different context-dependent roles in late industrialization, xii, 5, 21, 24-25; positive role for, 7, 20; and social structure, 10-11, 100; state's manipulation of, 98-99, 137-38, 140, 202-4, 229n103
traditionalism, 5, 19, 38, 218n40
Trentmann, Frank, 239n38
trichotomy approach, 29
trust: in the case of Italy, 242n2; competition to secure the president's, 125; family as strongest source of, 56-57; from network of social ties within high schools under colonial education, 40, 47, 49, 222n50; generated by *yangban* contribution to clan organizations, 52; main sources of, 59; neofamilial practices and, 142, 163, 172-75, 179-80; necessity to secure business opportunities, 170; secured from Park by ministries and stakeholders, 107
ture, 98

Ulsan, 2, 119
unemployment, 184-87, 195, 200

unilinear development pattern, 13; non-unilinear, 20
unintended consequences, 28-29
United States, 74, 150, 158, 177-78, 211, 215n4; hegemony, 13
universalism, 13-14, 36, 134, 142, 164, 215n4
universal consequences, 13-15, 202
untouchables, 50, 57, 222n54
urgency: as impetus for intervention in economic development, 23, 227n55, 236n75; induced from backwardness, insecurity, and inferiority, 5, 7, 11, 152, 202; Park Chung Hee's sense of, 64-66, 68, 72, 74, 77, 79, 90, 99-100, 104, 109-13, 125-26, 224n24, 226nn49-50, 233n29

values: "Asian values," 20; in civil society, 129, 141; conflicting, in colonial-era high schools, 43; Confucian, 18, 20; embedded, 159; in familism, 214n18; Japanese, 55; in relation to industrialization, 20; Korean non-modern cultural values, 131-32; universal, in bureaucratization, 112; used to reinforce authoritarian Yusin (Reform) regime, 99. *See also* traditional institutions and values
Veblen, Thorstein, 23
Vietnam, 149

Water Resources Management Corporation, 109
Weber, Max, 26, 95, 128, 217n34
Weberian template, 230n10
Western Europe, 63, 122
Western paradigms/models, 13, 131

"white man's burden," 34
white-collar workers, 91, 97, 146
"wild horse phenomenon," 108, 125, 233n26
working class, 2, 17–18, 140; movements, 17. *See also* blue-collar workers
World War II, 62
world-system theory, x, 215n5

yangban, 42, 49–55, 57, 59, 63, 222n64, 229n102, 230n106
Yeo-Soon revolt, 61
Yi dynasty, 51, 62
Yonsei University, 89, 91
Yŏsu, 118
Yusin (Reform) regime, 99, 230n104

www.ingramcontent.com/pod-product-compliance
Lightning Source LLC
Chambersburg PA
CBHW030606230426
43661CB00053B/1867